George Joffé is Lecturer in the Department of Politics and International Studies at the University of Cambridge. He has written extensively on the Middle East and North Africa, and is the editor of *Jordan in Transition: 1990–2000* (2001).

ISLAMIST RADICALISATION IN EUROPE AND THE MIDDLE EAST

Reassessing the Causes of Terrorism

EDITED BY
GEORGE JOFFÉ

I.B. TAURIS
LONDON · NEW YORK

Published in 2013 by I.B.Tauris & Co Ltd
6 Salem Road, London W2 4BU
175 Fifth Avenue, New York NY 10010
www.ibtauris.com

Distributed in the United States and Canada
Exclusively by Palgrave Macmillan
175 Fifth Avenue, New York NY 10010

Library of International Relations 51

ISBN 978 1 84885 480 2

A full CIP record for this book is available from the British Library
A full CIP record for this book is available from the Library of Congress

Library of Congress catalog card: available

Typeset by Newgen Publishers, Chennai

Printed and bound in the United States of America by Edwards Brothers Malloy,
Lillington, North Carolina

CONTENTS

MAPS

LIST OF CONTRIBUTORS

Arshin Adib-Moghaddam is Lecturer in the Department of Politics and International Studies at the School of Oriental and African Studies (SOAS), University of London.

Abdullah Baabood is the Director of the Gulf Research Centre at the University of Cambridge.

Roxane Farmanfarmaian teaches at the University of Utah and is a member of the Department of Politics and International Studies at the University of Cambridge.

Ezzedine Choukri Fishere is Professor of International Politics at the American University in Cairo.

Hugh Goddard is Director of the HRH Prince Alwaleed bin Talal Centre for the Study of Islam in the Contemporary World at The University of Edinburgh.

Ayla Göl is Director of the Centre for the Study for Radicalisation and Contemporary Political Violence at Aberystwyth University.

George Joffé is Lecturer in the Department of Politics and International Studies at the University of Cambridge. He has written extensively on the Middle East and North Africa, and is the editor of *Jordan in Transition: 1990–2000* (2001).

Clive Jones is Professor of Middle East Studies and International Politics at the University of Leeds.

Nasser Kalawoun is an independent scholar and the author of *The Struggle for Lebanon: A Modern History of Lebanese-Egyptian Relations* (I.B.Tauris, 2000).

Raphaël Lefevre is studying at the University of Cambridge.

Jose Liht is a member of the Faculty of Divinity at the University of Cambridge.

Johnny Ryan is at the Institute of International and European Affairs in Dublin.

Sara Savage is a member of the Faculty of Divinity at the University of Cambridge.

James Spencer is a consultant who served with British forces in Iraq.

Ryan J. Williams is a member of the Faculty of Divinity at the University of Cambridge.

1

INTRODUCTION: RADICALISATION AND THE ARAB SPRING

George Joffé

This book is based on the proceedings of a conference held in Cambridge in June 2009 under the auspices of the Faculty of Asian and Middle Eastern Studies and the Department of Politics and International Studies at the University of Cambridge. The conference itself, which also covered North Africa, formed part of a research project funded by the Economic and Social Research Council (ESRC) which was intended to elucidate the causes of radicalisation in the Middle East and North Africa (ESRC Reference RES-181-25-0022). The papers given at the conference on North Africa have now been published in a companion volume which appeared in mid 2011.[1]

Inevitably, the contents of this volume have undergone considerable change since the idea of publishing the original contributions to the conference first emerged, partly to provide a more complete coverage of the Middle Eastern region and partly to accommodate issues that did not at first appear to be important. One issue that is not covered, in detail, except in this introduction, although several chapters do refer to it, is the remarkable series of events that has transformed the politics of the Arab world during 2011. The reason for this is that, whilst some of the political situations which stimulated the arguments put forward here have undergone radical change the drivers, such as poor governance, ideological challenge and economic failure, that are addressed below have not. Indeed, in some cases they were responsible for the changes themselves by their role in radicalising the social movements that emerged to effect change.

Since the purpose of this volume has been to examine those drivers, rather than the outcomes they might produce, it seemed unnecessary to recast the volume to take the latest events into account. This is particularly true of the essential issue behind this volume, the concept of radicalisation, which should be contrasted with the parallel concept of extremism. Furthermore, the eventual outcomes of the Arab Spring are still very unclear and much more time may be needed to make anything but preliminary comments about them. Nonetheless, their connection with the key issue of this book is unmistakable and requires us to comment briefly upon them in order to give some substance to the concept of radicalism.

Radicalism and Extremism

'Radicalism' and 'extremism' are often used interchangeably, a usage which seems to be encouraged by the dictionary definitions of both terms.[2] It can be argued, however, that although both terms share the process of challenging an established order or hegemonic discourse, the outcomes they seek differ significantly. The challenge embodied in radicalisation is a process of contention designed to alter order and discourse but does not necessarily seek to destroy or replace the structures through which they are articulated – in the case of political radicalisation, the state or elites that support it. It involves dissent over the normative and hegemonic assumptions behind the definition of the state and can be organised into a social movement to contest them, once a sufficiently large number of people share an alternative, dissenting discourse. It is at this point that the structures of the state become contingent and thus open to a consensus about how they might be changed and in some instances – as in Tunisia and Libya – even entirely replaced with more legitimate structures.

Extremism, however, usually involves the active adoption of an ideology, and the praxis associated with it, to both delegitimise and then to eliminate the state and its associated elites through violence. The use of violence directed towards these ends is usually deliberate, often through asymmetric warfare, a feature which enables the state to characterise it as an aberrant form of criminal behaviour since it challenges the state's own monopoly of the legitimate use of violence,[3] indeed the very concept of the state itself.[4] Extremism, too, does not necessarily enjoy or even seek popular mass endorsement for, according to its own lights, its rejection of the state is inherently legitimate and even moral. It is therefore often expressed through social networks rather than social movements since its practitioners usually operate in isolation from the society around them as they seek to destroy and reconstruct the state itself.

Although it is clear that both forms of political action are very similar, there is a useful analytical distinction to be made between them, which is often related to the nature of their dialectical and antiphonal interrelationship with the state for, without that, neither has a meaningful existence. Indeed, state and opposition – whether radical or extremist – are dialectical in that it is their interaction that generates outcomes and they are antiphonal in that either one sequentially generates a reaction in the other in a pattern that can be repeated over time. Indeed, the kind of opposition that the state provokes will also reflect, at least in part, the nature and actions of the state itself. Yet, although it would appear to be the state that always initiates such a sequence, this need not necessarily be so, particularly in transitional circumstances, such as those of the Arab Spring, where the state itself may be vulnerable.

The distinction is that, for the radical, the state can, initially at least, be challenged in order to modify its hegemonic discourse whilst, for the extremist, the state is inherently illegitimate and must be replaced. Of course, to the degree that the state is unwilling to accept such challenges, regarding radical criticism as innately illegitimate and criminal, radicalism can mutate into extremism instead. Alternatively, mass opposition solidifies around the radical alternative, generating, in effect, a civil war instead, as happened with Libya. Such outcomes, too, can be influenced by external factors as well, in that the state receives external support for its refusal to deal with a radical critique. Such a development tends to support the view that the critique itself is essentially illegitimate and criminal – a securitising attitude typical of the decade after 11 September 2001. Yet, ironically enough, radicalism involves a legitimate critique of the state whereas extremism, by its total rejection of the state, does not.

An example of the way in which these processes can interact and become interdependent is provided by the experiences of the Algerian state after it achieved independence in 1962. An innate promise of the *Front de Libération Nationale* (FLN), which successfully led the struggle for independence, was that it would 'restore' the Islamic society destroyed by 132 years of French occupation. That promise was progressively betrayed over subsequent years, as the FLN itself was transformed from being a national liberation movement into a creature of the army-backed regime that took over the country. Inevitably, over time, widespread discontent emerged over this failure and increasingly coalesced into social movements challenging the state, to which the regime it encompassed responded with repression.

In response, an Islamist movement emerged as the dominant social movement that challenged the legitimacy of the regime on the grounds of its failure to honour its initial promise – a radical challenge. In October 1988, on the back of countrywide riots and the sudden reconstruction of the regime as a multi-party democracy, the *Front Islamique du Salut* (FIS) emerged as the dominant political party. Interestingly enough, its popularity was not derived solely from Islam but from the popular belief that it enshrined the original revolutionary legitimacy, subsequently betrayed, of the FLN.[5] It was on this basis that it was to contest control of the state through a legislative electoral process, whilst the presidency tried to use it to entrench presidential power. Yet its potential electoral success in December 1991 provoked renewed repression in the form of an army coup against the presidency, the suspension of legislative elections and the subsequent dissolution of the FIS itself.

This sequential interaction of opposed political forces was to generate its own quite specific outcomes, in the form of two movements challenging army rule; one radical and the other extremist. The radical movement, the *Mouvement Islamique Armé* (later to be transformed into the *Armée Islamique du Salut*) sought to coerce the new military regime into reinstating the electoral process, thus contesting power within the state. Its failure encouraged its extremist counterpart, the *Groupes Islamiques Armés* (GIA) (a coalition of disparate groups sharing a common objective), which simply sought to replace the state with an Islamic caliphate, in which violence in itself was the primary legitimating instrument by which political power could be achieved and maintained.

The upshot, of course, was the Algerian civil war, which lasted until 1999 with the loss of between 150,000 and 200,000 lives, when the GIA collapsed. Its remnants coalesced into yet another extremist group which has maintained a chronic but low level of rural violence ever since. It has also reconstituted itself into *al-Qa'ida in the Islamic Maghrib* (AQIM) which, despite its global claims, has been transformed into a largely criminalised movement still substantially directed against the Algerian state. External interest has also conflated its importance into a regional threat, thereby prolonging and intensifying the conflict between state and movement. Yet this is not the only way in which tensions between dissident and state can be resolved. The 'Arab Spring' provides us with a more recent and more acute example of the way in which popular radicalisation can find a solution to the problem of the illiberal and exclusive state.

The 'Arab Spring'

The purpose of the analysis of the 'Arab Spring' that follows is to highlight the interactive and antiphonal relationship between state and opposition which, if not resolved – either through violent confrontation or political contestation – becomes a statement about the rejection of the state. It is instructive to see to what degree the principles revealed by the Algerian experience are also relevant to an understanding of the convulsions throughout the Arab world in 2011. If the argument put forward above – that there is an inter-linkage between the state and the kind of resistance it generates through its abuse of its hegemonic position – is true, then it should emerge from the variegated experiences of Arab states in what has come to be called in the region the 'Arab Revolution' and abroad, the 'Arab Spring'. The Arab Spring, it should be recalled, began as a widespread protest in late 2010 over rapidly escalating food prices. Indeed, by the end of the year, the United Nations Food and Agriculture Office in Rome revealed that its food price index, started in 1990 at a base level of 100, had reached 231 – its highest level ever – at a time when oil prices also peaked.[6] In the Middle Eastern and North African region where levels of poverty are intense, with those living below the poverty line ranging from 20 to 40 per cent of the population on average, the consequences of such price rises are devastating. They are made worse by the growing national disparities in incomes, which are often a consequence of conventional policies of economic development. The consequence in 2010 was inchoate social discontent which expressed itself through mass popular protest.

This, in itself, however, is quite insufficient to explain the political events that followed in the wake of the mass protests. A similar regional situation in 2008, when food prices also suddenly spiked, also caused mass protest but there were no political consequences. Earlier there had been frequent mass demonstrations on a national basis over economic deprivation which, equally, had had no political consequences in countries such as Morocco, Tunisia and Jordan. Nor, surprisingly enough, had the wider failures of economic development in the Middle Eastern and North African region over many years ever generated a serious political challenge.[7] Not surprisingly, regimes did not apparently perceive political dangers arising from the demonstrations in 2010 either, for in general they responded as in the past with financial subsidies to bring down the cost of staple foodstuffs.

On this occasion, however, such perceptions turned out to be a mistake for, starting with Tunisia, the protests over economic deprivation were suddenly transformed into demonstrations challenging the political natures and failures of regimes across the region. Of course, it can be argued that there was a contagion effect in that events in Tunisia sparked off similar protests in Egypt and elsewhere, often significantly amplified by satellite television and social media.[8] In addition, there is no doubt that youth often frustrated and unemployed were key to the political protests that followed. However, none of these factors explains how such events should have been unleashed in Tunisia or why they spread in the way they did with such unpredictable and unpredicted effects. After all, there was no secret about the fact that governance throughout the region, with few exceptions, was repressive, excluded popular participation, and was exploited by corrupt and venal elites.

The answer to this conundrum may lie in two features of the governance situation in the Middle East and North Africa that are often overlooked. These were the existence of highly restricted and closely controlled civil society sectors in many regional states and the potential for organisations within them to mobilise as social movements in the appropriate circumstances. Such sectors were the consequence of pressure from the West on regional states to liberalise their political systems during the 1980s and 1990s. As a result restricted civil society arenas were created in many states, both in response to these pressures and to act as safety valves to prevent domestic demands for liberalisation from becoming too intense. Their purpose, in other words, was to enable the autocratic systems that tolerated such relatively autonomous civil institutions to perpetuate their rule. Such systems have been described by Daniel Brumberg as 'liberalized autocracies'.[9]

However, the organisations that were permitted to emerge – human rights organisations, trade unions, professional associations and even political parties – also enjoyed a degree of autonomous action, despite the strict controls that were placed upon them. In addition, by their very nature, they articulated political positions necessarily different from the prevailing orthodoxies, even if they were trimmed to avoid direct challenges to government. This meant, in effect, that they were potential social movements equipped with frames of reference that could easily be mobilised as frames of contention with the hegemonic discourses of regime and state. In short, they had immense potential for radicalisation, in the right circumstances.[10]

Moderate political Islamic movements formed a case apart, for regimes often tacitly permitted such movements, even if they were denied formal status, both to defuse social tensions and to co-opt them, if possible, as a mechanism for regime legitimisation.[11] Such movements, furthermore, had great potential as social movements through the mosque and charity networks they often controlled. It has been striking, therefore, to note that they played virtually no part, as movements, in the mass political demonstrations throughout the Arab world in 2011 that led to the changes now collectively labelled the 'Arab Spring', even if their members may have been individually engaged in them. One obvious reason has been the ambivalence such movements often felt towards the objectives of the demonstrators – demands for political participation, rather than ideological or cultural transformation often implicit and occasionally explicit in Islamist projects – since they had not initiated the demonstrations themselves. In any case, moderate Islamist movements will undoubtedly be amongst the major beneficiaries of the political and governance changes that have been brought about.

Not all of the autocratic regimes in the Middle East and North Africa accepted the 'liberalized autocracy' path in the 1980s and 1990s. Some simply did not tolerate the idea of meaningful civil society, even if under tight regime control, or otherwise, they allowed formal institutions to exist but denuded them of all content, so that they were no more than the state itself albeit under a different nomenclature. Such regimes also made it clear that no challenge to their authority would be accepted and they severely repressed any hint that emerged of potential dissidence. Indeed, challengers to their authority had to operate in clandestinity, through networks, and had no alternative but to seek to replace the regime itself, necessarily through violence. The history of the Libyan Islamic Fighting Group and its extremist confrontation with the Qadaffi regime in the late 1990s is instructive in this regard.[12] Indeed, should a direct challenge to the regime develop, as it did in February 2011 in Libya or a month later in Syria, the only outcomes could have been either the outright repression of dissident radicalism or the destruction of the regime, as occurred in October 2011 in Libya.

Amongst the liberalised autocracies, however, two further questions arise. First, what actually catalyses the emergence of social movements capable of challenging regimes and their discourses of power and, second, why do such regimes fail to repress such oppositions outright?

What the actual catalyst for contestation might be is purely arbitrary and unpredictable. In the current sequence of events it turned out to be the self-immolation of a fruit-and-vegetable seller in the South Tunisian town of Sidi Bou Zid on 17 December 2010. The event came to symbolise the tyrannical contempt (the same two terms that had characterised dissident discourse in Algeria during its civil war in the 1990s) of the Ben Ali regime towards Tunisians and it generated an immediate response, organised by local trade union branches[13], human rights groups, lawyers associations and journalists, in terms of peaceful protest and an essential demand for the removal of the regime. The Ben Ali regime itself collapsed, however, when the Tunisian army leadership, which had always been resolutely apolitical (unlike the politicised army leaderships elsewhere in the region) refused to obey orders to suppress the demonstrations and the effectively single political party, the *Rassemblement Constitutionnelle Démocratique,* which was the real heart of the regime, abandoned the presidency in order to preserve its own power. Demonstrations continued, however, until the party itself was disbanded by the Tunisian courts in March.

The effectiveness and the manner of the revolution in Tunisia certainly emboldened its sympathisers in Egypt where demonstrations erupted on 25 January 2011, just days after the Ben Ali regime collapsed. However, there had long been active challenges to the hegemonic power and discourse of the Mubarak regime. Since 2004, two movements within the politically-aware elite – *Kefaya* and *al-Ghad* – had been active. They had been joined in 2006 by a third movement, the April 6 Movement, stemming from unofficial trade union activity in the industrial cities of the Delta and, in 2010, a web-based youth movement coalesced around the image of the murdered Alexandrine youth, Khalid Said, who had been wantonly killed by two security officials. It was activists from this group that planned the initial demonstrations that caught the popular imagination in massive demonstrations against the Mubarak regime after Friday prayers on 28 January and, after weeks of continuous peace demonstrations involving millions of Egyptians, the regime was swept from power. Yet, once again, the final blow was struck by the Egyptian army command, which calculated that its interests would be best preserved by the removal of the regime in the face of such widespread popular protest. And, indeed, it is the army, which has been the core of ruling regimes in Egypt ever since the revolution in 1952, that has continued to exercise real power, despite the compromises it has made towards popular sentiment and the disgust of activists now cheated of the radical changes they had sought.

These two experiences of radicalised social movements challenging regimes, together with a series of less dramatic compromises in countries such as Morocco, Algeria and Jordan, must be contrasted with events in the Gulf, Libya and Syria. Yemen is a case apart, for it is the crucible for three, if not four, quite separate conflicts which are taking place simultaneously – a radical populist challenge to the ruling regime, now also challenged by tribal opposition, a longstanding rebellion in the north of the country, a secessionist movement in the south and a still-marginal extremist threat from al-Qa'ida in the Arabian Peninsula. In the Gulf, rulers have generally been able to buy off popular protest through financial largess. Only in Bahrain has a dispute involving economic and social discrimination masked as a sectarian quarrel challenged government, and there Saudi Arabia intervened, spurred on by its fears of Iran, domestic unrest in the Shi'a-dominated Eastern Provinces, and determination to preserve an existing order at all costs, ensuring that the challenge be neutralised — at least for now.

Libya and Syria represent two quite different situations. It is worth noting that in both cases the 'liberalized autocracy' option was never practised, although Syria experienced a brief false dawn at the start of 2000, in the 'Damascus Spring', with Bashar al-Assad's accession to power. The striking feature in both cases is that protests began as a result of internal issues and only after initial, localised protest took place was there a resonance at a national scale. In Libya, the issue was a demonstration in Benghazi over past, unsuccessful protests. It was only when a section of the army refused to fire upon protestors that the initial demonstrations escalated into a challenge to the regime itself. The inability of the regime to construct a response other than outright and total repression both incited a United Nations-sanctioned intervention by NATO to protect the civilian population (which rapidly escalated into an initiative to achieve 'regime change'[14]) and forced the opposition into the extreme position of seeking the destruction of the regime and the unique state structure associated with it – the *Libyan Arab Socialist Jamahiriyah*.

In Syria, protests began as a result of government repression in Dera'a, after a spate of anti-regime graffiti by youth there in March 2011. The unnecessary brutality of the official response provoked demonstrations which, in turn, stimulated ever greater regime violence as part of an escalating vicious circle. The amazing aspect of these antiphonal responses is that, until mid November 2011, the demonstrators were predominantly peaceful, despite the deaths of up to 4,200 people at the hands of the Syrian special forces, commanded by the president's brother, Maher Assad. The regime never wavered in its refusal to consider compromising with its opponents but, despite the typical demand of the demonstrators – 'the people want an end to the regime' – the opposition was by no means unanimous over its own objectives. There was, in fact, no unified response; representatives of the internal opposition sought accommodation, the external opposition sought regime replacement. Both, however, agreed on the principle of peaceful demonstration despite the brutality exercised by the regime.

Quite apart from the lack of unity amongst the Syrian opposition – which, by mid November, had moved into an extremist phase as army defectors began to mount their own challenge to the regime through the Free Syrian Army – the regime's irredentism reflected its own internal tensions. In many respects, the Syrian Ba'ath party had long forsaken its ideological roots. Instead it had become a party of minorities, ostensibly protecting Christians, Druze and Alawi, as well as the interests of commercial and economic elites, against the Sunni heartland. In addition, because of its internal structure, the Ba'athist old guard were quite unwilling to make concessions that might challenge its prerogatives. As a result, opportunity after opportunity was sacrificed for the chimera of maintaining unchanging political realities – with the result that a challenge that was radical and political in nature soon threatened the survival of the regime itself. In short, a challenge demanding reform became a demand for the destruction of the regime.

Implications

It is clear that the 'Arab Spring' overall was an example of the consequences of illegitimate, repressive government. It was the behaviour of government and state that provoked antiphonal mass popular resistance. In addition, it was the existence of proto-social movements within restricted civil society sectors that enabled inchoate anger to be channelled into coherent frames of contention to the hegemonic discourse of the state and into structures through which such contention could be meaningfully articulated. And, finally, it was the fragmentation of regimes under such pressure that produced dialectical outcomes that offered the possibilities of more hopeful futures. Essential to this process, however, was the initial compromise made by such regimes decades before to mobilise the potential of autonomous political action, albeit under strict control, as a mechanism for relieving the alienation and anomie[15] caused by unrestrained repression.

Interestingly, those states, such as Libya and Syria, in which no such mechanisms existed, found themselves engaged in effective civil war, once they were challenged, or their reactions to radical challenge forced extremist responses. In that respect, they emulated the experience of Algeria in the 1990s where an army-backed refusal to contemplate ideological and political compromise resulted in a five-year-long civil war. We do not yet know, however, what the ultimate outcomes of such confrontations on this occasion will be or how states will resolve the contradictions about outcomes that may emerge. Perhaps the most important aspect of the 'Arab Spring', however, consists of the way in which it has illuminated the effects of radicalisation within the process of democratic transition.

In the chapters which follow, the issues of radicalisation and the conditions which produce it are treated both in terms of literary archetypes and political praxis, as well as in the context of counter-radicalisation strategies. Although the dominant geographic arena is the Middle East, attention is also paid to spill-over effects in Europe and the United States, resulting from cultural tensions attendant on migration. The aim has been to provide, as far as possible, insights into the phenomenon of radicalisation in the post 11 September 2001 era and of perceptions of radicalisation that have emerged since then.

Thus Hugh Goddard examines the journeys of Ziauddin Sardar and Ed Husain from youthful radicalism as part of a search for identity towards mature appreciation of the true significance of Islam. Not all Muslims in migration achieve such outcomes alone; Jose Liht, Sara Savage and Ryan J. Williams describe a programme designed to help the process of deradicalisation whilst Johnny Ryan discusses the real role of the Internet in the radicalisation process. He points out that, although it has an enormous potential to disseminate the radical vision, it also has the potential to spontaneously undermine the degree of radicalism involved. Roxane Farmanfarmaian analyses the link between radicalisation and securitisation, as exemplified in Mohsen Hamid's *The Reluctant Fundamentalist*, an imagined monologue of a former emigrant to the United States and directed towards a mysterious and menacing American visitor to Pakistan.

The remainder of the book consists of a series of country studies of radicalisation in the Middle East. It begins with an analysis of political Islam in Egypt by Ezzedine Choukri Fishere who argues that, under the Mubarak regime and after the Tahrir revolution in 2011, the Islamist project(s) in Egypt have now become part of – perhaps the predominant part of – the political mainstream. Raphaël Lefevre analyses religious radicalisation in Syria, as seen in the development of the Muslim Brotherhood, which culminated in the Hama massacre of 1982, but which then reconstituted itself as a movement seeking peaceful engagement with the country's Ba'athist rulers. Nasser Kalawoun examines the role of Tripoli as the focus of Sunni radicalisation in Lebanon, finding its origins in the attempts of its leading families, cut off from their natural hinterland in Syria by the French mandate system, to break into the new national politics of Beirut.

Clive Jones reminds us that radicalisation in the Middle East is not just a Muslim phenomenon by examining the *Hardal* in Israel – the youth movement responsible for the creation of unofficial settlements in the West Bank which the Israeli government has been unable or unwilling to curb, despite the consequences this will have for any future peace arrangement between Israel and Palestine. James Spencer looks at radicalisation in Iraq during the insurgency that followed the American invasion in 2003, arguing that much of the so-called radicalisation identified by Western observers had more to do with national outrage at what had come to be seen as an occupation, rather than a liberation. Ayla Göl examines radicalisation amongst the Kurds, focussing on the Kurdish Workers' Party violence in Turkey in order to demonstrate the historical dialectic that is embedded in the evolution of such movements. Arshin Adib-Moghaddam discusses the concepts of radicalism and revolution in the context of contemporary Iran. He examines the trajectory of radicalism in the history of the Islamic Republic, arguing that this is of crucial importance in understanding the wider phenomenon in geopolitical and philosophical terms. Abdullah Baabood concludes the book by examining political Islam and radicalism amongst the Gulf states, thereby casting fresh light on a region normally dominated by discussions of commercial success and oil.

It is not possible within the confines of a single volume to treat all these issues as comprehensively as they require. Nevertheless, the aim has been to try to illuminate aspects of these issues that have tended to be ignored in the reconstruction of the Middle East and political Islam as a systemic and existential threat to Western concepts of universal civilisation. This was, after all, the consequence of the securitisation that external powers imposed on the region in response to the events of 11 September 2001.

Notes

1. Joffé, George. (ed.) 2011. *Islamist Radicalisation in North Africa: Politics and Process*. Routledge: London.
2. According to the *New Shorter Oxford English Dictionary*, a political radical is defined as someone 'advocating thorough or far-reaching change' whilst an extremist is a person who advocates 'drastic or immoderate measures'.
3. Weber, M. 1919. 'Politics as a vocation', in Weber M., Owen D.S., Strong, T.B., (eds.), Livingstone, R. (trans.), *The Vocation Lectures*.
4. 'The state is the actuality of the ethical idea', Hegel, G.W.F., (trans Knox, T.M.). 1991. *The Philosophy of Right*, prop.257.
5. Joffé, G. 2011. 'Trajectories of radicalisation: Algeria 1989–1999,' in Joffé, op.cit., pp.114–137.
6. FAO. 2011. http://www.fao.org/news/story/en/item/50519/icode/ : Accessed 29 April 2011. USEIA. 2011. http://www.eia.doe.gov/steo/ : Accessed 29 April 2011.
7. See, for example, Joffé, E.G.H. 2009. 'Morocco's reform process: wider implications', *Mediterranean Politics*, 14 (2), pp.151–165.

8. See Nanabhay, M., and Farmanfarmaian, R. 2011. 'From spectacle to spectacular: how physical space, social media and mainstream broadcast amplified the public sphere in Egypt's "Revolution"', *Journal of North African Studies*, 16 (4) (Special Issue: North Africa's Arab Spring), pp.573–603.

9. Brumberg argues that, from the 1980s to the 2000s, there was a transition away from authoritarianism and then back again, based on tactical political openings designed to sustain, rather than transform, autocracies there. This was mistaken by opposition actors in the region and external powers as an inherently unstable equilibrium giving way to competitive democracy, whereas the liberalised autocracies that were created, unlike full autocracies that made no concession to political sensitivities, were far more durable than imagined. In fact, the combination of guided pluralism, controlled elections and selective repression was not 'just a survival strategy by authoritarian regimes but a type of political system whose institutions, rule and logic defy any linear model of democratization'. Brumberg, D. 2002. 'The trap of liberalized autocracy', *Journal of Democracy*, 13 (4), p.56.

10. See Wiktorowicz, Q. 2004. 'Introduction', in Wiktorowicz, Q. (ed.) *Islamic activism: a social movement theory approach*, pp.1–9.

11. Algeria, once again, provides an example of this as early as the late 1980s in the way in which the Ben Chadli presidency tried to exploit the FIS. See Joffé, G. 'Trajectories of radicalisation'. op.cit., pp.114–137.

12. Gambill, G. 2005. 'The Libyan Islamic Fighting Group (LIFG)', *Terrorism Monitor*, 3 (6), 23 March 2005. See also Pargeter, A. 2008. *The new frontiers of Jihad: radical Islam in Europe*, pp.65–73.

13. The Tunisian trade union federation, the *Union Générale des Travailleurs Tunisiens*, had long been at odds with the regime, which had constantly tried to control it. Regime control, however, never reached down to local branches, even if the central leadership was controlled.

14. Roberts, H. 2011. 'Who said that Gaddafi had to go?', *London Review of Books*, 33 (22), 17 November 2011.

15. 'Anomie': a lack of social norms, fracturing of collective structures. See Durkheim, E. 1893, 1984. *The Division of Labour in Society*, 'Introduction'.

Bibliography

Brumberg, D. 2002. 'The trap of liberalized autocracy', *Journal of Democracy*, 13 (4).

Durkheim, E. 1893; 1984. *The Division of Labour in Society*. Macmillan: London; Coser: LA.

Gambill, G. 2005. 'The Libyan Islamic Fighting Group (LIFG)', *Terrorism Monitor*, 3 (6), 23 March.

Hegel, G.W.F. 1991. *The Philosophy of Right*, (translated by T.M. Knox). Cambridge University Press: Cambridge.

Joffé, E.G.H. 2009. 'Morocco's reform process: wider implications', *Mediterranean Politics*, 14 (2), July.

Joffé, G. (ed.) 2011. *Islamist Radicalisation in North Africa: Politics and Process*. Routledge: London.

—— 2011. 'Trajectories of radicalisation: Algeria 1989–1999,' in Joffé, G. (ed.) *Islamist Radicalisation in North Africa: Politics and Process*. Routledge: London.

Nanabhay, M., and Farmanfarmaian, R. 2011. 'From spectacle to spectacular: how physical space, social media and mainstream broadcast amplified the public sphere in Egypt's "Revolution"', *Journal of North African Studies*, 16 (4) Special Issue: North Africa's Arab Spring.

Pargeter, A. 2008. *The New Frontiers of Jihad: Radical Islam in Europe*. I.B.Tauris: London.

Roberts, H. 2011. 'Who said that Gaddafi had to go?' *London Review of Books*, 33 (22), 17 November.

Weber, M. 1919; 2004. 'Politics as a vocation,' in Weber, M., Owen D.S., (ed.), Strong T.B., (ed.), Livingstone, R. (translated), in *The Vocation Lectures*. Hackett Publishing Company: Indiana, Indianapolis.

Wiktorowicz, Q. (ed.) 2004. *Islamic Activism: A Social Movement Theory Approach*. Indiana University Press: Bloomington and Indianapolis.

2

A BIOGRAPHICAL APPROACH TO RADICALISATION: ZIAUDDIN SARDAR'S *DESPERATELY SEEKING PARADISE* AND ED HUSAIN'S *THE ISLAMIST*

Hugh Goddard

The genesis of the conference on which this volume is based, if I understand it correctly, is a research programme into 'radicalisation' in North Africa. The geographical remit of the discussion has been extended, however, to include other regions of the Middle East, and this chapter is going to push the boundaries out even further, firstly to the area beyond the eastern frontier of the Middle East, namely Pakistan, and secondly to the area beyond the western frontier of the Middle East, namely Europe, and particularly the United Kingdom. This might, I hope, offer some useful comparative insights, and the extension of the geographical focus of the discussion is a clear pointer, of course, to the extent to which, in the era of modern methods of transport and of communication, some of the traditional boundaries encapsulated in British Area Studies programmes are becoming redundant.

This chapter will focus, firstly, on biography (or autobiography), in order to, in a sense, personalise the discussion of a theme which is often investigated simply in terms of a social process, namely radicalisation; and secondly on the life stories of two significant British Muslims in particular, namely Ziauddin Sardar and Ed Husain.

Before we begin, however, it is worth noting that the key root word in the title of this book, 'radical', is a word which in an Islamic context is now almost always viewed negatively, so that 'radicalisation' is normally seen as a problem, in much the same way as is the case with 'fundamentalism'. In many other contexts, however, 'radical' is often seen in a very positive light, meaning 'thorough' or 'complete'. The word itself is therefore considerably more ambivalent than it often appears in the context of Islamic revivalism.

Ziauddin Sardar

The first of our authors, whose autobiography is entitled *Desperately Seeking Paradise: Journeys of a Sceptical Muslim* (London: Granta, 2004), was born in 1951 in the village of Dipalpur, in the province of Punjab, Northern Pakistan, in a 'contested area' near the frontier with India (p.21). The village was confirmed as part of Pakistan, but the author's father moved to London, to work in a car factory, presumably Ford at Dagenham, and the rest of the family followed soon after to live in Hackney. That was therefore where he went to school. Alongside this he describes in Chapter 3 the process of learning the Qur'an with his mother: 'with the skill of an F.R. Leavis...my mother was very good at confusing me' (p.43), while '[t]hroughout this conversation my father remained silent. His speciality was sitting quietly and fuming' (p.44).

The author describes how he established a branch of FOSIS (Federation of Student Islamic Societies) while still at school, as an act of youthful idealism. 'It fell to us to set the juggernaut of Islamic history back on the rails' (p.27). He heard the revivalist author A.A. Mawdudi in London in 1969, and was impressed by his rejection of revolution, and his espousal of an alternative 'reformative' method, but he also concluded that his vision was utopian, and he was certainly not impressed by Mawdudi's views on women, whom he decided

Mawdudi saw as 'innately inferior' (p.32). He looked at both the Muslim Brotherhood, as a Middle Eastern revivalist organisation, and the *Jama'at-i-Islami*, as a South Asian one, but his verdict was that 'the mindless slogans appeared to me nothing more than a prescription for totalitarianism' (p.36). They allowed no room for doubt: 'Islam, for them, was an ideology that allowed for no imperfections, no deviation, and, in the final analysis, no humanity. That is why I found so many of them so repugnant' (p.38).

He then migrated through, or round, firstly, the *Tablighi Jama'at* (a 'pietist' South Asian group), in which he became involved in 1972, participating in 'missions' to Sheffield and Glasgow which are described in some detail in Chapter 1 of *Paradise Awakened*; he describes *tabligh* (literally 'communication' or 'preaching') as 'the exact equivalent of ... earnest young Mormons' (p.3), but after these experiences he describes, on p.21, how '[i]t was evident the *Tablighi* route was not for me, but I could not dismiss the matter of paradise as easily'. The search of the title of the book had evidently begun.

He moved on to learn about what he calls the classical Islamic tradition, sitting at the feet of Jaffar Shaikh Idris, a Sudanese theologian who was working on a doctorate in philosophy in Cambridge: 'his eyes, far from reflecting monolithic certainty, refracted a mischievous curiosity' (p.47). He went on to study law, philosophy and exegesis, Qur'an, hadith and tafsir in an *usrah* family/study group: 'I encountered an outlook that was startlingly fresh ... These authentic voices ... were more critical and less certain of their opinions' (p.49). This study group provided 'a sustaining diet of critical thought' (p.52), but Sardar notes that Jaffar's views changed quite significantly later, when he took up a teaching position in Saudi Arabia (p.52).

In his mid 20s he was therefore leading a double life: 'During the week I was an "Islamic activist" in the sense that I circulated among the various activities of FOSIS and the doings of the Muslim community ... But at the weekends I became a socialist, active in the Hackney Citizens' Rights Group' (p.53). But '[w]eekdays or weekends, I met and mingled with idealist young people like myself, all with a burning desire to change the world for the better' (p.53), meaning that his world was one of 'across belongings' (p.53).

He went on to become the General Secretary of FOSIS, but underwent something of a crisis because of the reaction to the publication of 'what should have been the innocuous, underwhelming and entirely inoffensive *The Muslim Student's Guide to Britain*' (p.54) with Dawud Rosser-Owen. The latter was a Welsh Muslim studying International Relations at the University of Kent in Canterbury who had converted to Islam while serving with the British army in Malaysia (p.54). The problem was that some of the information contained in the *Guide* turned out to be inaccurate, and the strongly negative reaction to this on the part of some of the senior members of FOSIS brought about considerable disillusionment for Sardar.

He moved on to 'a different, "less arid", more tolerant and humane variety of Islam', represented by Sheikh Nazim Adil Haqqani, a Cypriot Sufi who had arrived in the UK in the early 1970s and claimed to be the 40th Grand Sheikh of the Naqshbandi Sufi order (p.61). Educated as a chemical engineer at Istanbul University he had 'a strong spiritual presence' and an 'aura of spirituality' (p.62).

Sardar's family then moved house to a new council flat, which turned out to be near the *zawiya* of another Sufi group, the Darqawi order whose local activities were co-ordinated by Sheikh Abdul Qadir, another (this time Scottish) convert to Islam who had embraced the tradition following a visit to Morocco. He found himself listening to a rather flowery commendation of him by his deputy, which is recorded on pp.64–65. The Darqawi *wird* (cf *dhikr*, literally 'litany') involved music, chanting, rhythmical breathing, and dance, and '[i]t was powerful, intoxicating stuff' (p.68). It was also, however, Sardar concluded, an example of 'the guru syndrome' of the 1970s, which 'was becoming a general epidemic' (p.69), a view which seemed to be confirmed when Abdul Qadir was 'electrified' by the teachings of Qadi Ayad, and moved from London to Norwich to establish 'a pure "Muslim village" which turned out to be a retreat-cum-military garrison' (p.70), and where Abdul Qadir's manifesto *Jihad: a ground plan*, 'a programme to establish the rule of Islam all over the world' (p.70) was published, including a call for the currency system throughout the Muslim world to be replaced by a gold dinar (p.71).

The author then decided to visit Fez for himself to learn more about the group. While admiring many aspects of the city's life, which had 'a powerful hypnotic effect' as a result of its ability to produce 'a time warp in which the parallel universes of past and present appeared to coexist' (p.72), nonetheless the experience also caused some concern as '[t]he whole panoply created by Sufi orders complicated, making different, special and abstruse what should be effortless and openly available...' (p.73).

He travelled on to Konya, to visit the tomb of Jalal al-din Rumi, and to Aksehir, to visit the tomb of Nasruddin Hoca, and as a result of further reflections on the basis of these experiences, did not reject Sufism per se but did conclude that 'as a collective spiritual path, Sufism does not produce a viable and equitable social order' (p.84).

I could go on, as I have summarised not even the first half of the book, but it is from this period, the mid 1970s, that Sardar began to travel more widely and to spend longer periods in different parts of the Middle East, 'a veritable Clapham Junction of routes to paradise' (p.88). He visited the wider Islamic world too, including Iran in 1974, Iraq, Syria, Jordan and the UAE, and then a longer period in Saudi Arabia on the staff of the Hajj Research Centre, for which he worked between 1974 and 1979, a period which merits two chapters in the book.

There are then further reflections on The Muslim Institute in London, under Kalim Siddiqui, the Centre for Policy and Future Studies at the East-West University in Chicago, directed by Dr Wasiullah Khan, and on the idea of the Islamisation of Knowledge, as associated with Isma'il al-Faruqi, before musings on his time spent in Pakistan in the era of General Zia (with all the debates at that time about the implementation of Shari'a), in China, in Turkey, and in Malaysia, with an intervening chapter about the Satanic Verses controversy. A recurring theme in this part of the book is the repeated raising and then dashing of the hopes inspired either by particular individuals (e.g. Anwar Ibrahim in Malaysia) or institutions or groups (such as the Ijmalis, established in Chicago, with 'their passionate commitment to liberating Islam from a fossilised tradition and religious obscurantism' (p.209), leading to 'despair, disillusion and dejection' (p.332).

For our purposes, however, it is the earlier part of the book which is more significant, tracing as it does with remarkable candour Sardar's attempts as a young man to find both a set of ideas and a group of people to which he could commit himself, in his search for meaning and identity.

Such searches, of course, are not a uniquely modern phenomenon. From the period of classical Islam it is possible to point to the experience of no less a figure than al-Ghazali, who in his *al-munqidh min al-dalal* (Deliverance from Error) outlines his personal life-pilgrimage through philosophy, theology, Shi'ism and Sufism, pursuing different options and schools of thought until finding what he eventually perceived to be the 'best option', namely Sufism. And there are obvious parallels in other traditions, including the lives of Justin Martyr and Augustine of Hippo within the early history of the Christian tradition.

Sardar remains a prolific author, of both books and journalism, about Muslim-majority societies and Muslims in Britain, and *Desperately Seeking Paradise* has been described by some as the *first volume* of his autobiography, so it will be interesting to see if he is able to carry the story forward, both in the sense of his own life journey and of his reflections on the wider journey of the *umma*.

Ed Husain (Muhammed Husain)

Secondly, as a representative of a different generation, and of a different part of the Islamic World, given that his ancestral connections are with Bangladesh, let us have a look at Ed (that is Mohammed) Husain, whose book *The Islamist*, when it was published by Penguin in 2007, aroused a huge amount of interest both within and beyond the Muslim community.

Born on Christmas Day 1975 in East London (Mile End), Husain's life journey is in one sense summarised in the subtitle of his book, 'Why I joined radical Islam in Britain, what I saw inside and why I left', and in the blurb on the back cover: '[w]hen I was sixteen I became an Islamic fundamentalist. Five years later, after much emotional turmoil, I rejected fundamentalist teachings and returned to normal life and my family.'

In slightly more detail, however, Husain describes his formative years in Limehouse, including the influence on his family of Shaikh Abd al-Latif, a Sufi *pir* from Sylhet, who was affectionately known in the family as 'Grandpa'. He helped (Muhamm)ed with his Qur'an recitation, which he undertook in mosques all over England and South Wales, and he comments '[i]n many ways, I suppose I was a sort of Muslim choirboy' (p.14).

Teenage rebellion, however, produced a desire for extra religious education even outside school hours – 'I desired everything to do with Islam' (p.20) – and the textbook which was used for this purpose by Mrs Rainey, the (Anglican) head of the Religious Studies department at the school, *Islam: Beliefs and Teachings* by Ghulam Sarwar, introduced Ed for the first time to the idea of the Islamic state, commending the activities of the Muslim Brotherhood and the *Jama'at-i-Islami* towards that end. This was an understanding of Islam very different from that which had been imparted within his family, so 'I, at sixteen, was already wondering why my parents had never spoken about this most important aspect of our religion, the Islamic state' (p.22). 'Perhaps Grandpa was wrong, I thought' (p.23).

This led to the assertion of a new identity, 'young, Muslim, studious, and London born' (p.23). Ed's allegiance shifted from the (Sufi-oriented) Brick Lane Mosque to the (Mawdudi-oriented) East London mosque. The book conveys very effectively the author's excitement at his first visit there, in comparison with the other mosque: '[t]here I was a young boy, in my father's shadow: here the place was buzzing with young, trim-bearded, English-speaking activists' (p.27), and not only that but they took an active interest in their new visitor: 'I felt I could easily become part of this highly organised robust network of brothers who led a mosque-centred life. At Brick Lane mosque the elders only stroked my head to acknowledge me. It was my father they engaged with; I was merely his little boy. The people here were interested in *me*. To an isolated schoolboy, that mattered' (p.28).

There followed a period of increasing tension with his parents as a result of Ed's involvement with the (Mawdudi-oriented) YMO (Young Muslim Organisation). The YMO provided friends, a place in the world, and answers (p.32). It also provided friends and a cause (p.33).

The author describes how he used to lie to his parents in order to attend Saturday evening sessions at the mosque (p.33). He read A.A. Mawdudi's *Let us be Muslims* (p.34). 'I was sixteen years old and I had *no* white friends. My world was entirely Asian, fully Muslim. This was my Britain. Against this backdrop, the writings of Sarwar's guru, Mawdudi, took me to a radically new level' (p.35).

He goes on to describe how he smuggled Mawdudi's books into the house with paper covers on them, as he knew that his father would not tolerate them. 'Now I was not a mere *Muslim*, like all the others I knew; I was better, superior' (p.36). He now thought of himself as a *true* Muslim.

His parents were seriously concerned about this sudden outburst of religious fervour, and the view that 'God...had to be sought out in activism, drive, energy, mobilising and expanding the Islamic movement. I had to be a "true Muslim", completely enmeshed in Islam, not a "partial Muslim" like my parents' (p.39). His father eventually came to find him at the mosque (pp.40–41), but then walked away, deeply hurt at his son's desertion of his family. YMO members, however, described the incident as a test of commitment, 'like the experience of the prophet Abraham' (p.41). Long debates followed with his parents, who were 'vehemently opposed to my version of Islam' (p.42). This led to an ultimatum: 'leave Mawdudi's Islamism or leave my house' (p.44).

Unable to accept two authorities, one night, late in the summer, I wrote a farewell note to my parents, left it on my pillow, and crept out of the house while they slept. I left home for the Islamic movement without a penny in my pocket and with only the clothes I was wearing (p.45).

He headed for the mosque, with mixed feelings. 'I felt it was a fight between my father and me: I had to win. By challenging me my father had challenged the Islamic movement' (p.45). His mother accused the mosque of kidnapping her innocent, naïve son' (p.46).

After three nights he returned home: his father was forgiving, his mother less so. 'She and my father on the Day of Judgement, before God, would no longer be responsible for my involvement with Islamism. From today I was answerable only to God. I had got my way and I was free to do what I wanted without my parents' interference. I was glad' (p.47). He went on to become President of the Islamic Society at Tower Hamlets College: 'with parental obstacles out of the way, my zeal and commitment to Islamism were unconfined' (p.47).

The works of Hasan al-Banna and Sayyid Qutb came to dominate the author's thinking, as represented by the 1960s slogan of the Muslim Brotherhood, 'Islam is the solution'. His father wept when he displayed a poster of a saying of Hasan al-Banna (p.52). He continued his campus *da'wa* activities, however. 'To offend us was to offend God. We had played on their sensitivities of guilt, shame, and humiliation' (p.63). 'In six months we had changed the entire atmosphere at college' (p.65).

Something of a challenge came, interestingly, from the Muslim sisters at college, who seemed to adopt the same 'holier than thou' attitude towards the male members of the YMO as they adopted towards others (p.68). Speakers began to be invited to college from other more 'radical' groups, such as *Jamiat Ihyaa Minhajj al-Sunnah* (JIMAS), the Movement for the Revival of the Prophet's Way) and *Hizb ut-Tahrir* (The Party of Liberation). New black, white and Asian converts seemed to 'leapfrog' over the Islamists in the strictness of their practice, particularly once again the female members, who displayed a 'holier-than-thou' attitude towards other women (p.71).

The author decided to consult his father, as the fount of traditional knowledge of Islam. These were Wahhabis, he explained, whose literalist approach was evidently attractive to many students. Several students left for jihad training in Afghanistan. 'Qutb's *Milestones* combined with Wahhabi literalism made a potent and dangerous cocktail' (p.73).

The Balkan crisis of 1993 radicalised many. *Hizb ut-Tahrir's* international nature and its specific proposal to re-establish the Islamic state, the *khilafa* or caliphate, proved highly attractive. 'I was disgruntled with YMO's obsession with the Bangladeshi community, lack of intellectual vigour, and complete failure to provide an answer to the Bosnia issue' (p.76). The YMO seemed parochial. The gradualism of

Mawdudi began to lose its attraction. *Hizb ut-Tahrir*, by contrast, was a radical organisation, with 'a clear methodology for dealing with all the problems of the world' (p.78). Islam was presented as being God's system of government, and *Hizb ut-Tahrir* as 'the only group in the world who really will implement it' (through a military coup) (p.78). David, a white convert, said that '[t]he West will shake and crumble. The flag of Islam will rise above Downing Street...' (p.79). 'David's sense of conviction was overpowering, his oratory unmatched by anything I had heard in Muslim circles before' (p.79). 'His ability to answer any question I put to him, his brimming confidence, and radical vision for a future world order were attractive to me, a disillusioned teenage Islamist' (p.79). David invited the author to a meeting at the London School of Economics which was to be addressed by Omar Bakri, the 'charismatic, pugnacious leader of Hizb ut-Tahrir' (p.80), who took the lecture theatre by storm. Many second-generation British Muslims and converts were seduced. The author himself joined, as the *Hizb ut-Tahrir* had 'a higher intellectual calibre' (p.85), and 'strategic vision' (p.86). It was 'global' (p.88), and transcended colour, nationality, and language (p.92).

There was 'an inbuilt culture of aggressive argumentation, dogged debate, and an inherent ability to cause offence that helped us thrive. We were taught "Never defend, always offend." With our radical ideas of world domination we set ourselves apart from the other Islamist groups in Britain' (p.100). Very few British Muslims could resist or stand up. 'We knew how to deny, lie, and deflect' (p.101).

Between 1992 and 1993 the group made a big impact on campuses. '[W]e had the loudest voices and the cleverest ideas' (p.105). Debates were organised with Paul Foot and Fred Haliday (sic). 'Our style of debate... was confrontational, designed to provoke outrage' (p.105).

A challenge came, however, from the members of the YMO, who opposed the author now that he had shifted his allegiance to *Hizb ut-Tahrir*. After a hostile meeting, he resigned, but the committee passed a vote of no confidence and expelled him from the Islamic Society (pp.108–110). The author's reaction was interesting: 'for the first time in months, if not years, I remembered Grandpa' (Shaikh Abd al-Latif, the Sufi *pir* from Sylhet who was affectionately known by this title within the author's family, as outlined above) (p.109), and '[o]n the bus home that day, for the first time in years, I cried' (p.110).

He continued, however, to confront mosque congregations, at the East London mosque, the Christian Street mosque, controlled by members of the *Tablighi Jamat*, and at the Regent's Park mosque. 'There was nothing Muslim about our conduct' (p.122). But these confrontations began to sow the seeds of doubt: 'What sort of human beings was the Hizb creating?' (p.128). This led to the realisation that 'my inner consciousness of God had hit an all-time low' (p.146). 'If we were working to establish God's rule on earth...then Hizb ut-Tahrir activists were the most unlikely candidates God could have chosen. My comrades were heady and headstrong young people' (p.146). 'I was no longer an observant Muslim' (p.146). 'I was getting older, and the Hizb seemed suddenly like pretentious, counterfeit intellectualism' (p.146). 'My life was consumed by fury, inner confusion, a desire to dominate everything, and my abject failure to be a good Muslim' (p.148). 'As an Islamist I had lost my ability to smile' (p.148).

Salvation, if that is not too strong a word, or perhaps deliverance, came through a good Bangladeshi woman, Faye (Fatima), whom the author subsequently married. Through their relationship the author describes how he was in a sense re-humanised, and found his spiritual relationship to God restored. She 'spoke of a God that was close, loving, caring, facilitating, forgiving, and merciful...I, by contrast, believed in a God who was full of vengeance, a legislator, a controller, a punisher' (p.149). When a Nigerian Christian student was murdered on campus a short time later, partly as a result of *Hizb ut-Tahrir's* rhetoric about separation and superiority, this proved a 'wake-up call' (p.153).

The next chapter of the book, Chapter Nine, is therefore called 'Farewell Fanaticism', and in it the author outlines how he realised that '[i]t was time to stand back and think again' (p.156). Intellectual liberation came through the study of history, at the University of North London. 'The Hizb's mental barriers were not easily broken down' (p.157), and particular acknowledgement is given of the contribution to this process of Professor Denis Judd, a historian of empire: 'he nurtured my mind with academic rigour, critical thinking, and fresh interpretation' (p.157). Studying provided a fresh experience of humanity. 'Were my intellectual heroes cardboard men?' (p.160). He began to think so, and encounters with the Islamic Society of Britain and the Muslim Association of Britain led to further reflection, and then to a chance to listen to a tape of an address by the American sheikh Hamza Yusuf Hanson. 'He explained Islam in a way that I could relate to' (p.175). Further input came from the Cambridge theologian Tim Winter and the American Sufi Nuh Keller (p.175). The conclusion of this period of reflection was that 'I had tried to be a Muslim and felt as though I had failed' (p.178). 'There was a sense of burnout' (p.178).

1997 represented, in a sense, a new beginning, both for the country, with the election of Tony Blair, and for the author, who joined the Labour Party, in clear defiance and rejection of the teachings of Hizb ut-Tahrir. He graduated, and joined HSBC, working at their branch in Holborn. 'I forgot that I had ever been an activist with Hizb ut-Tahrir...At HSBC I adapted well. The energy and drive that I had previously deployed in Islamist activities, I now used to advance my career and improve my life' (p.180). 'My parents at last had something to be pleased about' (p.182). 'But I was fooling myself as well as my loved ones. Really I was a sleeper Islamist, anti-American, anti-Israeli' (p.183).

Some disillusionment with the ethos of banking then followed. 'Mortgage slavery was not my idea of living the dream any more than the darkness of a life in Islamism' (p.183). 'My snappy silk tie began to feel like a corporate noose' (p.184). He therefore went on a mosque retreat for the last ten days of Ramadan on the eve of the year 2000 and the coming of the new millennium. Metamorphosis followed. 'I was in search of spiritual solace, meaning for my life, and whoever offered it would win my commitment' (p.186). The author investigated Buddhism, Hinduism, Judaism and Christianity. At the turn of the millennium, he decided that the way ahead for him lay in Sufism. 'Sufi-oriented scholars helped me anchor my soul after five years of political Islamism, a shallow, anger-ridden, aggression-fuelled form of political belief, based on exploiting Islam's adherents but remote from Islam's teachings' (p.190). Augustine of Hippo is quoted to the effect that 'the true philosopher is the lover of God' (p.190). 'Now, in humility, I found a new energy' (p.190).

August 2000 saw the author married, to Faye, with the honeymoon being spent in Turkey, which provided further opportunities for Sufi encounters. 'Such were the real men of God' (p.193). He had his first encounter with Rumi. 'For a thirteenth-century Muslim scholar, Rumi was remarkably liberal and insightful' (p.194). Shortly afterwards he met Dr Tim Winter in Cambridge: 'I discovered much that day in Cambridge, but one simple but crucial phrase stands out: "it depends"' (p.197). This was a call to consider alternatives, and '[t]o a former Islamist with a polarised view of the world, Dr Winter's nuanced response was a mighty eye-opener' (p.197). 'By the middle of 2001 I was committed to spiritual Islam.... Islamism...was distant, buried, history' (p.198). The events of 11 September 2001 revealed the persistence of some elements of Islamism, however. 'Any attack on the bullyboy of the world...was certainly good news for the rest of us' (p.203), he thought, so he prepared to celebrate. His Sufi friends, however, were aghast: '*astaghfirullah*'...Seek refuge in God' (or may God forgive you) (p.204).

Further study then followed, at the School of Oriental and African Studies (SOAS) in London and in Damascus, and '[m]y years of Islamist ranting now seemed so hollow, meaningless, and destructive' (p.215). Damascus, the city on the road to which St Paul saw the light, proved a good place to discuss inter-faith dialogue and the relationship between Islam and Christianity (p.219). He decided to change his name to Ed, and spent much time in the mosque above the tomb of Ibn Arabi, the patron saint of Damascus, who argued that the way to reach God 'combined virtue, knowledge, and experience' (p.220). His family visited, and through the study of the Arabic language he came to realise that '[t]he spirit of the Prophet's teachings has been lost among Muslims in the West' (p.223), particularly as a result of the harsh judgements which have been formulated there about others, for example Christians.

There followed some time in London and then in Jeddah, working for the British Council, before returning to England for postgraduate study at SOAS, and then helping to establish the Quilliam Foundation.

He attended a public debate on 'The Future of Islam' at the LSE, where the speakers were Ziauddin Sardar and Tariq Ramadan, who 'locked horns over their conflicting visions of "the future"', but 'were united in their call for a rereading of the Koran, and a fundamental reinterpretation of the meaning of the sources of Islamic law' (p.273).

'I returned to Britain because I believe it is my home' (p.282), even though the rise of the Far Right indicates that it is far from perfect. Many British Muslims 'are quietly developing a rich, vibrant Muslim subculture . . . incorporating the best aspects of their multi-faceted heritage' (p.284), even though many Muslims ask 'what are we supposed to integrate into. "Big Brother" lifestyle? . . . Binge drinking?' (p.284). The conclusion is that 'a British Islam is emerging', and '[t]he future of Islam is being shaped now' (p.286), in terms of which direction it will take.

Overall, *The Islamist* is thus a fascinating account of a 'radical' change of view and direction, and in the preface Husain himself draws some interesting comparisons with other people whose opinions changed radically during the course of their lives:

> Pope Benedict XVI, for a host of reasons, found himself a member of the Hitler Youth. St Paul, a Pharisaic persecutor of Christians, became a believer in Christ and spread the faith into Rome and beyond. Tony Blair, once an ardent activist in the Campaign for Nuclear Disarmament, ended up with his finger on Britain's nuclear trigger (p.xi).

And in his case his path has led from *Hizb ut-Tahrir* to being the Co-director of the Quilliam Foundation, which campaigns against extremism and for pluralism.

Discussion

Put together, these two books are vivid accounts of the spiritual journeys of two Muslim men from South Asian backgrounds growing up in Britain, and of their search for the authentic Muslim tradition, with all the travails, on many different levels, which that search involved.

Husain in particular comes close, with hindsight, to using the language of 'conversion' and 'deconversion', so radical was the nature of his change of world-view, but Sardar too, with his account of his spiritual journey, through a huge variety of schools of thought and organisations, sometimes seems to come close to this language too.

In a sense they might each appear to be classic examples of the 'angry young man', to quote the phrase based on the 1951 autobiography of Leslie Paul which came to be applied to the work of John Osborne, such as his 1956 play *Look back in anger*, and the work of other British playwrights of his generation. Husain in particular, however, has in a sense ceased to be angry, having mellowed considerably since parting company with *Hizb ut-Tahrir*, and there is an interesting contrast here with some of the next generation of angry young men in Britain, for example Christopher Hitchens and Martin Amis, who stayed angry, even if they changed what they were angry about!

In both autobiographies it is clear that a key role in the process of change is played by personal factors such as family dynamics, friendships and marriage, and this is portrayed particularly graphically by Husain. One other crucial factor seems to be the subject chosen to study, particularly at university level. It is quite difficult to ascertain the subject of Sardar's degree, but it was probably a scientific one, given the work he went to do for scientific journals in the 1980s. For Husain, however, it was clearly the study of history which had a dramatic effect on his intellectual journey.

In this context the very thorough 2007 Oxford Sociology research paper by Diego Gambetta and Steffen Hertog, entitled 'Engineers of the Jihad', is important. Based on an analysis of the biographies of 404 Islamists, they draw attention to the extent to which graduates in science, medicine and engineering figure prominently in Islamist movements both in Muslim-majority and Muslim-minority contexts, with engineers playing a particularly significant role in groups seeking to construct an Islamic state. They draw attention to the fact that this is a significant difference from the role of engineers in other radical groups.

If we are looking for analogies for the experiences of Sardar and Husain, in the sense of searching, as young men, for an authentic understanding of their religious tradition, perhaps the best ones are two: firstly, the experiences of many young Christians, particularly at university, with Christian Unions, which often provide a focus for meaning and identity at a time of radical change and challenge to many individuals.

The main difference between Christian Unions and some Islamist groups, of course, is the question of the legitimacy or acceptance of violence: evangelical Christians do not normally resort to instruments of violence, though there are of course exceptions such as the group called 'Commandoes for Christ' who burnt down a cinema in France back in 1988 for showing the film 'The Last Temptation of Christ', and, most recently, Dr George Tiller, who was shot dead in church in Wichita, Kansas, in May 2009, by Scott Roeder, because of his willingness to perform late-term abortions.

Philip Lewis' *Young, British and Muslim* also provides helpful analogies with Jewish and Christian experience through comments on Eva Hoffman's *Lost in Translation*, an account of the migration of her secular Jewish family from Poland to Canada in the 1950s, and John Cornwell's *Breaking Faith: Can the Catholic Church Save Itself?*, his autobiographical account of his religious formation in a Catholic seminary in 1950s England and his subsequent moving on from this rather terrifying example of enclave culture.

A second analogy, which perhaps works better with respect to the political dimensions of Islamism, is with the idealistic young Europeans who, in the 1930s, went off to fight, on both sides, in the Spanish Civil War, portrayed perhaps most famously with respect to their youthful idealism by Laurie Lee in his *As I walked out one midsummer morning*, first published in 1969, and their more modern successors, the Red Army Faction (often known as the Baader-Meinhof Group), which was active in Germany particularly in the 1970s, and the Red Brigades, active in Italy, also mainly in the 1970s. The former was disbanded by its own members in 1998, and the latter was broken up by the Italian authorities in 1984.

The study of these two works of autobiography is therefore helpful to the study of radicalisation in terms of illustrating, firstly, the importance of individual experience to the process of both becoming and ceasing to be a 'radical'; and secondly, the enormous diversity, and therefore range of choice, which exists within the contemporary Muslim community. There are indeed many readings of Islam, and while some appear to be particularly attractive to young Muslim men, their appeal does not necessarily last.

Bibliography

Cornwell, J. 2002. *Breaking Faith: Can the Catholic Church Save Itself?* Penguin: Harmondsworth.

Gambetta, D., and Hertig, S. 2007. *Engineers of the Jihad.* Sociology Working Paper No: 2007–10, Department of Sociology, University of Oxford.

Hussein, E. 2007. *The Islamist.* Penguin: Harmondsworth.

Lee, L. 1969. *As I Walked Out One Midsummer Morning.* Andre Deutsch: London.

Lewis, P. 2008. *Young, Muslim and British.* Continuum: London.

Mawdudi, A.A. 2002. *Let Us Be Muslims.* Al-Basheer Company for Publications and Translations: Denver, CO.

Qutb, S. 1993. *Milestones on the Way.* American Trust Publications: Oak Brook, Illinois.

Sardar, Z. 2004. *Desperately Seeking Paradise: Journeys of a Sceptical Muslim.* Granta: London.

Sarwar, G. 1998. *Islam: Beliefs and Teachings.* Muslim Educational Trust: London.

3

BEING MUSLIM BEING BRITISH: A MULTIMEDIA EDUCATIONAL RESOURCE FOR YOUNG MUSLIMS

Jose Liht, Sara Savage and Ryan J. Williams

How can we prevent young Muslims becoming attracted to violent radicalism? Although there are a myriad of possible reasons, individual and societal, why violent Islamic groups and ideologies have emerged at the turn of the twenty first century, and why some young British Muslims associate with them, we believe that it presents a characteristic that allows for intervention: it runs contrary to the natural developmental path to achieving value complexity. By this we mean that radical discourses usually emphasise one moral value (such as communalism, or justice for the oppressed) to the exclusion of other values (such as individualism or liberty). By facilitating the natural developmental process towards complexity (or when stunted, recovering it), our intervention strategy aims at preventing and reversing radicalisation processes that might lead to violence.

All mainstream religious traditions are value-plural. In responding to different challenges, mainstream religious traditions, such as Judaism, Christianity or Islam, evolve to maximise, within historically imposed limits, the multiple competing values of their communities.[1] By this we mean that religious traditions take into account the several priorities of their communities. For example when judging the appropriateness of the use of alcohol for pharmaceutical reasons, Islamic jurisprudence usually rules that alcohol is allowed to sterilise instruments or skin even when it is normally proscribed. In this way the precept of prohibiting alcohol is balanced against the modern benefit of its pharmaceutical use, exemplifying how the underlying value of purity (from contamination through contact with something considered *haram* or prohibited) is not an absolute when positioned relative to the value of health.

In contrast, fundamentalist splinter groups are much less inclined to work out value tradeoffs. In an effort to offer simple solutions to a complex world, those overwhelmed by modernity, including most Islamists, become highly selective within their own traditions; emphasising certain texts and interpretations while suppressing others.[2] In this process, they radically alter traditional underlying value hierarchies by increasing the importance of some values while dramatically decreasing that of others.

This lack of complexity in the domain of values can be seen, for example, in the absolute prohibition of the use and transportation of alcohol or the hardening of the demand for conducting business free from *riba* (interest), without consideration of the benefits lost to the community when *halal* (prescribed) loans are not available to finance businesses. And in the most extreme of cases, that of the suicide bomber, the glorification of Islam or the achievement of a political concession which furthers the group's objectives is given priority over the life of the perpetrator, those who love him, and all his victims. Consequently, these extreme versions of the tradition become less value-plural to the point of absolute value simplification (value monism). That is what we posit constitutes the 'radical' element in extremist Islamic groups. We also posit that the appeal of these groups can be countered by developing value complexity or, in other words, supporting people's developmental path towards complexity in the domain of moral values.

An important body of literature shows how individuals' cognitive development progresses from simplicity to complexity.[3] Moreover, a significant number of studies in persuasion and suggestibility show that individuals are most effectively influenced by messages with a complexity level similar to that of the receptor.[4] Consequently, we propose that fostering the natural developmental process of increasing value complexity can serve to create resilience to radicalism and thus prevent processes of radicalisation since radical groups are intrinsically value-monist.

Considering the increasing importance of religion for Muslims as a source of identity,[5] we posit that in order to achieve a successful integration of Muslim and British identities and their underlying values, individuals require more cognitive resources to successfully resolve the dissonance between religious and secular–rational value systems. If not engaged, this dissonance constitutes a risk for further radicalisation via the attractiveness of extremist groups, especially for people who are experiencing identity uncertainty or group status threat. By acknowledging that most Islamic positions espouse legitimate values, even the radical ones, as long as other value commitments are given equal importance, we aim to facilitate a non-dogmatic approach to the exploration of the full diversity of groups and ideologies. Therefore, we hold that promoting value complexity can be an effective intervention to prevent radicalisation.

Group Differences in Value Commitments

In order to understand how uncertainty and threat lead to value simplification, it is necessary to understand how different historical circumstances result in communities evolving different value priorities and how being exposed to multiple changing value systems engenders uncertainty which then needs to be resolved in order to function effectively.

A substantial amount of data from over 80 countries over the past four decades has revealed the different values espoused by poor nations in contrast to developed, post-industrialised societies.[6] The data reveals that the two defining cultural changes of modernity/postmodernity – secularisation and erosion of sources of authority – are both clearly linked to a particular economic base.[7] The majority of people living in advanced industrialised societies now take for granted the absence of the fear of starvation. Survival needs are generally assured.[8]

This economic prosperity (and its attendant specialisation and welfare provision) affords individuals a degree of freedom from traditionally prescribed roles and obligations. Freedom from threats to survival, brought about by the successful subjugation of nature through science and technology, has made belief in supernatural forces (believed to control nature) peripheral to society's functioning. As supernatural forces are no longer needed as guarantors of survival, institutions and culture invariably become secularised or religious belief ceases to have structural or institutional social or political significance.[9]

In the later stages of modernisation, the autonomy brought about by post-industrial specialisation (for example, in IT and communication technologies), along with the social flexibility enabled by the welfare state, has resulted in relational associations of choice (as opposed to duty) and a widespread rejection of truths emanating from traditional sources of authority. These are perceived to be at odds with individual's internal subjective experience. And so, modern culture has taken a 'subjective turn', and institutional religion is widely in sharp decline.[10] However, the increased cultural capital of wealthy, autonomy-loving societies fosters individuals' search for meaning, and this guarantees the survival of the religious niche, albeit within a non-authoritarian, individualised framework.

In short, economic development brings about two successive value changes: traditional religious values change to secular rational values and survival values change to self-expression values.[11] Freedom from survival needs and emancipation from authority means that traditional religious institutions are forced to accede their prior organising role, as shapers of the cultural world view, to the more scientific–technological domain, thus becoming marginal as conductors of society. They acknowledge the discoveries of science and the critical analysis of sacred texts, and begin to reformulate their dogmas in relation to these. Lastly they become tolerant of a broad range of lifestyles and personal choices that are not centred on survival of the group, including homosexuality, abortion, assisted death, and single parent families prevalent in post-industrial societies. This is the story of most mainline Christian denominations, and Reform Judaism in the West. It now threatens to be the story for Muslim populations.

We have argued elsewhere,[12] that the two consecutive phases of modernisation (first, secularisation and second, emancipation from authority) correspond to two discernible phases in the development of fundamentalist movements in the most prosperous Western societies, particularly the USA. The first wave came about as a reaction to the critical examination of sacred texts in the late nineteenth and early twentieth centuries (and coincides with widespread elimination of the fear of starvation). This first wave of fundamentalism was preoccupied mainly with the Darwinian theory and with Biblical criticism. The second wave has been, until now, an unexplained resurgence in the 1970s and 1980s in which Christian, Muslim, Jewish, Hindu, and other fundamentalisms exploded onto the world stage, much to the surprise of secularisation theorists. This we now understand as a reaction to the 'subjective turn': the loss of status enjoyed by religious authority, the increase of choice within post-industrial lifestyles, and the secular humanist morality that underpins it.

This second wave of fundamentalism also coincides with the rise in the service sector and information technologies that are foundational to the self-expression values of post-industrial, post-material society. The divide between the prosperous 'North' and the developing 'South' continues to amplify as the value differences between the two continue to diverge. An evermore connected world in which two cultures have evolved, one out of the richest of post-material society, and one which still holds a premodern spirituality, cannot avoid the confrontation of these two moral orders. These two ways of being, when confronted, cannot but threaten each other at both the levels of the international and of the international communities. However, the most threatened groups are usually the poorest or least prestigious ones.[13] The intrapsychic level of the subsequent reaction can be illuminated by research inspired by Terror Management Theory.

Terror Management Theory

Terror Management Theory advances the idea that a shared worldview provides individuals, in their day-to-day experience, with a defence from inevitable existential anxiety: the fear of death. Fear of death remains subconscious, but can become conscious – sometimes painfully so – when death is made salient in some way. A large body of research shows that subtle reminders of death increase the way people defend their cultural norms and their general worldview.[14]

A cultural normative worldview with its dos and don'ts minimises death anxiety by providing an understanding of the universe that has order, meaning and standards of acceptable behaviour. The latter, when upheld, confers self-esteem. Worldviews promise death transcendence to its members, for example, through religious beliefs in an afterlife, or through one's creative contributions transmitted to successive generations through culture. Even death transcendence, through extending one's family line, requires a worldview that supports family as an institution, and the handing on of family or socially shared memories. The defence of a worldview provides acts not only to postpone death anxiety (as in the temporary proximal relief achieved through suppressing or distracting thoughts of death from conscious awareness), but provides the existential shield necessary for day-to-day normal living.[15]

In short, Terror Management Theory shows how when death is made salient, people will intensify strivings for self-esteem and will respond positively towards people and ideas that support their cultural worldview. Conversely, they will respond negatively towards those people and ideas that undermine their worldview. When death is made salient, value commitments become intensified compared to normal control conditions. Moreover, violations to these value commitments, under death saliency, incur steeper punishments than under control conditions.

Conversely, the second main hypothesis derived from Terror Management Theory is that when the validity of a cultural worldview is threatened, then death anxiety will increase – a highly aversive experience, priming the search for resolution. Subjects made to read paragraphs challenging their value commitments can then imagine how dying will feel with greater detail and clarity.[16] Terror Management Theory is thus relevant for understanding religiously motivated militant activism in that the experience of conflicting worldviews and identities result in an intensification of one set of values leading to simplification in order to boost the existential protection provided by the subject's worldview.

Accordingly, we posit that promoting value complexity (in other words, developing high integrative complexity thinking in the domain of moral values) can be an effective intervention to prevent and reverse early stages of radicalisation. Our research findings to date – assessing our intervention based on this framework – appear to strongly support that achieving higher levels of value complexity serves as a preventative inoculation against uncertainty states that can be potentially exploited for violence and disruption.

Radicalisation interventions

Since 11 September 2001 and 7 July 2005 proactive strategies to stop people from becoming terrorists are increasingly recognised as important for security, alongside traditional military, policing and technology-based approaches. This involves intercession prior to individuals becoming violent. However, prevention presents a challenge considering the relative rarity of terrorist violence and the multiple, complex set of root causes for it. Furthermore, the presence or absence of these factors does not necessarily determine vulnerability or immunity.

The Channel Programme

One example of efforts to prevent violent extremism is the UK Home Office's Channel Programme. The Channel Programme is a referral-based programme that coordinates with local authorities and organisations in order to identify and address risk factors in individuals. These include, but are not limited to or necessarily determined by: (a) expressed opinions, including support for violence and terrorism; (b) possession of violent extremist literature or imagery, membership or contribution to violent extremist websites and/or chat rooms, or literature on weapons or bomb-making; (c) behaviour or behavioural changes including withdrawal from family and peers, hostility or association with extremist organisations; and finally (d) aspects of personal history including involvement in organisations espousing the use of violence or overseas military/ terrorist training.[17] Those who are referred to the Channel Programme are screened, assessed for needs, and have an action plan for support developed, according to these needs. Records detailing interactions with individuals are recorded in a database and retained for up to seven years (personal conversation, Channel Practitioner, 13 May 2010).

Primary Prevention

While the prevalence of a given social issue is decreased in secondary prevention by shortening the duration of symptoms once they are exhibited, primary prevention decreases prevalence by addressing causal factors. Primary prevention operates among the broadest segments of the population in order to cover the widest range of causal factors. In the attempt to cover as broad a base as possible to address root causes, the natural consequence is that individuals who are not at risk are subject to the same treatment as those who are vulnerable but whose symptoms are undetectable by the available diagnostic tools, or who may be vulnerable but do not exhibit any indicators. Thus school children are educated through anti-bullying and anti-smoking campaigns, even though some individuals will never be bullies or smokers.[18] The priority in primary prevention is to increase individual strengths and decrease individual weaknesses, increase social supports and decrease social stress, and to increase physical resources while decreasing physical pressures.[19] Such a paradigm, as described in Bloom's configural equation of primary prevention, has two complementary objectives, of supporting promotive factors whilst decreasing risk factors. In primary prevention the promotion of protective factors identified with individuals and within communities is as important as decreasing risk factors. There are several types of initiatives specific to the primary prevention of violent Islamist extremism that fall under the following categories: counter-ideology or alternative narratives, including the use of positive role models; identity strategies; addressing grievances and empowerment; and general education.

Counter-Ideology and Counter-Ideologue Strategies

It is not uncommon for rebuttals specific to ideological treatises to deconstruct the argumentation of authors espousing variants of Islamism that sanction the use of violence (*jama'a Islamayya* in Singapore for instance). This is more common in South East Asia, Egypt (where radicals have even offered rebuttals against their own writings), and Saudi Arabia, where official interpretations of Islam can readily be juxtaposed with deviant interpretations. In Britain counter-ideology is often embedded in Muslim youth culture involving youth magazines and forms of democratic activism (for example *Hear My Voice*, described further below) or in well-marketed initiatives that aim to flood the Muslim identity market and the religious seeker with alternative narratives. For example the Radical Middle Way (RMW) involves a series of influential speakers on various topics in Islam that hold talks across Britain. Speakers, who have included Shaykh Abdal Hakim Murad and the Grand Mufti of Egypt, Shaykh Ali Gomaa, provide alternatives to radical discourse. Through these figures RMW not only provides alternative narratives, but also provides alternative charismatic leadership to counter radicalisers such as the infamous Abu Hamza. Other positive role models or counter-ideologues include ex-radicals, which, not unlike the 'scared straight' programmes in the United States, utilise figures such as Ed Husain, author of *The Islamist* and founder of the Quillium Foundation, to inform broad audiences of the perils of radicalisers and of becoming radicalised.

Identity Strategies

Caplan's[20] model of prevention was informed by an Eriksonian notion of development, where a disorder, or in this case a social issue, arises because of maladaptation and maladjustment, and by altering the balance of forces, healthy adaptation and adjustment is possible. What guides primary prevention is the process of equipping communities with resilience to crisis – a triggering point in the onset of many social issues. In research on radicalisation, a crisis of identity is considered a risk factor. Where there are unresolved tensions in one's identity, the likelihood of a 'cognitive opening' to activism and vulnerability to radical discourses is increased.[21] One example in primary prevention is the emphasis on citizenship training, which aims to offer to immigrants a form of anticipatory instruction to safeguard or build resilience against potentially irreconcilable identity conflicts and stresses associated with immigration and displacement.[22]

Addressing Grievances and Empowerment

A third group of initiatives are those which broadly address grievances. The UK Home Office has set up a division called Research Information and Communications Unit (RICU) aimed at forestalling misinterpretation of counter-terrorism policy. More concretely, ombudsman initiatives involving representation for young Muslims to directly communicate with the government were established across Britain, serving as a primary prevention effort to safeguard against unaddressed grievances and perceptions of disempowerment. Organisations such as *Hear My Voice* offer alternative forms of activism through participation in democratic processes.

General Education Strategies

Davies[23] provides a systematic examination of extremism and a primary prevention platform through education. In her analysis, the prevention of violent extremism begins with root questions: How do we prevent people from becoming intolerant and absolutist? How do we prevent people from joining extremist or violent movements? How do we enable people to challenge extremism? These are the questions and challenges posed for primary prevention. Salient here is the 'process base' of her educational model, which underscores the role of critical thinking, as well as openness towards and presentation of alternative perspectives. Davies argues that such a strategy aligns with the tradition of *ijtihad*, promoted by the Washington think-tank, the Centre for the Study of Islam and Democracy, as well by Tariq Ramadan, the articulator of a European Islam.[24]

The 'Being Muslim Being British' Course

Being Muslim Being British (BMBB), the primary prevention course we developed in line with the framework described above (Savage and Liht, 2010), can be situated amongst the primary prevention interventions and shares characteristics with Davis's educational programme. However, while Davis, and in general other educational programmes, aims at reducing individual vulnerability to recruitment for terrorism by fostering a 'secular value system of human rights', BMBB posits that non-secular values need not be discarded or tempered in order to achieve social cohesion. BMBB rests on the premise that what fosters cohesion is a healthy equilibrium among value commitments, irrespective of whether they are couched in religious or secular terms.

BMBB explores the issues that affect young Muslims living in Britain and Europe today. This multi-media educational resource, over eight sessions (16 contact hours), uses DVD films and group activities led by trained facilitators to enable young people to develop value complexity (higher levels of integrative complexity in the domain of values). We believe that value complexity is a core-like skill for all people living in multi-cultural or globalised contexts today.

Our strategy for developing value complexity in BMBB works by exposing course participants to competing versions of Muslim opinion and teaching on key topics, thus revealing and affirming a wider array of under-girding values through the DVDs and activities. Throughout the sessions, 'Theatre of the Oppressed'-inspired group activities enable participants to work through the steps of raising integrative complexity, supported by trained facilitators.

An extensive research literature shows that thinking with higher levels of integrative complexity (IC) is related to lower conflict levels, greater capacity to find peaceful negotiated solutions and less dogmatic, more moderate social and political stances.[25] A motivating force for doing the extra cognitive work to raise IC arises from the desire to maximise more than one value – in a dilemma pitting two values against each other when both of these are deemed to have high importance in a personal hierarchy.[26] Thus, BMBB helps people to maximise a wide array of values. BMBB activities enable course participants to retain their own deeply held value commitments, and from there, to understand other viewpoints, find common values with them, and explore possible win/win solutions to complex problems in multi-cultural or globalised contexts.

Philosophy

The capacity to make free choices is fundamental to being fully human. In our approach to de-radicalisation, we reject authoritarian imposition of concepts of 'what is good'. People and communities are entrusted with working out their individual and collective value commitments in the knowledge that the limits imposed by the realities of human existence forces us to make choices. In the impossible task of maximising all values at all times and the recognition that it is impossible to place most values in a clear hierarchy of importance (incommensurability), our particular value commitments will be as valid as those of others choosing to prioritise different values, as posited by a value-pluralism political philosophy.[27]

For example, an interpersonal offence in a close relationship can evoke conflicting values of justice and mercy. Justice demands punishment of the offender and redress. Mercy compels us to understand the offender, and to find a way for the offender to be forgiven. The deep struggle of forgiveness is an effort to realise both values, justice and mercy, and prompts people to transcend their current level of complexity by achieving a solution where both justice and mercy are integrated. Nevertheless, it must be appreciated that, although one might desire to maximise both justice and mercy, this will be impossible and thus the final formula adopted will differ along individual and community lines especially if communities have different historical experiences. These assertions are in line with the Islamic principles of:

1. *Huq-uqul-ibad* (which places duty to people before duty to God – it is the meeting of human needs that pleases God),
2. The art of courteous disagreement (within Islamic Jurisprudence) and
3. Shura (consultation).

In this way, our philosophical approach can be couched in both core Islamic principles and in principles that are equally enshrined within Western democratic values.

By providing relevant information and skills, with ample opportunities for intellectual exploration on pressing issues for the Muslim community within an affirming religious context, this course aims to foster young people's capacity to approach complex religious and social issues with warranted complexity, in a safe and confidential environment. We argue that the faith of Islam, when freed of the distortions of radicalisers, has a moderating and peace-promoting affect. By providing opportunities for free reflection on intellectual and religious issues, and through the friendships that will arise through a pedagogy based on teamwork, the course aims to strengthen young people's commitment to a free and diverse society – one in which the greatest merit can be realised with the least compulsion.

Psychological Foundation

Our understanding of violent extremism is informed by Uncertainty Reduction Theory as well as Terror Management Theory (as described earlier). These psychosocial approaches maintain that people have two basic powerful motives: the need to adopt a worldview that allows one to make sense of the world, and the need to have that worldview validated in one's interactions with other people. Although people have the capacity to endure, and even actively look for, difference and diversity, serious threats to one's worldview will result in personal distress and a sense of threat (which lowers value complexity). This, in turn, can motivate forceful, even violent, collective resistance. Both of these normal motivations underlie radicalisation.

The Muslim experience in Europe involves the human dynamics engendered by immigration, deprivation and difference. These have played into the hands of destructive social movements and a single-narrative ideology that have capitalised on the vulnerability of young Muslims in the United Kingdom and the European Union. This ideology comprises a binary worldview that relies on, and produces, low value complexity.

We aim to prevent radicalisation by facilitating the exploration, negotiation and adoption of a worldview that honours religious faith, traditions and sense of identity of Muslims in the midst of western liberalism and multiculturalism. Far from opportunistically pitting one cultural system against the other, we recognise the good in both worldviews, and maintain that, in the absence of fear, a confluence of Muslim and European values holds the possibility of renewal and cross-fertilisation.

Educational Strategy

Our educational strategy, based upon psychological theory and research, takes place in three phases over an eight week period. The aim is to enable young Muslims in the UK and the EU to engage critically and creatively over personal key issues that have been harnessed and monopolised by radical Islamists. Radical Islamist ideology trades on the reaction to having an individual's worldview threatened, thus limiting young Muslims to their binary construction of social reality. Our aim is not to counter that position with a similarly dogmatic, but Western-inspired, counter-ideology; this, we think, would simply produce reactance. Rather we want to enable young people to think for themselves, to have the cognitive tools, the religious understanding, and enough confidence in their own personal identity within a supportive social environment, to enable them to voice their own opinions, weigh up the pros and cons of all relevant positions, to see the links and parallels between relevant positions, and to be able to compare and contrast different views on key issues, so that they may take responsibility for their own thinking, evaluate the array of positions available to them and draw their own conclusions. These cognitive tools will also involve the ability to identify and see through commonly used rhetorical strategies that prevent critical thinking, and to help people to understand their own vulnerabilities to being recruited, and to understand the gradual process of radicalisation that, for some, can lead to religious violence, with its increasingly limited freedom of choice as the stages of engagement progress.

Three Phases of Transformation

The first phase in our approach to de-radicalisation is to raise levels of thinking complexity (or IC). The first step in the journey towards raising IC is to enable participants to perceive multiple perspectives on social, moral and religious issues, and to be able to discover aspects of validity in each, by 'laddering' down to the deeper values that the different perspectives seek to defend.

The second educational strategy is to enable value complexity, in other words to embrace a wider array of values in one's moral reasoning. Typically, extremist ideologies concentrate, for example, on one value, such as 'justice', to the exclusion of 'liberty'. In our educational strategy, rather than relying simply on one value pole, we aim to enable young people to embrace a wider array of values (for instance justice and liberty). Cultural differences between Muslims and Westerners (for example, between a collective culture and an individualistic culture) will be easier to understand, and thus bridge from a vantage point of value complexity. From here it becomes possible to find higher order syntheses of apparently opposing perspectives (the second phase of integrative complexity). Value complexity is the necessary condition to enable the working out of integrated, win/win solutions to moral, social, religious issues. It is win/win solutions that protect the sacred values of different groups, and it is this protection of sacred values that enables peaceful resolutions to inter-group social and religious conflict.

Consolidating the Three Phases of Transformation

Religious validity: The three transformations described above (high IC, value complexity, and multiple epistemologies) are fragile in the early stages, and need to be consolidated. It is vital that the course content conforms to widespread Islamic norms, and shows an array of Muslim positions on various issues.

Learning by doing: None of the three phases of transformation will be 'explicit' or technically, intellectually conveyed. Rather, our approach is that the most powerful learning occurs through doing, and that human beings rarely 'do' anything meaningful outside of their social matrix. We argue that it is the mental/social work the young people do themselves that will enable the ability to perceive multiple perspectives, thus active, multi-media learning is key to the success of the course.

Social bonding: We also argue that it is the relationships that develop through the teamwork activities that will provide the 'glue' that will keep people returning to the course – to a group with whom they find belonging and support, as well as the liberation of honest discussion and exploration. The contrast between authoritarian, extremist groups that provide belonging, identity and support but require the sacrifice of honesty and exploration, will become evident over the duration of the course. We argue that the experience of being in a group that allows both belonging and honesty (value complexity) will serve as an 'inoculation' against the lure of authoritarian groups. Individuals' commitment to their team (and hence continued attendance) will be enhanced by the team project, to which all contribute in the last session.

In the piloting phase already conducted, we have heard young people repeatedly voice the view that they want to build better bridges with non-Muslims. This, the final session, will involve young people sharing their team project along with a celebration meal with invited non-Muslim guests. Thus, this last session is designed to foster relationships with non-Muslims. Moderate Muslim networks and resources will be listed in Participant's Booklets for people to pursue after the course is ended.

Sessions

The resources will consist of educational materials in the form of DVD based multi-media films, approximately a 20-minute film per session. Each of the DVD films features a 'narrator', a young Muslim who creates a 'home video diary' addressing issues of concern. Each session has a different narrator, an array of male, female, different ethnicities and implicitly different Muslim religious (Shi'a/Sunni/Sufi) backgrounds. The home video diary genre is one that is familiar and at the cutting edge in the media today, and one that we have seen, through piloting, that young people instantly relate to.

Each session explores a topic of interest for young Muslims and presents a balanced array of positions by well known Islamic personalities in the form of video clips. We aim to exploit the diversity of Muslim voices 'out there', most of which claim to be the 'one and only true expression of Islam', and to empower young people to make sense of, and make reasoned judgements, about that diversity.

The full BMBB course comprises eight sessions (two hours long each). Materials include eight films on DVD, Participants' Booklets and a Facilitator's Guide for leading the group activities. A Taster DVD and an Integrative Complexity Presentation provides an overview of the course and the background theory.

Values in Sessions

Schwartz's research has identified ten universal values: power, achievement, hedonism, stimulation, self-direction, universalism, benevolence, tradition, conformity, security.[28] These can be collapsed into two higher order dimension continua: conservation of tradition versus openness, and self-enhancement versus self-transcendence. Under the influence of threat, people's values can shift to the conservation of tradition or self-transcendence poles, excluding openness and self-transcendence, and in doing so they become more monist (one-sided), and less complex.[29]

Based on this structure and on how threat or worldview defence affects value commitments, each session is designed to develop complexity with regard to a pair of values that tend to fuse, with one or the other becoming dominant, under situations of threat.

The first session is dedicated to easing people into the course and introducing how competing versions of Islam on issues affecting Muslims living in the UK can be deconstructed into their underlying values and how these can be integrated into more complex value plural positions that maximise simultaneous competing values. By utilising 'Theatre of Oppressed' based activities, we aim to minimise the intellectual component and achieve our ends in an interactive and engaging way suitable for young people.[30] The subsequent sessions will be dedicated to developing complexity across the following competing values:

1. Communalism versus individualism underlying Islamic religiosity (Caliphate versus personal piety)
2. Communalism versus individualism in regard to relationships and marriage (arranged marriages versus romantic relationships)

3. Theism versus materialist scientism
4. Women and men as similar versus women and men as different vis-à-vis working out of equality
5. Economic liberty (free market capitalism) versus economic control (by Muslim clerics)
6. Activism versus fatalism in the context of democratic political means
7. Hedonism versus control of the body's desires (through abstinence or early marriage)

For example, the impact of the tension between communitarian versus individualist pressures is acted out in role play about marriage in which suitors try to sell themselves to a potential bride while group members play parents and community members and give their opinions of who will make the best husband. This activity is geared to enable participants to see new options, and new ways of working through the conflicts and pressures they often experience. From this experiential learning, the sessions enable participants to reflect on and articulate what they have learned.

Topics

Each DVD film is presented by a young Muslim narrator exploring, in an open-ended way, topics that impinge on young Muslims' social identity and their ability to fully participate in British culture. In consecutive sessions the narrator talks about how:

1. Daily tensions often pull young Muslims between traditional, secular, and religious influences. Distorted images of Muslims in the media make young Muslims feel defensive and alienated, while longing to relate better to the society of which they are part. How can we find a way of living in Britain that enables young people to flourish?
2. What different values underlie the way young Muslims and Westerners 'do' relationships – in families, at school, with friends?

Do these cultures inevitably clash? What makes you you? Are you Muslim, British, or both? How can people make the most of the potential richness of this mix?

3. Some say that Islam clashes irreconcilably with secular western, scientific culture. What underlies the so-called big differences? This session looks at age-old debates between science and religion, affirming Islam as a way of life that seeks knowledge and understanding, both scientific and moral.

4. Muslims are all equal in the sight of God. Islam's radical egalitarianism and Western notions of equality are noble – yet, how are these being lived out today? Men and women – different but equal? Contemporary voices often clash over these issues.

5. We all need money to live. How best to handle it? Can we do anything about modern greed and materialism? Is it a case of capitalism or Islam? This session explores Islamic principles of justice and finance, and examines the options that are being presented.

6. How can Muslims work to bring about an ideal (or at least better) society on earth? Can it be achieved through democracy? Must one live in a Muslim country in order to live a fully Islamic life? What is the true meaning of jihad? This session looks at ways of approaching positive social change.

7. Relationships, leisure, and self-esteem. It can be difficult balancing relaxation with work, human desires with moral principles. This session explores dilemmas facing many young people about how to behave in a consumerist and pleasure-oriented Western culture.

8. What is the goal of life? The beauty of Islam is a vision of peace. A celebration 'feast' marks this final session with an opportunity to invite guests. Invited guests (friends, family, community leaders, and non-Muslims), along with the Team, will explore some win/win solutions, and enjoy food together to celebrate.

To reinforce the learning, the final Session eight comprises participants sharing their own creative projects on a theme of their choosing, plus celebration feast with invited guests, handing out of Certificates and Next Steps handouts, and summary of IC though DVD film. Subsidiary tasks for sessions include:

1. Engendering perception of different ways of dividing up the in-group/out-group distinction, for example a visibly obvious member of the out group (such as a Western liberal), espouses values dear to the heart of the Muslim in-group (such as family values, human dignity, equality).
2. Avoiding an absolute polarity between Muslim and Non-Muslim, for example interview a somewhat radicalised Muslim who has gone back to the home country and encounters poverty, injustice, corruption. He realises that his Western life has some good features, and that he himself is partly Western. Introduce eclectic identities: Brit/Muslim mix.
3. Recognising and challenging stereotypes and caricatures of both the in-group and the out-group (for example media stereotypes of Muslims or stereotypes of Jews).
4. Recognising the rhetorical strategies of radicalisers that seek to present their version of reality as the only valid version; recognising the social processes that totalist groups employ to squash dissent and separate young people from their social networks of origin.

Conclusions

Response to BMBB from the outset has been overwhelmingly positive. So far, about two dozen Muslim clerics who have examined the material have regarded the principles of IC in line with Islam (for example, the art of courteous disagreement in Islamic jurisprudence and the practice of shura or consultation) and as contributing towards 'Islam as a high IC' resource. Clerics who received our one day facilitator training in various UK locations were even more positive at the end of the day.

Based on the responses of 33 individuals who participated in pre-piloting, the course has good face validity (please see Liht and Savage (forthcoming) for the full empirical assessment of seven pilot courses around the UK). Most participants of BMBB are enthusiastic in their embrace of the session topics and the activities. Young people very quickly perceive IC as 'fair', enabling reciprocity. Some have indicated a sincere and energetic embrace of IC: 'IC has changed my life' said one participant in our most recent pilot. Although it is difficult for some participants to sign up to eight sessions (and some groups only want to sign up to four sessions at a time), most groups are eager for more sessions by the end of the course.

We believe the success of our initial delivery on this project relies firstly upon not feeding young people with the 'right' answers and on presenting very different Islamic positions, from the most conservative to the most liberal, as genuine and of intrinsic value.

Our assessment research using a thick description provided by individual, interaction and social network level data and quantitative comparisons of IC before and after the intervention are soon to be available in journal article form (in submission at the time of writing). Our preliminary data shows that a critical feature of BMBB comes from the nature of the social interactions within the group, and this aspect of the research, along with our experience in training facilitators, provides insight into how to optimise the social dynamics to support the fostering of value complexity. These insights are now woven into the final resources and facilitator training materials and are informing new IC interventions for other extremisms.

Notes

1. Jinkins, M. 2004. *Christianity, Tolerance, and Pluralism: A Theological Engagement with Isaiah Berlin's Social Theory*. Routledge: London.
2. Marty, M.E., Appleby, R.S., and American Academy of Arts and Sciences. 1995. *Fundamentalisms Comprehended*. University of Chicago Press: Chicago.
3. Slugoski, B. R., Marcia, J. E., and Koopman, R. F. 1984. 'Cognitive and social interactional characteristics of ego identity statuses in college males', *Journal of Personality and Social Psychology*, 47 (3), pp.646–661.
4. Suedfeld, P., Leighton, D.C., and Conway, L.G. 2005. 'Integrative complexity and decision making in international confrontations', in Fitzduff, M., and Stout, C.E. (eds.) *The Psychology of Resolving Global Conflicts: From War to Peace. Volume 1, Nature vs. Nurture* (Vol. 1, pp.211–237). Praeger Security International: New York.
5. Choudhury, T. 2007. 'The role of Muslim identity politics in radicalisation (a study in progress)'. Retrieved 11 April 2009, from: http://www.communities. gov.uk/documents/communities/pdf/452628.pdf.

6. Inglehart, R., and Welzel, C. 2007. 'Modernization, cultural change, and democracy: the human development sequence', *American Journal of Sociology*, 112 (4), pp.1248–1250.

7. Ibid.

8. Norris, P., and Inglehart, R. 2004. *Sacred and Secular: Religion and Politics Worldwide*. Cambridge University Press: Cambridge, UK and New York.

9. Inglehart and Welzel, op.cit.

10. Heelas, P. 2005. *The Spiritual Revolution: Why Religion is Giving Way to Spirituality*. Blackwell Publishing: Malden, MA.

11. Inglehart and Welzel, op.cit.

12. Savage, S., and Liht, J. 2008. 'Mapping fundamentalisms: The psychology of religion as a sub-discipline in the understanding of religiously motivated violence', *International Journal for the Psychology of Religion*, 30 (1), pp.75–91.

13. Hogg, M.A., and Abrams, D. 1988. *Social Identifications: A Social Psychology of Intergroup Relations and Group Processes*. Routledge: London.

14. Bassett, J. F. 2005. 'Does threatening valued components of cultural world-view alter explicit and implicit attitudes about death?', *Individual Differences Research*, 3 (4), pp.260–268.

15. Greenberg, J., and Jonas, E. 2003. 'Psychological motives and political orientation: The Left, the Right, and the Rigid (Comment on Jost et al.)', *Psychological Bulletin*, 129 (3), pp.376–382.

16. Florian, V., and Mikulincer, M. 1997. 'Fear of death and the judgment of social transgressions: A multidimensional test of Terror Management Theory', *Journal of Personality and Social Psychology*, 73 (2), pp.369–380.

17. HO Government. March 2010. *Channel: Supporting Individuals Vulnerable to Recruitment by Violent Extremists*. Retrieved from http://security.home-office.gov.uk/news-publications/publication-search/prevent/channel-guidance?view=Binary.

18. Evans, R. I. 2001. 'Social influences in etiology and prevention of smoking and other health threatening behaviors in children and adolescents' in Baum, A., Revenson, T.A., and Singer, J.E. (eds.) *Handbook of Health Psychology* Lawrence Erlbaum Associates: Mahwah, New Jersey. pp.459–468.

19. Bloom, M. 1996. *Primary Prevention Practices* (Vol. 5). Sage: London.

20. Caplan, G. 1964. *Principles of Preventive Psychiatry'*. Tavistock: London.

21. Wiktorowicz, Q. 2005. *Radical Islam Rising: Muslim Extremism in the West'*. Rowman and Littlefield: Oxford.

22. Davies, L. 2008. *Educating Against Extremism*. Trentham Books: Stoke on Trent, UK.

23. Ibid.

24. Ibid., p.178.

25. Suedfeld, P., Leighton, D.C., and Conway, L.G. op.cit.

26. Tetlock, P. E., Armor, D., and Peterson, R. S. 1994. 'The slavery debate in antebellum America: Cognitive style, value conflict, and the limits of compromise', *Journal of Personality and Social Psychology*, 66 (1), pp.115–126.
27. Berlin, I., Espada, J.C., Plattner, M.F., and Wolfson, A. 2001. *Pluralism without Relativism: Remembering Sir Isaiah Berlin.* : Lexington Books: Lanham, MD.
28. Schwartz, S. H., and Boehnke, K. 2004. 'Evaluating the structure of human values with confirmatory factor analysis', *Journal of Research in Personality*, 38 (3), p.230.
29. Schwartz, S. H., and Huismans, S. 1995. 'Value Priorities and Religiosity in Four Western Religions', *Social Psychology Quarterly*, 58 (2), pp.88–107.
30. Boal, A. 1998. *Legislative Theatre: Using Performance to Make Politics.* Routledge: London.

Bibliography

Ashour, O. 2009. *Deradicalisation of Jihadism: Transforming Armed Islamist Movements.* Routledge: London and New York.

Bassett, J. F. 2005. 'Does threatening valued components of cultural worldview alter explicit and implicit attitudes about death?' *Individual Differences Research*, 3 (4), pp.260–268.

Berlin, I., Espada, J.C., Plattner, M.F., and Wolfson, A. 2001. *Pluralism without Relativism: Remembering Sir Isaiah Berlin.* Lexington Books: Lanham, MD.

Bloom, M. 1996. *Primary Prevention Practices*, Volume 5. Sage: London.

Boal, A. 1998. *Legislative Theatre: Using Performance to Make Politics.* Routledge: London.

Caplan, G. 1964. *Principles of Preventive Psychiatry.* Tavistock: London.

Choudhury, T. 2007. 'The role of Muslim identity politics in radicalisation (a study in progress)'. Retrieved 11 April 2009, from: http://www.communities.gov.uk/documents/communities/pdf/452628.pdf

Davies, L. 2008. *Educating Against Extremism.* Trentham Books: Stoke on Trent, UK.

Evans, R. I. 2001. 'Social influences in etiology and prevention of smoking and other health threatening behaviors in children and adolescents', in Baum, A., Revenson, T.A., and Singer, J.E. (eds.), *Handbook of Health Psychology.* Lawrence Erlbaum Associates: Mahwah, NJ. pp.459–468.

Florian, V., and Mikulincer, M. 1997. 'Fear of death and the judgment of social transgressions: A multidimensional test of Terror Management Theory', *Journal of Personality and Social Psychology*, 73 (2), pp.369–380.

Greenberg, J., and Jonas, E. 2003. 'Psychological motives and political orientation: The Left, the Right, and the Rigid (Comment on Jost et al.)', *Psychological Bulletin*, 129 (3), pp.376–382.

Heelas, P. 2005. *The Spiritual Revolution: Why Religion is Giving Way to Spirituality.* Blackwell Publishers: Malden, MA.

HO Government. March 2010. *Channel: Supporting individuals vulnerable to recruitment by violent extremists.* Retrieved from: http://security.homeoffice.gov.uk/news-publications/publication-search/prevent/channelguidance?view=Binary.

Hogg, M.A., and Abrams, D. 1988. *Social Identifications: A Social Psychology of Intergroup Relations and Group Processes.* Routledge: London.

Inglehart, R., and Welzel, C. 2005. *Modernization, Cultural Change, and Democracy: The Human Development Sequence.* Cambridge University Press: Cambridge and New York.

———. 2007. 'Modernization, Cultural Change, and Democracy: The Human Development Sequence', *American Journal of Sociology,* 112 (4), pp.1248–1250.

Jinkins, M. 2004. *Christianity, Tolerance, and Pluralism: A Theological Engagement with Isaiah Berlin's Social Theory.* Routledge: London.

Marty, M.E., Appleby, R.S., and American Academy of Arts and Sciences. 1995. *Fundamentalisms Comprehended.* University of Chicago Press: Chicago.

Norris, P., and Inglehart, R. 2004. *Sacred and Secular: Religion and Politics Worldwide.* Cambridge University Press: Cambridge and New York.

Savage, S., and Liht, J. 2010. 'Being Muslim Being British. A Multimedia Course for Young Muslims. Copyright the University of Cambridge'. Therefore, 9th reference will be a line rather than 'Savage, S., and Liht, J.

———. 2008. 'Mapping fundamentalisms: The psychology of religion as a sub-discipline in the understanding of religiously motivated violence', *International Journal for the Psychology of Religion,* 30 (1), pp.75–91.

Schwartz, S.H., and Boehnke, K. 2004. 'Evaluating the structure of human values with confirmatory factor analysis', *Journal of Research in Personality,* 38 (3), p.230.

Schwartz, S.H., and Huismans, S. 1995. 'Value Priorities and Religiosity in Four Western Religions', *Social Psychology Quarterly,* 58 (2), pp.88–107.

Slugoski, B.R., Marcia, J.E., and Koopman, R.F. 1984. 'Cognitive and social interactional characteristics of ego identity statuses in college males', *Journal of Personality and Social Psychology,* 47 (3), pp.646–661.

Suedfeld, P., Leighton, D.C., and Conway, L.G.I. 2005. 'Integrative complexity and decision-making in international confrontations', in Fitzduff, M. and Stout, C.E. (eds.), *The Psychology of Resolving Global Conflicts: From War to Peace. Volume 1, Nature vs. Nurture*: New York. pp.211–237.

Tetlock, P.E., Armor, D., and Peterson, R.S. 1994. 'The slavery debate in antebellum America: Cognitive style, value conflict, and the limits of compromise', *Journal of Personality and Social Psychology,* 66 (1), pp.115–126.

Wiktorowicz, Q. 2005. *Radical Islam Rising: Muslim Extremism in the West.* Rowman and Littlefield: Oxford.

4

THINKING CENTRIFUGAL: FECUNDITY AND HAZARD ON THE NET

Johnny Ryan

A constant theme of the policy debate in Western states about radicalisation and extremism, particularly with reference to political Islam, is the use made by radicals and extremists of the so-called 'new media' or 'social media'. This means of communication, based on the explosion in importance of the Internet to modern communications, is seen as a major threat to security because it is uncontrolled and, apparently, uncontrollable. Young militants, secure in their anonymity, can communicate with each other without fear of discovery, so the argument runs, thus rendering the security environment far more unstable than it used to be and making the tasks facing security services even more difficult than they were before. It is a concern not only to Western states but also to states in the Middle Eastern and North African regions, as the attacks in Morocco in 2007 – which began in an Internet café – make clear.

This is not necessarily the case, as this chapter will show, for the implications of the Internet for radical movements are far more ambivalent than they at first appear. It is true that the Internet is, by definition, a fecund medium in that it promotes the multiplication of means and pathways of communication; more so, perhaps, than any other comparable medium in history. Yet, at the same time, because of its uniquely interactive approach, it has potential to alter content as well as to multiply outlets. And this potential can both radicalise and moderate the message transmitted, both as a random process and because of the deliberate action of states and their security services. It is to the way in which these twin effects emerge from the intrinsic nature of the Internet and to the implications this may have for radical movements in the future that this chapter is directed.

The Nature of the Internet

The Internet has a 'centrifugal' character that is new and different. Understanding this centrifugal character is a first step toward a more practical, and more feasible, approach to online radicalisation. The premise on which the Internet and the technical protocols that govern communications across it were based explicitly lifted control from the centre and dispersed it everywhere throughout the network so as to make the network robust in the face of a nuclear strike.[1] Rather than there being a single controlling node at the centre, control rested instead within every participating node in the network. Thus, where the defining pattern of the industrial age was the single, central dot to which all strands led, the emerging digital age is different. The defining pattern of the digital age is the absence of the central dot.[2] In its place a mesh of many nodes is evolving, each linked by webs and networks. Within this mesh, each node – each individual person – is increasingly empowered to act on its own initiative.

The Internet provides militant movements with a means not only of circumventing restrictions on conventional media, but also of reaching out to peripheral supporters who might otherwise be impossible to identify or connect with. At the same time a countervailing force exists that distorts the militant message once it is communicated beyond the shelter of committed supporters' web forums and ventures on to the mainstream Internet to find prospective supporters. What this means is that the Internet, despite its marvellous fecundity for subversive ideas and communities, is also a hazardous environment for the militant Islamist message. The news is not so bad as might be assumed. Before the good news, let us start with the bad.

A Fecund Medium for Militants

Two years before the events of 11 September 2001, Jerrold Post wrote of the concept of a 'community of belief' in which informal groups of radicalised and mutually radicalising individuals might perpetrate particularly severe attacks.[3] Post was referring to 'Christian identity' right-wing sympathisers and far-right militants such as Timothy McVeigh who, though not formally associated with a militant group, might nonetheless undertake sympathetic operations in keeping with that group's ideology and goals as part of an informal and amorphous community rather than as a formal member of a defined group.[4] Benjamin Nathaniel Smith's racist shooting spree in 1999 showed that the Internet could facilitate such ties. In Smith's words:

> It wasn't really 'til I got on the Internet, read some literature of these groups that . . . it really all came together. It's a slow, gradual process to become radically conscious.[5]

In the context of militant Islamism the 'community of belief' that Post described might also be called 'leaderless resistance', as the militant strategist Abu Mus'ab al Suri phrased it in his own writing,[6] or 'leaderless jihad' as Marc Sageman termed it in 2008.[7]

The 'leaderless' language that Sageman refers to dates back to Ulius 'Pete' Louis Amoss. Amoss had been a member of the Office of Strategic Services during World War II,[8] and developed a concept of 'leaderless resistance' in 1953 in response to the prospect of a Soviet invasion of the US homeland.[9] Louis Beam, a white supremacist ideologue, took up Amoss' idea in 1983.[10] As government crackdowns increasingly threatened hierarchical organisation, Beam wrote, 'it will become necessary to consider other methods of organisation – or as the case may very well call for: non-organisation'.[11] Louis Bream reflected on the cell system used by the 'committees of correspondence' during the American Revolution in which information passed from local committee to local committee by letter, and each then acted independently 'without any central direction whatsoever'.[12] Yet this went beyond the old network strategies of previous underground movements because 'the option of belonging to a group will be nonexistent . . . [And therefore] this struggle is rapidly becoming a matter of individual action'.[13] Individuals, even those acting in isolation, who adhere to a common ideology will necessarily act in common, even if not in concert.[14]

This concept of a disparate group of individuals acting in isolation without hierarchical command has gained traction among many of those studying militant Islamists.[15] In essence, this view regards the Internet as an essential facilitator of radicalisation. According to this perspective the young Internet users to whom Web 2.0 (see below) is a native environment can tap in to communities that are sympathetic to militant Islamist objectives, and from whose members they can learn and develop a rationale that encourages them to seek opportunities to contribute to violent campaigns. Much of this online content capitalises on current events, resonates with readers' own personal experiences,[16] and can be particularly compelling to those with little prior knowledge of Islam. This may be particularly true of young second or third generation Europeans of Muslim extraction and to converts who, in the absence of a solid personal understanding of Islam, could be more easily swayed by crude, but strongly expressed, puritanical argument.[17]

Before the invasion of Afghanistan one militant Islamist strategist had already recognised its utility. In 1998 US Tomahawk strikes against suspected militant sites in Sudan and Afghanistan convinced Abu Mus'ab al Suri that a new approach was needed to confront such a militarily superior foe.[18] Al Suri argued for a new model of operation that focused on amorphous groups working with little top down coordination. This leaderless resistance would be a 'system, not organisation'.[19] Al Qa'ida itself was expendable so long as it prompted a wider participation in the struggle by other militant groups. His personal mission was to set down the doctrine of the overall movement for future generations to embrace as their own, much as Sayyid Qutb had smuggled the text of his last book from prison chapter by chapter, before his execution, in the hope of inspiring a vanguard of action.[20] This has to some extent been successful, and in 2008 Radio

Free Europe reported that the core of al Qa'ida accounted for 'a mere fraction' of militant Islamist media production.[21]

Network effects offer one approach to measuring the potential value of the centrifugal contribution to a militant campaign. The discussion that follows introduces three laws of 'network effects' to describe the enormous scale of the potential threat on the one hand, and the potentially enormous population of the assertive audience who might atomise the militant message on the other. As networks have changed, so have their effects. Thus each of the three laws mentioned in this section refers to a different stage of technological progress, beginning with one-to-many radio and television broadcasts, then discussing networked computers, and finally describing the so-called 'group forming networks' whose best example are the social networks such as Facebook.

The first law of network effects is from the era before digital networks. David Sarnoff, the founder of NBC, stated that the number of its viewers or listeners determined the value of a television or radio broadcast networks.[22] By virtue of the media with which it dealt, Sarnoff's Law conformed to a limited, centripetal logic. This was a simple one-to-many proposition. 'Network effects' are governed by a centrifugal logic. Theodore Vail, President of AT&T, offered a simple explanation of 'network effects' in 1908:

> a telephone – without a connection at the other end of the line – is not even a toy or a scientific instrument. It is one of the most useless things in the world. Its value depends on the connection with the other telephone – and increases with the number of connections.[23]

This suggested that a network should not simply be valued by how many people it could reach from a single point of broadcast, but how many users of the network could be reached by other users on the same network.[24] A more recent expression of this idea is 'Metcalfe's Law',[25] which holds that while an individual might only ever contact perhaps a hundred or so different people on a network of thousands, the value of the network is measured by the potential to contact many more.

Metcalfe's Law is a loose definition that states the value of a telecommunications network is proportional to the square of the number of users of the system. It refers to networks in the early years of internetworking, when simple functions such as e-mail and file transfer represented significant new capacities for organisations. Yet beyond these applications, network participants could provide value to each other in other ways too.

In the years since Metcalfe's Law additional services have become common on the Internet. Discussion groups, social networking, and chatrooms with many participants all represent an additional layer of service. Thus there should be an additional law to describe these new services on the Internet 'because it [now] facilitates the formation of groups in a way that Sarnoff and Metcalfe networks do not'.[26] David Reed, one of the early contributors to the TCP protocol and a computer scientist who spent much of his career working on networked group applications, expanded Metcalfe's Law with the 'Group Forming Law', also known as Reed's 3rd Law. From Reed's perspective 'group forming is...the technical feature that most distinguishes the Internet's capabilities from all other communications media before it'.[27] Reed's 3rd Law observes that the value of networks that allow their participants to form groups and collaborate on common goals scales in a far more dramatic way.[28] Group-forming networks such as online communities and discussion groups, argues Reed, do not scale linearly as Sarnoff's broadcast networks did, nor by the square number of the total number of participants as Metcalfe's Law suggests, but exponentially.

> If you add up all the potential two-person groups, three-person groups, and so on that those members could form, the number of possible groups equals 2^n. So the value of a GFN increases exponentially, in proportion to 2^n.[29]

This is because 'any system that lets users create and maintain groups creates a set of group-forming options that increase exponentially with the number of potential members'.[30] Thus where N equals the number of participants in the network the value of a network conforming to Sarnoff's Law is simply N; yet the value of a network conforming to

Metcalfe's Law is $N(N-1)$ or N^2; and the value of a network conforming to Reed's 3rd Law is 2^N-N-1. Furthermore, Reed says that 'the exponential, 2^N, is a sneaky function. Though it may be very small initially, it grows much faster than N^2, N^3 or any other power law'.[31] Herein lies the promise of the Internet for militant Islamists.

According to this the value to militant Islamism of large networks of sympathisers and activists would scale vastly, creating a sustainable, growing community.

> As networks grow, value shifts: Content (whose value is proportional to size) yields to Transactions (whose value is proportional to the square of size), and eventually Affiliation (whose value is exponential in size).[32]

Rather than simply creating new violent radicals who could communicate together as Metcalfe's Law would provide for, Reed's Law suggests the creation of new radicalisers who would act as focal nodes multiplying the value of the network to the militant cause. Not only could niche communities form online, but as Reed's 3rd Law reasons, their members can use their own initiative to contribute to and participate in the community's campaign. The way the individual works in an online community reflects the logic of the decentralised network itself. As Manuel Castells observes:

> A network has no center, just nodes. Nodes may be of varying relevance for the network. Nodes increase their importance for the network by absorbing more relevant information, and processing it more efficiently. The relative importance of a node does not stem from its specific features but from its ability to contribute to the network's goals.[33]

Nodal involvement in such a community need not necessarily mean active engagement or facilitation in militant campaigns. By gathering and redistributing militant material, individual community members can enhance their standing among their peers, much as participation in Wikipedia can gradually lead one to become a regular and active authority within the Wikipedia system.[34] Thus, for example, web forums could be self-perpetuating, and Reed's 3rd Law can be given effect:

> Administering the web forums can be carried out simultaneously by a limitless number of users, who can participate in the administration anonymously. In fact, many site administrators have no connection to actual members of jihadist groups and achieved their positions by being 'promoted' through the web forum's roster. They achieve promotion by their commitment to write new articles, post new material, and assist with other web forum tasks. This system helps to maintain the reliability of web administration; even if senior members of the website disappear or are killed, users located all over the world can continue to keep the site operational.[35]

David Galula, writing in *Pacification in Algeria, 1956–1958,* observed that despite the capture in 1957 of the top five leaders of the Algerian National Liberation Front, 'Their capture, I admit, had had little effect on the direction of the rebellion, because the movement was too loosely organised to crumble under such a blow'.[36] This appears to apply to al Qa'ida[37] but applies even more so to self-starters working to centrifugally disseminate militant media and messages on the Internet. Yet bleak though the outlook might seem, there is good news in the centrifugal character of the Internet too.

Hazards for militant narratives

While the evolution of digital networking and the norms of behaviour on it have enabled militant evangelists and their messages to proliferate, the norms of the Net also expose their content to the hazards of atomisation. The fecundity referred to above has a corollary: by virtue of its centrifugal character the Internet's users are far more assertive than their predecessors in the television age. Users increasingly dominate the medium. Their proclivities to edit, challenge, and criticise mean that the Internet is not only fecund, but also hazardous for the militant narrative. The disruptive behaviours of Internet users has brought a change to the nature of information that makes it plastic, and mutable, in a way that it has not been since before the invention of the printing press.

The first half of the 1990s were marked not only by the popularisation of the Web, but also by a kindling of interest among renaissance and medieval academics in oral culture,[38] which to some degree anticipated the development of what is now known as 'Web 2.0' – the interactive version of the Internet. In 1995 one specialist wrote that 'it is by now scholarly platitude to liken the customisation of a text possible through computer technology to a return to manuscript culture, when a similar customisation was standard'.[39] The previous year, in a seminal article in *Wired*, the Grateful Dead songwriter John Perry Barlow wrote 'information is an activity, not a noun'. 'As in an oral tradition', Barlow wrote, 'digitised information has no "final cut"'.[40] Earlier yet Marshall McLuhan had predicted the emergence of 'electric age' that 'succeeds the typographic and mechanical era of the past five hundred years'.[41] He argued that new communications may be "oral' in form even when the components of the situation may be non-verbal'.[42] McLuhan gives the example of musicians using 'all the techniques of oral poetry', in the 'electric or post-literate' time of the 1960s.[43] Much as the bardic tradition approached music in 'the terms of multiformity' because 'bards never repeat a song exactly',[44] so the new media would promote 'variability'. According to one specialist, 'a new medium object is not something fixed once and for all', but rather is 'variable', or in other words is 'mutable' and 'liquid':[45]

> Instead of identical copies a new media object typically gives rise to many different versions. And rather than being created completely by a human author, these versions are often in part automatically assembled by a computer.[46]

These various observations preceded the arrival of AJAX (see below) and the new web technologies that made them applicable to the general population. With the arrival of Web 2.0, however, information truly had become 'liquid' and 'mutable'. The first place where this was fully realised was within the software industry.

Beyond the narrow focus of terrorism studies a profound shift has occurred on the Internet that is changing how radicalisation occurs online. In 2004 Dale Dougherty coined the term 'Web 2.0'.[47] The '2.0' evokes the convention of appending version numbers after a piece of software's title to distinguish it from previous releases of the same package. Web 2.0 is a second iteration of the World-Wide-Web (WWW) revolution, and it crystallises the elements that make atomisation possible. Web 2.0 is the product of a number of factors. First, from 2004 onward a new generation of web technologies known as AJAX (AJAX stands for 'Asynchronous JavaScript and XML') allowed users to produce and distribute not only text and photos but video too.[48] AJAX now allowed users to do far more than simply read websites. In effect it extended websites into usable programs, transforming the web from a platform to read from to one to write on.[49] This transformed website readers into producers of content ranging from text to video. Social networking sites using AJAX were able to evolve into platforms where friends could play games against each other online. The second factor in the emergence of Web 2.0 is that faster 'broadband' Internet connections began to replace the far slower telephone line 'dial-up' connections during the same period.[50] This new speed allowed the emergence of music and then video as online media, since previous narrow band connections had been unable to transmit them in a satisfactory way. The third factor is the popularisation of the digital camera, which had been experimental since the early 1970s, and becoming a widespread consumer item.[51] Internet users embracing the culture of initiative discussed above began to create and watch amateur videos with gusto, and broadband connections to the Internet allowed them to upload them. Foremost among the new venues for user-created videos was the site 'YouTube', which launched its beta version to the public in May 2005. By mid 2007 YouTube users were uploading six hours of video every minute.[52] By mid 2009 they were uploading 20 hours of video every minute. Every video could be copied, rated and tagged by their peers.

The result of Web 2.0 was a user-driven revolution. PiperJaffray, a consultancy specialising in communications, reported in February 2007 that though the number of internet subscribers in the United States had grown by only 2 per cent in the previous year, the number using websites dependent on user generated content (such as Bebo, MySpace, YouTube, Wikipedia, Flickr or Facebook, to which Internet users contribute opinions, news, videos, ratings and comments on other users' content or images,) had grown by 100 per cent.[53] Thus a mere three years after the phrase Web 2.0 was coined, virtually all growth in Internet use in mature markets was driven by users viewing content generated horizontally by their peers or creating content themselves, rather than vertically by specialists in advertising agencies or delivered topdown, from an authority or government. Another way of putting it, in the words of one specialist, is 'mass-self communication', in which users become senders and receivers.[54]

Thus audiences who had been passive recipients of television and radio broadcast for most of the twentieth century were transforming themselves into the masters of content on the Internet at the beginning of the twenty-first. In late 2007 a Pew survey reported that 64 per cent of online teens in the USA had created and uploaded photos, artwork, or videos to the Internet.[55] Of the 50 most popular websites in the world at the beginning of 2009, 24 are reliant on Internet users creating their content.[56] Of the remaining 36, 16 are merely portal or search sites that link to other sites, and only ten are what could be considered conventional one-to-many, non-user driven sites such as CNN. com or Microsoft.com.[57]

Users, random and anonymous, are increasingly in control of the medium. For this same reason *Time Magazine* named 'You' the person of the year 2006, thereby breaking its standard practisce of nominating those who the Scottish historian Thomas Carlyle had called 'Great Men' whose acts made history.[58]

Look at 2006 through a different lens and you'll see another story, one that isn't about conflict or great men. It's a story about community and collaboration on a scale never seen before. It's about the cosmic compendium of knowledge Wikipedia and the million-channel people's network YouTube and the online metropolis MySpace. It's about the many wresting power from the few and helping one another for nothing and how that will not only change the world, but also change the way the world changes.[59]

Internet users have become the masters of online content, rather than simply passive receivers of information, and in turn they have begun to render information increasingly plastic and malleable.[60]

The dramatic growth of sites such as Wikipedia shows the increasing dominance that users rather than professional content producers have over the information on this increasingly plastic medium. From just under 20,000 articles in January 2002 the English language version of Wikipedia grew to over 2,500,000 by January 2009.[61] Virtually every single entry was created, edited, shortened or lengthened by people on the Internet who were neither Wikipedia staff nor professionals. This applies particularly strongly to controversial issues on the Internet. The Wikipedia article on George W. Bush has been edited 40,723 times as of 15 June 2009.[62] Heated editorial battles centred around his idiosyncratic pronunciation of the word nuclear, his national guard service, and whether it was appropriate to categorise him under the heading 'alcoholic'.[63] The Wikipedia entry on George W. Bush may in fact be one of the most edited pieces of text ever distributed in human history.[64] This remarkable plasticity is evident in other controversial issues on the Internet, in the interplay of ideas among people on Internet forums, and in comments on blog posts and video sites.

The users' increasing domination of Internet content has created what has become known as the 'perpetual beta' phenomenon.[65] In 2004 Tim O'Reilly outlined a new approach to software development that exemplified a new approach to user domination and anticipated the increasing plasticity of information.[66] The audience he was speaking to were familiar with an outmoded software development cycle in which progressive versions from an initial 'pre-alpha' build to a penultimate 'beta' version that is released for a period of testing by a small number of users before the final release candidate. From now on, O'Reilly told the gathered developers, Web 2.0 meant that software should never progress beyond the penultimate beta stage.[67] Instead it should constantly incorporate ideas and refinements from the global community of Internet users. Web 2.0 implied that there could be no final cut, no definitive version. The input of the empowered online audience of users would enrich products that remained flexible. Software, and much else besides, would remain in 'perpetual beta'. Software, media, and information would all be to some extent under the sway of their audience.

The phenomenon of the 'perpetual beta' is the result of the new dominance of user-generated content, which has made the Internet a horizontal rather than a top down medium. Another version of the idea was adopted in the analysis of new ways of running organisations, according to which 'permanently beta is a fluid organisational form resulting from the process of negotiation among users, employees, and organisations over the design of goods and services'.[68] In both versions perpetual beta conveys the concept of 'user as designer',[69] and of information increasingly being made plastic and malleable.

The perpetual beta and the attendant difficulties that the State faces in projecting preferred narratives online, is part of a seismic shift in communications. Taken in a broader context, the information environment is reverting to a model last experienced six centuries ago, before the printing press with movable type and printer's ink enabled the distribution of rigid, inflexible information. In Tom Pettitt's formulation, the half-millennium from 1500 to 2000 is the 'Gutenberg Parenthesis'.[70] Web 2.0 and the perpetual beta mark a reversion to normality. The difficult lesson for the State is that the comparatively brief spell of the print era is the anomaly in human history. This is a challenge that states will continue to face in the long-term.[71]

To fully comprehend the seismic scale of this change, and the challenge it poses to State narratives in the emerging environment of the perpetual beta and the user driven Internet, consider the communications problem faced by the Church in the centuries before the advent of the printing press. In AD 382 Pope Damascus commissioned Jerome to compile an edition of the Bible that became known as the 'Vulgate' edition.[72] Almost 1200 years later, in 1546, the Council of Trent decreed that St Jerome's Vulgate should 'be, in public lectures, disputations, sermons and expositions, held as authentic; and that no one is to dare, or presume to reject it under any pretext whatever'.[73] In other words the full weight of Rome was behind this particular text and no one should deviate from it. Yet in the absence of the print technology this kind of inflexible communication of information was simply not possible. Even a text as important as the Bible whose content underpinned the belief system of a continent and which was maintained by a centralised church with a cohort of highly disciplined monks underwent repeated alterations and re-edits. It was impossible to relay accurate information across Christendom for as long as the Church had attempted by relying on manual transcription. The mediaeval scribe was not a reliable repeater of text.[74] Thus, by the time the Council of Trent made its decree the original text of the Vulgate Bible had suffered generations of human error in transcription causing Erasmus to complain that there were as many Vulgates as there were Bibles.[75] Information, before the Gutenberg Press, was plastic.

The perpetual beta is a repetition of an earlier moment of change in the communication of ideas, from the bardic tradition of memorised learning to the written tradition of written learning. Harold Innis, in *Empire and Communications*, quotes Socrates in *Phaedrus,* who reports a conversation between the Egyptian god Thoth, the inventor of letters, and the god Amon. Amon accuses Thoth of creating forgetfulness in mens' souls:

> this discovery of yours will create forgetfulness in the learners' souls, because they will not use their memories; they will trust to the external written characters and not remember of themselves. The specific you have discovered is an aid not to memory, but to reminiscence, and you give your disciples not truth but only the semblance of truth; they will be hearers of many things and will have learned nothing; they will appear to omniscient and will generally know nothing; they will be tiresome company, having the show of wisdom without the reality.[76]

In the earlier era of plastic information before Pettitt's 'Gutenberg parenthesis',[77] authoritative text was relayed in two forms, according to Walter Ong. The first, chirographic, relied on citation to show authority; the second, oral, relied on resilience of the idea itself.[78] This first form is observable in the Islamic tradition of *ijaza*, the process by which a religious student who had memorised an important text to the satisfaction of the teaching *'ulama* would be empowered with an *iijaza* to teach the text to others.[79] In this tradition, when one wished to best understand a text one strove to hear it directly 'from a scholar whose *isnad*, or chain of transmission from the original author, was thought to be the most reliable', rather than simply to read it.[80]

Writing in the 1960s Eric Havelock reflected on the introduction of writing in ancient Greece and observed that, on the contrary to the God Amon's objections, it had created a new mental flexibility, a new plasticity of information that eclipsed learning by rote:

> The replacement of an orally memorised tradition by a quite different system of instruction and education...which therefore saw the Homeric state of mind give way to the Platonic.[81]

The Homeric state of mind, by virtue of requiring that poetic knowledge be retained in memory, rendered information necessarily rigid. Havelock suggests that Homeric education imparted in poetic narratives is 'essentially something [that the learner] accepts uncritically, or else it fails to survive in his living memory. Its acceptance and retention are made psychologically possible by a mechanism of self-surrender to the poetic performance...Only when the spell is fully effective can his mnemonic powers be fully mobilised'.[82] In short, 'his job was not to form individual and unique convictions'.[83] Poetic education before literacy created men of tradition. The perpetual beta from 2004 on introduces the same order of change as the transition from Homeric to Platonic, in the form of the passive broadcast audience that had previously been forced to watch, read, and listen uncritically, now emerging as an activist one in whom power to edit and remix is increasingly vested.

There is an additional aspect that goes beyond the individual users' power to edit: their power to peer-review. Internet users, with an unprecedented amount of information available to them, find it increasingly difficult to choose what information to view. This is what Joe Nye referred to some years ago as the 'paradox of plenty'.[84] What is scarce, when information is plentiful, is trust. Writing in the context of the so-called 'new economy', Kevin Kelly noted that prosperity and the increasing ease of producing physical goods inevitably diminished their value as they became plentiful. Under these circumstances, Kelly argued:

> ...those things that cannot be copied will become the true currency, the true sources of wealth. What cannot be copied? Trust. Authenticity. Immediacy. Presence. Experience. Relationships.[85]

Increasingly, this trust is the product of community vetting rather than top-down pronouncements. When faced with a rich supply of often-conflicting ideas and data, Internet users rely on something akin to the peer-review system of the academic world. The system dates to 1665, with the establishment by Henry Oldenburg of *Philosophical Transactions*.[86] Oldenburg created a process of peer-review to maintain the standard of the its articles, requiring authors wishing to publish in his journal would have to run the gauntlet of a review by other academics at the Royal Society. The process is summed up in one journal as 'a critical, judicious evaluation performed by one's equals'.[87] In practice, peer-review gives academics the power to approve or reject new developments in their respective areas,[88] yet peer-review also describes the open, democratic process by which information on the Internet is filtered by its readers. Our peers influence the review and reception of information and media content on the Internet, whether feedback on an eBay seller or a positive comment on the blog of a presidential candidate.

On an Internet where the Internet user is increasingly the creator or critic of content, word of mouth peer recommendation has a greater authority than normal one-to-many advertising. In the realm of commerce this quickly became a major factor in consumers' purchasing decisions. As of 31 March 2008, eBay members worldwide have left more than 7 billion feedback comments for each other regarding their eBay transactions.[89] Peer-review was an important contributor to YouTube's growth. Only after its introduction of comments and peer rating of videos did the site begin to attract large numbers of visitors. Yet peer-review presented a challenge to other enterprises. Amazon took a significant risk when it decided to allow users to write negative reviews under books on its site.[90] Conventional practice would have been to put an indiscriminately positive spin on all items. As Jeff Bezos told *Business Week*, allowing peer-review seemed counter intuitive to some:

> When we first did it, we got letters from publishers saying, 'Maybe you don't understand your business. You make money when you sell things.' Our point of view is, . . . negative reviews are helpful in making purchase decisions. So it's a very customer-centric point of view. Negative reviews will be helpful for customers, and that will ultimately sell more products than if you tried to cherry-pick the reviews.[91]

By allowing users to write negative reviews Amazon effectively put the fortunes of each retail item in the hands of its customers.

From the early 2000s onward word of mouth among users became the force that began to sift the good from the dross across the Internet, much as peer-review had done in academic circles since the mid 1660s. Kevin Kelly lamented that:

> As the Web expands in scope to include everything, the best gets overwhelmed . . . I want someone I trust to say to me: 'I've seen all the stuff, and I've used most of it, and this is the one you want.' I don't usually find that on the Web. First, trust is in short supply, and second, comparative evaluation is in short supply.[92]

Word of mouth became a collaborative sifting and categorisation, a 'folksonomy' in other words.[93] As Nicholas Negroponte and Mattie Maes wrote in 1996, 'the noise of the Net is its beauty, and navigating this noise will become easier and easier because of electronic word of mouth'.[94] In 2003 Joshua Schracter founded 'Del.icio.us', a directory of bits and pieces of Web content that users had tagged with reference phrases to denote that it was of interest for one reason or another.[95] Essentially, tagging became not only a way of categorising content on the Internet, but also a way of maintaining a personal library of book marked content and of finding like-minded peoples' tagged content.[96] Del.icio.us displayed details of users who created each tag, and allowed other users to look at collections of tagged content in other users' libraries. All Web content could thus be rated by 'social book marking', according to how many users thought it was worth tagging, and could be categorised according to what tags were used.[97] The user, therefore, is not only a creator of content but also an arbiter of what content is viewed by their peers. This is so acute that some advertisers are acknowledging the pivotal role of peer-review and user commendation and have begun to court influential bloggers to draw attention to their products using peer-to-peer, 'conversational' marketing.[98]

As Rupert Murdoch told the American Society of Newspaper Editors conference in April 2005:

> I'm a digital immigrant. I wasn't weaned on the web . . . Instead, I grew up in a highly centralised world where news and information were tightly controlled by a few editors, who deemed to tell us what we could and should know. My two young daughters, on the other hand, will be digital natives.

Islamist Discourse on the Internet

This critical and irreverent nature of 'digital natives' poses a challenge to any effort to enforce a rigorous and authoritative position on any subject. This is nothing less than a communications revolution, and has a potentially decisive impact on militant Islamist discourse on the Internet. These three aspects of Internet communications – namely that user-generated content dominates, that widely distributed information is now plastic in a way that it has not been for 500 years, and that community opinion has a decisive impact on how information proliferates – have turned the norms of communication upon their heads. The result is that individual Internet users are now the designers, editors, and contributors of content on the Internet, and that they trust their peers' opinions about what content merits attention.

None of this was necessarily clear to the al Qa'ida leadership in the days and weeks after 11 September 2001. Thus bin Laden took an imperious tone speaking in an interview with the Urdu media, *Karachi Ummat*, only weeks after 11 September 2001. He said 'Our silence is our real propaganda. Rejections, explanations, or corrigendum only waste your time . . . pulling you away from your cause'.[99] Yet conditions had changed by 2008 to the extent that Ayman al-Zawahiri decided to submit to an online question & answer exchange with Internet users in 2008. Indeed he adopted an open and accommodating tone in the introduction to his answers:

> I hope that those who sent in their questions have not become upset by the passing of some time between the posting of the questions and the giving of the answers. Allah knows that I did my best to make the answers come close after the questions.[100]

The tone of his apology for the delay in his responses to Internet users' questions suggests that al-Zawahiri understands better than most the growing power of the Internet audience to proliferate, distort, or reject his message.

Perhaps in part he was also moved by challenges arising from senior detractors within the broad militant Islamist movement. In March 2008, the same month that he published the first half of his responses to the Internet question and answers, al-Zawahiri also published *The Exoneration: a treatise exonerating the community of the pen and the sword from the debilitating accusation of fatigue and weakness* as a counter measure against criticisms of his violent campaigns from one of his peers, a senior militant ideologue.[101] In November 2007 Sayid Imam Abdel-Aziz al-Sharif, also known as Dr Fadl, the former grand mufti of Islamic Jihad in Egypt, published a book called *Rationalisations on Jihad in Egypt and the World*, serialised in the Egyptian paper *al-Masry al-Youm*, which repudiates al-Zawahiri's violent militant campaign.[102] Al-Sharif is the most senior Islamic scholar held in Egyptian prisons[103] and is an important and influential figure in the militant world. For example, his books have been found in the possession of disrupted militant cells in Germany and Italy in 2004.[104] Yet even if al-Zawahiri was partly motivated to respond to Dr Fadl's criticism, he nonetheless draws the readers' attention to the openness of his approach in the first of his two part responses to the almost two thousand questions he received in response to his invitation to an 'open meeting' on the Internet:[105]

> The listener... will notice that I have given more room to the opposing questions, despite them being less than the support-ing questions, and that is in order to encourage the opponents to bring their objections to light so they can be replied to and refuted and so the proofs of the *Mujahedeen* can be shown.[106]

As al-Zawahiri's statement acknowledges, a single, centralised and consistent narrative is difficult to maintain when exposed to a diverse population of online critics, commentators, and information hackers. The perpetual beta and the critical and irreverent nature of digital natives renders militant information campaigns vulnerable to distor-tion. Web 2.0 means that information is always open to challenge, always in 'beta', and that information campaigns that favour openness fare better than those that are top down. Authoritarian militant mes-sages are subject to the same irreverent challenge from digital natives that hinders the communication of top-down messages from hierarchi-cal authority. In order to appeal to new sympathisers, militants must reach beyond the locked web forums where their own devotees con-gregate. Once they engage in discussion in the wider, open Internet, militants fall prey to the same Internet phenomenon that renders governments powerless. The irony is that the Web that enabled the militant message to proliferate also subjects it to distorting, atomising pressures. The Internet therefore is a new high ground for which states and militants are in competition.

It should be noted that there are venues on the Internet that are not subject to the hazard of atomisation. These are the committed forums where those in outright support of militant campaigns gather. As Quilliam's recent survey notes, 'al-Qa'ida and its affiliate groups today largely communicate not through dedicated websites but instead through a range of online discussion forums'.[107] The software by which web forums are administered gives their managers broad power to prevent dissent if so minded. The popular vBulletin forum system allows for the establishment a hierarchy among users based on title, rank, reputation, and length of membership. This can create an inertia of opinion within each forum, entrenching high reputation individual's positions within its hierarchy and acting against the perpetual beta. vBulletin allows forum administers to establish hierarchies of forum members in the following ways. First, the forum administrator can establish a ladder of forum members based on the number of posts they have made.[108] According to a recent survey of militant forums there is an inbuilt bias on hard core sites against new arrivals:

> On Jihadist sites, moderators and members alike are usually very suspicious of new members posing news or discussing matters to do with the health of Jihadist leaders, strategies of Jihadist groups, or any other sensitive information, including the judicial or theological justifications for Jihadist tactics.[109]

On progression to senior membership new perks and functionality might be activated. vBulletin has further systems that allow for the establishment of entrenched hierarchy – provided they are enabled by a forum's administrator. A 'post count factor' takes account of the number of posts that a user has contributed to assign reputation points.[110] A 'reputation point factor' can add momentum to users with high reputations' further increase of their reputation.[111] Moreover, the 'minimum post count' option can be set by an administrator to prevent users who have made fewer than a set number of posts from giving or removing reputation points from another user, further entrenching the established hierarchy's reputation.[112] This can also be applied to users below a requisite level of reputation, using the 'minimum reputation count'.[113] Among other severe measures, forum software allows administrators to put users on a 'Coventry' list that puts that user in the ignore list of all other users meaning that while their own postings appear visible to them, they are invisible to others.[114]

The hazard of the Internet is less in effect in such controlled conditions where militants may be speaking among like-minded users, and ignoring dissenting voices. However, on the wider Internet, where the perpetual beta applies in full force, recent research by the author[115] proves that the core elements of the militant Islamist message lose consistency over time on forums that are less closely associated with militant groups. This is where the future of the militant movement lies, beyond the locked forums where comparatively small numbers of committed individuals congregate, in the wider Internet where disinterested millions conduct their affairs. Militant propagandists appear to realise this. Bari Atwan observes that a user writing under the alias 'al-Salem' on a hard core forum called al-Farouq posted a message entitled 'al-Qa'ida: the 39 principles of jihad', which included participating in other forums and spreading propaganda in support of militant campaigns.[116] The 2004 Madrid bombers, for example, visited both mainstream forums and committed forums.[117] Similarly, a posting on an the Arabic web forum *Shumukh* (Pride) by a member called Abu Dharr al-Makki that announced the establishment of an 'incitement brigade' that would operate across other forums and post recruitment propaganda.[118] The Quilliam Foundation's recent report on militant forums notes that:

> Forum members are encouraged to copy these releases into other forums and sites to achieve the maximum amount of publicity for the intended message. This is sometimes referred to on Jihadist forums as a 'Jihadist media incursion.[119]

This echoes Sayyid Qutb's 'vanguard',[120] which, as Lenin before him had written,[121] would carry a revolutionary Islamist message and transform wider society.

Metcalfe's and Reed's Laws suggest that the value of networks scale exponentially upward. Thus the sensible objective in countering online radicalisation should be a narrow one: the disruption of disturbance of the wider proliferation of militant ideas beyond the hard core locked militant forums. The irony is that the very factors that made the Internet so amenable to subversives also make the militant Islamist call to violence vulnerable to distortion and dilution. To grow one's network and appeal to the prospective self-starter, one must expose one's message to the hazards of the Internet – making it plastic and subject to the hazard of the perpetual beta. Once they engage in discussion in the wider, open Internet beyond the locked web forums where their own devotees congregate, militants fall prey to the same Internet phenomenon that frustrates state narratives. Only the most robust and resilient memes will endure. For example, Hegghammer has found that a 'hybridisation' of messages is occurring across various militant groups, whose rhetoric is increasingly becoming less particularist and more generic and simple to appeal to a wider body of supporters.[122]

Conclusion

In short, this suggests that the rhetoric of bin Laden and the core hierarchy of al Qa'ida is not virulent on the Internet – at least, not on the English speaking Internet. Therefore the challenge is not only to 'drain the swamp', but to see whether the waters subside of their own accord.[123] Fecundity and hazard have an antagonistic relationship that means niche communications can form, but also means that the exponential potential of Reed's 3rd Law[124] is unlikely to be realised. This allows the problem of violent radicalisation on the Internet to be redefined in a number of ways.

First, if the Internet is both fecund and hazardous, and is so in such a manner that the militant narrative does not perpetuate wildly beyond already committed forums, then the Internet does not represent an inordinate threat of violent radicalisation. Second, if the militant narrative is generally confined to committed forums it is possible to define and target this problem in a specific and focussed way rather than by Internet-wide measures such as web filtering. Finally, the existence of the online world in fact reinforces the importance of taking action offline. The prospect that a small proportion of citizens should be willing to kill their peers is a problem within society, rather than one of technology. Online radicalisation is a symptom of two factors: that the Internet is a medium of networks and relationships; and that there is a fundamental problem within society. The strength of society persists in a networked world, and offline measures to deal with violent radical sentiment within society should be pursued. Counter narratives need not necessarily be online, nor must they be Internet focused. Measures that succeed offline will necessarily make an impact online. It might seem too obvious to state, but the perpetual beta means that the more individuals across society that subscribe to the values of the State offline, the more vulnerable the militant message is to distortion online. Though the challenge is online radicalisation, the focus on offline society must not be obscured.

Alison Pargeter justifiably cautions against placing too much emphasis on the importance of the Internet as a means of radicalisation beyond Europe.[125] Yet this will soon change. Internet use in the Middle East grew by 1,825 per cent from 2000–10, and by 2,375 per cent in Africa, while growth in Europe and North America were only 352 per cent and 146 per cent respectively over the same period.[126] Statistics maintained by the International Telecommunications Union show that eventually, probably by 2019, the poorest nations will reach the point where one in every two people is an Internet user.[127] The Internet is also becoming a more engaging medium, and mobile connectivity and improved batteries will enable users in remote regions to spend ever longer periods of time online.[128] We are only now experiencing the first shocks of a communications change that will have an impact on security and society for many decades to come.

It is crucial to recognise at this early stage of the Internet's development that the Net, like the high seas, is part of the global commons, and any official approach to it at this early stage in its development must be considered from the long term perspective of building up a strong society of digital natives rather than by the short term imperative to act in the wake of a terrorist event. In the emerging digital era the State will be unable to control information as it has done in the past. Instead it must increasingly rely on its citizens and on the strength of its society so that the plasticity of information can work in its favour. One must respect the medium, but challenge the message. Subversives will persist online, but the more people in society who understand and oppose the violent narratives that threaten their society, the harder it will be for isolated militants to appeal with a consistent message across the wider Internet.

Notes

1. Paul Baran, 'On Distributed Communication Networks' (Santa Monica, 1962); Paul Baran, 'Summary Overview: On Distributed Communications' (Santa Monica, 1964), (URL:rand.org/pubs/research_memoranda/RM3767/), p.18; 'Recommendation to the air staff on the development of the distributed adaptive message-block network', 30 August 1965, (URL:www.archive.org/details/RecommendationToTheAirStaff, last accessed 29 January 2009). To those who argue against the importance of the nuclear factor, see Lawrence Roberts' own memorandum to the ARPA Director, in which he explicitly states that the ARPANET will be an experiment to test the ideas developed at RAND, 'Interactive Computer Network Communication System', Lawrence Roberts to E. Rechtin, Memorandum, 21 June 1968, p.1.

2. See Johnny Ryan, *A History of the Internet and the Digital Future* (London, 2010).

3. Jerrold Post, 'Psychological and motivational factors in terrorist decision-making: implications for CBW terrorism', in J. B. Tucker (ed), *Toxic Terror: Assessing Terrorist Use of Chemical Weapons* (London, 1999).

4. Ibid., pp31–2.

5. Brian Marcus, 'Online hate, communications, coordination, and crime', in Suzette Bronkhorst and Ronald Eissens (eds.), *Hate on the Net: A Virtual Nursery for Real Life Crime* (Amsterdam, 2004), p.41.

6. Al Suri's *Call for Worldwide Islamic Resistance*, December 2004, quoted in Lawrence Wright, 'The Master Plan', *The New Yorker*, 11 September 2006, p.51.

7. The subtitle of Marc Sageman's 2008 book *Leaderless Jihad*.

8. Richard Harris Smith, *OSS: The Secret History of America's First Central Intelligence Agency* (Guilford, CT, 2005, p.114).

9. 'The History, Definition, & Use of the Term "Leaderless Resistance"', Political Research Associates PublicEye.org, 2008 (URL: http://www.publiceye.org/liberty/terrorism/insurgency/leaderless-resistance.html, last accessed 2 December 2009); see also David C. Rapoport, *Terrorism: The Fourth or Religious Wave* (London, 2006), p.248.

10. George Michael, *Confronting Right-Wing Extremism and Terrorism in the USA* (New York, 2003), pp.114–5.

11. Louis Beam, 'Leaderless Resistance', 1983, reprinted in *The Seditionist*, Issue 12, February 1992 (URL: http://www.louisbeam.com/leaderless.htm, last accessed 2 December 2009).

12. Ibid.

13. Ibid.

14. Ibid.

15. 'From Dawa to Jihad: The various threats from radical Islam to the democratic legal order', Ministry of the Interior and Kingdom relations, translated in March 2005; see also 'Violent Jihad in the Netherlands: Current trends in the Islamist terrorist threat', Ministry of the Interior and Kingdom relations, 13 April 2006, p.17; 'Countering International Terrorism: The United Kingdom's Strategy', July 2006, HM Government (URL: http://security.homeoffice.gov.uk/news-publications/publication-search/general/Contest-Strategy, last accessed 30 October 2008), p.12; see also Dame Eliza Manningham-Buller, 'The international terrorist threat to the UK', at Queen Mary's College, London, 9 November 2006.

16. Marc Sageman, Speech at the Counter Terror Coordinator of the Netherlands Conference, the Hague, 24 October 2007.

17. Ibid.

18. Brynjar Lia, *Architect of Global Jihad: The Life of al-Qaeda Strategist Abu Mu'sab al-Suri* (London, 2007), p.6.

19. Abu Mu'sab al Suri quoted in ibid., p.7; see also Wright, 'The Master Plan'.

20. Ibid.; see also Fawaz Gerges, *Journey of the Jihadist* (Orlando, 2007), p.37.

21. Daniel Kimmage, 'The al Qaeda media nexus', RadioFreeEurope special report, March 2008, p.1.

22. Didier Lombard, *The Second Life of Networks* (New York, 2008), p.96.

23. 'Annual report of the directors of the American Telephone & Telegraph Company to the stockholders for the year ending December 31, 1908', p.21 (URL: www.porticus.org/bell/pdf/1908ATTar_Complete.pdf, last accessed 15 June 2008).

24. S. J. Liebowitz and S. E. Margolis, 'Network Externalities (Effects)', *The New Palgrave Dictionary of Economics and the Law*, MacMillan, 1998 (URL: www.utdallas.edu/~liebowit/palgrave/network.html, last accessed 15 June 2008).

25. George Gilder, 'Metcalfe's Law and its legacy', *Forbes ASAP*, 13 September 1993, (URL: http://www.seas.upenn.edu/~gaj1/metgg.html, last accessed 22 April 2009).

26. David Reed, 'Weapon of math destruction', *Context*, Spring 1999, (URL: http://www.contextmag.com/archives/199903/digitalstrategy.asp?process=print).

27. David Reed interviewed in the *Journal of the Hyperlinked Organization*, 19 January 2001, (URL: http://www.hyperorg.com/backissues/joho-jan19–01. html, last accessed 31 October 2009).

28. Reed, 'That sneaky exponential – beyond Metcalfe's Law to the Power of Community Building'.

29. David Reed, 'The law of the pack', *Harvard Business Review*, February 2001, vol. 79 (2)., p.24.

30. David Reed interviewed in Journal of the Hyperlinked Organization.

31. Reed, 'That sneaky exponential - beyond Metcalfe's Law to the Power of Community Building'.

32. David Reed, 'Reed's 3rd law: a scaling law for network value', (URL: www. reed.com/dpr/docs/Papers/reeds3rd.htm, last accessed 16 June 2009).

33. Manuel Castells, 'Informationalism, networks, and the network society: a theoretical blueprint', in Manuel Castells (ed), *The Network Society: A Cross-Cultural Perspective* (Cheltenham, 2004), p.3.

34. Coy Cheshire and Judd Antin, 'The Social Psychological Effects of Feedback on the Production of Internet Information Pools', *Journal of Computer Mediated Communication*, Vol. 13, No. 3, pp.705–27; see also Tim Stevens & Gilbert Ramsay contribution to Johnny Ryan et al., 'Study on non-legislative measures to prevent the distribution of violent radical content on the Internet'; Susan Bryant, Andrea Forte, and Amy Bruckman, 'Becoming Wikipedian: Transformation of Participation in a Collaborative Online Encyclopaedia', *Proceedings of GROUP: International Conference on Supporting Group Work* (Sanibel, FL, 2009), pp.1–10.

35. Torres Soriano, 'Maintaining the Message: How Jihadists Have Adapted to Web Disruptions', p.23.

36. David Galula, *Pacification in Algeria, 1956–1958* (Santa Monica, 2006), p.141.

37. Bruce Hoffman, 'American Jihad', *National Interest*, April 2010.

38. Leah S. Marcus, 'Cyberspace Renaissance', *English Literary Renaissance*, vol. 25 (3), 1995, p.395.

39. Ibid., p.393.

40. John Perry Barlow, 'The Economy of Ideas', *Wired* (March 1994); see also Ong, *Orality and Literacy: The Technologizing of the Word*; Marshall McLuhan, The Gutenberg Galaxy (Toronto, 1962); and Lars Ole Sauerberh, 'The Gutenberg Parenthesis - Print, Book and Cognition', *Orbis Litterarum*, vol. 64, No. 2, 2009.

41. McLuhan, *Gutenberg Galaxy*, p.3.

42. Ibid.

43. Ibid.

44. Alfred Lord, *The Singer of Tales* (New York, 1971), p.125.

45. Lev Manovich, *The Language of New Media*, (Cambridge, MA, 2001), p.36.

46. Ibid.

47. Tim O'Reilly, 'What is Web 2.0: Design patterns and business models for the next generation of software', 30 September 2005, Web 2.0 conference (URL: http://oreilly.com/web2/archive/what-is-web-20.html, last accessed 11 November 2010).

48. Jesse James Garrett, 'Ajax: A New Approach to Web Applications', 18 February 2005 (URL:www.adaptivepath.com/ideas/essays/archives/000385. php, last accessed 22 July 2009).

49. O'Reilly, 'What is Web 2.0: Design patterns and business models for the next generation of software'.

50. Time series data of broadband penetration from 2001 to 2005, in 'OECD Broadband Statistics to June 2006', (URL: http://www.oecd.org/documen t/9/0,3343,en_2649_34225_37529673_1_1_1_1,00.html, last accessed 11 November 2010).

51. 'European low end digital camera market growing 55% annually through 2005', InfoTrends Research Group press release, 12 July 2000 (URL: http://www. dpreview.com/news/0007/00071201eurodigicammarket.asp, last accessed 11 November 2010).

52. 'Zoinks! 20 Hours of Video Uploaded Every Minute!', Youtube blog, 21 May 2009 (URL:www.youtube.com/blog, last accessed 15 June 2009).

53. 'The user revolution: the new advertising ecosystem and the rise of the Internet as a mass medium', PiperJaffray Investment Research, February 2007.

54. Manual Castells, *Communication power* (Oxford, 2009), p.4.

55. 'Teens and Social Media', Pew Internet & American Life Project, 19 December 2007, p.i.

56. Alexa web service rankings, 24 January 2009.

57. Ibid.

58. Lev Grossman, 'Time's person of the year: You', *Time Magazine*, 13 December 2006.

59. Ibid.

60. Johnny Ryan, 'The Internet, the Perpetual Beta, and the State: The Long View of the New Medium', *Studies in Conflict and Terrorism*, volume 33 (8), pp.673–681.

61. 'Size of wikipedia', Wikipedia (URL: http://en.wikipedia.org/wiki/ Wikipedia:Size_of_Wikipedia, last accessed 15 June 2009).

62. Wikipedia most frequently edited pages, (URL: http://en.wikipedia.org/ wiki/Wikipedia:Most_frequently_edited_articles, last accessed 15 June 2009).

63. Wikipedia, archive of talk on George W. Bush page, (URL: http://en.wikipedia. org/wiki/Talk:George_W._Bush/Archive_index, last accessed 15 June 2009).

64. Ibid. – this is obviously impossible to verify.

65. O'Reilly, 'What Is Web 2.0: Design Patterns and Business Models for the Next Generation of Software'.

66. Ibid.

67. Ibid.

68. Gina Neff and David Stark, 'Permanently beta: responsive organization in the Internet era', in Philip Howard and Steve Jones, Society Online: the Internet in context (Thousand Oaks, CA, 2004), p.175.

69. Ibid., p.185.

70. Tom Pettitt, 'Before the Gutenberg parenthesis: Elizabethan-American compatibilities', MiT5, 'Folk Cultures and Digital Cultures', 2008, (URL: http://web.mit.edu/comm-forum/mit5/papers/pettitt_plenary_gutenberg. pdf, last accessed 24 July 2010).

71. Johnny Ryan, Speech at the Study Group on Intelligence, Royal United Services Institute, 'The Internet, Intelligence, the Perpetual Beta, and the State: The Long View of The New Medium', 29 January 2010.

72. Sparks, H, F, D, 'Jerome as Biblical Scholar', *The Cambridge History of the Bible: Volume 1, From the Beginnings to Jerome* (London, 1970), p.513.

73. 'Decree Concerning the Edition and the Use of the Sacred Books', Canons and Decrees of the Council of Trent, The Fourth Session, Celebrated on the eighth day of the month of April, in the year 1546 (URL: www.bible-researcher.com/trent1.html).

74. Bernard Cerquiglini, *Eloge de la Variante* [in praise of the variant text] (Paris, 1989), p.4 quoted in Pettitt, 'Before the Gutenberg parenthesis: Elizabethan-American compatibilities'.

75. John Sandys-Wunsch, *What Have They Done to the Bible?: A History of Modern Biblical Interpretation* (Collegeville, Minnesota, 2005), p.6.

76. Harold Innis, *Empire and Communications* (Toronto, 2007), p.78.

77. Pettitt, T, 'Before the Gutenberg parenthesis: Elizabethan-American compatibilities'.

78. Walter Ong, *Orality and Literacy: The Technologizing of the Word* (New York, 1982), p.2.

79. Francis Robinson, 'Crisis of authority: crisis of Islam?', *Journal of the Royal Asiatic Society of Great Britain and Ireland* (Third Series), 2009, p.342.

80. Ibid., p.343.

81. Eric Havelock, *Preface to Plato* (Cambridge, MA, 1963), p.198.

82. Ibid., pp.198–9.

83. Ibid., p.199.

84. Joseph Nye, 'Public diplomacy in the 21st Century', *The Globalist*, 10 May 2004.

85. Kevin Kelly, 'Pro-choice: the promise of technology', *Organisation and environment*, vol. 12 (4), December 1999, p.428; see also Kevin Kelly, 'Tools Are the Revolution', *Whole Earth*, issue 103, Winter 2000 (URL: http://www.wholeearth.com/issue/103/article/126/tools.are.the.revolution, last accessed 6 October 2008).

86. E.N.C. Andre, 'The birth and early days of the Philosophical Transactions', Notes and Records of the Royal Society of London, 1965.

87. 'Manuscript Peer Review: A Guide for Health Care Professionals: What Is Peer Review?', *Pharmacotherapy*, 2001 vol. 21 (4) (URL:www.medscape.com/viewarticle/409692, last accessed 26 April 2009).

88. Daryl E. Chubin and Edward J. Hackett, *Peerless Science: Peer Review and US Science Policy* (New York, 1990), p. 4.

89. 'eBay marketplace fast facts', eBay.com (URL:news.ebay.com/fastfacts_ebay_marketplace.cfm, last accessed 9 July 2008).

90. 'Jeff Bezos on word-of-mouth power', *Business Week*, 2 August 2004.

91. Ibid.

92. Kelly, 'Tools Are the Revolution'.

93. Thomas Vanderwal, 'Folksonomy Coinage and Definition', Vanderwal.net, 2 February 2007 (URL:vanderwal.net/folksonomy.html, last accessed 25 January 2009).

94. Nicholas Negroponte and Mattie Maes, 'Electronic word of mouth', *Wired*, October 1996.

95. 'Young Innovators under 35', *Technology Review Magazine*, 2006 (URL: http://www.technologyreview.com/tr35/?year=2006, last accessed 2 May 2010).

96. 'Learn more about Delicious', Delicious (URL: http://www.delicious.com/help/learn, last accessed 2 February 2010).

97. Tony Hammond et al., 'Social bookmarking tools', *D-Lib Magazine*, April 2005.

98. Ian Lurie, *Conversation Marketing: Internet Marketing Strategies* (Victoria, B.C. , 2006), p.36; 'Sponsored conversations', Izea.com (URL:http://izea.com/social-media-marketing/sponsored-conversations/, last accessed 25 July 2009).

99. 'Exclusive' Interview with Usama Bin Ladin on 11 Sep Attacks in US', *Karachi Ummat*, 28 September 2001, translated in *Compilation of Usama Bin Laden Statements 1994-January 2004*, FBIS, p.178.

100. Ayman al-Zawahiri, 'First Part of Responses by Dr. Ayman al-Zawahiri to Open Meeting Coordinated by al Fajr Center and as-Sahab', 2 April 2008 (URL: http://www.archive.org/details/Responses-1, last accessed 1 November 2008), p.1.

101. Peter Bergen and Katherine Tiedmann, 'The almanac of al Qaeda', *Foreign Policy*, May/June 2010; see also 'Zawahiri tries to clear name, explain strategy', Trasnnational security issues report, International Research Center, 21 April 2008 (URL: http://fas.org/irp/eprint/zawahiri.pdf, last accessed 6 December 2009).

102. Jarret Brachman, 'Leading Egyptian jihadist Sayyid Imam renounced violence', *Counter Terrorism Center Sentinel*, vol 1 (1), December 2007, p.12.

103. Ibid., p.13.

104. William McCants, Jarret Brachman, *Militant Ideology Atlas*, West Point Military Academy Counter Terrorism Center, November 2006, p.290.

105. See especially Ayman al-Zawahiri, 'First Part of Responses by Dr. Ayman al-Zawahiri to Open Meeting Coordinated by al Fajr Center and as-Sahab', 2 April 2008 (URL: http://www.archive.org/details/Responses-1, last accessed 1 November 2008), pp.1–2, and question 2/1 on p.15 to which al-Zawahiri answers with a pronounced tone of openness.

106. al-Zawahiri, 'First Part of Responses by Dr. Ayman al-Zawahiri to Open Meeting Coordinated by al Fajr Center and as-Sahab', p.2.

107. Mohammed Ali Musawi, 'Cheering for Osama: how Jihadists use Internet discussion forums', Quilliam, August 2010, p.4.

108. 'User titles', Bulletin manual (FAQ) (URL: http://www.vbulletin.com/docs/html/user_titles, last accessed 29 December 2009).

109. Mohammed Ali Musawi, 'Cheering for Osama: how Jihadists use Internet discussion forums', Quilliam, August 2010, p.19.

110. Ibid.

111. Ibid.

112. Ibid.

113. Ibid.

114. Ibid.

115. Johnny Ryan, 'Militant Islamist radicalisation: does the Internet atomize?', PhD thesis, University of Cambridge, 2010.

116. Bari Atwan, *Secret History of Al Qaeda*, pp.117–8.

117. List of URLs contained in the indictment of the Spanish court against the Madrid bombers, 11 April 2006 (URL: http://www.sofir.org/sarchives/005905.php, last accessed 9 November 2010).

118. Will McCants, 'How online recruitment works', Jihadica blog, 18 September 2009 (URL: http://www.jihadica.com/how-online-recruitment-works/, last accessed 18 October 2009).

119. Mohammed Ali Musawi, 'Cheering for Osama: how Jihadists use Internet discussion forums', Quilliam, August 2010, p.8.

120. Sayyid Qutb, *Milestones* (1964, PDF version online at majalla.org/books/2005/ qutb-nilestone.pdf, last accessed 19 January 2009), p.52.

121. Vladimir Ilyich Lenin, 'What Is To Be Done?: Burning questions of our movement', pamphlet, March 1902 (URL: http://marxists.org/archive/lenin/ works/download/what-itd.pdf, last accessed 3 February 2009), p.13.

122. Thomas Hegghammer, 'The ideological hybridization of jihadi groups', *Current trends in Islamist ideology*, vol. 9, 18 November 2009 (URL: http:// www.currenttrends.org/research/detail/the-ideological-hybridization-of-jihadi-groups, last accessed 4 December 2009).

123. Wade Merkel, 'Draining the swamp: the British strategy of population control', *Parameters*, vol. 36 (1), Spring 2006.

124. Blackmore, S. 1999, 'Instructions for carrying out behaviour, stored in brains (or other objects) and passed on by imitation', *The Meme Machine*, Oxford University Press, Oxford, p.17.

125. Alison Pargeter, *The New Frontiers of Jihad: Radical Islam in Europe* (London, 2008), p.108.

126. 'Internet usage statistics, world Internet users and population stats', 30 June 2010, (URL: http://www.internetworldstats.com/stats.htm, last accessed 1 November 2010).

127. Richard Heeks, 'Global ICT Statistics on Internet Usage, Mobile, Broadband: 1998–2009', ICTs for Development, 16 September 2010 (URL: https://ict-4dblog.wordpress.com/2010/09/16/global-ict-statistics-on-internet-usage-mobile-broadband-1998–2009/, last accessed 29 October 2010). This analysis uses ITU data.

128. Mary Meeker, 'Ten Questions Internet Execs Should Ask & Answer', presentation to the Web 2.0 Summit, 16 November 2010, San Francisco, CA, (URL: http://www.morganstanley.com/institutional/techresearch/pdfs/ten-questions_web2.pdf, last accessed 16 November 2010); see also regarding battery issues OLPC hardware, (URL: http://wiki.laptop.org/go/Laptop_ Batteries, last accessed 2 July 2010); regarding broadband penetration in BRICs countries in 2015 see Boston Consulting Group, *The Internet's New Billion: Digital Consumers in Brazil, Russia, India, China, and Indonesia* (Boston, 2010).

Bibliography

Baran, P. 1962. 'On Distributed Communication Networks', Santa Monica.
—— 1964. 'Summary Overview: On Distributed Communications' Santa Monica.

Bergen, P., and Tiedmann, K. 2010. 'The almanac of al Qaeda', *Foreign Policy*, May/June.

Blackmore, S. 1999. *The Meme Machine*. Oxford University Press: Oxford.

Brachman, J. 2007. 'Leading Egyptian jihadist Sayyid Imam renounced violence', *Counter Terrorism Center Sentinel*, 1 (1), December.

Bryant, S., Forte, A., and Bruckman, A. 2009. 'Becoming Wikipedian: Transformation of Participation in a Collaborative Online Encyclopaedia', *Proceedings of GROUP: International Conference on Supporting Group Work*. Sanibel: Florida.

Castells, M. 2004. 'Informationalism, networks, and the network society: a theoretical blueprint', in Castells, M. (ed.), *The Network Society: A Cross-Cultural Perspective*. Edward Elgar Publishing: Cheltenham.

—— 2009. *Communication power*. Oxford University Press: Oxford.

Cheshire, C., and Antin, J. 2008. 'The Social Psychological Effects of Feedback on the Production of Internet Information Pools', *Journal of Computer Mediated Communication*, 13 (3), pp.705–727.

Chubin, D.E., and Hackett, E.J. 1990. *Peerless Science: Peer Review and US Science Policy*. State University of New York Press: New York.

Galula, D. 2006. *Pacification in Algeria, 1956–1958*. RAND Corporation: Santa Monica, CA.

Gerges, F. 2007. *Journey of the Jihadist: Inside Muslim Militancy*. Harvest Books: Orlando.

Gilder, G. 1993. 'Metcalfe's Law and its legacy', *Forbes ASAP*, 13 September.

Grossman, L. 2006. 'Time's Person of the Year: You', *Time Magazine*, 13 December.

Hammond, T. (et al.). 2005. 'Social bookmarking tools', *D-Lib Magazine*, April.

Havelock, E. 1963. *Preface to Plato*. Harvard University Press: Cambridge, MA.

Hoffman, B. 2010. 'American Jihad', *National Interest*, April.

Innis, H. 2007. *Empire and Communications*. Dundurn Group: Toronto.

Kelly, K. 1999. 'Pro-choice: the promise of technology', *Organisation and Environment*, 12 (4), December.

—— 2008. 'Tools Are the Revolution', *Whole Earth*, 103, Winter.

Kimmage, D. 2008. 'The al Qaeda media nexus', RadioFreeEurope special report, March.

Lia, B. 2007. *Architect of Global Jihad: The Life of al-Qaeda Strategist Abu Mu'sab al-Suri*. Hurst & Co.: London.

Liebowitz, S. J., and Margolis, S.E. 1998. 'Network Externalities (Effects)', in *The New Palgrave's Dictionary of Economics and the Law*. Palgrave MacMillan: Basingstoke.

Lombard, D. 2008. *The Second Life of Networks*, Odile Jacob: New York.

Lord, A. 1960. *The Singer of Tales*. Harvard University Press: Cambridge, MA.

Lurie, I. 2006. *Conversation Marketing: Internet Marketing Strategies*. Trafford Publishing: Victoria, BC.

Manovich, L. 2001. *The Language of New Media*. Massachusetts Institute of Technology Press: Cambridge, MA.

Marcus, B. 2004. 'Online hate, communications, coordination, and crime', in Bronkhorst, S., and Eissens, R., (eds.) *Hate on the Net: Virtual Nursery for Real Life Crime*, Ashgate Publishing Limited: Hampshire, UK.

Marcus, L.S. 1995. 'Cyberspace Renaissance', *English Literary Renaissance*, 25 (3).

McCants, W., and Brachman, J. 2006. *Militant Ideology Atlas*, West Point Military Academy Counter Terrorism Center, November.

McLuhan, M. 1962. *Gutenberg Galaxy*. University of Toronto Press: Toronto.

Merkel, W. 2006. 'Draining the swamp: the British strategy of population control', *Parameters*, 36 (1), Spring.

Michael, G. 2003. *Confronting Right-Wing Extremism and Terrorism in the USA*. Routledge: New York.

Neff, G., and Stark, D. 2004. 'Permanently beta: responsive organization in the Internet era', in Howard, P., and Jones, S., *Society Online: The Internet in Context*, Sage Publications: Thousand Oaks, CA.

Negroponte, N., and Maes, M. 1996. 'Electronic word of mouth', *Wired*, October.

Nye, J. 2004. 'Public diplomacy in the 21st Century', *The Globalist*, 10 May.

Ong, W.J. 1962. *Orality and Literacy: The Technologizing of the Word*. Marshall McLuhan, The Gutenberg Galaxy: Toronto.

Pargeter, A. 2008. *The New Frontiers of Jihad: Radical Islam in Europe*. I.B.Tauris: London.

Perry Barlow, J. 1994. 'The Economy of Ideas', *Wired*, March.

Post, J. 1999. 'Psychological and motivational factors in terrorist decision-making: implications for CBW terrorism', in Tucker, J.B. (ed.), *Toxic Terror: Assessing Terrorist Use of Chemical Weapons*, Massachusetts Institute of Technology Press: Cambridge, MA.

Rapoport, D.C. 2006. *Terrorism: The Fourth or Religious Wave*. Routledge: London.

Reed, D. 1999. 'Weapon of math destruction', *Context*, Spring.

—— 2001. 'The law of the pack', *Harvard Business Review*, 79 (2), February.

Robinson, F. 2009. 'Crisis of authority: crisis of Islam?', *Journal of the Royal Asiatic Society of Great Britain and Ireland* (Third Series).

Ryan, J. 2010. 'The Internet, the Perpetual Beta, and the State: The Long View of the New Medium', *Studies in Conflict and Terrorism*, 33 (8), pp.673–681.

—— 2010. 'Militant Islamist radicalisation: does the Internet atomize?' PhD thesis, University of Cambridge.

—— 2010. *A History of the Internet and the Digital Future*. Reaktion Books: London.

Sandys-Wunsch, J. 2005. *What Have They Done to the Bible?: A History of Modern Biblical Interpretation*. Michael Glazier Inc: Collegeville, Minnesota.

Sauerberg, L.O. 2009. 'The Gutenberg Parenthesis: Print, Book and Cognition', *Orbis Litterarum*, 64 (2).

Sparks, H.F.D. 1970. 'Jerome as Biblical Scholar', *The Cambridge History of the Bible: vol.1, From the Beginnings to Jerome*, Cambridge University Press: Cambridge.

Smith, R.H. 2005. *OSS: The Secret History of America's First Central Intelligence Agency*, Lloys Press: Guilford, CT.

Torres, S. 2009. 'Maintaining the Message: How Jihadists Have Adapted to Web Disruptions', *CTC Sentinel*, 2 (11).

5

RELUCTANT RADICALS: HEARTS AND MINDS BETWEEN SECURITISATION AND RADICALISATION

Roxane Farmanfarmaian

To define radicalisation as the contestation of a hegemonic discourse enables analysis to focus on the process in which practices of contestation constitute a prevailing discourse as a threat to a marginalised community. This process is analogous, if in many ways opposite, to the Copenhagen School's rhetorical formulation of securitisation, in which threats are constructed through speech acts as an existential security issue for the community. Radicalisation can be seen as a response to the rhetorical process of being rendered 'Other' in the course of securitising society. Both processes are social and inter-subjective and depend on the securitising or radicalising leadership successfully winning the hearts and minds, and thereby, the authorisation of a target audience to adopt extraordinary measures to protect Us from Them. It is the struggle for support of this audience as a collective identity community, that, it is claimed here, has been under-theorised as the importance of community engagement is what distinguishes radicalisation from extremism, a point that gains salience when the use of extraordinary measures, including force, does not fall within the purview of the state, and its monopoly on violence. Likewise, this highlights the importance of persuasion, with implications for the nature of the speech act. To better understand the ambivalent pulls and pushes on the audience, Mohsin Hamid's *The Reluctant Fundamentalist* serves as a source of illustration, in that it captures the role of pride and shame in the inter-subjective construction of identity threat in marginalised communities and the contrast between post-9/11 securitisation and radicalisation processes. By mapping individual and social identity as subjects of security, Hamid's work exposes the effects of post-colonialism on perceptions of social survival, and the consequences of reluctant community radicalism on both radicalisation and securitisation.

If radicalisation is defined as contestation of a hegemonic discourse (see introduction in this volume), this immediately renders it an ongoing rhetorical process in which the contestation itself is discursively produced and given meaning. Discourse, 'the enactment of meaning in use', attains hegemony, according to Gramsci, by incorporating, whether by force or persuasion, the majority into an Us.[1] To contest that hegemony is to promote a position outside the Us. This is because those adopting that position are signified as a threat to the security of society at large and therefore as Other; alternatively, the contesters perceive the hegemonic discourse as threatening the identity and security – and if sufficiently powerful, the survival – of their own community. Because Self and Other are referential, as well as self-referential, they are mutually threatening. The existence of the Other implies a differentiation, rather than homogeneity, of values and practices, a situation, though critical to the construction of bounded collective identity, is also anathema to it, the site of 'foreignness', hostility and fear.[2] Indeed, as Bauman describes the nation state and its hegemonic practices:

> National states promote 'nativisim' and construe its subjects as 'natives'. They laud the ethnic, religious, linguistic, cultural *homogeneity*. They are engaged in incessant propaganda of *shared* attitudes. They construct *joint* historical

memories . . . They breed, or at least legitimise and give tacit support to, animosity towards everyone standing outside the holy union.[3]

Thus, radicalisation can be understood as contestation by the Other in response to what is perceived as a discursively produced existential threat, and therefore rendered a security issue for the identity community in question and, in mirror form, for the (larger) society producing the contested hegemonic discourse. In this reading, radicalisation of a community is frequently a reflexive process, constituted by, but likewise, constituting a threat.

As a process, contestation can be understood as an inter-subjective community discourse composed of speech acts. These are utterances that are themselves actions in that they not only give expression to perceptions of insecurity, injustice, lack of power or other cultural antagonisms toward the way the hegemonic discourse is affecting societal security, but likewise, through expression, 'the utterance of the sentence is, or is a part of, the doing of an action'.[4] Balzacq sees this as an example of Austin's concept of the 'perlocutionary speech act', in which a dialectic emerges between leader and audience, in that the utterance 'does something' to the receiver, and then is re-constructed back to the originator.[5]

Viewed in this way, radicalisation, like securitisation, discursively interlinks and grounds the identity of a political community with the security of that community.[6] Indeed, it is argued here that when viewed in terms of community, radicalisation and securitisation are symbiotic, and represent two sides of the same rhetorical process, in that their manifestations and responses are similarly constructed. According to the Copenhagen School's definition of securitisation, three rhetorical steps are necessary for its logical accomplishment: a) a discourse of existential threat to the community, b) the proposed adoption of extraordinary measures to combat or contain the danger to the community, and c) obtaining the support of the target audience. These same steps will be shown to describe equally well the process of radicalisation, a claim that will be elaborated theoretically in the first section of this chapter.

Radicalisation, unlike securitisation, is often narrowly defined as representing a discourse of low integrative complexity, that is, a binary world view tending to violent intergroup conflict.[7] However, radicalisation, as the Arab uprisings of 2011 indicated, can be a broader-spectrum phenomenon that includes the pursuit of or support for changes in the social order more generally. Because radicalisation can be discursively expressed as contestation to protect a given identity community (which may be the society at large) against an existential threat by the surrounding hegemonic discourse, it describes a range of contestations: when lacking audience support, it can describe violent extremism at one end of the spectrum; when enjoying audience hearts and minds, but lacking either charismatic leadership to translate community identity concerns into a persuasive rhetoric, or alternatively, lacking access to extraordinary means (and thus, appearing on the surface to be in conformity with hegemonic practices), it can describe latent social radicalisation at the other end.

The radicals that prior to the Arab Spring were securitised in their societies (through hegemonic 'no alternative' discourses, for example, that equated calls for democratic reforms with the take-over of Islamic extremists), were inspired by a surfeit of humiliation and outrage to rise up and contest the regimes of Ben Ali's Tunisia, Mubarak's Egypt and Qadaffi's Libya.[8] At other times, in other settings, similar speech acts against the hegemonic power – and discourse – had been labelled 'radical'. In Bahrain, counter-measures of an extraordinary nature were justified by the state on the basis that such speech acts, the emotions they elicited and the actions that followed, were an existential threat: 'The government cannot and will not stand for those who call for violence and attempt to destroy the very fabric of Bahrain's society'.[9]

However, the movements that overthrew the regimes of Ben Ali, Mubarak and Qadaffi, established new hegemonic discourses, based on popular desires for 'dignity' and 'pride' after years of shaming. These new discourses were accepted by the international community, suggesting that what previously was seen as 'radical' rhetoric had won the hearts and minds of the global commons. Indeed, the uprisings can be understood as a process of securitisation for the specific identity communities that rose up to contest the prevailing authoritarian discourses, which for decades had been hegemonic both locally and within the international theatre. The successes of the Arab Spring, therefore, not least because of their acceptance across the international community, illustrate the interchangeability of securitisation and radicalisation.

To obtain popular support for action, the radicalising (and securitising) agent(s) must be able to persuade through the use of speech acts, the power elite, and/or the identity of the community in order to gain momentum in opposition to the constructed Other (the enemy). Only then can an existential threat be perceived by the target audience as endangering the very survival of the community, and be accepted as credible, providing grounds for support, and action. This is a process that necessitates a relationship of trust between community leaders and the community at large, the level of the agent's social capital being, to Wæver, of particular importance. I argue here that equally, if not more germane as a motivator in the process, is the agent's ability to pinpoint and draw out emotions of shared pride in the collective Self, and shared shame in the experience of community alienation, deprivation, angst, fear, and other responses to group perceptions of political violation.[10] Research in Intergroup Emotion Theory (IET) indicates that strong group identity leads to intense group emotions, and 'a group's emotions determine the group's action tendencies (inclinations toward a specific behaviour) and thus, actual behaviour'.[11]

Though society functions on established rules, and is composed of communities reluctant to face the unknown consequences of changing those rules, the motivation to do so comes about when the indignity (shame) of continuing within the status quo is understood by the group as being too great, and/or the fear becomes critical that the basic survival of the community is at risk.[12] The relationship between pride/shame and the ability to convince a given population through discourse to dispense with existing rules and support extraordinary measures will be explored in the second section.

Mohsin Hamid's *The Reluctant Fundamentalist* neatly explores the nexus in language between hegemonic and radical discourses, and the emotional political ambivalence in the responses of the silent majority targeted in the securitising/radicalising moves of the agents courting its support. Persuading the hearts and minds of reluctantly radicalising individuals within identity communities reveals itself a slow and painful process, reflecting the risks of contending against the hegemonic discourse, as well as the imperatives of post-colonial identity reconstruction from both the hegemonic and radical perspectives. The ambivalence is exquisitely caught in Hamid's title, and the narrative that shifts individual pride and social shame to individual shame and social pride by following the twisting path of a Möbius strip – the straight and rational ending up on the opposite side of where it began.

The book is deceptively simple in structure for it consists of a monologue by its main character, Chengez, over tea with an American visitor to Lahore. They have met, apparently, by happenstance, although as the pages turn, it becomes increasingly ambiguous who in fact the American is, and how chance the encounter actually has been. Chengez's winding monologue reveals the experiences he has had in the USA and later Pakistan, that have taken him, step by step, through the terrain of radicalisation. At the same time, he interrupts his monologue to respond to the American, who becomes increasingly sinister as the light falls on the afternoon. The novel closes in uncertainty as to whether Chengez's radicalisation spills over into extremism or whether the visitor is on a securitising mission with Chengez its object, and ultimately, its victim.

Using passages from *The Reluctant Fundamentalist* to illustrate the dichotomies at play, analysis will tease out the mirroring processes of securitisation and radicalisation, and the competing tensions between those vying for and dependent on the public's support. The power of Hamid's work lies in his ability to map these processes by revealing the self-deception that arises first from repressed shame in both the individual and social contexts, second the initial search for pride that attempts to locate identity in hegemonic practices that provide an inadequate and hollow Self, and at last, awareness that, in rejecting the hegemonic discourse so readily embraced before, recognises itself, if reluctantly, as radical against the backdrop of the hegemonic order, and open to supporting radicalising contestation.

In the third section of this chapter, an examination of the concepts and language of shame and pride in the context of Hamid's work will throw light on the political implications of their expression for obtaining the authorisation of targeted audiences to support processes of radicalisation, and the importance of reluctance in the face of adopting extreme measures. The question that remains, and which is addressed in the conclusion in the context of the Arab uprisings of 2011, is whether in the course of instrumentalising similar logics, self-knowledge and social reflexivity renders the agent a 'reluctant', or 'radical', securitiser.

Securitisation and Radicalisation: Two Aspects of the Same Theoretical Coin

In the current debates on the broadening of the meaning of security, the Copenhagen School has been one of the most important contributors. This is not only because of its constructivist approach to security as a course of social action, rather than as an objective condition, but equally, because of its conception of security as located not just in the military sector (where it has to do with the protection of territory), but likewise in other sectors, including the *political* (where it engages the question of norms), and the social (where it addresses the issue of human security).[13] Weber and Lacy argue that this broadening of the state's security agenda reflects not only the means it now uses to mobilise security for its citizens, but because, 'as new and unexpected threats and risks proliferate in contemporary life, modern citizens expect and demand increased levels of security, protection and comfort in all aspects of life – not just traditional military security but also transport, finance, health and home – to a level unimaginable in past generations'.[14]

The Copenhagen School's contention that security is a 'speech act' and therefore, 'located in the realm of political argument and discursive legitimation' not only expands the reach of the state's security contract with its citizenry, but the role of security across society.[15] In this formulation, security 'securitises' behaviours and threats through a specific kind of speech act defined by a rhetorical structure that can be broken into three discrete (and to some degree, sequential) elements, though the elements are, in fact, closely intertwined, each constituting and constitutive of the others. According to Waever, the securitising speech act must: a) represent a threat as existential – that is, endangering the very fabric of society – and therefore, b) construct the threat as requiring immediate and 'extraordinary measures' to counter it. The third element involves the legitimation of the speech act through the acquiescence or outright support of its intended audience. It is argued here that this element – the role of the audience – has been under-theorised, and yet is critical[16] as it is the location in which radicalisation and securitisation overlap most closely, and upon which their success ultimately depends.[17]

By defining security as an inter-subjective course of social action outside any purely military procedure, securitisation as a set of practices is freed of any necessary linkage to hegemonic power or discourse, and simply linked to the protection of identity communities. As a set of speech acts, they are political and social, but not linked to established locations of power. Rather, they are a specific rhetorical structure that can be instrumentalised from the top down to protect the hegemonic Us from an external or internal Them; or, they can be instrumentalised from the bottom up to counter a threatening hegemonic discourse that produces and empowers Them, until a shift (using extraordinary measures) can be brought about to empower the Us. The processes are similar no matter from where within society the securitising speech acts emanate, or to which audience they are addressed. Habitually, and drawing from the original theorising of Wæver and Buzan in regards to Europe, if the speech acts are directed to protecting the hegemonic discourse and centre of power, the process is labelled 'securitisation'; if it is to contest and counter that discourse with the intent of protecting and empowering an audience that perceives its identity threatened by that discourse, it may be labelled 'radicalisation'.[18]

The importance of the audience role reflects upon the very nature of our understanding of the speech act itself, and whether it is constructed to reflect and engage group identity and emotion, whether it is instead a signalling mechanism to the community in question that those with agency have determined that action regarding that community's security will take place, or whether it is a self-authorising act by dictators or extremists.[19] Thus, the participatory aspect of authorisation is at issue for comprehending the speech act and the location of agency. Debate among securitisation theorists has centred on whether the speech act is illocutionary (a one-way meaningful utterance coupled by performative force), what Wæver contends, or perlocutionary (a two-way meaningful utterance designed to persuade, and hence something is brought about in someone/something else), the position taken by Balzacq.[20] The distinction is important, for an illocutionary speech act is not inter-subjective, but relies on the social capital of the actor, who, because of personal power or position within the elite either does not need an inter-subjective conversation with a wider audience for the performative force of securitisation to take place, or because the elite, as the decision-making audience, does not need further persuading.[21] A perlocutionary speech act, on the other hand, engages the audience as a critical element in the process of securitisation (and radicalisation), the building of emotional buy-in and eventually, consensus, being a key step in the dynamic of internalising and externalising agency by individuals within the context of collective societal identity.

The debate has continued as shifts have taken place within the Copenhagen School itself regarding the power of the agents, and therefore, the purpose of the speech act. Initially, the contention was that the power of the speech act was to establish meaning outside the recognised context, being radically open and indeterminate, rather than socially prefigured.[22] However, debate shifted to the social capital of actors, whether institutional and representative of power at the centre, or, if outside the institutional, nonetheless operating within the framework of hegemonic power – politicians, police and others in leadership roles. In teasing out the role of the identity community in processes of radicalisation, by contrast, and the role (and power position) of the radicalising agent(s), it becomes clear that without the engagement and active support of the audience, the speech act in the hands of the radicaliser becomes an expression of individualised alienation and self-authorisation, which defines extremism. This is in contrast to radicalisation within and by an identity community searching for a 'balance between freedom and order, liberty and license'.[23] Moghaddam, who discusses radicalisation in terms of a staircase of floors, sees the extreme (individualised and morally disengaged) as located on the top floors, while the generalised anomy of an identity community struggling with ways to contest the oppression of the hegemonic order as occupying the ground floor, which he labels, 'Perceived options to fight unfair treatment'.[24] For our purposes in looking at the grammar and agency of radicalisation, the point is theoretically important, as to view the speech act as perlocutionary avoids the pitfall of reifying society as a passive, unchanging entity 'which never speaks [as] it is only there to be spoken for'.[25]

In fact, Theiler locates securitisation firmly in the realm of societal security by defining society as a 'social, cultural and psychological formation' that constitutes a source of group belonging through the satisfaction of 'certain cognitive and emotional needs'.[26] The act of defending the society, group or other identity community is itself self-signifying and self-affirming on both an individual and collective level, and although societies may become sedimented, the individuals inside them remain responsive and part of an ongoing dialectic of creating and protecting the salience of the collective identity, not least because to them, the boundaries of their 'groupness' are of intrinsic value.[27] Indeed, for Conway, society and language must come together equally if the speech act is to have success.[28]

Defining radicalisation as a discursive process in which speech acts contest the hegemonic discourse and which otherwise follow the same contours as securitisation, however, reconfigures the way in which adopting extreme measures is understood – for in the hands of those outside the hegemonic discourse, the use of such measures is viewed as illegitimate if they involve the use of force or violence, as opposed to the legitimate use of such means by the state.[29] Radicalisation has the propensity to be perceived, therefore, especially from the vantage point of those identifying themselves with the hegemonic discourse, in terms of extremism. Here the audience role is again critical, as the element that distinguishes radicalisation from acts of extremism is the dialectic between agent and audience, and the support of the latter for the measures being proposed, a necessity for the former, not so for the latter. If extremism is defined as 'advocating drastic or immoderate measures to challenge the state' (see introduction to this volume), it is simply illocutionary – promoting performative force – and is therefore self-authorising.

The literature on extremism is extensive, and radicalisation at this upper limit is not of primary concern to us here, though the analysis used to unpack the theoretical linkage between securitisation and radicalisation remains consistent even for this most violent and fanatical of interpretations. For example, Huysmans' elaboration of war as the outer limit of securitisation closely parallels definitions of radical extremism. In Huysmans' view: 'The political significance of war does not reside in its actualisation but in its radicalisation of the exception into a real limit...War pushes the significance of the enemy to its most extreme realisation...It is at the limit that one finds the radical open condition which allows for calling into being new rules, a new community'.[30] In effect, it can be argued that any form of contestation, even the most non-confrontational, against the hegemony of a dominating discourse, is a call for new rules and a new form of community, a premise that applies equally to all securitising acts, whether conducted under a hegemonic umbrella, or a radicalising one.[31] Van Munster and Williams both argue that the friend–enemy antagonism is at the heart of the existential, and therefore, the most political and the most extreme of social constitutions.[32] As Buzan, Wæver and de Wilde elaborate in *Security: A New Framework for Analysis*, 'That quality is the staging of existential issues in politics to lift them above politics'.[33]

Huysman's argument captures the risk entailed in adopting extreme measures – whether to protect or contest the hegemony of a discourse – because in so doing, norms are abrogated in the name of security that may never be reprised, and hence the very identity of the community which such measures set out to protect, may change fundamentally. As Gromes and Bonacker observe, 'securitisation [can] foster damaging democracy'.[34] Indeed, Williams suggests that the mundane process of 'securitisation creep' may lack the intensity of the single and distinct securitisation act, but affect the normative construction of society in equal if not greater measure, routinely securitising potential threats, and the risk of threats, as existential, as in the case of the War on Terror.[35] This offers a paradigm for understanding the escalation of opposite and competing processes of securitisation and radicalisation, as both can be seen as developing into grammars of risk management, 'a regulating form of security that permanently identifies, classifies and constitutes groups/populations on the basis of the risk ascribed to these groups'.[36] Securitising and radicalising communities see in each other not only a unified enemy, but fragmented, elusive and shape-shifting Others, disrupting 'the link between space and order' and rendering society permanently securitised and radicalised.[37]

Alternatively, war often provokes self-authorisation (as does authoritarianism) within a hegemonic discourse, which in the name of protecting against existential threat at any and all costs enables a 'self-based violation of the rules'.[38] If this occurs in the name of the state it may lead thereafter to prosecution of such acts as war crimes. If it occurs on the part of individuals in the name of the community, it may be constituted as criminal or terrorist.[39] In both cases, the degree of audience authorisation is unclear, and will vary according to the level of conflict and the nature of the act. What can be defined, however, is the nature of extremism, which results from over-individualised actions insufficiently tempered by the dialectical exchange between the wider audience and agent in the course of socially constructing community identity, the choice of the agent trumping the voice of the community in methods used and costs engendered.

In sum, the discursive grammar of the illocutionary speech act, which defines an existential threat in a way recognisable to a target community can be seen to describe the logic of radicalisation as much as securitisation. Both rely on the interplay of security and identity, in that the construction of the Other as the existential threat ultimately defines the Self, which accounts for the chiaroscuro relationship between the two, and the mirroring processes of their logics. Without the support of the audience within the identity community they both define and secure, however, the rhetorical processes of securitisation/radicalisation become vulnerable to violating the rules through expressions of extremism, the use of violence untempered by community authorisation.

Winning the Hearts and Minds of the Audience

To effectively move beyond the assertion of existential threat to the adoption of appropriate extraordinary measures requires popular support, and it is in the struggle to win over the hearts and minds of the target population where the tension between securitisation and radicalisation becomes acute. Convincing the audience that protection of its security necessitates a transfer 'to the agenda of panic politics' – whether for the sake of strengthening the hegemonic discourse or contesting it – is the key to the success of the effort, since 'security (as with all politics) ultimately rests neither with the objects nor with the subjects but *among* the subjects...'[40]

An issue does not become securitised until the intended audience approves this 'transfer to panic politics', a process of struggle to win hearts and minds that is neither predetermined, nor necessarily total.[41] This winning of hearts as well as minds to the point that there is group support for extraordinary action, is a three-step process: establishing the rhetorical logics of in-group identification, developing in-group emotion through discursive economies of opposition to out-groups, and, motivating certain behaviour through group emotion and identity.[42] How threat is framed determines whether group identity becomes salient in public debate, and can trigger the intensity of emotions that promote action. Framing translates thought into a specific formulation of language, moving ideas from the individual to collective, and thereby, into public discourse. How well the framing promotes the thought depends on what Eriksson and Noreen have termed the 'speech costume' – the choice of substance and presentation by which the speech act is constructed.[43] Audience perception that the threat as constructed endangers group, community or society's existence as they would wish it to be preserved, is critical for arousing emotions in support for action. Indeed, emotions can be argued to be rational feelings of import that promote intention, and desire makes pursuit of a goal intelligible as worthwhile.[44]

What Buzan, Wæver and Wilde do not define is the range of threats that constitute existential dangers. Instead, it is the discursive construction of plausibility that is important, since, as Theile observes, 'anything can be perceived as a security threat once it has been effectively securitised'.[45] To construct an existential threat, therefore, is to construct threatened identities, a political 'staging' of issues in such a way that they are bound up with the community's preservation. Threatened identities imply not only the physical, but ontological – that is, 'the subjective sense of who one is, which enables and motivates action and choice'.[46] To ensure survival by adopting extraordinary measures is to promote a move beyond politics, for 'extraordinary' delineates actions that lie outside the accepted norms and practices of society.

To achieve audience buy-in, the threat as articulated must argue that to regain security requires temporarily dispensing with the routines that order the social environment, what Jennifer Mitzen calls 'the inter-societal...routines [that] help maintain identity coherence for each group'.[47] Yet, the proposition that extraordinary means be used to re-assert the social order introduces further uncertainty, for such means lie outside the quotidian routines that 'serve the important emotional function of "inoculating" individuals against the paralytic, deep fear of chaos'.[48] As routines sustain identity, discourses that support overriding them must convince that some uncertainties are better than others – a tautological argument, that in effect contends that the transgression (however temporary) of the very structures of society that define and are existential to the identities of its inhabitants will in effect protect those same norms and social practices.[49] In this manner, securitisation can 'alter the premises for all other questions' because 'if we don't deal with this problem, everything else will be irrelevant'.[50] Indeed, psychological uncertainties such as perceived social injustice, and threats to cultural tradition, for example, have compelling salience as existential dangers, and can temporarily trump routines producing stability, for the sake of regaining identity traction.[51] (In the 'leaderless' revolutions of Tunisia and Egypt, this role can be seen to have been taken up by the organisers of demonstrations, and the managers of social media organs.[52] It requires, in sum, a leap of faith, whether conscious or unconscious, on the part of the intended audience.

Though there is debate as to what constitutes sufficient audience approval, or in fact, what constitutes approval, the language game has certain constraints.[53] To be persuasive, the securitising/radicalising move must construct a recognisable narrative of shared experience and meaning, publicly articulating, and thereby rendering political, a target audience identity through a process of interpreting and negotiating 'feelings of deprivation that arise because of the position of an individual's group relative to that of other groups'.[54] Thus, authorisation is obtained through an 'amalgamation of actors and audience...' in the construction of a subjective dialectic of threat, and an issue becomes securitised (or radicalised) only when the target audience is integrated into the process.[55]

Moghaddam argues that 'From the French revolution to the Iranian revolution and other collective uprisings in modern times, it is perceived injustice and relative rather than absolute deprivation that coincide with collective non-normative action'.[56] Following on from this point, since the identity community or society is the 'primary locus of identification for its members...and subjectively, the repository of shared meanings', the feeling of belonging forms a wellspring of self-referential pride.[57] If that feeling is perceived as being trampled – because the identity community perceives itself as being ignored, marginalised, insulted, dishonoured – the collective suffers a sense of injustice, isolation, or betrayal which signals that the locus of shared identity, the very value of the community itself, is at risk.

Pride transgressed by the Other, and moved from individual feeling and thought to collective discourse, becomes an existential threat, and if acknowledgement and reparations are not made to overcome the sense of transgression and a sense of fairness reintroduced into the process, the frustration and anger that ensue become the fodder for securitising–radicalising speech acts.[58] Sasely notes, for example, that worldwide Muslim responses to the Danish cartoon depictions of Mohammad were inspired not because 'the cartoons showed them as individuals in a funny light, but because the cartoons insulted the "Muslim" view of what is proper for "Islam", and thus angered the group as a whole'.[59] This, it is argued, is a general characteristic of identity – one which applies to any identity community, whether hegemonic or contesting, and underpins speech acts that successfully translate existential threats into security threats for both.

In fact, Scheff, based on marital dispute experiments by social psychologist Retzinger, argues that unacknowledged shame (the opposite of pride) *always* precedes anger, and that recursive, unacknowledged shame is *sufficient* motive for those within a given identity community, to provide their support for the adoption of extreme measures to protect the societal.[60] Alone or in combination, shame shapes, and is shaped by, shared meanings of deprivation and infringement, effectively ensuring salience for utterances that link shame to survival of the Self, and the necessity of overcoming the former to ensure the latter. It makes possible the leap of faith in the capability of extraordinary means to restore the pride of the collective, as well as the individual, self. The compelling securitising–radicalising speech act makes it clear that ordinary means have failed to deliver pride in the subjective sense of who one is, and worse, have enabled instead, the perpetuation of shame. How shame engages both individual and social identity in the construction of existential threat, and constitutes a key component in developing agency as the product of practice in the winning of hearts, and then minds of an audience in the radicalisation–securitisation process, is the focus of the next section.[61]

Shame within Securitising Discourse: Illustrated by *The Reluctant Fundamentalist*

Shame and pride are core emotions that critically affect all human exchange.[62] Both are at the heart of how self and other are perceived and ordered because of the human propensity of what Cooley called 'living in the minds of others'.[63] Shame perpetuated as a historical and cultural mechanism (as in post-colonial societies) infects social perceptions of Self and social positioning in regards to Other as a form of ongoing trauma that is continuously reconstituted within society.[64] Fierke contends that the process of giving voice to social trauma, and infusing meaning to the discourse surrounding it, is a political one, an act of leadership. As she explains, 'The emotions may remain disguised in individuals, but to be translated into political agency and identity, they must be put into words by leaders, who give meaning to the individual experience by situating it in a larger context of group identity'.[65] Sasley takes this a step further by noting that 'Activation of social identity is more likely among those who can claim to represent and speak for a given identity group'.[66] When the banner for an identity group is taken up by actors inside that group but outside the hegemonic order, the translation of social distress into a political dialectic refracts the hegemonic grip – a process of radicalisation as much a function of those reflecting the social disquiet as those imposing it.[67] If the ensuing lacuna is dismissed or belittled by either party, tensions will tend to rise, the discourse of shame percolates within the target audience, and the adoption of extraordinary measures, a product of unacknowledged shame, becomes more likely.[68]

Because shame and pride are so important within the discourse of both securitisation and radicalisation, it is important to understand how they operate, and when shame, or false pride (hubris) can trigger violence. Shame and pride are social emotions in that they arise only when another's view is engaged, that is, when self-worth is perceived through the eyes of another.[69] These two categories of emotion are likewise emotions of reflexivity, since, as Sartre pointed out, 'self-monitoring from the viewpoint of others gives rise to self-regarding sentiments'.[70] Thus, pride and shame establish status and hierarchies between parties, and reflect cultural norms as well as motivations. Yet, in many modern societies, particularly in the West, the words 'shame' and 'pride' are rarely used, and instead, are evoked through a wide variety of linguistically rich variants.[71] Shame might be articulated, therefore, as embarrassment, humiliation, indignity, insecurity, self-righteousness or other variations of anger, guilt or fear. The euphemisms for pride can include honour, respect, trust, solidarity, prestige, security, and friendship. This is particularly important to recognise in the study of discourses surrounding radicalisation, as the language itself conspires to deny the existence of pride and shame, and hence, disguise the logic of emotions in actions and decisions.[72]

Second, according to research by sociologist Thomas Scheff and social psychologist Suzanne Retzinger, repressed shame that is neither acknowledged nor resolved (on the part of either the Self or the Other), leads to violence. Thus, 'shame causes and is caused by alienation, pride causes and reflects solidarity'.[73] According to this argument, shame and pride constitute key elements in the process of attunement between parties, providing the emotional security (or insecurity) of a relationship's bonds. This does not mean that parties within a well-attuned relationship do not have disagreements or fights, but that they fight fairly, their communication of respect toward the other reflecting the secure bond of pride in the other, and by reflection, in themselves.[74] Acknowledged, shame passes quickly, having acted as a signal that a bond was at risk and in need of repair. Thus, a conflict over interests does not per se lead to violence, for parties in attunement can acknowledge the other's needs sufficiently to find compromise – a disagreement in this situation often leads to a strengthening of the bridges binding individuals or societies, and encourages further cooperation.

It is in those relationships where the other's legitimate needs are devalued, or ignored, that shame festers. The denial of shame (through silence and guilt, or though the overt expression of anger to 'save face' or exact retribution) leads to further shaming of the other in the form of disrespect (to overcome pain or humiliation, for example), begetting a perpetuated spiral of recursive strife. A state of isolation ensues, in which the insecure linkages are perpetually chafed through suspicion, pain and anger.

How does this translate into radicalisation? First, Ruggie, drawing on Durkheim, suggests that 'social facts are constituted by the combination of individual facts through social interaction', a point of departure for developing the concept of collective signification, and group intentionality.[75] This describes how meanings gain and change currency within societies, incorporating both individual and social contexts.

In *The Reluctant Fundamentalist*, we can follow, through observation of speech acts, the process of recursive shame as a social fact within the hearts and minds of a silent majority, as expressed by the individual experiences of the protagonist, Chengez, who is from Lahore, Pakistan. Chengez – and the society he represents – reflect a quietist subordination to the hegemonic discourse, fitting the pattern of power relations between 'oppressors and subordinates' as articulated by James Scott, in which 'the latter can and do feign ideological conviction – put on masks – and keep false faith with a dominant ideology'.[76] This is the stage in which the identity community, according to Kuran, 'may well loathe an oppressor, [but may] still fail to develop 'cognitive autonomy' precisely because of the social conditions created by the oppressor'.[77] When we reach the stage of the radicalising move, the existential threat to the identity community develops salience in contrast to a threat to the hegemonic discourse. It is here Chengez begins to develop an alternative discourse of contestation, exhibiting a political agency 'achieved on the basis of practices that alter the subject'.[78] As such, Chengez is both a member of an identity community and a radicalising agent, articulating social shame as an argument for the adoption of extraordinary measures (demonstrations; re-configuring the Western discourse), which garners an enthusiastic audience. In the third stage, it translates into the conditions for possible violence – though how important Chengez's ambivalence is, as the radicalising agent actively contesting the securitisation of his interlocutor, renders the outcome unclear. The beginning lines immediately engage the contradictions and the unease:

> Excuse me sir, but may I be of assistance? Ah, I see I have alarmed you. Do not be afraid of my beard; I am a lover of America. I noticed that you were looking for something; more than looking, in fact you seemed to be on a *mission*.

In this terse introduction, Hamid combines the offer of a local reaching out to an American visitor, with the disquieting image of fear – establishing an instant relationship of reversals. It is a specific fear – of the terrorist, the *jihadi* – something any Western reader understands immediately and viscerally. Yet Chengez wears his beard despite that – one surmises as a show of pride for the habits of his own society, new and old, political and traditional. Nonetheless, though evoking the image of the young Pakistani radical, he hastens to add: 'I'm a lover of America', an offer, not just of comfort, but of assurance that he holds similar values – if not interpretations – to the American', a statement that a silent majority living anywhere along thousands of miles from Lahore to Casablanca, would understand immediately and viscerally as well.

The Reluctant Fundamentalist begins as a story of a talented young man on a quest to beat the West at its own game – it is his way to assuage, even avenge the social shame of an old culture, whose cities are ravaged by modern urban blight, and whose intellectual elite, from which he springs, is threadbare and nostalgic. For this he goes to Princeton; afterwards, he interviews with the director of a top financial valuations firm in New York for a job:

> I said I was from Lahore, the second largest city of Pakistan, ancient capital of the Punjab, home to nearly as many people as New York, layered like a sedimentary plain with the accreted history of invaders from the Aryans to the Mongols to the British. He merely nodded. Then he said, 'Are you on financial aid?'[79]

Here we have pride – or is it hubris? – ignored, unacknowledged. The response is a form of shaming – however rational the question might have been. It is also a dialogue in which the social valuations of two cultures are brought into conflict – a process of establishing status – but at what cost for the radicalising heart and mind?

In this passage, still speaking to the visiting American, he offers the following impression of walking into a lobby on the forty-fourth floor of his Manhattan office building:

> This I realised was another world from Pakistan; supporting my feet were the achievements of the technologically most advanced civilisation our species had ever known. Often, during my stay in your country, such comparisons troubled me. In fact, they did more than trouble me; they made me resentful. Four thousand years ago, we, the people of the Indus River basin, had cities that were laid out on grids and boasted underground sewers, while the ancestors of those who would invade and colonise America were illiterate barbarians. Now our cities are largely unplanned, unsanitary affairs, and America had universities with individual endowments greater than our national budget for education. To be reminded of this vast disparity was for me to be ashamed.[80]

Chengez's individual pride in Self is contrasted here with the social shame of his background and culture, but it is an inchoate shame, that goes unacknowledged by the society which commands the hegemonic order, and which he aspires to join. Hamid thus invokes the trauma of comparison that falls short, of history and culture transgressed, of resentment, the roots of radicalisation. It is a reflexive shame as well, for not only does Chengez bemoan his own society's modern failures, but he does so feeling ashamed at how the Americans must view Pakistan, and how specifically, the American sipping tea across from him must view it, as he hastens to offer this explanation. Nonetheless, though he chafes at the presumptions of his American colleagues, he takes pride in outshining them despite being Pakistani – reflecting Kuran's point that his subject position within the discourse renders him unable to develop cognitive autonomy. In fact, the pride his American counterparts take in him helps him to believe that *he* is the new American dream, the living example of how his adopted hegemonic discourse makes no distinction when it comes to quality, and equality.

Until 11 September 2001. That evening he turns on the television to see the World Trade Center being attacked – and *smiles*. 'Yes, despicable as it may sound, my initial reaction was to be remarkably pleased,' he admits to his American interlocutor in Lahore. 'But surely, you cannot be completely innocent of such feelings yourself?' he goes on. 'Do you feel no joy at the video clips – so prevalent these days – of American munitions laying waste the structures of your enemies? ...But you are at war, you say. Yes, you have a point. I was not at war with America.'

Yet the smile belies this last claim, even as Hamid plays with the ambiguity of the collective and the individual – the 'I', the you – in who is at war. In his reactions to 9/11, Chengez comes up hard against the established hegemonic order, and finds that pride does not allow him to proceed in the same direction as his American colleagues, who identify with the discourse of securitisation surrounding terrorism, which takes hold in New York after 9/11. Though his sudden self-awareness is not inspired by Islamic identifications, Chengez feels more strongly the collective post-colonial trauma and sensibilities expressed by the World Trade Center attackers than the shame expected by the society surrounding him, an imposed and personalised shame because, in the pervasive American discourse, the attackers are seen as being from his world, and as a young Pakistani man, he is seen as possibly like them. He comes to see his quest to out-shine the Americans as what Scott called 'false faith', and finds, in rejecting the dream, that he has, however reluctantly, become as much in his own eyes, as theirs, mysterious, a radical. In formulating a new discourse of contention against the hegemonic one surrounding him, he finds himself identifying with the out-group, the Other. Anger, dismay, hatred – all follow as it becomes in fact his war against the hegemony of America.

Hamid's power lies in his ability to map the process of radicalisation by revealing the fraught search for pride through discourses of contention, and eventually, the adoption of extraordinary measures, as constituting its antidote. Although Hamid's chosen character is from the elite, his is an odyssey of reluctant radicalism repeated throughout the east as an alternative identity community – an exposé of the social effects of colonialism, post-colonialism and globalisation as out-group deprivation, and the desperate consequences of the ambivalence toward Self and Others that has ensued.

Toward the end of the story, he reveals to the American, how his views of American civilisation have changed. Chengez pours out his radicalised view of how the attackers articulated, through their actions, a new meaning to his perceptions and a new power situated in the practice of agency expressed in perlocutionary speech acts.[81] Though he never supports the terrorists' choice of means – ensuring the actions of 9/11 remain in the realm of extremism – he notes that he has become a university teacher, whose lectures have become wildly popular among the students, and that he 'persuaded them of the merits of participating in demonstrations for greater independence . . . demonstrations that the foreign press would later, when our gatherings grew to newsworthy size, come to label anti-American'.[82] In this way, he reveals that he has become the agent of a discourse of contention that offers the identity community new meanings and approaches toward the hegemonic order, 'My office hours were soon over-run by meetings with politically minded youths."[83] But he also admits, 'I have received official warnings on more than one occasion' and that the protests, and indeed, one of his students, have garnered the ire of the authorities, prompting Chengez to be interviewed on international television.

> It seemed to me then – and to be honest sir, seems to me still – that America was engaged in posturing. As a society, you were unwilling to reflect upon the shared pain that united you with those that attacked you. You retreated into myths of your own superiority. And you acted out these beliefs on the stage of the world, so that the entire planet was rocked by the repercussions of your tantrums, not least my family, now facing war thousands of miles away. Such an America has to be stopped not only in the interests of the rest of humanity, but also in your own.[84]

Here, shame and pride have informed the process of individual radicalisation through alienation, resentment, lack of acknowledgement, and rejection, producing a discourse of contention that articulates an existential threat to the society. The agency exhibited by Chengez through the speech acts he uses to arouse the target audience (his students), themselves constitute the extraordinary measures in this case, threatening the US and its alliance with Pakistan officialdom.

> It seems an obvious thing to say', says Chengez on the last page, 'but you should not imagine that we Pakistanis are all potential terrorists, just as we should not imagine that you Americans are all undercover assassins.[85]

Yet, it is not clear whether either point is true. The American, though without actual voice in the book, develops into a furtive, doctrinaire figure who carries unusual high-tech gadgetry and glances frequently over his shoulder. He remains distant in the face of Chengez's warm and hospitable chatter, as though on a mission, indeed, possibly, a nefarious one. The contrast between the two men is stark – the agile Pakistani pouring out his contentious discourse to the stolid representative of the hegemon. Each reflects an identity community experiencing existential threat, a face-off between the idealistic, infinitely polite radical offering tea as a possible precursor to a death blow, and the almost silent, technologically provisioned Western agent tasked to carry out extraordinary measures for the sake of securitisation. It is a dangerous encounter and Hamid maintains the ambiguity to the bitter end.

In conclusion, it has been argued that if radicalisation is understood as contention against the hegemonic discourse, securitisation and radicalisation, when focused on the community, engage similar rhetorical instruments and processes. Indeed, securitisation and radicalisation are intricately intertwined, as each is a logic of measures to protect the Self against the Other, the one having little meaning outside the duality of both. The identity community's support for the process becomes important in analysing the integrated nature of securitisation and radicalisation, however, since without the moral protection of the state's monopoly on the use of force, the same process in the hands of a non-state actor (and community) risks being labelled extremist. This brings up the nature of the utterances being used in the discourses of securitisation and radicalisation, and it has been shown here that for an inter-subjective relationship between agent and community to be established, and hence, for the hearts and minds of the target audience to be engaged in the adoption of extraordinary measures, the speech acts must be perlocutionary, that is, persuasive and integrative.

In this way, unpicking the similarities and difference between securitisation and radicalisation has thrown new light on the common ground they occupy and the political identities and boundary-producing practices they constitute.

Notes

1. Milliken, J. 1999. 'The Study of Discourse in International Relations: A critique of research and methods', *European Journal of International Relations*, 5 (2), pp.225–254.
2. Buzan, B. 2004. *The United States and the Great Powers: World Politics in the Twenty-First Century*. Polity: Cambridge, p.18; see also Campbell, D. 1998. *Writing Security: United States Foreign Policy and the Politics of Identity*. University of Minnesota Press: Minnesota.
3. Bauman, Z. 1991. *Modernity and Ambivalence*. Cornell University Press: Ithiaca, NY, p.64, emphasis in original.
4. Austin, J.L. 1962. *How to do Things with Words?* p.5.

5. Balzacq, T. 2005. 'The Three Faces of Securitization: Political agency, audience and context', *European Journal of International Relations*, 11 (2), p.175; and Taureck, R. 2006. 'Securitization Theory: The Story So Far: Theoretical inheritance and what it means to be a structural realist'. Paper presented at the at the 4th annual CEEISA convention, University of Tartu, 25–27 June, p.20. The classic example is the phrase, 'I do', used in a marriage ceremony, an utterance that itself changes the status of the individuals, and hence, is an action, as much as a semantic phrase. See also Austin, op.cit.

6. Campbell, op.cit; Kowert, Paul A. 1991. 'National Identity: Inside and Out', *Security Studies*, 8 (2/3), Winter-Spring, p.1; and Van Munster, R. 2005. 'Logics of Security: The Copenhagen School, risk management and the War on Terror', Political Science Publications Series, p5.

7. See Sara Savage, in this volume.

8. Filiu, J.P. 2011. *The Arab Revolution: Ten Lessons from the Democratic Uprising*, pp.76–78.

9. Bahrain News Agency. 2011. 'Bahrain's News Statement on the Conviction of 21 Protestors', 24 June; http://www.bna.bh/portal/en/news/462286.

10. Moghaddam, F.M. 2005 'The Staircase to Terrorism: A psychological exploration', *American Psychologist*, 60 (2), p.163; see also Scheff, T.J. 2000. *Bloody Revenge: Emotions, Nationalism and War*, pp.39–54.

11. Sasely, B.E. 2011. 'Theorizing States' Emotions', *International Studies Review*, 13, pp.462–463.

12. Buzan, B., Wæver, O., and de Wilde, J. 1998. *Security: A New Framework for Analysis*, p.26.

13. Williams, M. 2003. 'Words, Images, Enemies: Securitization and International Politics', *International Studies Quarterly*, 47, p.513.

14. Weber, C., and Lacy, M. 2011. 'Securing by Design', *Review of International Studies*, 37 (1), July, p.1023.

15. Wæver, O. 1995. 'Securitization and Desecuritization', in Lipshutz, R. (ed.) *On Security*, p.55; see also quote in Williams, op.cit., p.512.

16. Taureck, op.cit., p.19; see also Wæver, 2003.

17. For an argument against the securitising process as inter-subjective, see Taureck, ibid., p.21.

18. Buzan, et al, op.cit; see also Moghaddam, op.cit., and Wæver, 1995, op.cit.

19. Taureck, op.cit., p.21.

20. Balzacq, T. 2005. 'The Three Faces of Securitization: Political agency, audience and context', *European Journal of International Relations*, 11 (2), p.175; Taureck, ibid, p.22; and Wæver, 2003, p.12.

21. Taureck, op.cit., pp.19–20.

22. van Munster, op.cit., p.3.

23. Zakaria, F. 2009. 'Learning to live with Radical Islam', *Newsweek*, 28 February, p.5.

24. Moghaddam, op.cit., p.163.

25. Theiler, T. 2003. 'Societal Security and Social Psychology', *Review of International Studies*, 2 (2), pp.253–255; Buzan, et al, op.cit., p.188; the concept of consultation and consensus between leaders and society is a key element in Islamic concepts of good governance, see Joffé, E.G.H. 1997. 'Democracy, Islam and the culture of Modernism', *Democratization*, 4 (3), Autumn 1997 and Joffé. 2008. 'Democracy and the Muslim world'.

26. Theiler, op.cit., pp.263–264.

27. Ibid., p.267; Sasley, op.cit., p.460.

28. Conway, M. 2005. 'The Media and Cyberterrorism: A study in the construction of "reality"', paper presented at the first International Conference on Information Revolution and the Changing Face of International Relations and Security, p.8.

29. Weber, M. 1958. 'Politics as a Vocation', in Gerth, H.H., and Wright Mills, C. (eds.) *From Max Weber: Essays in Sociology*, pp.77–78.

30. Huysmans, J. 1998a. 'The question of the Limit: Desecuritisation and the aesthetics of horror in political realism', *Millenium*, 27 (3), p.581.

31. van Munster, op.cit., p.4.

32. Ibid., Williams, op.cit., p.516.

33. Buzan, et al, op.cit., p.26.

34. Gromes, Thorsten and Thorsten Bonacker. 2007. 'The Concept of Securitisation as a Tool for Analysing the Role of Human-Rights-Related Civil Society in Ethno-Political Conflicts', Center for Conflict Studies, University of Marburg, Shur Working Paper Series, March, p.7.

35. van Munster, op.cit., p.6; Williams, op.cit., p.521.

36. van Munster, ibid., p.6.

37. Ibid., p.7.

38. Buzan, et al, op.cit., p.26.

39. Fierke, K. 2009. 'Agents of Death: The structural logic of suicide terrorism and martyrdom', *International Theory*, 1, pp.155–184. Fierke argues that the language that constitutes extreme acts is itself politicised, as in the contrasting discourses of 'martyrdom' and 'suicide bombing', the former a politicising label, the latter a depoliticising one. In politicising, 'martyrdom' constitutes the human bomb as a moral agent in pursuit of justice, who is empowered vis-à-vis an earthly and a divine community. In depoliticising, 'suicide terrorism' constitutes the agency of states vis-à-vis a moral deviant and an abject other who is outside politics and is thus the object of legitimate violence.

40. Buzan and Wæver, 2003, p.71.

41. Sasley, op.cit., p.463.
42. Erikson and Noreen, p.10.
43. Ibid.
44. Helm, B.W. 2009. 'Emotions as Evaluative Feelings'. *Emotion Review*, 1, July, p.249.
45. Theiler, op.cit., p.252, fn7; Scheff, op.cit; Scheff, T. quoting Goffman, E., notes that *'any* issue can become a *causus belli'* Scheff, 2000, p.3.
46. Mitzen, J. 2006. 'Ontological Security in World Politics: State identity and the security dilemma', *European Journal of International Relations*, 13 (3), pp.341–370.
47. Ibid., p.352.
48. Ibid., p.347.
49. Theiler, op.cit., p.251.
50. Buzan et al., op.cit., p.24.
51. Moghaddam, op.cit., p.162.
52. Filiu, op.cit., esp. chapters 3 & 4. See also Taurek, op.cit.
53. Taurck, ibid.
54. Moghaddam, op.cit., p.163.
55. Conway, op.cit; Gromes and Bonacker, op.cit., p.7.
56. Moghaddam, op.cit., p.163.
57. Scheff, 2000, op.cit; see also quote in Theiler. op.cit., p.251.
58. Moghaddam, op.cit., p.163.
59. Sasely, op.cit., p.452.
60. Retzinger, op.cit; Scheff , 2000, op.cit., p.4, p.65.
61. Väyrynen, T. 1997. 'Securitzed Ethnic Identities and Communal Conflicts: A need for problem-constructing conflict resolution?' *Peace and Conflict Studies*, 4 (2), December, http://www.gmu.edu/programs/icar/pcs/vayryn.html, p.7.
62. Scheff, 2000, op.cit., p.66.
63. Cooley, C.H. 1922. *Human Nature and the Social Order*. Scribner's: New York, p.184.
64. Doty, R. 1996. *Imperial Encounters*.
65. Fierke, K. 2004. 'Whereof We Can Speak, Thereof We Must Not Remain Silent: Trauma, political solipsism and war', *Review of International Studies*, 30 (4), p.484.
66. Sasely, op.cit., p.468.
67. Bisley, N. 2004. 'Counter-Revolution, Order and International Politics', *Review of International Studies,* 30 (1), January, pp.49–70.
68. Scheff, 2000, op.cit.
69. Scheff and Retzinger, op.cit., p.8.

70. Sartre, J.P. 1956. *Being and Nothingness: An Essay on Phenomenological Ontology*, trans. Barnes, H., p.347, fn.
71. Scheff and Retzinger, op.cit., p.19.
72. Ibid.
73. Ibid., p.3.
74. Ibid., p.2.
75. Ruggie, J.G. 1998. 'What Makes the World Hang Together? Neo-utilitarianism and the social constructivist challenge', *International Organization*, 52, (4), p.858.
76. Scott, J. 1990. *Domination and the Arts of Resistance: Hidden Transcripts*, p.110.
77. Kuran, p.175.
78. Scott, J. 1990. *Domination and the Arts of Resistance: Hidden Transcripts*, p.1.
79. Hamid, M. 2007. The Reluctant Fundamentalist. Penguin: London, p.8
80. Hamid, M. 2007. The Reluctant Fundamentalist. Penguin: London.
81. Väyrynen, op.cit., p.7.
82. Ibid., p.203.
83. Ibid., p.204.
84. Ibid., p.190.
85. Ibid., p.209.

Bibliography

Austin, J.L. 1962. *How to do Things with Words?* Clarendon Press: Oxford.

Bahrain News Agency. 2011. 'Bahrain's News Statement on the Conviction of 21 Protestors', 24 June, http://www.bna.bh/portal/en/news/462286.

Balzacq, T. 2005. 'The Three Faces of Securitization: Political agency, audience and context', *European Journal of International Relations*, 11 (2).

Bauman, Z. 1991. *Modernity and Ambivalence*. Cornell University Press: Ithica, New York.

Bisley, N. 2004. 'Counter-Revolution, Order and International Politics', *Review of International Studies*, 30 (1).

Buzan, B. 2004. *The United States and the Great Powers: World Politics in the Twenty-First Century*. Polity: Cambridge.

Buzan, B., Wæver, O., and de Wilde, J. 1998. *Security: A New Framework for Analysis*. Lynne Rienner: Boulder, CO.

Buzan, B., and Wæver, O. 2003. *Regions and Power: The Structure of International Security*. Cambridge University Press: Cambridge.

Campbell, D. 1998. *Writing Security: United States foreign policy and the politics of identity*, Manchester University Press: Manchester.

Conway, M. 2005. 'The Media and Cyberterrorism: A study in the construction of "reality"', paper presented at the first International Conference on Information Revolution and the Changing Face of International Relations and Security, Lucerne, Switzerland, 23–25 May.

Cooley, C.H. 1922. *Human Nature and the Social Order*. Scribner's: New York.

Doty, R. 1996. *Imperial Encounters*. University of Minnesota Press: Minneapolis.

Eriksson, J., and Norreen, E. 2001. 'Setting the Agenda of Threats: An Explanatory Model', in 'The Politics of Threat Images', The Swedish Agency for Civil Emergency Planning, www.pcr.uu.se/digitalAssets/18/18591_uprp_no_6.pdf.

Fierke, K. 2004. 'Whereof We Can Speak, Thereof We Must Not Remain Silent: Trauma, political solipsism and war', *Review of International Studies*, 30 (4).

—— 2009. 'Agents of Death: The structural logic of suicide terrorism and martyrdom', *International Theory*, 1.

Filiu, J.P. 2011. *The Arab Revolution: Ten Lessons from the Democratic Uprising*. Hurst and Co: London.

Gromes, T., and Bonacker, T. 2007. 'The Concept of Securitisation as a Tool for Analysing the Role of Human-Rights-Related Civil Society in Ethno-Political Conflicts', Center for Conflict Studies, University of Marburg, Shur Working Paper Series, March.

Hamid, M. 2007. *The Reluctant Fundamentalist*. Penguin: London.

Helm, B.W. 2009. 'Emotions as Evaluative Feelings'. *Emotion Review*, 1, July, p.249.

Huysmans, J. 1998. 'The question of the Limit: Desecuritisation and the aesthetics of horror in political realism', *Millenium*, 27 (3).

Joffé E.G.H. 1997. 'Democracy, Islam and the culture of Modernism', Democratization, 4, 3, Autumn 1997.

—— 2008. 'Democracy and the Muslim world,' in *The International Politics of Democratization: Comparative Perspectives*, Texeira, N.S. (ed), *The International Politics of Democratization: Comparative Perspectives* Routledge: London.

Kowert, P.A. 1989–99. 'National Identity: Inside and Out', *Security Studies* 8 (2/3), Winter-Spring.

Kuran, T. 1995. *Private Truths, Public Lies: The Social Consequences of Preference Falsification*, Harvard University Press: Cambridge MA.

Milliken, J. 1999. 'The Study of Discourse in International Relations: A Critique of Research and Methods', *European Journal of International Relations*, 5 (2).

Mitzen, J. 2006. 'Ontological Security in World Politics: State identity and the security dilemma', *European Journal of International Relations*, 13 (3).

Moghaddam, F. M. 2005. 'The Staircase to Terrorism: A psychological exploration', *American Psychologist*, 60 (2).

Retzinger, S. 1991. *Violent Emotions: Shame and Rage in Marital Quarrels*. Sage: Newbury Park, CA.

Ruggie, J.G. 1998. 'What Makes the World Hang Together? Neo-utilitarianism and the social constructivist challenge', *International Organization*, 52, (4).

Sartre, J.P. 1956, *Being and Nothingness: An Essay on Phenomenological Ontology*, translated by Hazel Barnes. Philosophical Library: New York.

Sasely, B.E. 2011.'Theorizing States' Emotions', *International Studies Review*, 13.

Scheff, T.J. 2000. *Bloody Revenge: Emotions, Nationalism and War*. Lincoln, NE: Authors Guild Backinprint.com, iUniverse.com Inc.

Scheff, T.J., and Retzinger, S.M. 1991. *Emotions and Violence: Shame and rage in destructive conflicts*. Lexington Books: Lexington, MA.

Scott, J. 1990. *Domination and the Arts of Resistance: Hidden Transcripts*. Yale University Press: New Haven.

Taureck, R. 2006. 'Securitization Theory: The Story So Far: Theoretical inheritance and what it means to be a structural realist', Paper presented at the at the 4th annual CEEISA convention, University of Tartu, 25–27 June.

Theiler, T. 2003. 'Societal Security and Social Psychology', *Review of International Studies*, 2 (2).

Van Munster, R. 2005. 'Logics of Security: The Copenhagen School, risk management and the War on Terror', Political Science Publications Series, Department of Political Science and Public Management, Syddansk Universitet, October.

Väyrynen, T. 1997. 'Securitzed Ethnic Identities and Communal Conflicts: A need for problem-constructing conflict resolution?' *Peace and Conflict Studies*, 4 (2), December: http://www.gmu.edu/programs/icar/pcs/vayryn.html.

Waever, O. 1995. 'Securitization and Desecuritization', in Lipshutz, R., (ed.), *On Security*. Columbia University Press: New York.

Weber, C., and Lacy, M. 2011.'Securing by Design', *Review of International Studies*, 37 (1).

Weber, M. 1958. 'Politics as a Vocation', in Gerth, H.H. and Wright Mills, C. (eds.), *From Max Weber: Essays in Sociology*. Galaxy: New York.

Williams, M. 2003. 'Words, Images, Enemies: Securitization and International Politics', *International Studies Quarterly*, 47.

Zakaria, F. 2009. 'Learning to live with Radical Islam', *Newsweek*, 28 February.

6

EGYPT: MAINSTREAMING RADICALISM

Ezzedine Choukri Fishere

In its generic definition, radicalism refers to political projects aiming at creating an order that is sharply different from the existing reality, coupled with preparedness to take severe measures including violence in order to materialise it. Sociologically, radicalism is not only about 'bringing about change but controlling such change so as to drive history onward'.[1] Radicalism, accordingly, is a trans-ideological phenomenon, an approach to social change that could be adopted by very different groups. In this sense, modernisers who seek to engineer social change as well as traditional fundamentalists resisting it could both qualify.

In this chapter, I argue that Islamic revivalists as well as nationalists are part of a radicalism born out of Egyptians' encounter with modernity. Both are attempts to take control of the modernisation process and to steer it towards a constructed vision of social order. The relative failure of the State to achieve this goal discredited nationalism under whose banner it acted, and allowed Islamic revivalists to benefit alone from Egyptians' frustration with the consequences of a distortive modernisation. This, added to eight decades of active socio-religious advocacy and political mobilisation, allowed Islamic revivalists to redefine Egypt's political mainstream[2]. Ultimately, Islamic revivalists pushed most of the political actors, including the State, to respect this new mainstream, and marginalised the rest.

The chapter begins by analysing the link between Egyptians' encounter with modernity and the birth of radicalism in Egypt, in both Islamic revivalist and nationalist versions. A second part looks at the political contest between nationalists and Islamic revivalists during the last few decades. A third section analyses Islamic revivalists' success in placing their radical discourse in a hegemonic position. Finally, a conclusion looks at the implications of this success for the future of Egypt, taking into account the changes in its political scene since the overthrow of President Mubarak in February 2011.

I. The Challenges of Modernity

At the root of Egyptian radicalism lies the problematic relationship between social actors and the dynamics of modernity. The dominant narrative of modernity in Western Europe is one of multi-layered struggle. Capitalism, bureaucratisation, and human emancipation 'disembed' social interactions from their immediate contexts and relocate them across indefinite time–space. Some actors resist, deploying various strategies in order to protect tradition and regain control over the 'juggernaut' of modernity. On the Left as well as on the Right, these radicals aim at 'regaining' control over social interactions that were left out of their local/immediate social context and transferred to a political bureaucratised centre, an invisible hand in markets or an abstract social order composed of atomised individuals who are yearning for a foundation.[3] In Egypt, where the dynamics of modernity are imported and deliberately promoted, both the modernisers and their opponents find themselves engaged in a *radical* project. The modernisers construct a model for their societies and try to *steer* social change towards it. The defenders of 'tradition' turn into radicals as social reality changes and their 'tradition' becomes more and more an elusive souvenir if not an outright imagined narrative. Just like the environmentalists who seek to protect a Nature that is no longer there, radical fundamentalists and revivalists *reconstruct* tradition, if not make it up from scratch. They then seek to impose this new vision of the past on the existing social order. Radicalism, in this sense, is modern in every sense, even when it seeks to resist modernisation.[4] In this sense Islamists are not advocates of a return to the past; 'Islam becomes a reserve on which the promoters of new identities draw'.[5] From Fascism to Fundamentalism, radical projects reflect social actors' determination to control modernisation and its consequences.

Egyptians' reaction to modernity was marked by the specific historic conditions in which this encounter took place, namely its association with imperialism, its intertwinement with cultural alienation, and the deliberate and selective character of its expansion. Let us deal with each of these in turn.

First, Egyptians' encounter with modernity took place in mayhem and in blood. It is true that the French expedition of 1798, which occupied the Ottoman-ruled Egypt for three years, brought within its ranks scientists who dazzled Egyptians with their knowledge, skills and capabilities. But the expedition was primarily a military one, inflicting destruction, humiliation and foreign domination on the country. It announced to the Egyptians that a whole new world was emerging in science, politics, administration and social organisation and – at the same time – that their country was falling under the rule of the foreign masters of this new order. The association can rarely have been stronger, and if some had doubts about the causal link between modernity and foreign domination, they were convinced when the French artillery repeatedly crushed their revolts. When finally the French were driven out, it was the equally modern British who did this, not the Egyptians or their Ottoman protectors. These crucial three years 1798 to 1801, conditioned the Egyptians' take on modernity. And when an Ottoman soldier, backed by an anxious populace, propelled himself to rule Egypt, his approach to modernisation was to be first and foremost military-oriented. The construction of a strong modern army led the modernisation of Egyptian economy, administration, and education throughout the nineteenth century. The return of the modernity masters in 1882, this time to anchor Egypt in the British Empire for 70 years, would once again reinforce this association Egyptians make between modernity and foreign domination.[6]

Second, Egyptians associated modernity with the 'Christian West'. The country's political and military leaders were no strangers to the steady decline of Ottoman power and its corollary debates regarding the possible borrowing of modern inventions from the Christian West, especially in armament, training and organisation.[7] But the French expedition exposed the weaknesses of the Ottoman Empire to the public and shocked the unsuspecting Egyptians out of their complacency. Suddenly, they realised that the 'inferior infidels' of Western Europe had become superior to the 'nation of faithful'. Both Lewis and Khalidi present a detailed account, albeit with opposed interpretations, of the reaction to this shock.[8]

Third, Mohammed Ali's project of 'importing modernity', starting in 1805, established a deliberate and selective approach to modernisation that would also be followed by his successors. For two centuries the Egyptian modernisers, mainly the leadership of the State, imported the aspects of modernisation that they deemed 'befitting'. State-administered modernisation, for example, prioritised the importation of methods and products that enhanced the military, economic, and certain organisational capabilities of the state. While the modernisation process inevitably expanded, as testified to by the rise in demands for democratic reform in the 1880s or the debate over secularism in the 1920s, those who controlled the state – the ruling family and their British protectors – kept a watchful eye and a certain level of control over the pace and scope of modernisation.

It is against this background that modern Egyptian radicalism was born. The early nationalists and Islamic revivalists sought to *re-appropriate* modernity and attributed existing 'backwardness' to the deviation from Egyptian/Muslim tradition. Embracing an equally selective approach to modernity, they maintained that the values and social principles underpinning Egyptian heritage, including Islam, shared the modern emphasis on science, innovation and reason. Although they identified 'obstacles' to modernisation in some of the prevailing social practices, they blamed the decline of Egypt on foreign domination or religious stagnation, or both. Egyptian nationalists borrowed from the 'Western lexicon' of nationalism and socialism, especially Saint-Simonism, but they also built their edifice on Islamic teachings and directed their rhetoric against European domination.[9]

Both Islamists and nationalists wanted the same thing: first and foremost *al-Nahda*; the rise or renaissance of their country. This rise included independence from foreign powers and modernisation in all its aspects: political organisation, economic development, and social welfare. Islamic revivalists and nationalists alike reserved an important place in their competing discourses for both religion and nationalism.[10] Both movements drew a narrative of some past where the nation, be it Egyptian, Arab or Muslim, was prosperous, strong and just. It was this vision that had to be reconstructed.

Islamic revivalists and nationalists shared the same tactics, from political mobilisation to the use of violence. Nationalists found their way sometimes through liberal evolutionary politics, as expressed by the popular *al-Wafd* party in 1920–50, and sometimes in radical ways, as did the Free Officers who seized power in 1952. Islamic revivalists also combined evolutionary politics with violence, as did their most powerful representative, the Muslim Brotherhood. They shared the goal of transforming society and state to fit a vision of a modern, strong and independent Egypt. The main difference between them was the degree to which they emphasised the Islamic dimension of Egyptian identity. But when a community is mobilised to face what it perceives as an imminent danger coming from the outside, it does so by mobilising its diverse components; reducing this mobilisation to one of its elements, or attributing it to the deliberate strategy of one component, would be to miss the complexity of social mobilisation and the constant changes in the composition of this mobilisation.[11]

Living up to the challenge of modernity was, and remains, the basic goal of Egyptian nationalists, as exemplified by the contributions of Refa'a Tahtawi, Abdullah al-Nadim, Qasim Amin, Ahmad Zaghloul, and Ahmad Lutfi al-Sayed. They all called for disentangling the Egyptian nation from Ottoman *and* European influences. Their writings could not be more clear on the matter: the current state of Egypt was one of decay and confusion, its identity had been 'corrupted' by centuries of foreign domination, and the 'duty' of enlightened Egyptians was to rise and 'reclaim' a new, modern, Egyptian-centred identity.[12] These nationalists spent a considerable amount of their energy on cautioning against the foreign domination risks involved in unconditional acceptance of modern norms that some advocated. It was their attachment to the 'national identity' that led them to find common ground with Islamic revivalists. Tahtawi was an al-Azhar graduate and teacher, and his writings can easily fit Islamic revivalist lexicon. Al-Nadim and Amin used Islamic references extensively. Mustafa Kamil's National Party was launched with encouragement of the leading Islamic revivalist Jamal-al-din al-Afghani and direct involvement of his disciple Mohammed Abdu. Sa'ad Zaghloul, the founder and leader of *al-Wafd* party who would dominate the political scene until 1952, was a close friend and collaborator of Abdu, and so was his brother Ahmad.[13] They both followed Abdu's goal of making Egypt part of the modern world while avoiding a breach with its identity. Finally, Lutfi El-Sayed, who stated that Afghani's influence on him was 'overwhelming', is considered 'the central figure in Egyptian modernism after the death of Mohammad Abdu'.[14]

The common ground between nationalist and Islamic revivalist discourses did not decrease with time. When Nasser and his colleagues seized power in 1952, they radicalised the nationalist discourse further, but they also brought on board the same Islamic identity discourse found in early nationalist writings. Esposito[15] refers to some of the ways Islam was employed by Nasser to expand his legitimacy, such as the use of Islamic language and symbols, the establishment of platforms broadcasting Islamic religious content and the extension of state control over al-Azhar. Yet, this is only a part of the story; Nasser was not a secular figure forced by political imperatives to adopt an Islamic gear. His 'Charter', the best articulation of his ideological platform, includes *foundational* references to Islam, which is presented as a fundamental component of Egyptian identity. It portrays faith 'in God, his prophets and his sacred messages' as a fundamental element of the 'nation' struggle for its liberation and progress'. It emphasises the role of Islam in guiding the Egyptian nation and enabling it to make significant contributions to human civilisation. Citing the Qur'an extensively, Nasser's Charter demonstrates how Islam remains contemporary and responds to today's needs for freedom, justice and equality.

It invokes Islam's practice of *Zakat*[16] as means to achieve social justice. It praises the contributions of Islamic revivalists such as Mohammed Abdu, and the role of al-Azhar in defending the nation's interests and Islam. It also asserts that the 'revolution', i.e. the regime, made the instruction of religion compulsory in schools, made the *shari'a*[17] a basic source of legislation, and was promoting gender equality 'according to al-shari'a'.[18]

As much as nationalists showed awareness of the importance of protecting 'Egyptian identity' in the course of modernisation, Islamic revivalists were not blind to the nationalist dimension of their modernising project. In fact, one way of looking at the birth of Islamic revivalism in Egypt and the Arab world is to see it as a foil to direct colonial pressure.[19] Islamic revivalists saw in secularism not only an affront to Islam, but a form of 'symbolic dispossession', a Trojan horse of the occupier.[20] The emphasis here is clearly put on the dichotomy foreign/ national. Jamal-al-din al-Afghani (1838–97), whom Esposito pointedly describes as the father of *Muslim Nationalism*, used the religious tradition of renewal, *al-tajdid* to turn Islam into a mobilising force against colonialism and for modernisation. Islam, according to al-Afghani, was not only compatible with modern thought and values, it was the catalyst for Muslim societies to rid themselves of the darkness of centuries of stagnation. To do this, they must reclaim Reason, which had been integral to Islamic civilisation until reactionary forces closed the door of *ijtihad* – use of reason in interpreting religious texts – and coming up with new rulings. Islam, in this sense, is the catalyst for reform and modernisation and the tool to repel colonial designs. Al-Afghani's call was not to return to a glorious past but to construct a strong and thriving society capable of rising on its own feet and facing the future. For this to happen, he counselled neither a rejection of modernity nor an unconditional embrace of its dynamics. His project calls for constructing a new, modern social order that would be *guided* by the principles of Islam. This included, in his view, supporting constitutional rule and parliamentary governments as well as a strong emphasis on education and modern sciences, all of which are based on principles that Islam called for. The thrust of his Islamic reform project is therefore to return Islam to a position where it becomes the mobilising force in the lives of modern Muslims. Mohammad Abdu (1849–1905) developed this approach further: Islam and Reason were complementary and the decline of Muslims was due to their abandoning of Reason in favour of what he describes as un-Islamic, irrational thinking and blind imitation of predecessors. Abdu distinguished between the core of Islamic creed, which he considered immutable, and the outer layer of provisions administering transactions and relationships among the people, which he presented as subject to change. Abdu, who became the head of the al-Azhar, was often criticised by its traditional sheikhs for his modernist penchant. The Syrian Rashid Reda (1865–1935), who learned with Abdu at the hands of Afghani, became more hostile to the West in his later writings and saw in modernist rationalism a prelude to increased Western influence in Egypt.[21] In the minds of these revivalists, the national concern was never divorced from their vision of the role of Islam.

Hasan al-Banna (1906–49), who founded the Muslim Brothers along similar principles, was not seeking to reconstitute the Islamic Caliphate, but to modernise and reform Egypt. He launched his movement when it became apparent that the attempts to restore the Caliphate were doomed (the last of these attempts was carried out by none other than the Egyptian 'king'). The Muslim Brotherhood was not pan-Islamic as a political organisation; it did not seek to reunite Muslim countries, even if it provided a model for addressing similar weaknesses in other Muslim countries. In fact, other than the obvious Palestine question, which galvanised support for the organisation, the Muslim Brothers have rarely taken a position on non-Egyptian matters. Its external links, which would lead to the creation of the so-called international organisation of the Brotherhood, would happen later, and would be constituted by individuals carrying the advocacy to other Muslim countries, establishing similar organisations there. By and large, the Brotherhood was a nationally oriented organisation.[22]

Al-Banna was not an intellectual though; he was first and foremost a mobiliser. He built his organisation's platform progressively, as he dealt with political constraints and opportunities of the 1930s and 1940s. But the messages he articulated were guided by an eclectic reading of al-Afghani and his two disciples, Abdu and Reda, as well as the traditional Azhar-based Islamic thought. Practically, al-Banna's political project started where Abdu ended: recognising that public education was the key to building a modern Islamic society. He urged his followers to focus on *ad-da'wa* – advocacy or social preaching – leaving the quest for political power to a much later stage. This does not mean that the Brotherhood's advocacy neglected politics. Far from that, politics constituted a fundamental component of its 'preaching'. But al-Banna emphasised the distinction between political advocacy and seeking political power. The latter would be futile unless it was *preceded* by changing the social base upon which the political order stands. If the Muslim Brothers seize political power before the society is ready for it, it will have to force Islamisation on society, which is neither sustainable politically nor acceptable religiously. Instead, al-Banna prescribed what a Gramscian analyst would call a *war of position* to build a counter-hegemonic culture. In al-Banna's terminology, he sought to change the moral and political beliefs of the society and through this mobilise social pressure on the rulers to introduce matching changes in the political system, a change from the bottom up. Changing society, in his view, would obviously take longer, but it would be more sustainable and less disruptive than forcing change by seizing political power.[23] In fact, this choice is consistent with Abdu's later writings, in which he counselled educational and social reforms as the only way to promote a modern interpretation of Islam in Muslim societies. This choice is the key to understanding the Muslim Brothers' relationship with politics, including their anti-revolutionary stance and their ambivalence regarding establishing a political party. When the transformation of society approaches completion, when society has sufficiently been re-Islamised, then the Brotherhood would have reached what al-Banna called the 'empowerment phase'. In this phase, the re-Islamised society itself would bring rulers who followed the teachings of Islam.

Drawing on al-Afghani and his disciples, al-Banna articulated a vision for a re-Islamised society based on three principles. First, place Islam in the centre of social life, inseparable from politics and other societal spheres. Islam was *Din wa dawla*; literally a religion and a state. Second, Islamic values and principles together with its creed constitute an immutable core, but their application was left to *ijti-had*, the use of reason. The aim of the Brotherhood was not therefore to restore the past, but to use its underlying principles and values in constructing a new future. For example, Islam ordained that decisions pertaining to public affairs be taken through consultation, *shura*. This, in al-Banna's view, was stronger and more reliable than democracy. Third, the anti-colonial drive also took on an anti-Western flavor. The West, according to al-Banna, was morally bankrupt: its institutions and ideologies had failed to protect the universal ideals of global fraternity, peace, freedom, justice, social welfare, work ethics, science, order and religion. Islam was better equipped to realise and protect these ideals, which are also its own. Although Reda's influences, especially regarding the self-sufficiency of Islam, can be easily identified in al-Banna's writings, so can Abdu's modernism and openness towards modern (and outright Western) ideals, institutions and models.[24] This ambivalence enabled the Brotherhood to appeal to various audiences. But it also allowed Sayyid Qutb and his followers to develop a vision that became the ideological platform of violent fundamentalist groups in the 1970s and afterwards.

In practice, the Brotherhood operated as a regular political organisation. Al-Banna even ran for legislative elections twice; in 1942 he withdrew in return for political concessions by the government to his movement, then ran again in 1945 and lost. Like others in its time, the organisation had indoctrination sessions for its members and physical training programmes, especially for the youth. It also established a secret military wing, and became entangled in political assassinations.[25] Al-Banna also paid special attention to army officers, and the Brotherhood entered into an alliance with the 'Free Officers' movement. The violent episode of the movement was a severe crisis in its time, and still clouds it today. Although most of its military operations were directed at the British interests in the Suez Canal area and the Zionists in Palestine, these inevitably expanded to include the Egyptian authorities. The confrontation with the latter ended in the dissolution of the Muslim Brothers in 1948 and the imprisonment of many of its leaders, followed by the assassination of Prime Minister Mahmud Fahmi al-Nuqrashi and, two months later, of al-Banna himself. A second round of violence occurred in October 1954 when a Muslim Brotherhood member was accused of attempting to assassinate Nasser during a public speech in Alexandria. Nasser ordered a second dissolution of the Brotherhood and threw thousands of its members in jail. Many of its leaders were put on trial, leading to the execution of six of them.[26] In addition to the dissolution of the organisation, the executions and the subsequent heavy repression (which led to the execution of Sayyid Qutb himself in 1966) led to a profound soul searching within the ranks of the Brotherhood, where a conflict between the Qutbists and the others was resolved in favour of the latter. To reaffirm its new orientation, the organisation published a platform called 'Preachers not judges' in which it reaffirmed its peaceful advocacy strategy and renounced any link to violence and extremism.[27]

Experiencing Modernity: The Nationalists and Their Brothers

As a result of these turbulent experiences, especially its controversial use of violence, Nasser's repression and the schisms all this left on its members, the Muslim Brotherhood hibernated. The nationalists, now led by Nasser, took command of the state and led a wide ranging modernisation project, probably the most profound since Mohammed Ali's time.

Disappointing Nationalists

As the nationalists extended their control to engulf all the institutions of the state, Egyptians expected them to live up to the challenges of modernity: asserting the country's independence vis-à-vis the domineering Western powers, protecting national identity against the alienating Western culture, and enabling Egypt to rise to the place it deserved among the nations. This might be too tall an order for any regime, but Nasser's promises were not less ambitious. His record, though, was mixed. Nasser's anti-imperialist policies bought him by staunch support from the population. His assertive rhetoric engendered a sense of pride among a population for long subjugated to foreigners.

His social and economic reforms were equally popular, and covered to a large extent – together with his charisma – his political failures. The inconsistencies of the new regime's identity discourse were relegated to a secondary position, given the primacy of a successful national mobilisation behind the two other goals of modernisation; independence and development. But this worked only for a while: when the external assertiveness came crumbling down in June 1967, all the other flaws of the regime became painfully apparent.

The defeat of June 1967 stunned the Egyptians: the extent of the military humiliation, the loss of territory, the brevity of the war, the finality of its outcome, and above all, the identity of the enemy – insignificant Israel – brought down the edifice of national pride and assertive independence that Nasser had built. The regime, believed to be a Third World leader supporting revolutionary movements near and far, turned out to be incapable of protecting its own territory. If in 1956 Israel occupied Sinai, it did so in collision with two empires who led the attack. This time around there was no empire to blame; only the Zionist entity that the regime belittled and dismissed. The shock of the Egyptians explains the mass rallies of 9th and 10th June, 1967, after Nasser acknowledged the defeat and took responsibility for it. The masses who took to the streets shouted 'we will fight' – not 'long live Nasser'. They wanted to fight for what they had lost; not merely Sinai, but their independence in the broadest possible sense. This is largely why Sadat's reconciliation with Israel was – and remains – unpopular. Many Western analysts fail to understand that Egyptian attitudes towards Israel are not solely a function of sympathy towards the Palestinians. It is also part of Egyptians deep-seated revulsion of Western domination. In their eyes, the creation of Israel, and the continued support it receives, is a consequence and a sign of this loathed domination. Israel plays the role of a lightning rod for Western domination; its presence and policies reflect the destructive power of the 'West'. For many Egyptians, accepting Israel is tantamount to surrendering the dream of standing up to 'Western domination' as much as it is accepting the loss of Palestinian rights.

The 1967 defeat dealt an indirect but strong blow to the discourse of nationalist identity. Nasser's regime was not particularly successful in articulating a coherent discourse on identity to start with. For him, choosing between the competing identity discourses in the 1940s meant alienating parts of the population. Discourse coherence was unnecessary from the nationalists' point of view; it was neither a priority nor something they could not circumvent. In the shadow of full state control over media and education, coherence was a lesser concern. Discourse coherence was also impossible to achieve, for the free officers gathered in their ranks a heteroclitic collection of shades of political opinion and identity. The nationalists made up for a lack of coherence by patriotic rhetoric, which worked well with the population. Later, Nasser assembled an eclectic discourse on identity, combining elements of socialism, traditionalism, Egyptian, pan-Arab and Islamic discourses together. As with the 'Socialist Union' – Nasser's political organisation – charisma and state powers compensated for the weak ability of the regime to convince. Nasser, when the leader who embodied the nations' will, and sometimes dictated it, could afford a weak political organisation and a polyvalent identity discourse. But the defeat of 1967 shattered his standing, and the cracks in the dominant identity discourse started to appear, in journalists' writings as well as in drama and literature.

Sadat's policies widened the cracks in more than one way. Wary of Pan-Arabism, which served his Nasserite political foes, Sadat emphasised the Egyptian and Islamic elements in the prevalent identity discourse. This was also in line with his vision of what Egyptian foreign policy should look like. After the October 1973 war, perceived in Egypt as unquestionable military victory, Sadat's credentials allowed him to be more assertive in pursuing this vision. He led the state not only into accepting Israel, but to an alliance with the United States; a quite unpopular vision. After more than three decades of this shift, and tens of billions of dollars in aid, the government still finds it difficult to publicly endorse American policies. In fact, state leaders find it politically attractive to engage in anti-American rhetoric, partly as a cover for effective cooperation with Washington. The Egyptian alliance with the United States is frequently described in the media as *inbitah*; a not-very-eloquent term meaning 'lying down in surrender'. Even those who control the State, oddly enough, frequently lament that their country's independence from the dominant West has not been achieved, and probably will not be. For those who are not in charge of the State, the culprit is quite obvious.

Sadat's version of nationalism emphasised the Islamic dimension of Egyptian identity more than any of his predecessors. In order to balance the Nasserite and leftist influences in Egypt's limited public space (mainly universities and trade unions), Sadat tolerated Islamic revivalists' activities and released scores of Muslim Brothers from prison. At the same time, he relaxed state control over the media and allowed competing political voices to emerge. Pan-Arab nationalists and leftists who were familiar voices in state-controlled media were inevitably associated with the State and suffered from its credibility deficit. By contrast, Islamic revivalists were fresher voices, untainted by the failures of the State. Their discourse sounded anachronistic sometimes, but their overall message resonated with the popular perceptions of morality and capitalised on Egyptian anxieties regarding 'decadence' and the loss of a distinct identity.

Nationalists were losing the battle on the account of both independence and identity preservation. As for the third challenge of modernity – remedying domestic weakness and generating an overall rise in the country – it was obviously the area where the nationalist state failed most. This is not the place to detail the shortcomings of Egypt's state-sponsored development; the United Nations' Arab Human Development Report (2002) provides an excellent analysis of the state of Egyptian development in its various aspects. But to put the macro-economy figures in context, the analyst is well served by trying to witness how a majority of Egyptians experience this state of development. Visiting any of the slums inside and around Cairo is one way of doing that, where poverty, and absence of clean water, sanitation, or any form of public services, have become a fact of life for millions of people who simply gave up hope that their living standard would improve. A visit to a random public school, university, hospital, government office, or a police station could also show the analyst how the macro-economic figures are translated into reality. Another way is to attempt – or watch someone attempting – to start a business and go through the Kafkaesque layers of corruption – big and small – and bureaucratic absurdities. Local newspapers and contemporary Egyptian literature abound with accounts of how a majority of Egyptians perceive their daily life: new buildings collapsing, ambulances and fire brigades unequipped or unable to make it to their target in time, medical malpractice and industrial accidents 'discovered' years later and yet enjoying impunity, weak or non-existent public health controls over food and drugs, frequent transportation mega-accidents, frequent small accidents where people are electrified by a loose electric wire, fall in a hole in the road, or crash in unannounced and unilluminated traffic checkpoints. Egyptians experienced these failures as a form of undeserved decadence, a confirmation of their country's declining fortunes, or as put eloquently, with a deep sense of 'sorrow'.[28]

These sorrows are part and parcel of Egypt's modern experience. Giddens[29] suggests that a modern social order is dependent on the creation of functioning 'expert systems', which are a 'system of technical accomplishment or professional expertise that organise large areas of the material and social environment in which we live today'. A school, or an elevator, is an expert system. When you send your child to a school, you 'trust' that this school will provide the child with proper education and care. This trust is in fact a trust in multiple 'expert systems'; those in charge of developing the curriculum, of protecting the children, of designing and building schools, of training the teachers, as well as trust in the supervisory systems that reviews and corrects the flaws of these expert systems. When systems fail frequently, overall trust is eroded. The dysfunctions and unreliability of expert systems, together with the well-studied phenomena of weak capitalist transformation and authoritarian bureaucratisation, gave Egyptian modernisation the traits it now has. Weak self-reflexive capabilities meant that many of these malfunctions remain unattended. Caught between a distorting modern order and inoperative tradition, Egyptians often suffer from the worst of both worlds. In addition to the usual social dislocations associated with modernity, they have to endure higher levels of hazards, lower levels of achievement, and weaker mechanisms through which to remedy the pains of modernisation.

In addition, modernist administrators since Mohammed Ali have avoided – as much as possible – the most politically troubling aspects of modernity and yet the most fundamental; human emancipation.

Human emancipation, the 'disenchantment of the world',[30] refers to the freeing of the individual from external obligations and his transformation into a master of himself and the world. This emancipation, which started with the European Enlightenment, also means a shift of fundamental morality from an external source, whether it is divine or man-made as in the case of 'tradition', to internal sources, whether it is personal commitment or intersubjective reason. Egypt's modernist administrators had neither interest nor desire to push for such a shift. Nor is it certain that they would have succeeded had they tried. Demand for modernity was more concerned with the material products modernisation can achieve: from weapons to schools. Demand for philosophical transformations was rather limited, often restricted to a minority of intellectuals. And even then, they were constrained by a majority that felt threatened in its identity by the association it made between modernity and cultural alienation. State leaders had no dogs in such a fight. Far from that, many of them were actually imbued with traditional philosophical discourse and averse to human 'emancipation' both as individuals and as political actors who saw in the 'emancipation' a source of political trouble.

This does not mean that the philosophical discourse of modernity is absent, or that Egyptian social order is based exclusively on a traditional philosophical discourse. There is a long list of Egyptian intellectuals who advocated, with varying degrees of political correctness, a philosophical transformation in line with Enlightenment principles. And even if the majority of Egyptians dismissed the most extreme of these calls, some of its elements penetrated the dominant discourse and often influenced the religious discourse itself, such as that of Mohamed Abdu. But ultimately, the idea of human mastery remains unpopular, with a clear majority safely anchoring morality in its external source: divine guidance.

Islamic Resurgence: The Journey from al-Afghani to Afghanistan and Back

While the credibility and appeal of nationalists were eroding by the end of 1960s, the Muslim Brothers were hibernating in exile or in prison. Interestingly, the demand for Islamic revivalism persisted despite the absence of what is generally thought of as its primary motor. A new breed of Islamists composed of university students; *al-Gama'at al-Islamiya* – the Islamic groups or communities – started to appear as early as 1969.[31] Their popularity rose instantly, and by 1976 they controlled student unions in almost all Egyptian universities. Their messages built on the accumulated thinking of Islamic revivalism as transmitted by the Brotherhood, especially through Qutb's writings. But *salafi* thinking – the more literalist orthodoxies of Islam – also influenced them. Fearing for its position, the Brotherhood stepped in and convinced the leaders of *al-Gama'at* to collectively join its ranks. This move saved but also changed the Brotherhood; with the injection of fresh young members into its structure, the Brotherhood gained additional strength which compensated in part for its absence from the political scene. But it also injected a lot of dynamism into an essentially old and stagnant organisation, which would translate itself in repeated and increasing demands for change from within. At the same time, the Brotherhood began to negotiate with President Sadat over the possibility of establishing a political party. But ultimately the Brotherhood desisted; either because Sadat attached too stringent conditions to the offer or because its leadership deemed that the organisation was not ready yet for such a step.[32]

If some leaders of *al-Gama'at al-Islamiya* joined the Brotherhood, many others – especially in Upper Egypt – rejected it and developed their own vision of Islamic revivalism.[33] Combining the writings of Qutb with *salafi* readings of Islam, *al-Gama'at* built its revivalist vision around three main pillars. First was the determination that the current Arab and Muslim regimes were *apostates*, because they did not rule according to divine legislation. Consequently, participation in state institutions – including parliaments and courts – was prohibited. Second, Muslims who violate Islamic rules were also apostates, even if the violations were committed as a result of ignorance. What constituted a 'violation' was a long list of acts, including the use of state courts. Thirdly, the road to revive Islam was through the 'spiritual separation' of *al-Gama'at* members from their apostate societies and the active advocacy of the 'true path'. In the course of their advocacy, *al-Gama'at* members could determine who was responding well to their call and who was bent on embracing apostasy. The latter became a fair target for punishment.[34] Reflecting this dual role of its members – advocates and judges – *al-Gama'at* quickly started to use violence in addition to its work of advocacy. It continued to use violence until 1997.

Gama'at Al-Jihad was born as another of these student groups, especially in the campuses of Upper Egypt and was itself splintered until 1981. The *al-Jihad* revivalist vision differed from its sister groups on two accounts. While *al-Jihad* agreed that current Arab and Muslim regimes were apostates (including state institutions and their staff), they did not consider Muslim individuals apostates. Muslim ignorance that their actions violated Islamic rules exonerated them. Second, the road to reviving Islam was not bottom-up advocacy; it was armed struggle aimed at seizing political power and using it to Islamise society from above. Accordingly, *al-Jihad* targeted the 'apostate rulers' and their servants in state institutions. And if these rulers and their servants hid behind innocent Muslims, it was acceptable to sacrifice the innocent. Fighting these regimes has priority over fighting the 'Jews of Palestine' (until this ruling was reversed in 1998 when *al-Jihad* joined al-Qa'ida in prioritising fighting 'the Jews and Crusaders').[35]

If both *al-Gama'at al-Islamiya* and the Brotherhood spoke in the name of Islamic revivalism and in response to the challenges of modernisation, they disagreed on the nature of such a response. In fact, as Burgat notes,[36] it is partly through *al-Gama'at*'s criticism of the Muslim Brothers that we realise the extent to which the latter have appropriated modernity. Al-Zawahri, the former second-in-command to Osama Bin Laden and the leader of the Egyptian Jihad, wrote a whole book criticising the Brotherhood. In his view, the Brotherhood's embracing of democracy and Western constitutional tradition was a deviation from the Islamic path and an affront to God's exclusive sovereignty. Giving the power of legislation to men is sharing God's power to legislate for his creatures. This position is not unique to al-Zawahri: it is a common reference in the literature of *al-Gama'at*, *al-Jihad* and in *salafi* thinking.

In fact, *al-Gama'at*'s reading of Islamic revivalism is not more or less radical than that of the Muslim Brothers – in the sense radical- ism is used in this chapter. Both articulate a constructed vision of social order and seek to 'steer history' towards achieving it. What distinguishes their reading from that of the Brothers is its funda- mentalist approach and its violent strategy, which are closely inter- twined. As Giddens suggests,[37] globalised modernity questions traditional practices that were looked upon as given and requires that these practices 'explain themselves'. Fundamentalists refuse to explain tradition or engage in dialogue over its practices. Instead they opt for defending it *in a traditional way*. In the case of *al-Jihad*, the traditional way includes the use of *Jihad*, the religious duty of fighting in defence of Islam.

Redefining the Egyptian Mainstream

The most important characteristic of Islamic revivalism in Egypt is its move from the margins to the mainstream: today, leading an Islamic way of life is no longer an exception but a choice made by increasing numbers of men and women from various social back- grounds and profiles.[38] Islamic revivalism, which started as a radi- cal vision of society, has today become hegemonic in Egypt. Even if the Muslim Brotherhood as an organisation is not, the discourse it advocates has become dominant. The state itself has for all practi- cal purposes adopted this discourse, even as it continued to exclude the Brotherhood from power. Islamic traditional authorities, for their part, have been ambivalent about the Brotherhood, but they definitely share its revivalist discourse. As for secular and liberal political play- ers, they have either adapted their discourse to avoid clashing with Islamic revivalism or stood firm on their principles and lost public support. Finally, the violent Islamists who originally competed against the Brotherhood have moved back to positions commensurate with organisation's version of Islamic revivalism. In sum, the Brother's dis- course has become hegemonic.

Starting in the mid 1970s, while *al-Gama'at al-Islamiya* occupied the violent margins of Islamic revivalism, the Muslim Brotherhood moved to occupy its political centre. Although the Brothers declined Sadat's offer to form a political party, they were keen on avoiding activities that could curtail the freedoms granted to them by the 'faithful President'. Throughout the 1970s, the Brotherhood focused on rejuvenating their structures and improving its outreach. The ban on its magazine, *al-Da'wa,* was lifted and the Brotherhood operated more like an Islamic revivalist 'interest group' than a political party.[39] However, just before his death, its 'General Guide' counselled his colleagues to work towards the establishment of a political party.[40] The Brothers did not follow his advice in the 1980s, but they joined the political game almost as a political party. In 1984 the Brotherhood built an electoral coalition with the former nationalist/liberal party, *al-Wafd* and fielded candidates for legislative elections. They won seven seats. In 1987, they struck another electoral alliance, this time with the 'Labour Party' (a rather empty shell that started decades earlier as a nationalist/Islamic political party) and the politically insignificant but legalised 'Liberals Party'. This time the Brothers won 36 seats. In 1990 they boycotted the legislative elections in coordination with opposition parties. They then ran in the elections of 1995 despite harsh restrictions, repression and interference, and won only one seat. The electoral record improved again in 2000, with 17 seats won (more than the seats won by all opposition parties combined). But it is in 2005 that they stunned by their electoral victory: winning 88 seats, one-fifth of the Parliament, despite fraud and heavy governmental intervention in the electoral process. In the 1980s the Brotherhood also became active in trade unions and professional associations. By competing for their governing boards (but not for the politically sensitive posts of secretary-generals), the Brotherhood managed to at least partly control key unions.[41] The Brotherhood used their influence in these unions to mobilise support among their followers through expanding social services and setting a model for participatory management of their boards.[42]

But in addition to gains in political support, the Brotherhood was in fact transformed by their experience in parliamentarian and associative politics. Political transactions necessary for mobilisation, horse-trading and negotiation, added to the Brotherhood penchant for political pragmatism and refined it. This experience served as training for their mobilisation and negotiation skills, which grew exponentially. But this experience also empowered younger leaders and indirectly increased internal pressure for renewal.[43] Their success in parliamentary and associative politics gave momentum to the idea of establishing a political party. But as state repression increased, a harder-line leadership emerged and gave the Brotherhood a more traditional outlook.[44] Frustrated by the foot-dragging of the older leaders, a group of the younger generation decided in 1996 to establish a political party on their own. But their attempt failed: the authorities – and courts – denied them a licence, and the Brotherhood leadership ostracised them. After the 2,000 elections, the Brotherhood called once again for the establishment of a political party of their own.

The immersion in parliamentary and associative politics not only influenced the Brotherhood's political and organisational capabilities but also its discourse, bringing them closer to the political realities of Egyptian society. By 1996, in response to pressures from outside and inside the organisation, the Brotherhood issued a 'Statement on Democracy,' in which they clarified their positions on key issues such as the use of violence, the status of non-Muslim Egyptians, the relationship between religion and politics, as well as human rights. The statement was clear in rejecting violence as means of re-Islamising society and reaffirming the Brotherhood commitment to peaceful advocacy. They asserted that the Brotherhood's 'position regarding our Christian brothers in Egypt and the Arab world is [. . .]: they have the same rights and duties as we do'. The statement also asserts the 'fusion' of the religious with the political but gives it a stark secular spin: 'the legitimacy of government in a Muslim society should be derived from the consent and choice of the people [who] have the right to invent different systems [. . .] that suit their conditions, which definitely would vary according to time, place, and living conditions'. The Brotherhood statement also asserts respect for human rights, regardless of differences in language, colour, or race.[45]

In addition to the evolution resulting from direct experience in parliament and associations, their revivalist discourse was also expanded by deliberate contributions of a broader circle of intellectuals who did not necessarily belong to the Brotherhood itself. For example, Tariq al-Bishri, Adel Hussein and Hasan Hanafi moved from socialist and nationalist positions to embrace a more Islamic discourse. The transformation of their political orientation seems to have been influenced mostly by re-integrating identity politics and cultural heritage arguments in their analysis, while keeping some of the fundamental aspects of their earlier writings about social change. Khaled Mohamed Khaled moved from liberal constitutionalism to a discourse based on accepting the unity of state and religion. Yet, Khaled did not move all the way to embrace the divine sovereignty advocated by *al-Gama'at* or, albeit in a lesser manner, by certain segments of the Brotherhood. Instead, he preserved the idea of a 'social contract' between the ruler and the ruled as a foundation for the political order. But he emphasised the consistencies between this contract and the implementation of Islamic law. Some analysts see in these writings a deliberate attempt by its authors to use Islam in order to legitimise a positivist approach to politics. Others see it as a natural evolution of their thinking, inspired by the same changes and disappointments that affected Egyptian society as a whole. But ultimately the result is the same: the 'acknowledgement of the political nature of Islam played into the hands of the Islamists in their demand to establish an Islamic system of governance in Egypt'.[46] This is certainly the case, but they also enriched and expanded the Islamist discourse. What is interesting about these writers – and others who embarked on similar attempts – is that they completed the circle that al-Afghani and Abdu started. If al-Afghani and Abdu started from the question of how to revive Islam in response to the challenges of 'Western' modernity, these writers started from the 'modern' thinking and moved back to Islamic revivalism. In doing so, they inserted their modern understanding of governance, reason, and social change into Islamic conceptual frameworks. It is this combination that makes their writings an enrichment of the otherwise narrow Islamist vision based on Rashid Reda's reading of revivalism.

Al-Ghazali, al-Qaradawi and Imara are closer to the core of the Brothers' discourse on modernity, but their work also expanded it. All three brought a fresher look to the nature of Islamic teachings and their role in the daily – and political – lives of contemporary Muslims. They articulated what they described as a centrist view, defining liberal secularism and *al-Gama'at's* fundamentalism as extremes. In their view, neither a secular nor a theocratic form of state is acceptable. Similarly, neither a literalist reading of Islamic teachings nor a one that treats these as a menu one can pick from at leisure is acceptable. Instead, Islamic teachings must be viewed as *foundational*: they establish the basis and the boundaries for Muslims' lives – both in individual and public domains. Freedom of interpretation is granted, but within these boundaries and on these bases alone. Three categories of Muslims had ignored one aspect or another of this equation. Secularists and Westernisers ignored Islamic teaching altogether, and failed. Traditional *ulama* ignored the pivotal role of Islamic teaching in the public domain especially in politics. They also ignored the need to reinterpret religious texts in ways that make them useful to contemporary challenges, and, in their failure they hurt the standing of religion in the lives of Muslims. Fundamentalists share with the latter category their neglect of the need to reinterpret texts, and adopt a literalist view of them in ways that put them at odds with the Islamic community and the true instructions of God. A centrist position that uses reason as an approach and Islam as a foundation is the true path of Islam. Using this approach, the centrists concluded, for example, that *shura* is an obligation on the ruler towards the ruled and therefore consistent with democratic principles. The same goes for the traditional Islamic *bay'a* – the declaration of one's allegiance to a new ruler – and the modern practice of voting.[47]

State strategy towards Islam and identity contributed to rendering the Islamists' discourse hegemonic. Nasser reserved a place in his discourse for religious references, probably as an attempt to bolster support for his nationalist project. But he also laid the institutional foundations for the next generation of Islamists. Sadat went further, trying to tap the pool of support for Islamic revivalism by rebranding himself and his regime in Islamic terms while repressing Islamists. Repression of Islamists was not a novelty; but the State adopting Islamic revivalist references was. The decision by the State, which tightly controls the public space, to adopt Islamic revivalist references empowered those who control its production. As al-Azhar (and even the Brotherhood) was losing authority over defining Islam to the younger and rebellious *al-Gama'at al-Islamiya*, relying on Islamic references was bound to backfire – and it did. The assassination of Sadat cannot be understood in isolation from his own strategy. Under Mubarak this strategy was nuanced, but not abandoned. The repression of the Islamists has grown and the confrontation with *al-Gama'at* militants reached, by the mid 1990s, an unprecedented scale.[48] The adoption of Islamic revivalist references was also nuanced; Mubarak never presented himself as the head of the faithful as his predecessor did. But overall, the State continued to promote and protect Islam as the point of reference and to abstain from opposing Islamic revivalism in its controlled media as well as in its educational and cultural institutions. Although it allowed dissenting liberal intellectuals to express their views, this tolerance has been consistently bounded by the avoidance of 'offending the public's religious feelings'. This unwritten ban included the publication of novels, poetry or even academic research papers that raised Islamist objections. It also included at times banning the teaching – inside university classes – of classic books now deemed un-Islamic.[49] When an obscure Danish magazine's cartoons of Prophet Mohammed became a controversy, it was the State who took the lead in the campaign to 'defend Islam'. Engaging the Danish government, the European Union, the United Nations General Assembly and the Human Rights Council, among other instances, was deemed part of the state's 'duty' to defend the Islamic references. This strategy has probably succeeded in preventing Islamic revivalists from capitalising politically on the affair, but it contributed significantly to strengthening the discourse of the Islamists.

The traditional Islamic authorities, represented by al-Azhar, have adopted the radical vision of Islamic revivalism long ago. Al-Azhar played a leading role in calling for the implementation of the Islamic law in the 1970s. Its Shaikh Gad al-Haq undertook a serious effort to push the State towards this end, and when the latter hampered his efforts he took the matter to public opinion and – at least for a while – resigned in protest. In a context where other players were making the implementation of Islamic law a priority, al-Azhar was clearly worried about losing its religious leadership if it did not do so. But this zeal also translated a deep-seated belief among al-Azhar scholars and leaders that Islam is a *Din wa Dawla*. In this, al-Azhar was in agreement with the basic tenet of Islamic revivalism if not outright fundamentalism. Its objection, as Hatina puts it, was directed at the extremist interpretations of Islam including Muslim militant accusations of other Muslims that they were apostates.[50] In other words, al-Azhar was opposed to the visions articulated by *al-Gama'at* (not the one presented by the Brotherhood) of how religion and state can be integrated, not to the principle of their integration. In the 1980s and beyond, al-Azhar leaders and other traditional religious leaders played an instrumental role in promoting Islam as a framework for both personal and public affairs, relegating the idea of separating religion and politics to a marginal place, if any, in the public debate.

The violent margins of Islamic revivalism have, after a bloody and lengthy confrontation with the state, moved back to the revivalist discourse as articulated by the Muslim Brothers. In 1997, after a complex process, the militants of *al-Gama'at al-Islamiya* unilaterally declared an end to their recourse to violence. Ten years later, *al-Jihad's* prominent theoretician and former *Emir* followed suit[51]. Ending violence developed quickly into comprehensive reviews of *al-Gama'at* vision and tactics. This is not the place to discuss these reviews, which by their depth, comprehensiveness and the credentials of their authors could have dramatic implications for the use of violence in the name of Islam worldwide.[52] The most basic aspects of these reviews are two: abandoning the belief that current Muslim societies and regimes are apostate and, consequently, accepting that the only acceptable means of reviving Islam is peaceful advocacy, not armed struggle.[53] In so doing, *al-Gama'at*, together with the Egyptian Jihad[54], moved right back to the 'mainstream' Islamic revivalist discourse in its definition of the challenges Egyptian society faces, the need for reviving Islam in order to meet them, and the need for *ijtihad* to achieve this revival. All this should be promoted solely through public education and advocacy, not through violence or attempts to seize power from above. It goes as far as suggesting dialogue as a permanent state of relations with non-Islamic civilisations. In this revised vision, one can still see nuances from the revivalist discourse as adopted by the Brotherhood, but not fundamental differences.[55]

The liberals and other secular political players – and their discourses – have moved to the margins, if not to irrelevance. The performance of their political parties in legislative elections has always been bad, and they explain their lack of popularity by the long years of electoral fraud and security harassment of their supporters. But these are the same conditions under which the Brotherhood operated. In the 2000 legislative elections, the Brotherhood won 17 seats – more than the total seats won by all other 15 'secular' opposition parties combined (who won 16 seats). In 2005, the Brotherhood won 88 seats – a full 20 per cent of the seats in the Assembly. The extent of this victory should be assessed in light of the fact the Brotherhood fielded candidates for only a quarter of the seats in an attempt to reassure the regime that they did not seek to threaten its two-thirds majority in the Assembly. All 'secular' opposition parties combined won nine seats. The decline of the liberals is not only in electoral performance; it can also be seen in the size of their parties' membership as well as their lack of mobilisation power. This general weakness, compared to the strength demonstrated time and again by the Brotherhood, reflects the marginality of the secular movements in Egyptian public life, both in practice and in discourse. The strength of the Brotherhood cannot be explained solely by its extraordinary organisational skills; it sits on top of a broad adherence to the discourse it articulates. Secular players, by contrast, are sitting on a discourse that they can hardly embrace in public. Their basic premise of secularism is no longer a serious political proposition. In newspaper editorials, opinion articles, talk shows, and the like, some intellectuals and opposition figures still advocate the principle (which they cushion in apologetic terms because of Islamic preferences). But these calls are either ignored or harshly criticised as extreme positions. Being *'almani*, a secularist, has become more of an accusation than a positive claim[56]. The core proposition of Islamic revivalism, framing Islam as the purported foundation of the social order, as a *din wa dawla*, has become the hegemonic discourse in Egypt.

Conclusion: Putting Islamic Revivalism to the Test

If what al-Banna meant by the 'empowerment phase' is a time when the Brothers' discourse would become so hegemonic that rulers will have either to act accordingly or step aside, then this time has come. This seems to also be the conclusion many leaders in the Brotherhood have made. It is consistent with the organisation's decision in January 2007 to finally launch a political party. Its 'General Guide' at the time, Mahdi Akef, indicated that the party would be based on Islamic principles, the *marja'iyya Islamiyya,* and that the Brotherhood would continue as an organisation focusing on public education.[57] Six months later the Brotherhood released a draft of the party's political programme, causing uproar by its emphasis on the role of 'religious authority', among other things. The disagreements around the political programme were not only outside the Brotherhood; many within its ranks were unhappy with its language. Unable to find internal consensus on the needed amendments, the Brotherhood withdrew the draft and shelved it. The political developments in the Brotherhood, especially its latest internal elections, slowed down the organisational moves in this direction.[58] In the aftermath of Mubarak's fall, the *al-Wasat* party was finally legalised (after 15 years of legal battles) and a number of 'Islamic' parties were announced. The Brotherhood announced in turn its intention to launch its own political party; 'Freedom and Justice'.

But political party or not, the Muslim Brothers are aware of their power, and their many internal divisions. The 'Egyptian revolution' brought two major changes to the Egyptian political scene: it created an opportunity for the unknown quantity of liberals to come together and organise themselves, and accentuated the internal conflicts in the Brotherhood. The 'youth' who took to the streets of Egyptian cities included segments from the Brotherhood who challenged their old leaders' instructions not to demonstrate. Later, when the Brotherhood stepped in to recover the victories achieved on Liberation Square, the internal divisions – especially the generational gap – made themselves felt. The Egyptian political scene is still in flux, but the hegemony of the Islamic revivalist discourse remains certain. What is less certain is how this hegemony will manifest itself concretely and practically in the political and social realm.

Islamic revivalism is a general framework, but the definition of what it means in practice is still open to dispute. Mubarak's authoritarianism shielded the Muslim Brotherhood from political scrutiny. The political space was tightly controlled and occupied by the regime, and the Brotherhood relied on its members for survival. Its electoral victories reflected its organisational capabilities in addition to a dose of protest vote. Under these conditions, the Brotherhood could afford to maintain a general (and vague) language on the main questions facing Egyptian society. When the political space widened in 2005 and it announced its intention to form a political party, it had to draft a platform. This process included answering some of the questions it had so far avoided. It failed, mainly because of internal divisions. But instead of going through a needed – and painful – process of internal struggle, the closing up of the political space enabled it once again to delay the exercise of self examination and go back to its vague positions. With the establishment of a new party, and the mushrooming of competing Islamic parties, this choice will no longer be available. The Brotherhood will have to face its own demons, and answer the difficult questions about citizenship, political rights of women, minorities and individual freedoms. It will also have to answer a host of other questions about Egypt's relations with the rest of the world. If indeed Egypt adopts a political system based on free and fair election of those in power, the Brotherhood – as well all other Islamic revivalists – will have to compete for the people's votes, which means that it will have to provide them with concrete answers to their concrete questions. This will be more so if the liberals, now energised by their Liberation Square experience, manage to form a relevant political force. If this competition becomes the dominant pattern, Islamic revivalists will be forced to define these answers, which they have so far avoided.

In this context, the main question about Egyptian radicalism changes. Instead of the simple question about their chances of seizing power, we should explore four different sets of questions. First, which reading of the heterogeneous Islamic revivalist discourse will prevail: one closer to Abdu or to Qutb? Secondly, how will Islamic revivalist discourse itself evolve as it increasingly serves as a source of legitimation for political power? Third, how would the outside world deal with the Egyptian assertion of its identity: with integrating understanding or antagonising rejection? And how would the world's reaction influence Egypt's identity formation? Fourth, how will Islamic revivalists develop their discourse on social issues? By this I am not referring only to the obvious questions regarding the status of women and non-Muslim citizens or personal freedoms. I am more concerned with the 'foundation' of social order. So far, Islamic revivalism has sought to construct a model of endogenous modernity that combines two aspects of 'Western' modernity with a traditional or divine foundation. It is unclear whether this attempt, once allowed enough space to be experienced on a large scale in society, will work and how. If successful, this could begin to resolve the built-in tension between identity and modernity in Egypt. Theoretically, a postmodern (or an ultra-modern) world, tolerant of eclecticism and wary of grand narratives could be more hospitable to such experiments. But it is yet unclear whether the Egyptian actors could develop this eclecticism into a coherent and functional model. So far these attempts juxtaposed contradictory elements of modernity that contributed further to the distortions and pains of modernisation in Egypt. This, in my view, is the main challenge facing Egyptians in the coming decade.

Notes

1. Giddens, A. 1994. *Beyond Left and Right: The Future of Radical Politics*. Stanford University Press: Stanford, CA. p.1.
2. Munson, Z. 2001. 'Islamic Mobilisation: Social Movement Theory and the Egyptian Muslim Brotherhood', *The Sociological Quarterly*, 42 (4), pp.487–510. Modernity, in this chapter, is not a pre-defined structure that imposes consequences on social actors: it is rather a group of dynamics that create opportunities and constraints for social actors. In this sense, there is no contradiction in approaching Islamism as a reaction to modernisation and at the same time approaching Islamist movements using social movement and mobilisation analysis.
3. Giddens, A. 1990. *The Consequences of Modernity*, Stanford University Press: Stanford, CA.

4. Giddens, 1994, op.cit., pp.84–88. Following Giddens, modernity here is presented as inclusive of these three dynamics. Obviously, Marxists would emphasise the primacy of Capitalism and its consequences, Realists would focus on the role of bureaucratised politics – the State and its institutions, and Liberals would underline the modern process of human emancipation and its consequences. But regardless of the primacy debate, all three traditions would recognise that the modern rupture, in economy, politics or social organisation, generated social dislocations and strong social reactions.

5. Halliday, F. 2003. *Islam and the Myth of Confrontation: Religion and Politics in the Middle East*. I.B.Tauris: London. p.115.

6. For the specific period of Egyptians' encounter with the French Expedition and its impact on the way they perceived politics, modernity and the West, see El-Raf'ay, A.R. 1929. *Tarikh Al-Haraka Al-Qawmya Fi Misr*. Dar El Maaref: Cairo. pp.330–348. For a broader discussion of the subject, see both Khalidi,R., 2004 and Esposito, J., 2005.

7. Lewis, B. 2002. *What Went Wrong: The Clash between Islam and Modernity in the Middle East*. Weidenfeld and Nicolson: London.

8. Ibid., Khalidi, R. 2004. *Resurrecting Empire: Western Footprints and America's Perilous Path in the Middle East*. Beacon Press: Boston.

9. In fact, there is room to argue that Islamic revivalism and nationalism are philosophically intertwined. What Gellner, E. 1983. *Nations and Nationalism*. Cornell University Press: Ithaca, NY, pp.3–4 labels 'Reformism' (or Protestantism) and 'Nationalism' are both responding to the same ethical, philosophical, and social imperatives, and they both reinforce each other in practice.

10. Burgat, F. 2008. *Islamism in the Shadow of al-Qaeda*. University of Texas Press: Austin, Texas. pp.31–37.

11. Ibid., pp.17–20.

12. Ahmad, J. 1960. *The Intellectual Origins of Egyptian Nationalism*. Oxford University Press: Oxford.

13. Hourani, A. 1960. 'Introduction' in Ahmad, J. 1960. *The Intellectual Origins of Egyptian Nationalism*. Oxford University Press: Oxford.

14. Ahmad, op.cit., pp.86–87.

15. Esposito, J. 2005. *Islam: The Straight Path*. Oxford University Press: New York. p.170.

16. A religious individual obligation to pay a tax on one's assets to the poor (or certain purposes of public interests).

17. Divine Law.

18. Nasser, G.A. 1962. *Al-Mithaq*. Ministry of Education: Cairo. pp.148–158.

19. Burgat, op.cit., pp.32–33.

20. Ibid., pp.10–11.

21. Esposito, op.cit., pp.128–134.

22. Abdel-Meguid, W. 2009. 'Al-Ikhwan Al-Muslimoon bayna al-mahlya wal alamya', in Shobaki, A. (ed.) *Azmat Al-Ikhwan Al-Muslimeen*. Al-Ahram: Cairo. pp.229–265.

23. Habib, R. 2009. 'Roaya lilmostaqbal al-syassi lil Ikhwan Al-muslimeen', in Shobaki, A. (ed.) *Azmat Al-Ikhwan Al-Muslimeen*. Al-Ahram: Cairo. pp.31–34.

24. Esposito, op.cit., p.150.

25. Zahid, M., and Medley, M. 2006. 'Muslim Brotherhood in Egypt and Sudan', *Review of African Political Economy*, 33 (110), pp.693–708.

26. Munson, op.cit., p.489.

27. Habib, K. 2009. 'Al-elaqa bayna Al-Ikhwan wal gamaat Al-Islamyia al okhra', in Shobaki, A. (ed.) *Azmat Al-Ikhwan Al-Muslimeen*. Al-Ahram: Cairo. pp.149–152.

28. Ajami, F. 1995. 'The Sorrows of Egypt', *Foreign Affairs*, 74 (5), pp.72–88.

29. Giddens, 1990, op.cit., p.27.

30. Habermas, J. 1993. *The Philosophical Discourse of Modernity*. Massachusetts Institute of Technology Press: Cambridge, MA.

31. Awa, S. 2006. *Al-Gamaa Al-Islamyia Al-Muslaha Fi Misr*. Dar El-Shorouk Aldawlia: Cairo. p.66.

32. Habib, Rafik , op.cit., pp.41–43.

33. Awa, op.cit., p.82.

34. Habib, Kamal, 2009, op.cit., p.137. Whether Qutb himself meant his writings to be taken in this way is questionable. But this became the established reading of his texts.

35. Ibid., p.141.

36. Burgat, op.cit., p.79.

37. Giddens, 1994, op.cit., p.85.

38. Esposito, op.cit., pp.173–174.

39. Shobaki, A. 2009. 'Al-Ikhwan Al-Muslimon bayna mushkilat al-hader wa tahadyat al-mustaqbal', in Shobaki, A. (ed.) *Azmat Al-Ikhwan Al-Muslimeen*. Al-Ahram: Cairo. p.72.

40. Habib, op.cit., p.43.

41. El-Ghobashy, M. 2005. 'The Metamorphosis of the Egyptian Muslim Brothers', *International Journal of Middle East Studies,* 37 (3), pp.373–395.

42. Gaafar, H. 2009. 'Tagrobat Al-Ikhwan Al-Muslimoon fil niqabat almehanya fi misr', in Shobaki, A. (ed.) *Azmat Al-Ikhwan Al-Muslimeen*. Al-Ahram: Cairo. pp.97–128.

43. Habib, R., op.cit., p.45.

44. El-Ghobashy, op.cit., p.386.

45. Ibid., p.385.

46. Hatina, M. 2007. *Identity Politics in the Middle East: Liberal Thought and Islamic Challenge in Egypt*. Tauris Academic Studies: London. p.42.

47. Ibid., pp.138–148.

48. Awa, op.cit., pp.132–146.

49. Mehrez, S. 2008. *Egypt's Culture Wars: Politics and Practice*. Routledge: London.

50. Hatina, op.cit., pp.35–36.

51. His name is Sayed Imam el-Sherif, but he is widely known under his assumed names of Dr. Fadl and Abdel-Kader Bin Abdel-Aziz.

52. For more details, see the account of Nageh Ibrahim in 2008, a former key leader of Al-Gama'at.

53. Rashwan, D. 2008. 'Al-muragaat: al-syaq - al-maghza -al-dilalat', in Rashwan, D. (ed.) *Al-muragaat: al-syaq al-maghza al-dilalat*. Al-Ahram: Cairo. pp.12–13.

54. But not yet its 'outside' branch, which is led by Ayman Zawahri whose positions on the matter have differed from those of Dr Fadl in a rather dramatic fashion since 1994.

55. Ibrahim, N. 2008. 'Al-Gamaa Al-Islamya bayna al-mubadra wal muragaa', in Rashwan, D. (ed.) *Al-Muragaat min Al-Gamaa Al-Islamya ela Al-Jihad*. Al-Ahram: Cairo. pp.44–54.

56. Tibi, B. 2009. *Islam's Predicament with Modernity*. Routledge: London. pp.268–289, for an interesting discussion of how Egyptian education, and social change process in general, led to the marginalisation of secular elites.

57. *Al-Masri al-Youm*, 13 January 2007, Cairo.

58. Shobaki, op.cit., p.77.

Bibliography

Abdel-Meguid, W. 2009. Al-Ikhwan Al-Muslimoon bayna al-mahlya wal alamya, in Shobaki, Amr, ed. *Azmat Al-Ikhwan Al-Muslimeen*.Al-Ahram: Cairo.

Ahmad, J. 1960. *The Intellectual Origins of Egyptian Nationalism*. Oxford University Press: Oxford.

Ajami, F. 1995. 'The Sorrows of Egypt', *Foreign Affairs*, 74 (5).

Al-Masri al-Youm, 13 January 2007, Cairo.

Awa, S. 2006. *Al-Gamaa Al-Islamyia Al-Muslaha Fi Misr*. Dar El-Shorouk Aldawlia: Cairo.

Burgat, F. 2008. *Islamism in the Shadow of al-Qaeda*. University of Texas Press: Austin.

El-Ghobashy, M. 2005. 'The Metamorphosis of the Egyptian Muslim Brothers', *International Journal of Middle East Studies*, 37.

El-Raf'ay, A.R. 1929. *Tarikh Al-Haraka Al-Qawmya Fi Misr.* Dar El Maaref: Cairo.

Esposito, J. 2005. *Islam: The Straight Path.* Oxford University Press: New York.

Gaafar, H. 2009. Tagrobat Al-Ikhwan Al-Muslimoon fil niqabat almehanya fi misr, in Shobaki, Amr, ed. *Azmat Al-Ikhwan Al-Muslimeen.* Al-Ahram: Cairo.

Gellner, E. 1983. *Nations and Nationalism.* Cornell University Press: Ithaca, NY.

Giddens, A. 1994. *Beyond Left and Right: The Future of Radical Politics.* Stanford University Press: Stanford, CA.

—— 1990. *The Consequences of Modernity.* Stanford University Press: Stanford, CA.

Habermas, J. 1993. *The Philosophical Discourse of Modernity.* Massachusetts Institute of Technology Press: Cambridge.

Habib, K. 2009. Al-elaqa bayna Al-Ikhwan wal gamaat Al-Islamyia al okhra, in Shobaki, Amr, ed. *Azmat Al-Ikhwan Al-Muslimeen.* Al-Ahram: Cairo.

Habib, R. 2009. Roaya lilmostaqbal al-syassi lil Ikhwan Al-muslimeen, in Shobaki, Amr, ed. *Azmat Al-Ikhwan Al-Muslimeen.* Al-Ahram: Cairo.

Halliday, F. 2003. *Islam and the Myth of Confrontation: Religion and Politics in the Middle East.* I.B.Tauris: London.

Hatina, M. 2007. *Identity Politics in the Middle East: Liberal Thought and Islamic Challenge in Egypt.* Tauris Academic Studies: London.

Hourani, A. 1960. 'Introduction' in Ahmad, J., *The Intellectual Origins of Egyptian Nationalism.* Oxford University Press: Oxford.

Ibrahim, N. 2008. Al-Gamaa Al-Islamya bayna al-mubadra wal muragaa, in Rashwan, Diaa, ed. *Al-Muragaat min Al-Gamaa Al-Islamya ela Al-Jihad.* Al-Ahram: Cairo.

Khalidi, R. 2004. *Resurrecting Empire: Western Footprints and America's Perilous Path in the Middle East.* I. B. Tauris: London.

Lewis, B. 2002. *What Went Wrong: The Clash between Islam and Modernity in the Middle East.* Weidenfeld and Nicolson: London.

Mehrez, S. 2008. *Egypt's Culture Wars: Politics and Practice.* Routledge: London.

Munson, Z. 2001. 'Islamic Mobilisation: Social Movement Theory and the Egyptian Muslim Brotherhood', *The Sociological Quarterly,* 42 (4).

Nasser, G.A. 1962. *Al-Mithaq.* Ministry of Education: Cairo.

Rashwan, D. 2008. Al-muragaat: al-syaq al-maghza al-dilalat, in Rashwan, Diaa, ed. *Al-Muragaat min Al-Gamaa Al-Islamya ela Al-Jihad.* Al-Ahram: Cairo.

Shobaki, A. 2009. Al-Ikhwan Al-Muslimon bayna mushkilat al-hader wa tahadyat al-mustaqbal, in Shobaki, Amr, ed. *Azmat Al-Ikhwan Al-Muslimeen.* Al-Ahram: Cairo.

Tibi, B. 2009. *Islam's Predicament with Modernity.* Routledge: London.

Zahid, M., and Medley, M. 2006. 'Muslim Brotherhood in Egypt and Sudan', *Review of African Political Economy,* 33 (110).

7

BETWEEN PRAGMATISM AND RADICALISM: THE SYRIAN MUSLIM BROTHERHOOD AND THE BA'ATH REGIME

Raphaël Lefevre

Despite its recent rejection of violence, the Syrian Muslim Brotherhood – the Ikhwan Muslimin – has not yet emerged from the obscurity it was thrown into over thirty years ago, when its bloody struggle against the Syrian Ba'ath brought the regime to the verge of collapse. From the time of the Ba'athist takeover of Syria's political, economic and security institutions in 1963 to the massacre of thousands of alleged Muslim Brothers at Hama in 1982, the Ikhwan had constantly hesitated between adopting a pragmatic or a radical stance towards the regime, eventually opting for the latter with dramatic consequences for the future of the Islamist movement itself. Forced into exile, the Muslim Brotherhood thereafter strove to gain acceptance from the Syrian Ba'ath by reinventing itself as the pragmatic organisation it had been when it was founded. However, this strategy has not proved successful as the Ba'athist regime remains haunted by the vivid memory of the violent Islamist challenge to its rule, a memory that has been revived by widespread demonstrations throughout Syria in 2011.

The Socio-Ideological Roots of the Struggle
between the Ba'ath and the Ikhwan

After the Ba'athist takeover of Syria in March 1963, the Syrian Muslim Brotherhood rapidly rose to become the new regime's fiercest ideological and political opponent. From its secular outlook to its socialist programme, virtually every aspect of the Syrian Ba'ath seemed to put it at odds with the Ikhwan. Founded as the Syrian branch of the Muslim Brotherhood by a group of Islamic scholars who brought together several religious organisations that had emerged throughout the country in the 1930s, the Islamist movement had traditionally emphasised the unique role of Islam in Syrian society and politics. This had led to early clashes between the Ikhwan and supporters of the Ba'ath when, in April 1950, Ikhwani leader Mustapha al-Sibai pushed forward a draft constitution which would have made Islam the official state religion, had it been passed.[1] This infuriated the historical founders of the Ba'ath such as Michel Aflaq and Salah Eddine al-Bitar who, despite viewing Islam as the highest expression of the 'Arab spirit', nonetheless displayed a fierce secularism summed up in the slogan 'religion is for God, country is for all'.[2]

Soon after the Ba'ath Party's ascent to power, clashes between the two groups intensified. Violent anti-regime protests led by the Ikhwan broke out at Hama, a bastion of religious conservatism, as early as April 1964. As a consequence, and in order to curb the power of the religious sheikhs allied with the Ikhwan, the new Ba'athist rulers brought the *Waqf* (religious endowments) under governmental control and prohibited religious teaching outside of mosques. The resentment cultivated by the *'ulama* (religious establishment) and the Ikhwan against such manifestations of Ba'athist secularism culminated in massive street protests throughout Syria's major urban centres when, in January 1973, Hafiz al-Assad, now controlling government, proposed a draft for a new constitution which was fiercely criticised for not including a clause requiring that the president must be a Muslim.[3] By that time, however, the Islamist anger displayed at the seeming atheism of the Syrian Ba'ath had also been directed at the religious roots of a new generation of rulers. In November 1970, Hafiz al-Assad had become the first Syrian president to come from the Alawi confessional group, putting a formal end to the long-standing political and social domination of the country by its Sunni majority and, by the same token, bringing Syria to the brink of sectarian strife.

Syria had indeed become, by the mid 1970s, a country whose political, economic and security institutions had become disproportionately dominated by members of the Alawi minority, comprising no more than 10 per cent of the population. Historically oppressed by the Sunni majority, which had tended to see its members as heretical Muslims ever since the time of Ibn Taymiyya's fourteenth-century fatwa against the 'Nusayri' community, the Alawis had had to struggle in order to survive. Alongside other minority communities, such as the Druzes, the Christians and the Ismailis, the Alawis vested in two institutions in which their power would ultimately prevail in post-independence Syria: the Army and the Ba'ath Party. After the latter took over the country through the coup of 8 March 1963, an internal struggle for power took place within both institutions, which was played out along sectarian, regional and socio-economic lines. Inside the Syrian Ba'ath, the 'old guard' of Sunni Ba'athists was eventually marginalised from power when the more radical, minority-dominated 'neo-Ba'ath' took over following the coup of 23 February 1966. Inside the Armed Forces, the non-Alawi minority factions, namely the Druzes and the Ismailis, were sidelined after 1969, paving the way for an intra-Alawi confrontation between the country's strongman, Salah Jedid, and the defence minister, Hafiz al-Assad, which the latter eventually won through his 12 November 1970 coup.[4] The aggregate result of these bitter power struggles within the Ba'athist regime was that, in both the Syrian Ba'ath and the armed forces, the number of Alawis rising to posts of responsibility increased in numbers disproportionate to their demographic presence in Syrian society. Whilst the proportion of Alawi officers in the armed forces rose from 30 per cent in 1963–66 to 42 per cent in 1966–70, the share of Alawis within the Syrian Regional Command – the Ba'ath Party's most influential decision-making body – increased from 14 per cent to 23.4 per cent during the same period.[5]

As the Assad regime came to reflect in a more obvious manner the emergence of an Alawite ruling class, the confrontation between the Ba'ath and the Muslim Brotherhood gradually assumed a sectarian nature. By the mid 1970s, many Sunnis who did not hold particularly strong religious views became increasingly attracted by the subtly antagonistic tone towards the regime and the Alawi dominance within it conveyed by the Brotherhood. The movement had indeed started to emphasise the distinctively 'Nusayri' nature of the Ba'athist regime, in an implicit reference to Ibn Taymiyya's radical *fatwa* condemning the religious minority. Equally, despite claiming to be playing down the sectarian dimension, the Muslim Brotherhood's political programme clearly emphasised the religious illegitimacy of the Alawi regime through statements such as 'a minority cannot forever rule a majority'.[6] By the end of the 1970s, an atmosphere of quasi-civil war most visibly fought along sectarian lines had become palpable. In June 1979, gunmen affiliated with *al-Talia al-Muqatila*, an armed organisation loosely linked to the Syrian Ikhwan, massacred 83 Alawi cadets at the Aleppo Artillery School; ushering in a period of violent sectarian tension between Alawis and radical Sunnis which would culminate in massacre of thousands of Muslim Brothers at Hama, in February 1982, allegedly on the orders of Rifaat al-Assad, the president's brother and commander of the special brigades used for domestic control.

Deeply troubled by the Alawi-dominated nature of the secular Ba'athist regime, the revolutionary socialist programme put forward by Syria's new rulers also profoundly concerned the Muslim Brotherhood. The 1963 coup had indeed brought to power a radically new political and economic elite whose deprived social background intensified their commitment to land reform and nationalisation. Often coming from the rural areas surrounding Latakia and, to a lesser extent, Dara'a and Deir ez-Zor, the Ba'athist rulers were committed to put into practice their slogan, 'The land to him who works it'.[7] The aggregate effect of the successive land reforms carried out by the new ruling class soon proved quite effective, as the number of Syrians belonging to the upper landowning class decreased fourfold between 1963 and 1970.[8] However, the socialist programme implemented by the Syrian Ba'ath also came to have a devastating effect on the livelihood of the growingly vocal middle class urban traders, harmed by the rise in the price of commodities, the expansion of state bureaucracy, controls on imports and exports, nationalisations and soaring inflation.

The Muslim Brotherhood, which had been since its creation the natural ally of the socially conservative and economically liberal *souk*, soon came to the defence of these endangered small traders and artisans. Led by the Ikhwan, strikes broke out in 1964 and 1967 in the *souks* of Aleppo, Homs and Damascus, where the powerful Chamber of Commerce demanded the repeal of restrictions on foreign trade and guarantees against further nationalisations. By the mid 1970s, Hafiz al-Assad's promise of liberalising the economic system had been only partially fulfilled. Persisting state restrictions on private capital and trade infuriated the small traders and *souk* merchants who took their anger to the streets. In a deliberate act of defiance, the cooperative stores, which had become a symbol of failed Ba'athist socialist policies, were among the first establishments to be destroyed by members of the Brotherhood during the mass protests which took place at Aleppo in March 1980.

According to one commentator, the Syrian Ikhwan had therefore become by the late 1970s 'the most implacable opponent' to socialist Ba'athist policies as well as 'the forward arm of the endangered urban traders'.[9] This was reflected through the Brotherhood's political programme which, when it was published in 1980, made much play of the defence of values such as the 'right of ownership of private property', the 'freedom of trade' and the 'encouragement of private investment in the national economy'. In addition, the nature of the language employed was unambiguously tailored to the attention of an economically liberal social group, with a reference to the public sector suggesting that it should be 'purified' of its 'laziness and incompetence'.[10] According to one analyst, it is thus quite clear that 'the pro-capitalist, anti-statist bias of most of [the Muslim Brotherhood's 1980 political] programme is unmistakable'.[11] With socio-ideological roots opposed on all accounts to those of the rulers, the public political discourse put forward by the Syrian Ikhwan gradually came to represent a fierce challenge to Ba'athism.

Between Pragmatism and Radicalism

Just as the Syrian Muslim Brotherhood rose to become the Ba'athist regime's most implacable ideological and political opponent throughout the 1970s, the message which the Islamist movement strove to convey also became blurred. While most members of the Ikhwan agreed on the general objectives of the struggle against the Syrian Ba'ath, the movement's discourse became fragmented between those advocating preparation for *jihad* and those favouring restraint and peaceful resistance. To understand the extent to which internal divisions came to play such a prominent role in the movement, a brief historical glance at the circumstances surrounding its creation is needed.

Despite the name suggesting the existence of a single coherent organisation modelled on its Egyptian counterpart, the Syrian Ikhwan was in fact the product of an attempt to unify the many religious organisations which had sprang up throughout Syria in the 1930s. The most important of these, *Dar al-Arqam*, had its centre of activities in Aleppo, a city which logically became the main headquarters of the Syrian branch of the Muslim Brotherhood upon its official foundation in 1937. Sensing the approach of independence in 1944, however, the society moved its activities to the capital, thereby unleashing a sense of bitterness which would come to dominate the attitudes of Aleppine members of the Brotherhood towards their Damascene brothers. Nevertheless, these underlying frustrations did not come to the fore immediately, as the society was at the time led by Mustapha al-Sibai, a charismatic and consensual figure from Homs who did his utmost to keep up a geographical balance within the leadership.

Various divisions, however, soon came to plague the relations between Ikhwani decision-makers, weakening the grip of the Brotherhood's leadership on its followers and blurring the message it strove to convey. Issam al-Attar, an Islamic scholar who by 1957 had become the society's General Guide, did not seem to display the same interest as his predecessor in trying to retain a degree of internal cohesion within the organisation's ranks, thereby raising criticisms that he too often confused 'being a great speaker with being a great leader'.[12] Originally from the capital, the new leader came to rely almost exclusively on a small group of Damascene followers, neglecting the ties which linked the society's headquarters to the rest of the country. This led a former Syrian Brother to note that, despite claims of representing the exact opposite of the Ba'ath Party, the Ikhwan came to rely on a geographic factionalism similar in many respects to that of its rival.[13] Issam al-Attar's religious roots, originating in Salafism, also became problematic. Salafists aim at closely following the *salaf* ('the ancestors', a reference to prominent Muslims of the Prophet's generation and the Rashidun period) and, therefore, strongly condemn later Islamic traditions which developed around Sufism. However, many of Syria's *ulama*, such as the powerful Hama-based Sheikh al-Hamid, were Sufis. All in all, it seemed as if Issam al-Attar was forgetting the legacy of his predecessor, al-Sibai, whose motto had been: 'Islam is *'amal* [action] not *jadal* [controversial argumentation].'[14]

It is against this backdrop that the leadership crisis which seized the Ikhwan in 1969 should be viewed. In addition, members of the 'Aleppo faction', who were challenging the 'Damascus wing' led by al-Attar, complained that the exile of the Ikhwani leader – who had been forced to settle in West Germany after the Ba'ath takeover – was making the society's work on the ground more difficult. In reality, Issam al-Attar's exile had only exacerbated existing tensions and came to represent a window of opportunity for other members of the Brotherhood to emerge as new leaders. His authority was thus challenged by prominent Syrian Brothers who originated from various cities to the north of Damascus, mainly from Aleppo and Hama. Led by a historic Aleppine figure, Sheikh Abdel Fattah Abu Ghuddah, the group comprised young rising stars of the movement, such as Said Hawwa and Adnan Saadeddine from Hama. The leadership crisis which ensued dealt a fatal blow to the organisation, as each camp refused to compromise with the other.

By 1970 the tensions which had poisoned relationships between Ikhwani factions were running so high that the Egyptian Muslim Brotherhood, as the mother-organisation, had to intervene in order to set up a special committee tasked with organising new internal elections.[15] However, when these took place, Issam al-Attar's 'Damascus wing' decided to boycott them and subsequently did not recognise Abdel Fattah Abu Ghuddah's victory. At the time, many followers of al-Attar left the organisation, perhaps because of the Sufi background of the new leadership, according to the former Ikhwani spokesman, Obeida Nahas.[16] By the time Abdel Fattah Abu Ghuddah was officially recognised by the international body of the Muslim Brotherhood in 1972, the Syrian Ikhwan's two factions had effectively become separate branches. This rupture would persist until the height of Ikhwani confrontation with the Ba'athist regime, when the two branches came back together in 1981 to form a short-lived Islamic Front. The geographical factionalism displayed by the Brotherhood, which stemmed from questions of leadership, also came to reflect the crisis of identity experienced by the Syrian Ikhwan after 1963.

By the early 1970s, it had become clear that the geographical fault lines separating the 'Damascus wing' from the 'Aleppo faction' largely overlapped with generational and ideological ones as well. Despite the repression the Ikhwan suffered from Ba'athist rule, Issam al-Attar, whose intellectual roots drew on a quietist tradition, had constantly rejected growing calls for the advent of an armed opposition and had instead insisted on restoring 'parliamentary legitimacy'. When the anti-regime assassinations campaign started, in the mid 1970s, he condemned the use of violence in unequivocal terms and questioned the political motives of those advocating it.[17] By that time, however, Issam al-Attar and his Damascene followers were already a minority within the organisation. The more militant 'Aleppo faction' had taken control of the society's leadership, with the backing of most members on the ground, in a historical turn which would profoundly alter the nature of the Syrian Ikhwan.

Frustrated by the moderate and passive stance of the 'Damascus Wing', many Brothers from Hama and Aleppo came to the conclusion that, since a compromise with the Ba'athist regime seemed out of reach, the only remaining option which would ensure the Brotherhood's survival was to directly confront Syria's rulers. While not officially endorsing complete *jihad* against the regime before 1980, the Brotherhood's new leadership nonetheless began to flirt with the idea of preparing its troops for armed struggle. It therefore seems fair to suggest that the push for violence came from the 'Aleppo faction' of the Syrian Ikhwan. A Syrian Brother who was interviewed, himself originally from Aleppo, suggested that the divergence of the two branches in their approach towards the regime might be due to cultural differences stemming from local identities. Accordingly, while Damascene

Brothers would be more 'flexible and compromising' towards the ruling elites, given their proximity to the centre of power, Aleppine and
Hamawite Ikhwanis would tend to be 'tougher and more suspicious'
towards the regime.[18]

Within the 'Aleppo faction', a new generation of Ikhwani militants was indeed emerging whose youth gave them a 'more daring
and reckless' outlook than their elders, claimed a former leader of the
Brotherhood.[19] The new activists, often university students, also came
in disproportionate numbers from the city of Hama, which by the
1970s had become the birthplace of over 60 per cent of the Muslim
Brotherhood's cadres.[20] They strongly resented the Ba'athist regime,
whose shelling of the Sultan Mosque as the result of the April 1964
anti-regime riots had infuriated many. Furthermore, they were profoundly influenced by the anti-secular radicalism of the popular
Sheikh Muhammad al-Hamid. Said Hawwa was the living example of
this younger, more militant generation of Ikhwani activists. A young
Islamic scholar from Hama, he had become in 1975 the Syrian Muslim
Brotherhood's 'chief ideologue',[21] advocating an Islamic revolution in
which waging *jihad* against the *kafir* (heathen) boiled down to militarily confronting the Ba'athist regime. The popularity of Said Hawwa
among the rank and file of the Brotherhood was such that, by the mid
1970s, books he had authored, such as *Jund Allah* (Soldiers of Allah),
were distributed by thousands in mosques and underground religious
bookshops.[22] His writings also came to reflect the spillover into Syria
of the debate on the use of violence, which, in the mid 1960s, had
pitched the Egyptian Ikhwani leader, Hassan al-Hudaybi, against the
radical Sayyid Qutb.

The Emergence of al-Talia al-Muqatila

The impact of the Egyptian Muslim Brotherhood's radicalisation, subsequent to the growing influence of Sayyid Qutb within its ranks, was
to prove a determinant factor in its Syrian sister's slide into violence.
A Syrian Brother for instance recalls: 'We were studying *Signs on the
road* at that time, rather than *Preachers, not judges.*'[23] In the 1960s, a
few Syrian Brothers who had left their country and gone to Egypt

for their studies became immersed in the ideological debate taking place within the Egyptian organisation. This was the case with Marwan Hadid, an Ikhwani student in agricultural engineering from Hama who was at the time completing his studies in Cairo, where he befriended Sayyid Qutb, before becoming one of his most outspoken supporters. In *Ma'allim fi'l tariq* ('Signs on the road'), which quickly became a significantly influential work, the radical Ikhwani ideologue had laid out a doctrine for action aimed at combating non-Islamic Arab governments, such as the Nasserist regime in Egypt. Upon his return to Hama in 1963, Marwan Hadid started to advocate the immediate necessity for the Brotherhood to wage an armed struggle against the Syrian Ba'ath as, in his view, the Islamist movement was bound to be quashed whether or not it took up arms.[24]

However, as he started to publicly call for immediate *jihad* against the regime from his hometown of Hama, he was quickly sidelined by the 'Damascus wing' then in control of the Brotherhood's leadership, which categorically rejected his ideas and did not wish to be associated with him. The split came to the fore when the Syrian jihadist emerged as a charismatic and popular figure in the anti-regime riots of Hama in 1964, as a result of which the Ba'athist rulers forced the Brotherhood's leader, Issam al-Attar, into exile for not being able to control his followers. Even though Marwan Hadid could count on the tacit support of prominent Ikhwani members Adnan Saadeddine and Said Hawwa, the Brotherhood's leadership, which by the early 1970s had switched to the 'Aleppo faction', was not yet prepared to endorse his actions, for fear of further Ba'athist retaliation and a lack of consensus. The group, which Marwan Hadid developed around Hama throughout the 1960s and early 1970s, therefore became a 'fringe movement on the periphery of the Brotherhood', according to one commentator.[25]

Nonetheless, following the constitutional crisis of 1973, which seemed to confirm the secular orientation of the regime, Marwan Hadid's views became sufficiently influential to gather a sufficient number of committed followers in order to carry out the targeted killings of prominent members of the Ba'ath's security apparatus. His goal was clear and well summed up in the name he gave to his group, *al-Tali'a al-Muqatila lil-Mujahidin* (The Fighting Vanguard of the Mujahidin). By taking the initiative to kill prominent representatives of the regime, he hoped to trigger a retaliation which would ultimately convince the Brotherhood's leadership of the inevitability of armed struggle. In other words, his ambition was to revolutionise the Syrian Ikhwan. With the help of commando training received from the Palestinian group *Fatah* in its Jordanian and Lebanese camps, the troops of Marwan Hadid soon became so efficient that the Ba'athist regime concentrated its resources on tracking down their leader, who was arrested in June 1975.[26] His subsequent death one year later, allegedly through poison, provoked a cry of outrage so loud that it was heard not only by Hadid's admirers but also by many within the Brotherhood, who admired his courage and lonely struggle and sought revenge for his death.[27]

According to Husni Abu, a Syrian Brother from Aleppo, it was as a result of Marwan Hadid's death that many radicals, who had been sensitive to his call for armed struggle but were spread throughout Syria, decided to set-up a more coordinated, nationwide organisation tasked with carrying on his enterprise.[28] From Hama, the militant Abd-us-Sattar az-Za'im took on this task, bringing together under the general umbrella of *al-Talia al-Muqatila* the various armed cells which, beyond Hama, had spread in Quneitra and Aleppo under the local leadership of Ikwhani radicals Adnan Uqlah and Husni Abu. The organisation soon became very effective, assassinating Major Muhammad Gharrah, the chief of the Hama branch of General Intelligence in early 1976, most certainly in an act of retaliation for the torture which Marwan Hadid was rumoured to have undergone while in prison.[29]

Various other personalities of the regime were targeted and killed, creating by the late 1970s an atmosphere of paranoia among senior Ba'athist officials, even in the capital, Damascus. If the Alawi confessional status of almost all the victims had made the sectarian nature of *al-Talia al-Muqatila*'s actions plain from the beginning, the shift into the indiscriminate mass killing of Alawites made it even clearer. This came about in June 1979 when Adnan Uqlah, who by that time had taken over the armed organisation's leadership, directed the killing of the 83 Alawite cadets at the Aleppo School of Artillery, with the help of the Ba'athist Ibrahim Yusef. However, the analyses of this event remain confusing. While the regime conveniently accused the 'Syrian Muslim Brotherhood' of being behind the massacre, many analysts point out that the core Ikhwani leadership did not know about the incident until after it happened. Adnan Saadeddine, who had in 1975 become the organisation's leader, subsequently condemned it.[30] Nevertheless, Syria's former vice-president, Abdel Halim Khaddam, notes that if Ibrahim Yusef was secretly part of *al-Talia al-Muqatila*, he might also very well have been a member of the Brotherhood.[31] This, in turn, raises the complex question of the ambiguity of the Muslim Brotherhood's links to the armed organisation and, in a more general manner, of its attitude towards the use of political violence.

Extremism: The Ikhwan and Political Violence

By 1980, the ideological shift ushered a decade earlier when the 'Aleppo faction' had taken over the Muslim Brotherhood's leadership finally came to a head. At a Congress held that year in Amman, the Ikhwani leaders had indeed officially endorsed the use of violence as a legitimate means to fight a Ba'athist regime which had by then sharply increased its repression of the Islamist movement.[32] The Syrian Muslim Brotherhood's statements regarding the use of violence at the time are thus unsurprisingly filled with references to 'self-defence' and the 'option of last resort'. In an April 1980 issue of *An-Nadhir*, an information letter published outside Syria by the Muslim Brotherhood, Ikhwani leaders for instance stressed that, 'We did not begin our *jihad* until the oppressors had begun to exterminate Islam and until after having received the broken bodies of our brothers who had died under torture'.[33] In fact, it is undeniable that increased state repression did have a polarising effect on the political situation in Syria. This is even retrospectively recognised by Syria's former vice-president Abdel Halim Khaddam, according to whom 'the regime made a mistake by increasing the repression after the Aleppo Artillery incident [of June 1979], as it only further radicalised many Brothers who came to feel they had no option but to use violence'.[34] The repression faced by the Muslim Brotherhood sharply accentuated over the months, especially after an attempt to assassinate President Hafiz al-Assad nearly succeeded, on 26 June 1980. The next morning, two units of Rifaat al-Assad's Defence Companies were sent to Palmyra, where they slaughtered at least five hundred suspected members of the Syrian Ikhwan who were jailed in a prison located in the surrounding desert. On 8 July, the Syrian Parliament passed the notorious 'Law No. 49', which made it a capital offence to belong to the Muslim Brotherhood. An exiled Syrian Brother recalls, 'We were being tracked by the security services; and if they found us we faced four options: prison, torture, death, or one after the other'.[35]

In such circumstances, the leadership of the Syrian Ikhwan soon became overwhelmed by increasingly loud demands from rank-and-file members to act more violently against the regime. In many ways, the 1980 endorsement of the use of violence by the Ikhwani leadership also reflected its increasingly marginalised position on the ground, as *al-Talia al-Muqatila*'s popularity was rapidly growing. Indeed, by 1980 the armed organisation had gained the title of the 'Internal Muslim Brotherhood', a reflection both of the prominent political influence it possessed over the Syrian Islamist movement and of the marginalisation of the traditional Ikhwani leaders, who had been forced to flee Syria after 1979 in order to find exile in places such as Saudi Arabia and Jordan. By the late 1970s, membership to the Muslim Brotherhood was about to drop as many of its activists were joining *al-Talia al-Muqatila*. In the words of a former Syrian Brother, the Ikhwan was thus in the midst of a 'struggle for control', doing its utmost to prevent its influence on the ground from further declining.[36] It could therefore very well be that, by declaring *jihad* against the Ba'ath regime, the exiled leadership of the Syrian Ikhwan was trying to reassert its political position inside Syria and regain some of the popularity which it had lost after it had had to leave the country.

The political opportunism displayed by the leadership of the Muslim Brotherhood finally came to a head late in 1980 when the Ikhwan officially decided to join forces with *al-Talia al-Muqatila*. As evidence of the opportunistic dimension of such an alliance, even the Damascene followers of Issam al-Attar joined the new group, notwithstanding their historical reluctance to use violence and their quarrels with the Aleppo-led Ikhwani leadership. A joint command of 12 men was set up, headed by the Damascene Brother, Hassan Houeidi, with four members representing each of the three factions, in an effort to put differences aside. This would culminate in early 1981 in the creation of the short-lived Islamic Front.[37]

Retrospectively, the Syrian Muslim Brotherhood argues that its alliance with Adnan Uqlah's *al-Talia al-Muqatila* represented a mere 'joint venture'; a short term enterprise in which both organisations shared the same ambition of overthrowing the regime and therefore briefly joined forces, despite sharp organisational and ideological differences.[38] The argument is convenient for the Ikhwan, as it seems to imply the absence of a deeper relationship between the two groups preceding the advent of the Joint Command in 1980. This would allow Ikhwani leaders, in turn, to blame the killing of 70 Ba'athists in Hama which led to a bloody governmental retaliation on 'Adnan Uqlah's own recklessness'.[39] But was the short-lived alliance between the Muslim Brotherhood and *al-Talia al-Muqatila* really just a one-off 'joint venture'?

The nature of the relationship between the two organisations had been, from the very beginning, a complex one. Marwan Hadid's armed exploits had made the prospects of an Islamic revolution in Syria more likely and had increased the popularity of the Muslim Brotherhood, yet in so doing he had also brought down the wrath of the Ba'ath regime upon the whole of the movement. The Ikhwan therefore adopted a policy which, at first glance, appeared in many respects to be contradictory. On the one hand, the Muslim Brotherhood's leadership strictly prohibited its rank-and-file members from belonging to both organisations and from attending the sermons of Marwan Hadid and Adnan Uqlah.[40] On the other hand, however, many inside the society suspected that Ikhwani leader Adnan Saadeddine was holding secret coordination talks with the leaders of *al-Talia al-Muqatila* as early as 1977.[41] The rationale behind this secret alliance was clear: while the Muslim Brotherhood was aware that it could potentially benefit politically from the armed struggle waged by Adnan Uqlah's organisation against the regime, it also knew that this could backfire, were the regime to find out about the bridge being established between the two.

The willingness to secretly join forces was also reinforced by a shared feeling inside the Brotherhood's leadership that Adnan Uqlah, whilst a very effective commando leader, was also an unpredictable and unreliable character. Those who have met him describe his personality as being 'very charismatic' yet 'overzealous' and even 'irrational'. The goal of the Ikhwan was therefore, in the words of an exiled Syrian Brother, to 'retain control' of Adnan Uqlah by secretly joining forces with him and, thereby, weigh on his agenda in a direction favourable to the Ikhwan's ambitions.[42] The secret coordination could, for instance, have taken the form of clandestine joint meetings and large money transfers made by the Brotherhood to *al-Talia al-Muqatila*, most often through the intermediary of Riyath Jamour, who was acting as secret link between the two organisations.[43] However, the middleman was caught by the regime in early 1979, ushering in a few months of dysfunctional coordination between the two groups. This seems to confirm that Adnan Saadeddine did not have prior knowledge of the Aleppo Artillery massacre before it happened, in June 1979. But what was the degree of involvement of the Ikhwani leadership in the events which led to the violent showdown with the regime at Hama in February 1982?

Hama and the End of the Double Game

Pushed to self-criticism by subsequent decades in exile, the Syrian Ikhwan set up a 'truth seeking committee' tasked with producing an internal assessment of what had led to the situation encountered by the regime in Hama. The document, not publicly available, reportedly lays much of the blame on the former leader, Adnan Saadeddine, and his ideologue, Said Hawwa, for their secret links to *al-Talia al-Muqatila*. It is quite clear, however, that these two personalities, who were no longer members of the Ikhwan when the evaluation report was produced during the mid 1990s, seem to have served as convenient scapegoats for the whole of the movement going astray. If individual mistakes were made, much of the blame lay on the collective failure of the movement to restrain its most radical members from becoming involved in the events of February 1982 at Hama. One faction of the Brotherhood appears to have been particularly implicated in the violence which seized the city at the time: the local Hama leaders of the Ikhwan.

Despite the coordination which existed between the Muslim Brotherhood and *al-Talia al-Muqatila*, the two organisations had generally remained two institutionally distinct entities. Yet, things appear to have been different in Hama, where the line between both groups was blurred. A former Syrian Brother for instance reports that while the national leadership of the Ikhwan strictly prohibited its members from belonging to both organisations, the local Ikhwani leaders in Hama showed 'tolerance' towards this policy of non-duplication of memberships.[44] In practice, this meant that, in Hama, an Ikhwani militant could also be an activist of *al-Talia al-Muqatila*. In the city, the lines were blurred to such an extent that even Umar Jawad, the local leader of the Ikhwan, is thought to have also belonged to Adnan Uqlah's organisation.[45] In other words, at Hama the two groups had almost entirely merged.

It was the close cooperation between Adnan Uqlah and Umar Jawad which seems to have sparked the crisis at Hama in February 1982. The leader of *al-Talia al-Muqatila* had visited the city several times in the January of the same year and both men had come to an agreement that the local Ikhwani militants would stage a full-scale rebellion there upon reception sometime in April of a code word sent by Adnan Uqlah on the radio. However, the national leadership of the Ikhwan never endorsed these active preparations for imminent *jihad* as it did not feel that the movement was strong enough to sustain an open confrontation with the regime. Hassan Houeidi, who by 1980 had become the leader of the Muslim Brotherhood, thus reportedly asked his lieutenant, Said Hawwa, to deliver a message to Umar Jawad, making it clear that the Ikhwani leadership categorically rejected the idea of an early full-scale *jihad* in Hama. The message, however, never reached the local leader of the Muslim Brotherhood, who called upon the whole city to rise when he received Adnan Uqlah's orders soon after an abortive governmental raid on the group's weapons cache on 2 February 1982.[46] The outcome is well-known; after having distributed weapons to the inhabitants of Hama, local Ikhwani militants slaughtered seventy Ba'athist officials and led violent street riots which, in turn, provoked the troops of Rifaat al-Assad into bloody acts of revenge against the city's inhabitants, culminating in the deaths of between 10,000 and 20,000 people.[47]

Even if the current leadership of the Muslim Brotherhood is aware of the ways in which the events unfolded, it still insists that, 'The unanswered question remains that of who neglected to pass on Hassan Houeidi's message to Umar Jawad'.[48] According to a high-ranking member of the Syrian Ikhwan, it is clear that Said Hawwa did not deliver the message to the local leader of the Muslim Brotherhood in Hama, thus raising questions on the Ikhwani ideologue's commitment to the Brotherhood's agenda, an organisation from which he would resign in 1983. It is striking, however, that individuals such as Said Hawwa, Adnan Saadeddine and Adnan Uqlah have been heavily blamed by the Brotherhood leadership for what happened, yet it does not seem to have fully grasped the consequences of its own attempt to enter into a fatal double-play with the regime.

Struggling for Relevance

The Syrian Muslim Brotherhood is still remembered for the extremism into which it had fallen in the early 1980s and has not yet emerged from the obscurity of exile, despite its repeated attempts to gain recognition from the Ba'athist regime by softening its stance. Decades of exile seem to have pushed the Ikhwan into mellowing its 1980s 'discourse of crisis', a shift which can be seen through the lens of Ali al-Bayanouni's own evolution. A long-time radical member of the 'Aleppo faction', he had by the early 2000s made his new-found commitment to non-violence, the protection of minorities and the promotion of democracy the cornerstone of Ikhwani discourse in exile.

As General Guide of the movement (1996–2010), his first steps were to soften the image of an organisation tainted by its links to the violence of the early 1980s. In 2001, he pushed Ikhwani members to adopt a National Honour Charter which condemned in unequivocal terms the use of violence against one's own government.[49] According to Zouheir Salem, often considered as the current chief ideologue of the Syrian Ikhwan, 'We learned from the failure of armed struggle and now believe that the only way to oppose the regime is through peaceful means on the model of Mustapha al-Sibai'.[50] Ali al-Bayanouni is also often considered to be the main driving force behind the publication in 2004 of the Muslim Brotherhood's political programme, a document emphasising notions such as political pluralism and civil liberties. In an effort to make this more substantive, the Ikhwani leader even went as far as pledging that the organisation would respect election results even if a woman or a Christian were chosen as President of Syria.[51]

This effort at moderating the society's doctrine on many points was coupled with a willingness to engage in a political dialogue with other Syrian opposition forces, including various prominent secular or left wing figures such as the Christian Michel Kilo and the Communist Riad al-Turk. Negotiations over a common opposition platform culminated most notably in 2005 with the signing of the Damascus Declaration, of which the Muslim Brotherhood became a key component.[52] However, it was the defection of Vice-President Abdel Halim Khaddam in December 2005 which provided a real opportunity for the Syrian Ikhwan to prove that it was once again a pragmatic movement willing to go as far as engaging with former Ba'athist officials. According to the former vice-president, it was the Brotherhood which initiated a dialogue with him, after Ali al-Bayanouni and Abdel Halim Khaddam had both taken part in a show broadcast on Al-Jazeera in January 2006.[53] The two parties to the dialogue agreed to form a joint opposition platform, which culminated with the creation of the National Salvation Front (NSF) at a meeting at Brussels in March 2006. For the Brotherhood, the alliance with the former Ba'athist vice-president also represented a golden opportunity to regain a measure of relevance in the landscape of Syrian politics.

According to Obeida Nahas, who was the political adviser to General Guide Bayanuni and the man behind the alliance with Khaddam, 'This was a serious enterprise, as we thought our partnership with a former prominent Ba'athist would attract more defections on the part of regime officials'.[54] At the time, the belief that the NSF was gaining momentum was also shared by many inside the Ba'athist regime who expressed 'fear' at the emergence of such an alliance precisely when

Bashar al-Assad's grip on power was being greatly weakened by the forced Syrian withdrawal from Lebanon and the threats of external intervention coming from Washington.[55] However, as Ikhwani hopes for 'regime change' in Damascus progressively declined, it became 'embarrassing' for the Brotherhood to remain associated with a former prominent Ba'athist figure who had participated in the massacre of its own members.[56]

In January 2009, Ikhwani leaders suspended their opposition activities, officially in order to show support for the Syrian regime's anti-Israel stance during the war in Gaza. This, however, was described as a 'mere pretext' by Abdel Halim Khaddam, who claims that the real aim behind the Brotherhood's withdrawal from the NSF was in fact an Ikhwani willingness to negotiate its way back to Damascus with the Syrian regime.[57] This is confirmed by Obeida Nahas, according to whom a 'mediation' between the Ikhwani leadership and the Ba'athist rulers took place sometime between 2009 and 2010, although he insists that, 'The talks never moved beyond the mediation phase'.[58] Nevertheless, this newfound willingness on the part of certain Ikhwani leaders to initiate a dialogue with the Syrian regime was never fully accepted within the society's ranks as ideological differences within the Muslim Brotherhood came again to the fore.

Divisions within the Islamist Movement

In many respects, the issue of the attitude which the Muslim Brotherhood should adopt towards the Ba'athist regime has remained, ever since 1963, the dominant ideological fracture within the movement's ranks. The division which in the early 1970s had separated the 'Damascus wing' from the 'Aleppo faction' over the question of armed struggle soon re-emerged during the mid 1980s. Aware that its advocacy of the use of violence had led to a catastrophic situation, members of the 'Aleppo faction', led by Sheikh Abdel Fattah Abu Ghuddah, started to reflect on their past actions and to call for negotiations with the Ba'athist regime. They were opposed by the 'Hama group' led by Adnan Saadeddine who continued to argue for armed struggle from his Iraqi exile, where he could count on a close relationship with the

Saddam Hussein regime, given its chronic hostility towards the Ba'ath in Damascus, to raise funds and obtain weapons.[59]

By 1986, the divisions which had emerged between the 'Aleppo faction' and the 'Hama group' were running so deep that the two wings had effectively become separate entities, despite having together formed the core of the Ikhwani leadership throughout much of the 1970s. The ideological divergence on the use of violence had, once again, geographical roots. Indeed, while the Ikhwani leaders who were born in Hama had felt directly targeted by the fierce governmental repression of February 1982, the Aleppine Brothers often showed more emotional detachment because Aleppo had not been as badly affected as Hama. This meant that they were often more conciliatory to a Syrian regime towards which the Hamawi Brothers still expressed strong resentment and bitterness.[60]

The split between the two groups effectively came to a head when Abdel Fattah Abu Ghuddah was elected as leader of the Muslim Brotherhood in April 1986, in a fiercely contested election, after which Adnan Saadeddine left the movement to create his National Front for the Salvation of Syria, a Baghdad-based group advocating *jihad* against the Syrian regime. In the meantime, members of the 'Aleppo faction' had chosen to follow a new moderate path, arguing that carrying out negotiations with the Ba'athist regime could bear more fruit than wielding violence against it. This newfound quietism was encouraged by Hafiz al-Assad, who asked his chief of military intelligence, Ali Duba, to open negotiations with the Ikhwani leaders of the 'Aleppo faction'.[61] However, the two rounds of talks carried out by Ali Duba in Frankfurt in 1984 and 1987 never seemed to represent genuine willingness on the part of the regime to find a political settlement acceptable to both parties. Instead, former Vice-President Khaddam suggests that, at the time, negotiations were opened with members of the Syrian Muslim Brotherhood, with the sole aim of provoking divisions amongst its members, thus weakening it.[62]

The regime's 'divide and rule' strategy proved successful, as the rift between Adnan Saadeddine and the rest of the Ikhwani leadership by then ran so deep that, despite his repeated attempts to reintegrate the movement, the former leader of the Muslim Brotherhood had to wait until he fell seriously ill before his membership to the society was reinstated, just two years before he died in 2010.[63] If Adnan Saadeddine appears to have become a convenient scapegoat for the divisions within the Ikhwani leadership, his Hamawite followers were nonetheless spared their Aleppine brothers' anger and were reintegrated into the movement in 1992, shortly after the election of Hassan Houeidi, as an Ikhwani leader prepared to find compromises between the various factions, as General Guide. A few years later, the Muslim Brotherhood published its National Honour Charter which, by officially denouncing the use of violence against one's own government, seemed to put an end to the ideological divisions over armed struggle. But has it really meant the end of divisions inside the movement's ranks?

Despite Ali al-Bayanouni's willingness to play down internal divisions during his three terms as leader of the Syrian Ikhwan (1996–2010), some of the decisions he took, such as teaming-up with Abdel Halim Khaddam and opening a new negotiation channel with the regime, proved controversial inside the movement. According to a Syrian Brother exiled in Paris, the decision to ally with the former Ba'athist vice-president was validated by only a narrow majority of Ikhwani members.[64] However, Ali al-Bayanouni's leadership is widely credited for having put the movement back into the spotlight after decades of irrelevance. Many Ikhwani members have also praised him for being a consensual figure who, despite being from the northern metropolis of Aleppo, has striven to bridge the gaps between Hamawite and Aleppine Brothers by putting together a collective leadership representative of these geographical differences. On this point, the election of Hama-born Mohammad Riyadh al-Shaqfih as General Guide in September 2010 seems to have re-opened old wounds. A long-time member of the 'Hama group', the new leader is said to have adopted a more hard-line stance towards the regime than his predecessor, perhaps as a result of his own violent past inside the organisation. His conservative credentials and over-reliance on the Hama group have led a few members of the Syrian Brotherhood to resign from the movement.[65] All in all, it seems as if the clannishness, which has characterised the movement since its very beginnings, is bound to remain a fundamental fault line for some time to come.

Despite efforts at moderating its stance on key issues, the Muslim Brotherhood has not yet been able to convince the Syrian Ba'ath that it does not represent the violent threat to its rule that it once did in the late 1970s and early 1980s. Today as before, the message which the Ikhwan strives to convey is being blurred by the internal divisions which since 1963 have regularly seized the organisation on the issue of the attitude to adopt towards the Ba'athist regime. Furthermore, despite its condemnation of the use of violence, the Syrian Ikhwan has been very reluctant to address its responsibility in the bloody events which struck Syria 30 years ago. While this is certainly due to the fact that many of the figures responsible at the time for supporting the cycle of violence are still in charge of the organisation, this is an issue from which the leadership will not be able to shy away, should the Ikhwan ever be in a position to return to Syria.

Notes

1. Teitelbaum, J. 2004. 'The Muslim Brotherhood and the "Struggle for Syria", 1947–1958: between accommodation and ideology', *Middle Eastern Studies*, 40 (3), p.143.

2. Carré, O., and Michaud, G. 1983. *Les Frères Musulmans 1928–1982*. Gallimard: Paris. p.34.

3. Humphreys, S. 1979. 'Islam and political values in Saudi Arabia, Egypt and Syria', *Middle East Journal*, 33 (1), p.14.

4. Batatu, H. 1999. *Syria's Peasantry: The Descendants of its Lesser Rural Notables, and their Politics*. Princeton University Press: Princeton. pp.170–176.

5. Van Dam, N. 1978. 'Sectarian and regional factionalism in the Syrian political elite', *Middle East Journal*, 32 (2), pp.208–210.

6. Abd-Allah, U.F. 1983. *The Islamic Struggle in Syria*. Mizan Press: Berkeley. p.211.

7. Hinnebusch, R. 1982. 'Rural politics in Ba'thist Syria: a case study in the role of the countryside in the political development of Arab societies', *The Review of Politics*, 44 (1), p.117.

8. Longuenesse, E. 1979. 'The class nature of the state in Syria', *MERIP Reports*, 77, p.4.

9. Batatu, H. 1982. 'Syria's Muslim Brethren', *MERIP Reports*, 110, pp.16–19.

10. Abd-Allah, op.cit., p.162.
11. Hinnebusch, R. 1990. *Authoritarian Power and State Formation in Ba'thist Syria: Army, Party and Peasants.* Westview Press: San Francisco. p.284.
12. Abd-Allah, op.cit., p.95.
13. Interview with Obeida Nahas, 2011.
14. Abd-Allah, op.cit., p.95.
15. Pargeter, A. 2010. *The Muslim Brotherhood: The Burden of Tradition.* Saqi Books: London. p.69.
16. Interview with Obeida Nahas, 2011.
17. Hinnebusch, 1990, op.cit., p.281.
18. Interview with Ahmed al-Uthman, 2011.
19. Adnan Saadeddine quoted in Batatu, 1982, op.cit., p.20.
20. Manna, D. 1985. 'Histoire des Frères Musulmans en Syrie', *Sou'al*, 5, p.76.
21. Weismann, I. 1993. 'Sa'id Hawwa: the making of a radical Muslim thinker in modern Syria', *Middle Eastern Studies*, 29 (4), p.619.
22. Pargeter, op.cit., p.73.
23. While *Signs on the road* (1964) represented Sayyid Qutb's most prominent advocacy of armed struggle against non-Islamic Arab regimes, *Preachers, not judges* (1969) is often seen as Hassan al-Hudaybi's refutation of Sayyid Qutb's thesis, (quoted in Pargeter, 2010, op.cit., p.73).
24. Abd-Allah, op.cit., p.95.
25. Ibid.
26. Manna, op.cit.
27. Interview with Zouheir Salem, 2011.
28. Husni Abu quoted in Carré and Michaud, op.cit., p.152.
29. Interview with Zouheir Salem, 2011.
30. Batatu, 1999, op.cit., p.267.
31. Interview with Abdel Halim Khaddam, 2011.
32. Pargeter, op.cit., p.82.
33. Abd-Allah, op.cit., p.109.
34. Interview with Abdel Halim Khaddam, 2011.
35. Interview with Ahmed al-Uthman, 2011.
36. Interview with Obeida Nahas, 2011.
37. Batatu, 1999, op.cit., p.268.
38. Interview with Obeida Nahas, 2011.
39. Adnan Saadeddine in Batatu, 1999, op.cit., p.269.
40. Interview with Ahmed al-Uthman, 2011.
41. Interview with Obeida Nahas, 2011.
42. Interview with Ahmed al-Uthman, 2011.
43. Batatu, 1999, op.cit., p.267.

44. Interview with Obeida Nahas, 2011.
45. Interview with Ali al-Bayanouni, 2011.
46. This account is based on extensive discussions with Obeida Nahas, Ali al-Bayanouni and Zouheir Salem.
47. Interview with Abdel Halim Khaddam, 2011.
48. Interview with Zouheir Salem, 2011.
49. Zisser, E. 2005. 'Syria, the Baath regime and the Islamic movement: stepping on a new path?', *The Muslim World*, 95 (1), p.56.
50. Interview with Zouheir Salem, 2011.
51. Weismann, I. 2010. 'Democratic fundamentalism? The practice and discourse of the Muslim Brothers movement in Syria', *The Muslim World*, 100 (1), p.8.
52. Landis, J., and Pace, J. 2009. 'The Syrian opposition: the struggle for unity and relevance, 2003–2008', in Lawson, F.H. (ed.) *Demystifying Syria*. Saqi Books: London. p.129.
53. Interview with Abdel Halim Khaddam, 2011.
54. Interview with Obeida Nahas, 2011.
55. Interview with US Embassy in Damascus, 2006.
56. Interview with Obeida Nahas, 2011.
57. Interview with Abdel Halim Khaddam, 2011.
58. Interview with Obeida Nahas, 2011.
59. Kutschera, C. 1987. 'Syrie: l'éclipse des Frères Musulmans', *Cahiers de l'Orient*, 7 (3), p.5.
60. Interview with Obeida Nahas, 2011.
61. Batatu, 1999, op.cit., p.276.
62. Interview with Abdel Halim Khaddam, 2011.
63. Interview with Obeida Nahas, 2011.
64. Interview with Ahmed al-Uthman, 2011.
65. Interview with Obeida Nahas, 2011.

Bibliography

Abd-Allah, U.F. 1983. *The Islamic Struggle in Syria*. Mizan Press: Berkeley, CA.

Batatu, H. 1999. *Syria's Peasantry: The Descendants of its Lesser Rural Notables, and their Politics*. Princeton University Press: Princeton.

—— 1982. 'Syria's Muslim Brethren', *MERIP Reports*, 110.

Bayanouni, A. 2011. Interview with author, 21 June. London.

Carré, O., and Michaud, G. 1983. *Les Frères Musulmans 1928–1982*. Gallimard: Paris.

Pargeter, A. 2010. *The Muslim Brotherhood: The Burden of Tradition*. Saqi Books: London.

Hinnebusch, R. 1990. *Authoritarian Power and State Formation in Ba'thist Syria: Army, Party and Peasants*. Westview Press: San Fransisco.

—— 1982. 'The Islamic movement in Syria: sectarian conflict and urban rebellion in an authoritarian-populist regime' in Hillal Dessouki, A.E. (ed.), *Islamic Resurgence in the Arab World*. Praeger: New York.

—— 1982. 'Rural politics in Ba'thist Syria: a case study in the role of the countryside in the political development of Arab societies', *The Review of Politics*, 44 (1).

Humphreys, S. 1979. 'Islam and political values in Saudi Arabia, Egypt and Syria', *Middle East Journal* 33 (1).

Khaddam, A.H. 2011. Interview with author, 23 June. Paris.

'Khaddam's and Bayanouni's Faustian pact'. 18 April 2006. *US Embassy in Damascus' Cable to State Department* (C-NE6–00262).

Kutschera, C. 1987. 'Syrie: l'éclipse des Frères Musulmans', *Cahiers de l'Orient*, 7 (3).

Landis, J., and Pace, J. 2009. 'The Syrian opposition: the struggle for unity and relevance, 2003–2008' in Lawson, F.H., *Demystifying Syria*. Saqi Books: London.

Longuenesse, E. 1979. 'The class nature of the state in Syria', *MERIP Reports*, 77.

Manna, D. 1985. 'Histoire des Frères Musulmans en Syrie', *Sou'al*, 5.

Nahas, O. 2011. Interview with author, 30 June. London.

Pargeter, A. 2010. *The Muslim Brotherhood: The Burden of Tradition*. Saqi Books: London.

Salem, Z. 2011. Interview with author, 21 June. London.

Seurat, M. 1989. *L'Etat de barbarie*. Le Seuil: Paris.

Seale, P. 1988. *Asad of Syria: The Struggle for the Middle East*. I.B.Tauris: London.

Teitelbaum, J. 2004. 'The Muslim Brotherhood and the "Struggle for Syria", 1947–1958: between accommodation and ideology', *Middle Eastern Studies*, 40 (3).

Uthman, A. 2011. Interview with author, 2 June. Paris.

Van Dam, N. 1978. 'Sectarian and regional factionalism in the Syrian political elite', *Middle East Journal*, 32 (2).

—— 1996. *The Struggle for Power in Syria: Politics and Society under Asad and the Ba'th Party*. I.B.Tauris: London.

Weismann, I. 1993. 'Sa'id Hawwa: the making of a radical Muslim thinker in modern Syria', *Middle Eastern Studies*, 29 (4).

—— 2010. 'Democratic fundamentalism? The practice and discourse of the Muslim Brothers movement in Syria', *The Muslim World*, 100 (1).

Zisser, E. 2005. 'Syria, the Baath regime and the Islamic movement: stepping on a new path?', *The Muslim World*, 95 (1).

8

TRIPOLI IN LEBANON: AN ISLAMIST FORTRESS OR A SOURCE OF TERROR?

Nasser Kalawoun

Tripoli in Lebanon has acquired an unenviable reputation for radical violence in recent years. At the start of the 1980s, for example, it was the home of the *Harakat al-Tawhid al-Islami* (Islamic Unity Movement), which became the largest radical Sunni movement in the country until its militia was crushed by the Syrian army in 1986. At around the same time, it was the place where Lebanon's *Salafi* movement began. And, of course, it was in Tripoli that *Fatah al-Islam* confronted the Lebanese army at the Nahr al-Bared Palestinian refugee camp in 2007, until the movement was dispersed and the camp destroyed, rendering over 30,000 refugees homeless. Yet the city and its surroundings are predominantly Sunni and it has always enjoyed a reputation for religious conservatism. In effect, the city suffers from none of the social or sectarian tensions of the capital, Beirut, which emerged after the creation of the Lebanese state. Its violence, in short, is not a consequence simply of recent events but is rooted in its long historical past.

The city's natural hinterland was Syria, but with the French mandate at the beginning of the 1920s it was forced into a new political structure. Thus, it became the second largest city in the country, after General Gouraud declared his intention to establish the new state of Lebanon on 1 September 1920. The new regional order thus created – built on the ruins of the Ottoman Empire – has not served Lebanon or Tripoli well through the intervening years up to 2010. Traditional issues of identity, ideology, economic development and urban planning, together with entrenched religious and sectarian sentiment, profoundly weakened the newly created state of Lebanon while eventually culminating in the terrorist violence that has characterised the region.

Such terrorism may have been born out of radicalism challenging the hegemony of the state or extremism seeking to replace it, or indeed from both tendencies working together, for that matter. After all, these factors generating violence have been frequently expressed in Tripoli or wider afield; in Lebanon itself, or Syria, Israel/Palestine or even in the wider Middle East region ever since 1948. The creation of Israel and its imposition by force has reignited the fears of sectarian elites in the region – Christian and Muslim alike in the context of Lebanon – and inspired accommodation with Tel Aviv or defensive action against the Zionist project. Often, these reactions have emanated from weak Arab states and regimes, as well as from the mosaic of sects or tribes, the ethnic and sectarian groups that make up the modern Middle East.

Perhaps the most obvious manifestation of this has been the development over the past 60 years of refugee camps, vast agglomerations of people displaced by these struggles that had, by default, evolved into semi-permanent anarchic population centres. Tripoli, for instance, has had to welcome its share of the fallout from the Palestinian *Nakba*, in the shape of two refugee camps, the al-Bared and al-Baddawi camps, located on its northen outskirts. This development intensified political rifts and tensions that had already existed with the new centre of the Lebanese state in Beirut. It is a development that has also played its part in the radicalisation of Tripoli ever since.

That central conflict has also stimulated struggles for power and influence that are ostensibly based on much more local issues as well. Tripoli has been particularly prone to such events, as outlined above and as is discussed in more detail below. Often, such tensions bubble below the social surface for very long periods of time without necessarily erupting into overt violence, which however they continue to reflect. This situation has been typified in recent years by an attack, published by Omar Tadmouri, on a pamphlet that appeared on 1 August 2008 on the website of the Phalange Party.[1] His attack, which was published in *Al-Bayan*, a local newspaper, was entitled, interestingly enough, 'Tripoli's history: from the Crusaders to the Salafis', thus highlighting Omar Tadmouri's belief in the importance of Tripoli's history in explaining the present-day struggle for power there between Muslim and Christian.[2]

Conquest and Power in Tripoli's History

Tripoli's earliest history was born in violence, for the city was lost to the Crusader invasions for 180 years during the twelfth and thirteenth centuries until the Mamluk Sultan, Mansour Qalawoun, re-took it in 1289 CE. In effect, Tripoli had become a Crusader kingdom during this period and was one of the last Crusader centres to be recovered by Muslim armies after a month-long siege. Acre, the last Crusader outpost, fell two years later, thus bringing the era of the Crusader kingdoms in the Levant to an end. Tripoli's loss was a consequence of its betrayal by the Venetians and the Pisans, who conspired with the sultan to attack the city after its ruler, Lucia, Countess of Tripoli, had allied herself with the Genoese in a local struggle with the Commune of Tripoli for power.

This historical episode has also entered the world of fiction because of a much earlier myth popularised by one of the greatest of the troubadours, Jaufré Rudel, a nobleman from Blaye in France, born in 1125 CE who wrote in Provençal. In his poems, he declared his love for Lucia, a mythical Countess of Tripoli whose fame and virtue had been spread by returning Crusaders as she had allegedly been forced to retire to a convent after being jilted. The myth claims that Jaufré Rudel joined the Second Crusade in 1147 CE and travelled to Tripoli via Palestine. On the journey he fell ill, to die in his beloved's arms on arrival in Tripoli.

The myth seems to be based on Hodierna, Countess of Tripoli, who lived from 1110 to 1164 CE and was married to Raymond, Count of Tripoli, rather than Lucia, who lived 100 years later. It was turned into an opera, *L'Amour de Loin*, written by the distinguished Lebanese author, Amin Maalouf, and based on Jaufré Rudel's own *La vida breve*.[3] Both the myth and the actual history of Tripoli at the time highlight the way in which the city was at the heart of a history of violence throughout the medieval period in both the Islamic and Crusader worlds, pitting all the major powers in the Mediterranean at the time against each other in a complex pattern of alliance and betrayal.

Later, the Mamluks rebuilt the old city around St Gilles's castle, a Crusader edifice which has since been much restored, thus celebrating the city's combined Christian–Muslim medieval history, with both surviving to this day as physical symbols of this shared past. Thereafter, Tripoli became a major port trading with Europe and with its Syrian hinterland. The Ottoman history of the city has been unearthed since the mid 1990s, as part of Turkey's new and active policy towards the Middle East.[4] Even up to the late nineteenth century, Tripoli remained an important Ottoman port and the Great Powers constantly monitored the province in which it was situated. Britain, given its command of the seas and its complex relationship with the Porte, was a major player in this respect, as was testified by the sinking of HMS Victoria, on 22 August 1893, off the coast of Tripoli during manoeuvres by the British Mediterranean fleet — designed to impress the Ottomans. All this was to change, however, with the defeat of the Ottoman empire after the First World War.

Post-Ottoman Tripoli: Only Faisalieh Remains

As soon as the last Ottoman governor left Tripoli, the new Arab government in Damascus, created by Emir Faisal of Mecca, the leader of the Arab Revolt, appointed Saadi al-Monla as his successor. However, local notables ignored the telegram advising them of this decision and chose instead the Mufti of Tripoli, Abdul Hamid Karami, who founded a political dynasty in Tripoli with ambitions that were eventually to reach national prominence. He was, nonetheless, willing to recognise the authority of the Emir in an interesting blend of local interest and national aspiration. The arrival of the British and French troops barely a week later, however, blocked this initiative by the fledgling independent Arab government of Syria to integrate the old Ottoman provinces into a new political structure.

In the face of European insistence on their own plans for the region, the local elite wavered and split between cooperating with the French, as a result of the division of the Levant as laid out in the Sykes–Picot Agreement, or waiting, as Abdul Hamid Karami wanted, for the Emir Faisal to extract an agreement from the Great Powers for some sort of Syrian kingdom. A visit by Faisal, in the winter of 1918 to Tripoli, had kindled Karami's dream that the city should become Syria's main port on the Mediterranean. This tension between European designs and an independent state was to last for many months, until France installed its Mandate. Before this happened, some signs of Tripoli's commitment to the Emir and to an independent state did emerge.

Three symbolic gestures indicating Tripoline willingness to support a Syrian Kingdom survived these eighteen months of political confusion in post-Ottoman Tripoli. First, Faisal succeeded in recruiting a local former Ottoman army officer, Fawzi al-Qawuqjee, to join him in Damascus following his self-declaration as King of Syria, thus providing a link with Tripoli — which was to become important decades later. Al-Qawuqjee came from a religious Sunni family and had fought the British in Iraq under the Ottoman flag. Second, Karami persuaded the notables of the town to build a miniature palace along the lines of the Al-Hamra in Granada, the long-lost Muslim kingdom in Andalucia, for the Emir. However, when the Emir Faisal's plans for an Arab kingdom failed, Karami himself decided to occupy this structure, which still exists and is now known as the mansion of Karm al-Qilleh. Third, in the end, Faisal's legacy has survived only in the form of a local sweet called al-Faisalieh – in a similar fashion to a previous kind of sweet which had been called 'al-Osmanlieh' to honour the former Ottoman rulers of Tripoli![5]

French Mandate Tripoli: Elite Splits

The initial near unanimous welcome to the Emir Faisal by Tripoli's elite was not to last. French pressure gradually split the elite between realists and Arabists. The former accepted the new political game in Beirut established by the French. It included, amongst others, the Muqaddams (soon to become the rival of the Karamis), the al-Jisrs, the al-Ahdabs and the al-Bissars. The Arabists clustered around the Karamis and their stronghold in the Bazaar, under an anti-French and pro-Syria banner.[6] The confusion over Syria's future status, which lasted until 1937 at least, added to the feeling of marginalisation in Lebanon's second city; while Beirut's pro-French elite accumulated affluence and power. It also created growing tensions between the two branches of the elite in Tripoli itself. Perhaps the project to deliver drinking water from Rashe'in, in early 1935, to substitute a typhoid-infested Abu Ali River was the last occasion of peaceful cooperation before violent conflict erupted between them, although it set Abdul Hamid Karami and Rashed al-Muqaddam at loggerheads.[7]

There were two violent episodes which underlined this interaction between local, Lebanese, Syrian and French political interests, and affected Tripoli's future up to 1975. The first involved Adbul Hamid Karami directly, as a result of an incident in the city's main cafe, the Mariette Pasha, next door to the local government building, the *al-Saraya*. In early May 1935, Sufi processions were marching down Tripoli's main streets to celebrate the Prophet Muhammad's birthday when a Syrian politician, Fakhri al-Baroudi, unwittingly set off a serious row. Baroudi who, ironically enough, was visiting the city as a mediator, reprimanded the leaders of one procession for mixing religion with politics by chanting slogans supporting Karami and his allies in Damascus. In response, the demonstrators wrecked the Mariette Pasha cafe, which was owned by the Muqaddam family.

This, in turn, led to another fracas later in the day, in which Abdul Hamid Karami shot dead Abdul Majid al-Muqaddam and was arrested.[8] After a spell in prison, Karami was tried in Beirut, his trial being an occasion in which many leaders of the new elite in the capital were involved as lawyers and officials; personalities such as Bishara al-Khoury, Habib Abu Shahla and Fouad Ammoun. In short, the local affairs of Tripoli now had a national stage. Abdul Hamid Karami was found to have acted in self-defence as a *mufti*, a man of religion, after he had been attacked with a stick and a knife. As a result, he was freed while the al-Muqaddams withdrew their complaint. Moreover, Riyad al-Sulh, independent Lebanon's future first premier between 1943 and 1945, presided over a group of the Beirut Sunni elite which helped to conclude a new accord between Abdul Hamid Karami and his rival, Rashed al-Muqaddam, in the autumn of 1935.[9]

The second violent episode involved most of Tripoli's elite at virtually the same location, just after the withdrawal of French troops from Lebanon. On 4 March 1947, the Muqaddam clan arranged a popular reception for the return of Fawzi al-Qawuqjee to his city – after 25 years away. He had just been freed by the French from a Berlin prison, as he had accompanied Haj Amin al-Hussaini of Palestine in an anti-British initiative during World War II. At the same time, he had acquired the status of a popular hero for having supported rebellions in Syria and Palestine against the French and the British respectively, hence the reception arranged for him in Tripoli.

Abdul Hamid Karami had tried in vain, whilst Fawzi al-Qawuqjee was in Beirut, to convince him not to play internal politics in Tripoli – especially on the eve of parliamentary elections in Lebanon. In fact, Karami's concerns were legitimate despite the fact that he had been able to secure his own position in the new independent state by winning easily in the 1943 parliamentary elections in Tripoli over Omar al-Muqaddam. He was also to serve as prime minister in 1945. By contrast, Nafiz al-Muqaddam had just returned from exile in a British colony, with the aim of claiming his father's (Rashed's) mantle after he had died in 1944. This inevitably revived the rivalry between the two clans of the Karamis and the al-Muqaddams, each of whom may have had allies and foes in Beirut and amongst the security services in Tripoli, but both had pan-Arab credentials amongst the Tripoline public. The problem was to be that neither could let the ballot box resolve the rivalry between them.

There was much at stake as support in Tripoli or Beirut could grant legitimacy to aspiring candidates for the Lebanese premiership, now that it had been agreed that the post would be entrusted to a Sunni Muslim in Lebanon's new consociational political system under the 1943 National Pact. In such a complex situation, an intervention by Fawzi al-Qawuqjee could have had national consequences as well as tipping the balance to the al-Muqaddams locally. His public reception on return to Tripoli started with a fete, held over a two kilometre stretch of road from Tripoli's southern entrance to its central square at Al-Tal, with streets full of Sufi bands and armed men firing jubilantly in the air. However, the day ended with a tragedy when a violent duel between two clan leaders (*qabadays*) developed into a massacre engulfing the security forces as well. As a result, al-Qawuqjee was ordered to go into exile again, while the government blocked an official investigation of the incident.[10] Later, the Arab League appointed al-Qawuqjee as commander of the Arab Salvation Army, but he failed to prevent the creation of the Israeli state whilst his city, Tripoli, later absorbed its share of the Arab defeat in the shape of the two Palestinian camps — which were to appear in its northern suburbs.

Tripoli and Pan-Arabism: Modernise or Die?

President Sham'un's pro-West policy in the mid 1950s transferred regional splits in the Arab world onto the national Lebanese political scene. In the case of Tripoli, Rashid Karami sided with the oppositionist Arabist camp, alongside Syria and Egypt under Nasser, as a protest at the marginalisation of his city, both politically and economically, by the Beirut and Mount Lebanon elite. This duality of attitudes between Arabism and the West came to a head in the mini civil war in the country in 1958 – thus earning Tripoli the label of a rebel city. However, President Nasser, now head of the United Arab Republic of Syria and Egypt, was instrumental in ushering in a new order in Lebanon, with Fouad Shihab as President and Rashid Karami as premier.[11] The opportunity that Rashid Karami now had to restore Tripoli's glory was translated into a number of modernisation projects emanating from a foreign aid and development programme for the city.

Symbolically, this success was made manifest in the centrepiece of a new boulevard running through the city which was dominated by a statue of Rashid Karami's father, Abdul Hamid Karami. He had died in 1950 and the statue showed him as a secular statesman and not as a *mufti*, thus indicating how values and status had evolved from the days of the Ottomans. However, despite the new projects and the success of its local sons in achieving national political status, Tripoli remained marginalised from national politics. In a lecture in May 1966, Nazih Kabbara acknowledged the investments in the port, the Abu Ali River project and a new exhibition centre for the city, but complained of the centralisation of power and services in Beirut whilst Tripoli had been cut off from its natural hinterland in Syria. In addition, he lamented the absence of tourism, basic industries, an airport and a motorway to link the city with Beirut as a gesture to compensate it for 'severing the economic link' with Syria.[12]

Despite his concerns little was done, so that Tripoli continued to be peripheral to the Lebanese state such that its sense of alienation constantly increased up to the outbreak of the civil war. The Arabist faction of the Tripoline elite also saw itself marginalised with the demise of Nasserism. Rashid Karami tried to exploit nascent Islamism, as opposed to left-wing political parties, as a new tactic to advance Tripoli's interests and keep his own position as a powerbroker. However, the tactic was to fail and his loss was translated symbolically by the destruction of his father's statue, just a stone's throw away from the al-Hamra Mansion, now the Karami residence although originally constructed for the Emir Faisal.[13]

Islamism in Tripoli: Extremist, Radical or Neither?

The civil war in 1975–76 saw the destruction of the new Mediterranean façade to the city that had been built through the modernisation projects of the 1960s. This exposed the sad state of Tripoli's urban heritage, despite its renowned 44 major monuments. More important, perhaps, was the fact that the city's social fabric was also torn away, not only through the polarisation of Christians and Muslims in the civil war but also in terms of a confrontation between the Sunni and 'Alawi communities. The pattern of Arab polarisation within the Middle East region pushed the Sunnis of Tripoli into alliance with the Palestine Liberation Organisation, now present in the two Palestinian camps in the suburbs, while the 'Alawis and some right-wing Christian groups allied with Syria. The result was a continuing conflict, dormant or active, over the few assets contained in the Bazaar, port, municipal council and IPC refinery.[14]

When Yasser Arafat was evicted from Tripoli in 1984 by the Syrian army, his legacy to Tripoli took the form of a radical Sunni anti-Syrian alliance: *Harakat al-Tawhid al-Islami*. By 1987, Tripoli had become the target of hostility from left-wing, right-wing and pro-Syrian parties, on top of the ongoing disintegration of the country through the civil war. In his description of Tripoli, Kabbara captures the poor state of the city's social, economic, political and commercial life as a result of the war, for it was at the mercy of 'bombs and bullets fired daily indiscriminately'.[15]

The violent recapture of Tripoli by the Syrians and their allies in the mid 1980s involved the suppression of the *Harakat al-Tawhid al-Islami*, and was followed by the assassination of Rashid Karami, by then premier for the eighth time, presumably by a Christian militia. This may have contributed to the radicalisation and alienation of the city's traditional elite and its professional classes. The only remnant of Islamist symbols – the word 'Allah' – was left in al-Noor/Karami Square, on the site of Adbul Hamid Karami's statue which had been destroyed some years earlier. The city's slogan, 'Tripoli: The Fort of Muslims welcomes you', was removed for a while then reinstated however. Thereafter, Islamic festivals became the occasions when the 'Sunni character' of the city and its historical heritage were commemorated.[16]

Even though Syria's objective of enforcing the Taif's Accords was to end the civil war in 1991, Tripoli did not benefit from the reconstruction boom managed by the new prime minister, Rafiq Hariri, which was centred on Beirut. It was said that the local *zaim*, Omar Karami, had vetoed any extension of the prime minister's reconstruction programme to Tripoli because he feared Hariri's encroachment into his fiefdom. Others suspected a Syrian veto for geopolitical reasons and because of sectarian balances and power games in Lebanon and beyond the border.

Paradoxically, one of Karami's election campaign managers confided that 'the Syrians played a role in robbing him of victory' in the Tripoli elections despite Karami's reputation of having become pro-Syrian.

Moreover, Ibrahim al-Misri, by then the head of *al-Jamaa al-Islamia*, complained of a veto by Hizbullah to block any 'Sunni fighters' from playing a role in South Lebanon prior to Israel's withdrawal in May 2000.[17] That was a decision which, if true, would be bound to severely marginalise the Sunni population of Tripoli in national matters. At the same time, the lack of a development model within the central government may have opened the way for GCC petrodollars to try to balance heavy Iranian investment into the social welfare system of the now rival Shi'a community. However, Tripoli's share was restricted to projects which were 'too-little too-late', whilst religious colleges and mosques mushroomed at the expense of other urban structures, such as clubs, cinemas and theatres.

Quite apart from the chaos of the civil war, these developments, not surprisingly, have made Tripoli unattractive to tourism despite Arab Development Fund and EU projects in the old city.[18] By early 2000, bloody clashes between the Lebanese army and Arab Afghans in Tripoli led to the city and its two Palestinian camps being tarnished as a 'refuge for outlaws and terrorists'. The political class, however, has tried to win parliamentary and local elections by championing welfare projects whilst laying claim to modernist and Islamic, particularly Sufi, credentials.[19] In fact, local elections in May 2004 saw absolute gains by this coalition, backed by the prime minister, Rafiq Hariri, at the expanse of Omar Karami's faction, whilst the radicals – *al-Tawhid* and the Salafis – failed to win a single seat. One reason for this may have been that the major donors to welfare projects in the city had been princes and sheikhs from the GCC. They may well have had an interest in supporting Sunni institutions – albeit under Syrian tutelage.[20]

Post-Syrian Withdrawal: No Real Change

They may have seriously miscalculated, for Rafiq Hariri's shocking assassination in Beirut, on 14 February 2005, hit a raw nerve amongst

Tripoli's religious and secular elites who, in general, like most Lebanese, suspected a Syrian hand in his death. His successor, Saad Hariri, riding high on the anti-Syrian wave, managed to win all 28 parliamentary seats allocated for North Lebanon in the elections of July 2005. The subsequent Syrian military withdrawal from Lebanon buried the widespread conviction in the city that had developed during the previous 29 years, namely that Tripoli was part of 'Syria's share', should Lebanon disintegrate.[21] Thus, in a sense, Tripoli finally accepted its Lebanese identity as a result of the assassination.

However, at the same time it was far from clear how far a Sunni Muslim leader, representing Tripoli, would go in antagonising Syria, for economic and strategic reasons if for no other. As a result, external players sought to reinforce the anti-Syrian sentiment that had developed in the city. Sa'ad Hariri, for example, boosted his legitimacy there by patronising social welfare networks and Islamist organisations, whilst his elder brother Bahaa and aunt Bahia took care of the long-neglected al-Mansour Qalawoun Mosque. Other local players, with similar agendas, joined the fray, bringing in regional allies as well. For instance, official Turkish patronage was welcomed by all to 'reclaim and celebrate' the city's Mamluk and Ottoman past.[22] At the same time, Salafist groups opposed the removal of any religious symbol deemed to render the city unattractive to tourists, because 'nobody dares to remove unappealing portraits of Shi'a ayatollahs in the vicinity of Beirut Airport' – an implicit attack on Hizbullah.[23]

The real challenge to stability in Tripoli, however, occurred when a mysterious extremist group, *Fatah al-Islam*, began terrorist attacks in the city's streets in the early summer of 2007. The group had emerged in November the previous year as the result of a split in a Syrian-backed Palestinian group, *Fateh Intifada*, which itself had originated from a split in *Fateh*, the dominant group inside the *Palestine Liberation Organisation* (PLO). It involved Lebanese, Syrians and Palestinians, united around a Salafi-Jihadi Islamist agenda, led by Shaker al-Absi, with alleged links to *al-Qa'ida*. It clashed with Lebanese security forces in May 2007 when they were investigating a series of bank robberies in Tripoli. After the clashes, the movement seized control of security outposts around the Nahr al-Bared refugee camp.

The government in Beirut decided that the Lebanese army should deal with this virtual insurrection. Eventually, the prime minister, Sa'ad Hariri, obtained a fatwa from the Sunni Chief Mufti, Mohammad Rachid Qabbani, to authorise the elimination of the group by the Lebanese army. Although most Sunnis approved of his actions, there was certainly muted opposition to his decision because of its implication of confronting Palestinians. The issue was therefore used, by the pro-Syrian and Hizbullah propagandists, to attack the prime minister's Arab nationalist credentials. The criticism touched on Saudi support of Salafist sheikhs, such as Da'i al-Islam al-Shihhal, who may have been exploited, albeit unwittingly, by some members of the *Fatah al-Islam* group previously, but were now wreaking havoc in the city and the al-Bared camp.[24]

It soon became clear that popular perceptions of the consequences of the polarising effect of interventions in Lebanon by Arab regimes, coupled with long-standing Iranian backing of Hizbullah, generated fears, genuine or otherwise, among sects and foreign powers that an 'Islamic Emirate' might develop in North Lebanon – paradoxically in a Palestinian camp. To protect Tripoli from extremists, the Lebanese army was left to deal with the crisis on its own, an operation which it completed successfully, albeit at the cost of 167 dead and the destruction of the refugee camp. The incident underlined the dangers of sectarian extremism in Lebanon and restored public confidence in the ability of the Lebanese army to handle such incidents, apart from the unresolved challenge of Hizbullah. The latter may have benefited in stressing that extremism was a Sunni problem, despite the fact that the Sunni political and religious class united behind Sa'ad Hariri, and the Lebanese state, to reject this poisoned chalice.

Perhaps the most important outcome of the incident was a public determination to establish a truce with the underlying causes of violence in Tripoli. The episode may have also contributed to an intensification of relief and aid programmes to Christian and Muslim communities in the North as a means of cementing this newly-formed detente. Of course, political agendas and calculations play a role in this; Tripoli, as has been demonstrated in the past through the saga of the Karami family, can provide any potential national politician with access to the political scene in Beirut.[25] In addition, the passage of time has led to the cooling of regional tensions and the growth of detente between Riyadh and Damascus which has helped to bury the issue of 'Tripoli's extremists' for a couple of years. At the same time, the city's elite aimed to benefit from Turkey's regional shift in policy towards restoring its old 'Ottoman' ties with the Arab Middle East.[26] Thus, the question of where Tripoli's real position, loyalty, identity and, above all, economic interests lie, has been reopened after nearly a century of roaming through what has proved to be a cultural, historical and geopolitical minefield.

Conclusion

Violence in Tripoli stems from a long history reaching back to medieval times but has recently intensified because of the regional changes that have occurred since the Ottomans left the Mediterranean port in 1918. It has proved very difficult to impose a uniquely religious or ideological label on the various aspects of social groups, elites or mob behaviour that have occurred since then but there have been some factors which are peculiar to Tripoli within Lebanon:

- First, violence has been practised by individual religious and political figures against one another, as well as by their clients on their behalf. Often this has been done as part of securing a national, as well as a local arena, as the success of the Karami family has shown.
- Second, there has been inter-linkage of political and religious factors — whether based on Sufi, Salafi or Revivalist Islam — with economic factors in the creation of new leaders and in securing the influence exercised by old leaders as well.[27] It is no coincidence, incidentally, that leading figures in political competition with one another keep their Islamic credentials bright by patronising religious associations.
- Third, new extremist forces have emerged around the city in recent years. They are normally linked to other transnational terrorist organisations and tend to be clustered around poverty-stricken districts such as the Nahr al-Bared and the Baddawi Palestinian

refugee camps. Thus, Arab radicals who flocked from abroad to join *Fatah al-Islam* in 2007 were mainly based in the Nahr al-Bared camp and not in Tripoli proper.

- Fourth, Tripoli's economic interests have suffered immensely from the city's neglect by the Beirut and Mount Lebanon ruling elites, from which it received little support for nearly three decades, during the Syrian occupation of Lebanon.

- Fifth, despite the city's predominantly Sunni character and the relative absence of sectarianism, religious differences can play a part. Paradoxically, for example, the city's agrarian Bazaar at Bab al-Tabbaneh is divided on Muslim sectarian lines between Sunni and Alawi.

- Sixth, recurrent violent clashes in the city over the decades have been, at root, an expression of a struggle to control the few economic prizes that exist, whatever the label with which they have been described. For example, Faisal tried his luck as Qawuqjee and Arabism, anti-French, pro-Nasserist, pro-Palestinian, opposed to Christian domination, anti- or pro-Syrian, and finally local or foreign Islamist forces.

- Seventh, Arab polarisation between moderate and radical has adversely affected Tripoli but has been neglected by the foreign media unless there was an element of international terrorism involved. A possible exception to this general rule occurred when PLO leader, Yasser Arafat, was trapped inside the city by the Syrian army in the mid 1980s. Quite apart from anything else, this incident resulted in ecological disaster as a result of the destruction of the IPC refinery in the fighting.

- Eighth, and last, the clash of collective identities in the city is also an open battleground between old and new elites. This has been especially true since the removal of Tripoli's marginal secular elite at the outset of the civil war between 1975 and 1986.

Tripoli's underlying Ottoman and Islamic identity also has to accommodate other levels of identity such as Christian, Lebanese, Mamluk, Mediterranean, Arab and Levantine. But the real challenge for its elite in the future will be to maintain the push for modernity and cosmopolitanism while not slipping into sectarianism and warring spheres of competing ambitions and attitudes. Perhaps, Turkey's ascent will offer a litmus test to see if the Tripoli's elite has learned from past failures of successive models in the post-Ottoman world, ranging from Emir Faisal, the French Mandate, shaky independence, Arabism and the many varieties of Islamism.

Notes

1. www.kataeb.org.
2. *Al-Bayan* published a series of articles by Omar Tadmouri under this curious title, with the final section appearing on 13 July 2010. As the most notable recorder of Tripoli's Islamic history, Omar Tadmouri sought to 'correct' claims that the city's famous clock tower and some of its mosques had been built by Christian hands. The ulterior motive, however, was to block the candidacy of a Phalange candidate, Samer Saadah, for the city's Maronite Christian seat in the upcoming elections. The tactic failed; in the elections in June 2009, Samer Saadeh won, despite the opposition of a powerful local *zai'm* (powerbroker), Omar Karami, who had also been Lebanese prime minister. Mr Saadeh, however, had enjoyed the strong backing of Sa'ad al-Hariri, the son of the assassinated Rafiq Hariri and himself a future Lebanese premier.
3. Libretto by Amin Maalouf and music by composer Kaija Saariaho, first shown in Salzburg in 2000; then in Santa Fe, Bergen and London.
4. *Attamaddon Weekly*, 16 February 2007. A survey by Omar Tadmouri of a project, running since 1972, to translate and publish millions of Ottoman documents related to Tripoli and other Syrian provinces. His son, Khaled Tadmouri, a graduate of Sinan University in Istanbul, has also embarked on another project designed to strengthen Turkish efforts to preserve Tripoli's Ottoman and Islamic monuments.
5. *Attamaddon Weekly*, March 2010, three successive weekly articles commemorating the city's undocumented political history.
6. *Al-Hayat*, 2 August 2008. Abdulwahhab, M.H., review of 'Al-Jisr family of Tripoli' by Abdullah Said. Abdullah Said argues that the notables of Tripoli shifted from focussing on religion and Sufism under the Ottomans in the nineteenth century to political and professional activities during the twentieth century, which increasingly brought them into the national arena. This transformation affected not only the al-Jisrs, leading to Sheikh Mohammed al-Jisr's bid for the highest office in Lebanon in 1932, but also other major families, such as the Karamis, Rafi'is, Hussainis, Ahdabs, Qawuqjees and Mikatis.

7. *Al-Afkar*, 31 March 1997. Interview with the sons of Abdul Latif al-Bissar and Rushdi Salhab. The interview highlighted the role of the two branches of this new middle class in the face of indirect opposition from the zai'ms of Zghorta (a Christian Maronite town) and Tripoli. It is claimed that Abdul Hamid Karami opposed financing the project from non-governmental sources, fearing the growing role of the new professional class. He wanted to rely on central government financing instead. The article included a photograph of Karami, in religious garb, sitting in the middle of a group of notables, including his new rival, Rashed al-Muqaddam.

8. Al-Afkar magazine, April 1999. The first four articles in a series of 33 articles on this affair written by the editor, Walid Awad, himself a Tripoli publisher. Awad's style is kind to all concerned, relying on different archives and accounts with the aim to 'bury all remaining hatred for ever'.

9. Ibid., 31 May–28 June 1999. Series 9–14. Riad al-Sulh is credited with having chosen the mansion of Christian leader, Shibl Issa al-Khouri, in Bisharri as the place in which a truce was sealed. His aim had been to 'block the French Mandate administration from sowing discord among Christians and Muslims'. As a result, blood money of 4,500 Gold Liras was paid by Karami to his rivals.

10. Ibid., 25 October–8 November 1999. Also, *Attamaddon*, March 2010. The first source ended its series with an open verdict on who was responsible while the second hinted, in a series of three articles, that the Karami camp may have been more to blame. As a result, Karami did not run for election in the north of Lebanon, thus paving the way for his opponents, especially, Mayez al-Muqaddam, the brother of the murdered Nafiz, to win. Also, Mustafa Karami, brother of Abdul Hamid, was leaned upon to resign as the leader of Tripoli's municipal council. The massacre took the lives of 25 Lebanese and 40 Syrians (followers of al-Qawuqjee) and there were also scores of injured. The interior minister imposed a ban on publishing photographs of the incident, whilst national schools curriculum never mentioned this sorry saga in Tripoli's history. In a way, there is a comparison to be drawn between the troubadour, Jaufré Rudel, and the mujahid, Fawzi al-Qawuqjee, who died unknown and forgotten in 1977.

11. Kalawoun, N. 2000. *The Struggle for Lebanon*. I.B.Tauris: London. pp.42–72.

12. Kabbara, N. 1995. *Lizikra wa zaman al-ati*. North Lebanon Cultural Council: Tripoli. pp.48–76.

13. Kalawoun, op.cit., pp.134–160.

14. Ibid., pp.160–5.

15. Kabbara, N. 1995. *The Silver Jubilee of the Cultural Council of North Lebanon*. Jarrous Press: Beirut. pp.3–5 and pp.50–58. A memorandum was submitted

to the then Prime Minister Rashid Karami to complain of the deterioration occurring not only in Tripoli but also in its Muslim hinterland.

16. *Al-Diya'*, Issue 2 (June 1989). This issue commemorated the 700th anniversary of the liberation of Tripoli from the Crusaders by the Mamluk Sultan al-Mansour Qalawoun. Although the *Islamic Salvation Front*, a middle class group, and other Islamists championed this tradition, Prime Minister Omar Karami, Mufti Taha Sabunjee and historian Omar Tadmuri played the central role in this project.

17. Interviews with Marwan Mawwas and Ibrahim al-Misri, Lebanon, July 2001.

18. *Al-Afkar*, 11 August 1997. Interview with Nicolas Fattoush, minister of tourism. He complained that the north of the country lacked an atmosphere that would attract tourists and warned that 'without hotels, there is no hope for tourism to thrive in Tripoli'.

19. *Tripoli Post*, Issue 29, 25 March 2004. This glossy free-sheet was patronised by Mohammad al-Safadi, a parliamentary deputy, in order to promote his philanthropic activities in North Lebanon. In a similar manner, another parliamentary deputy, Najib Mikati, patronised *al-Azm wa Assaadah*, a mildly Islamist local society.

20. *Al-Rakib*, 29 April 2004. A list of top donors to the new private wing of the Islamic Hospital, which is also frequented by the city's poor, includes the Saudi princes Sultan, al-Waleed and Bandar al-Saud, as well as many names from the UAE, Kuwait, and Saudi Arabia, while most Lebanese donors donated less than $10,000 each.

21. *Al-Mustaqbal*, 20 June 2005. The main headline in the issue reads 'Muslim-Christian battle in North Lebanon against past Syrian hegemony'.

22. Tripoli municipality newsletter, May 2006.

23. Statement by Zakaria al-Misri, Committee of Islamic Revival Association, April 2006.

24. *Assafir*, 29 May 2007. An anti-Saudi propaganda essay was published under the headline 'Tripoli Islamists: from students in Saudi Arabia to the army of the Sunnis'.

25. *Al-Majalla*, issue 1462, 23 February 2008. Interview with former minister Laila al-Sulh, vice president of the al-Walid bin Talal Humanitarian Foundation. The foundation acts in all Lebanese areas and does not discriminate between religions and sects.

26. *Asharq al-Awsat*, 23 February 2010. An effort by Tripoli's Mufti, Malek al-Shaar, to bring 'disgruntled Islamists' under his wing. The aim was to gather 200 Sunni personalities in order to refute accusations that Tripoli is tainted with terrorism.

27. Traditionally, the Karamis sought to hold the key to control of the city through control of its list of parliamentary deputies, the municipal council, the port authority, the IPC refinery and the Bazaar. Any new challenger, therefore, had to fight them with local or external support to gain a political foothold. New elite figures, with Gulf backing have, however, been creating new power-centres by investing in religious, social, and much needed educational fields.

Bibliography

Al-Afkar. March 1997.
—— August 1997.
—— April 1999.
—— May-June 1999.
—— October-November 1999.
Al-Bayane.13 July 2010.
Al-Diya'. June 1989.
Al-Hayat. August 2008.
Al-Majalla. February 2008.
Al-Mustaqbal. June 2005.
Al-Rakib. April 2004.
Asharq al-Awsat. February 2010.
Assafir. May 2007.
Attamaddon Weekly. February 2007.
—— March 2010.
Kalawoun, N. 2000. *The Struggle for Lebanon*. I.B.Tauris: London.
Kabbara, N. 1995. *Lizikra wa zaman al-ati*. North Lebanon Cultural Council: Tripoli.
—— 1995. *The Silver Jubilee of the Cultural Council of North Lebanon*. Jarrous Press: Beirut.
Tripoli Post. Issue 2004.

9

ISRAEL'S INSURGENT CITIZENS: CONTESTING THE STATE, DEMANDING THE LAND

Clive Jones

In September 2008, a small pipe bomb exploded outside the Jerusalem home of the academic and peace activist Ze'ev Sternhall, causing shrapnel wounds to his legs. A leading advocate of Israeli withdrawal from the occupied territories and a two state solution with the Palestinians, Israeli security forces were in no doubt that the attack was perpetrated by elements from within the religious–nationalist community.[1] While preoccupied by the violent challenge presented by sub-state Islamist movements – most notably *Hamas* and the Lebanese *Hizbollah* – the attack was an unwelcome reminder that individuals or groups within the Israeli body politic remain willing and able to engage in acts of violence against those whose support of territorial retrenchment is deemed inimical to their particular *Weltanschauung*. Memories in Israel still remain raw over the assassination of Premier Yitzhak Rabin in October 1995, an act motivated according to his assassin, Yigal Amir, by the need to destroy a political process that threatened to desecrate God's name – *hillul hashem* – and with it, bring an end to any hope of realising the messianic era. It should be noted from the outset that such acts of extreme violence remain at the margins of Israeli society but equally, they have a resonance that questions Israel's proud claim to be the only true manifestation of stable political pluralism in the contemporary Middle East.

To be sure, other cleavages have long determined the contours of political discourse in Israel. Communal divisions between Ashkenazim Jews and those of a *Mizrachi* background, religious dissonance between the *Haredim* (Ultra-Orthodox Jews) and the main body of secular Israelis, and the continued marginalisation of Israel's own Palestinian Arab minority stem in no small part from ongoing debates within Israeli society over the very nature of Zionism itself and how an Israeli identity is therefore to be defined. Moreover, the very idea of a state being both Jewish and democratic is seen by some to be a contradiction in terms, the apparent ethno-religious basis of what it means to be an Israeli being antithetical to the idea of nationality and citizenship grounded in territorial affinity and cultural pluralism.[2] For the most part however, such tensions have been contained and regulated within structures and institutions that have, however imperfect, regulated political exchange across the Jewish state: the *Knesset*, an independent judicial system, and indeed, the Israel Defence Forces (IDF).

Religious nationalism however has always had a rather ambivalent relationship to the state in Israel. Its emergence as a powerful political discourse is testament to the very success of Zionism in state creation but equally, its inherent logic posits an inversion of classical Zionist thinking that regarded settlement of the land as the means to achieve statehood whereas, for religious nationalists, the state exists to redeem land under a sacred covenant between God and the Jewish people. Any attempt by the state to renege on this covenant strikes at the very core value system of some Jewish settlers who have always been vexed by the suggestion that the West Bank, or 'Judea and Samaria', should become part of a Palestinian state. Much has been written about the Jewish settlers, the development of umbrella organisations such as *Gush Emunim* (Bloc of the Faithful) and their emergence as a potent political force in Israeli politics across four decades.[3] Less attention however has been paid to the generational shift among their number and how consequently, their 'ideo-theology' – best illustrated in the emergence of the *Hardal* or hill top youth – has moved beyond the wider settlement project to deny agency and legitimacy to Israel as a predominantly secular ideal.

This chapter pays particular attention to the *Hardal*, framing as it does an understanding of their worldview through the work of Ted Gurr and the idea of 'relative deprivation' outlined in his classic work, *Why Men Rebel*.[4] Despite the passage of time, it remains a useful tool for conceptualising the gap between the 'value expectations' of a group or movement, its actual 'value capabilities' and the extent to which the disjuncture between the two not only underpins the sense of alienation from the state but equally, a growing distance from the settler community itself.

Religious Nationalism and the Settlers

While Israel's stunning military victory in June 1967 first saw the emergence of religiousnationalism as a true force in the politics of the Jewish state, the contours of its ideo-theology – a moniker that captures the fusion of biblical precedence and *halachic* jurisprudence with the belief that Zionism, as a largely secular ideology, heralds the beginning of the messianic era – had begun to emerge in the pre-state *Yishuv* or Jewish settlement in Palestine. In particular, the ideas of Rabbi Avraham Yitzhak HaCohen Kook (1865–1935), Chief Ashkenazi Rabbi of the Jewish community in British Mandate Palestine, were influential in challenging the rejection of Zionism by the majority of Orthodox Jews who regarded Zionism as an apostasy, and a rejection of their core belief that only the coming of the *Meshiach* could reunite the Jews with *Eretz Yisrael* (The Land of Israel). Moreover, although classical Zionism was largely seen as a secular nationalist movement – the idea of being a Jew was defined on grounds of ethnicity – Kook argued that Zionism heralded the beginning of the messianic era with Zionists, the unknowing tools of God, hastening the redemptive process by settling once more in *Eretz Yisrael*.

As such, the June 1967 war and, with it, the capture of the West Bank and East Jerusalem, the biblical heart of *Eretz Yisrael,* against seemingly overwhelming odds acquired messianic overtones for the religiousright. In particular, Rabbi Zvi Yehuda Kook, the son of Rabbi Avraham Kook, placed Israel's military triumph within the continuing evolution of the messianic era. His vision encompassed a preordained Jewish right to settle the newly captured territories, a process that was encouraged by Kook among the students of the Yeshivat Merkaz Harav in Jerusalem. They formed the spearhead of early settlement drives, leading to the establishment of settlements such as Kiryat Arba next to Hebron.[5] Furthermore, Kook adapted the ideas of his father to add theological legitimacy to the use of force in order to achieve and maintain the unity of *Eretz Yisrael.* Such ideas found a receptive audience among the wider religious right, offering as they did a *carte blanche* that divorced settlement activity from more humanistic considerations.

The real impact of the religious nationalism however was to redefine the normative character of Zionism. Never a single cohesive ideology, Zionism was nonetheless an amalgam of ideas drawn from Jewish philosophy, history and religion and fused with the universal values of freedom, democracy and justice for its citizens, values identified with Western civilisation. This early incorporation of universal values marked the development of an *Israeli,* rather than a *Jewish,* identity. The June 1967 war marked a watershed in this process. Capture of the West Bank and East Jerusalem with its sacred Jewish sites witnessed not only the emergence of a belief in the 'covenantal relationship between "People, God and promised land"', but in the process, the reaffirmation, of particular Jewish, rather than universal, values in determining the character of the State of Israel.[6]

Although such thinking within the Israeli parliament or *Knesset* came to be associated with the National Religious Party, it was an extra-parliamentary movement formed in the aftermath of the October 1973 war, the *Gush Emunim,* that conflated religious conviction with the practical politics of security.[7] It was to prove a heady mix, able to exploit the vagaries of coalition government and which in turn, enjoyed the patronage and approbation of successive Israeli administrations from 1974 to 2002. As one-time member of *Gush Emunim*, Rabbi Yehuda Amital stated:

> This [ReligiousNationalist] Zionism has not come to solve the Jewish problem by the establishment of a Jewish State but is used, instead, by the High Providence as a tool in order to move and advance Israel towards its redemption. Its intrinsic direction is not the normalisation of the people of Israel in order to become a nation like all nations, but to become a holy people, a people of living god, whose basis is in Jerusalem and a king's temple is its centre.[8]

This was a clear rejection of the secular ethos of *mamlachtiyut* (statism) whose contours had determined the scope of political discourse in Israel until 1967. As long as successive Israeli governments – albeit on security grounds – continued to value Jewish control over the territories captured in the June 1967 war, a clear symbiosis of objectives existed with the religiousnationalists. Nonetheless, by regarding the land as central to the redemptive process of the Jewish people, it followed that any attempt to trade land for peace usurped the will of God, and therefore, had to be opposed.

This absolute belief in the redemptive process has, however, been tempered by both time and context. The total number of Jewish settlers in the West Bank, including East Jerusalem, is now well in excess of 250,000, with the very term settler becoming synonymous with an ideological type, unwilling to compromise over the partition of land deemed to be their patrimony. But as Yehuda Ben Meir reminds us, 'The residents of Ma'aleh Adunim, Ariel and Alfei Menashe are different from the residents of Elkana, Efrat and Paduel who in turn are different from those of Itamar, Har Bracha, Yizhar and Tapuah.'[9] While undoubtedly sympathetic to the original security rationale behind their construction, the inhabitants of the first three settlements attach relatively little religious importance to the process of settlement. They remain predominantly secular enterprises, and while religious piety may be observed, their growth is a reminder that many of those living in such settlements do so out of socio-economic consideration, most notably access to affordable housing beyond Israel's densely populated coastal strip.

Moreover, even in settlements where adherence to the ideology of *Eretz Yisrael* provided the *rationale* for their establishment, high levels of socio-economic affluence have served to dim the ardour of religiousnationalism. Finally, since 2002 the construction of Israel's security barrier now visibly challenges the accepted shibboleths surrounding the sanctity of the land. For most Israelis, it is justified by military necessity, designed as it was to prevent the infiltration of Palestinian suicide bombers from the West Bank into Israel proper following the outbreak of the *Al-Aqsa intifada* in September 2000. Suicide bombings amounted to only 3 per cent of recorded attacks against Israelis between 2000 and 2005, but accounted for 39 per cent of civilian casualties. While the average monthly figure for Israeli civilian casualties had been 36 between September 2001 and September 2002, the total number for the whole period from 2004 and 2005 (after construction of the barrier had begun along a line contiguous with, but not located on, the old pre-1967 border) was 56 fatalities.[10]

The barrier now incorporates major settlements established just over the Green Line such as Elkana, Sha'are Tiqva, Etz Efrayim. It would be folly to suggest that all settlers view the barrier with favour but many have come to accept, however reluctantly, that it represents a new contract with state: it will not evacuate them from their homes but equally, they must accept that the attainment of *Eretz Yisrael* no longer equates with regional realities. By definition therefore, the security barrier *is* a political boundary, not just in demarcating Israel's external boundaries with the Palestinians, but by setting the limits of political discourse within Israel itself. If the security barrier had followed the Green Line, this would not have been possible. Rather, the settlers of all political and ideological hues would have comprised an insurmountable obstacle, unmoved by recourse to moral argument or international opprobrium as justification for ideological retrenchment.

The intellectual hegemony the barrier now exercises over Israelis is best seen in public reaction to the withdrawal from Gaza in August 2005, the national election results of March 2006, and the subsequent fissures within the ethno-religious discourse that threaten irrevocable

splits from the State.[11] Contrary to some of the more alarmist predic-
tion, Israelis were not 'traumatised' by the withdrawal of just over
8000 settlers from Gaza. While many expressed sympathy with the
pain of those losing their homes, the sight of some of the inhabitants of
Gush Katif, the largest settlement bloc in Gaza, bedecked in Orange
(the colour of the Jewish municipal council in Gaza) and sporting the
Star of David drew the ire of many Israelis who resented the moral
equivalence with the Holocaust.[12] What trauma did exist remained
confined to those settlers whose belief in divine intervention, be it
in the form of widespread refusal among the Israeli security forces to
implement the evacuation or by some more perceptible act of celestial
intercession, remained conspicuous by its absence.[13]

Relative Deprivation and the Hill Top Youth

In his assessment of the impact that the security barrier was having upon the political landscape of Israel, the late sociologist, Baruch
Kimmerling, argued that it '[S]mashes to smithereens the ideology
of *Eretz Yisrael* and knocks the ideological and political infrastructure out from under the feet of Jewish fundamentalism'.[14] A crisis of
identity certainly exists among some whose worldview, grounded in a
particular eschatological determinism, regards maintenance of Jewish
sovereignty over all the Occupied Territories as central to the realisation of a messianic era. The failure of the *Yesha* Council – an umbrella
organisation dominated by religious nationalists but which represents the interests of all settlers – to adopt more proactive measures
to prevent the evacuation of the Gaza settlements saw accusations of
political naivety levelled against prominent Rabbis representing the
Yesha, such as the veteran Pinhas Wallerstein. For the most part, these
accusations have come from a younger generation of settlers who have
known no other homes but the settlements. They have demonstrated a
willingness to take more proactive measures to protect and expand the
physical reality that informs their cosmic worldview.

This call to the barricades has a particular resonance among the
ultra-Orthodox religious-nationalist youth, all too ashamed at the
apparent timidity of their elders in the *Yesha.* Known as the hill

top youth or *Hardal* their origins can be traced back to 1989 and the increasingly militant activities of young settlers from Bat Ayin close to Hebron. Inspired by Rabbis such as Dov Lior from the settlement of Kiryat Arba that overlooks Hebron and Elyakim Levanon of Elon Moreh, these settlers represented a new generation whose outlook had been totally shaped by having been born and raised in settlements whose close proximity to a predominantly Palestinian urban milieu only served to accelerate the process of radicalisation. As such, they have proven to be far more confrontational in their dealings with the Palestinians, and increasingly with the IDF across the West Bank. Under an umbrella organisation, *Maginei Eretz* (Defenders of the Land), the *Hardal* have formed themselves into several groups, most notably *Ne'emanei Eretz Yisrael* (Faithful of the Land of Israel), *Komemiyut* (Sovereignty), *Mate Tzafon* (Northern Quarters) and *Halev Ha'Yehudi* (The Jewish Heart). It remains hard to discern the relative strength of such groups and their cohesion as a collective social movement, not least because membership is often shared between them. But the emphasis upon a Jewish, as opposed to an Israeli, identity is something that marks them off from both mainstream Israeli society as well as the older generation of settlers.[15]

Given their increasingly vexed relationship with the state, the *Hardal* are best described as 'insurgent citizens', claiming allegiance to the Jewish norms of the state but willing to confront it by extra-legal means when it denies efficacy to religious claims over land and *deprives* them of the resources deemed necessary to realise their worldview or, to use Ted Gurr's phrase, their 'value expectations'. These expectations relate directly to viewing the state as a vassal, limited to providing the means of enabling redemption but whose unwillingness to do so breeds dissatisfaction and eventually grievance when such means are limited or indeed denied. The often closed nature of such groups means that such grievance can become amplified into a cosmic struggle with the central belief that divine right entitles the group to those resources necessary to attain a particular vision above and beyond their existing capabilities. The greater the gap between capabilities and expectation, what Gurr calls 'relative deprivation' only serves to increase the likelihood of violent confrontation with the state. [16]

In the case of the *Hardal* however, this sense of relative deprivation is magnified by adherence to a more extreme discourse associated with the theological legacy of the late Rabbi Meir Kahane, the most radical of thinkers among right-wing religious opinion in Israel. Containing a clear veneration, if not outright sanctification, of the use of violence in order to maintain the integrity of *Eretz Yisrael*, Kahanism takes issue with the prevailing view among the religiousnationalists concerning Zionism as the necessary precursor to the messianic era. In a little read essay, *Hillul Hashem*, published in 1976 Kahane maintained that the Jewish State was established not because of the righteousness of the Zionist cause, but rather because God could no longer tolerate the continued persecution of his chosen people by Gentiles. Thus Israel was created by God as a punishment to the Gentiles, not a reward to the Jews. But this also led Kahane to conclude that the newborn State was virtuous not because Zionists were a pious people – clearly they were not – but because of what a Jewish State 'inflicts upon the Gentiles'. [17]

In a very real sense, Kahanism views violence as a cleansing process, one that has set the Jewish people free from the persecution and servitude of the Diaspora. It moves from the radical to the extreme by consciously adopting a metahistorical approach which applies the term *Amalekh* to describe all enemies, past, present, and future of the Jewish people. The *Amalekh* were a biblical tribe whose destruction was demanded of the Israelites by God according to the *Torah*[18]. As such the term was applied by Kahane to include all enemies of the Jewish people in general, and the Palestinians in particular. Therefore, if God's name is to be sanctified *(Kiddush Hashem)*, it is incumbent upon the Jews to destroy the *Amalekh*, thus ushering in the true messianic era. Such logic, a priori, underscores the fact that concessions over territory threaten the very core tenet of the *Hardal* over what it means to be a Jew, let alone an Israeli. In this respect, Kahanism is crucial in understanding an environment that not only condones acts of civil disobedience, but, through the prism of its ideo-theology, sanctifies recourse to violence. For example, the ideas surrounding *hillul hashem* had a particular resonance among the settlers of Kiryat Arba, a settlement renowned for the militant activism of some of its members. Continued tension between settlers and local Palestinians over access to the al-Ibrahimi mosque/Tomb of the Patriarchs in Hebron was equated with the metahistorical struggle against the *Amalekh*, a confrontation that Kahanist logic embraced if God's glory was to be redeemed – *kiddush hashem*. As such, the massacre of 29 Palestinians by Dr Baruch Goldstein from the settlement was therefore entirely consistent with the most radical interpretation of Kahanist ideo-theology. The community of Kiryat Arba not only felt itself threatened in a physical sense by the overwhelming Palestinian presence in Hebron, but also by the spiritual atrophy of a secular State that had negated the redemptive process. Indeed, it was reported that on February 24, 1994, on the eve of the festival of *Purim*, a crowd of Palestinians approached the Tomb shouting '*Itbah al-yahud*', death to the Jews, an incident thought to have provoked Goldstein's bloody actions. The massacre has to be understood, therefore, within the context of a Kahanist interpretation of *hillul hashem,* and not just as a brazen attempt to destroy the peace process.[19] Influenced by an ideo-theology that refuted normative values in dealing with the Israel–Palestine dispute, the actions of both Goldstein and Yigal Amir were in a very real sense preordained.

It should be noted that such bloody acts remain exceptional events. Even so, they demonstrate how the volatile mix of a shared sense of communal deprivation, social alienation and an extreme interpretation of *Hillul Hashem* carries the potential to visit bloody violence upon Palestinians and Israelis alike. In their analysis of Jewish terrorism, Ami Pedahzur and Arie Perliger note the powerful counterculture that exists among many of the members of the *Hardal* whose styptic worldview is often underpinned by strict ideological adherence to charismatic clerics who, in turn, brook no compromise in their interpretation of *Halacha*. Such relationships, while not unique to radical Jewish groups, are reinforced in the case of the *Hardal* by 'primordial' ties that deepen a sense of collective belonging to the group at the expense of ties to a wider community or society. The Spartan conditions and isolated locations of many of the hill top settlements, a physical expression of their inhabitants belief in a theocratic idyll governed in accordance with a strict interpretation of the *Halacha*, serves to underline still further the cultural alienation of the *Hardal* from both the Israeli mainstream and indeed the wider settler movement.[20] For Pedahzur and Perliger, these settlements represent a 'further radicalisation of the Kahanist ideology', standing as they do 'in defiance of the state sovereignty that only serve to reinforce still further 'the de-legitimisation of the existing socio-political order'.[21]

Among the *Hardal* however, opposition to Israeli government policy over the future evacuation of settlements has to date remained non-lethal if still violent. The forced evacuation and destruction of nine prefabricated buildings at Amona, an illegal settlement established by *Hardal* members, close to the larger and well-established settlement of Ofra, remains the most turbulent event to date. Its destruction had been ordered by the Israeli High court of Justice. When, on Wednesday, 1 February 2006, the border police and IDF troops moved in to enforce the court decision, they were met by a hail of stones, burning cinder blocks and buckets of paint from *Hardal* youth. The reaction of the security forces was the direct antithesis of the restraint, indeed tears, so publicly shed in front of the international media the previous August over the evacuation of Gaza. Using mounted police wielding truncheons, the security forces evicted the protestors from their redoubts but not before over 200 were injured, several seriously. Interviewed in the immediate aftermath of the violence, Rabbi Avi Gisser from the settlement of Ofra noted that the seeds for such violence were sown not only in the growing estrangement of settler youth from the institutions of the State, but also from the Yesha. He concluded, 'Amona is the price the Yesha Council paid for the loss of Gush Katif' (in the Gaza Strip).[22]

In the aftermath of Amona, one protestor from the settlement of Beit Al, Asaf Baruchi, was reported to have stated that 'It is now a war between cultures. The Left is trying to liquidate religious Zionism, the only alternative.' Another, describing confrontations with the security forces, this time in Hebron, claimed that 'This is an army of Israelis who hate the Jews'.[23] While care must be taken to place such statements within their emotive context, they remain of a piece with the more sober (yet no less profound) pronouncements emanating from those close to *Hardal* feeling. The refrain therefore that '[I]f the State of Israel withdraws from the Land, then we are withdrawing from the

State of Israel', is not uncommon when describing prevailing sentiment among religious-nationalist youth.[24] The logic of this position
has found expression in calls for a separate State of Judea or what some
have termed *mishtar torah* – the Torah State – where free from the las-
situde of a corrupt, secular polity, the messianic era can be realised.

For now, such separatist tendencies remain on the margins, not least
because the right-wing coalition government of Benjamin Netanyahu,
in power when this chapter was written, was deemed to be sympathetic to the wider settlement project. Even so, the idea of separatism does enjoy some support from settlers across the West Bank
who are not *Hardal*. An opinion poll conducted in spring 2010 by the
Hebrew University in Jerusalem suggests that some 21 per cent of
settlers believe that 'all means must be employed to resist the [future]
evacuation of settlements, including the use of arms [if necessary]'.[25]
Of more immediate concern to Israelis however are the open levels
of dissent now being displayed towards the IDF by *Hardal* youth. In
February 2010, settlers from Yitzhar, near Nablus attacked soldiers
they believed had been sent by the government to evict them from
their temporary homes, leading one senior IDF official to label the
settlers 'scum'. Again, care should be taken over contextualising such
remarks, but they are indicative that the national approbation enjoyed
by the IDF across Israeli society and not least among the religious-
nationalist community has become frayed. The motivation to serve
in the elite units of the IDF remains exceptionally strong among the
religious-nationalist community, but recent displays of open defiance
by young soldiers towards the military hierarchy have shocked many
Israelis. The most widely reported incident was the unfurling of ban-
ners at a recent passing-out parade where recruits demonstrated their
refusal to evacuate any settlements should they be ordered to do so.[26]

But while the widespread use of lethal force against groups and
individuals representing the state has yet to be realised, members of
the *Hardal* youth have perpetrated numerous acts of violence against
Palestinians, ranging from drive-by shootings to the burning down of
a mosque in the Palestinian village of Yasuf in December 2009. Prior
to this, on 29 April 2002, it was only a combination of luck and the
prompt actions of two Israeli policemen in East Jerusalem that led to

the arrest of a terrorist cell of *Hardal* youth from the settlement of Bat Ayin. Part of a wider network, Shlomo Dvir-Zeliger and his accomplice Yarden Morag had been attempting to set the timing device on a car bomb next to a girl's school, the timer having been set to detonate the following morning as children arrived for lessons. It was only the fact that they, as Jews, were present in the Palestinian half of the city at the height of the *Al-Aqsa intifada* that aroused the suspicion of a passing police patrol. Had the bomb detonated, the immediate carnage and longer term political impact amid an already bloody conflict can only be imagined.[27]

For the time being however, the expressed desire for a State of Judea parallel to the State of Israel remains a pipe dream. The number of settlers involved, let alone paucity of resources that only the State could provide determine as much. However deep the theological and emotional turmoil the construction of the security barrier may cause among those settlers attached to the integrity of Judea and Samaria, the majority, with their relative economic affluence, the knowledge that their homes will not be dismantled, and their continued existence within the boundaries of a predominantly Jewish dispensation has been enough to reconcile all but the most extreme to the security barrier and the logic of finite borders.[28] As Rabbi Gisser noted somewhat wearily:

> For Israeli society, the conflict [with the Palestinians] and the price we pay for it has become intolerable. For 100 years the agenda of [Israeli] society here has been belligerent, combative. The Israeli public wants a different agenda, a civil one. Today, the three largest parties (Kadima, Labour and the Likud) are talking about two states for two people. Twenty years ago that was the mantra of the New Communist List ... We [the settlement movement] did not submit to the people of Israel a sufficiently realistic political plan because we found it emotionally difficult to mark borders in the heart of the land of our forefathers, in the heart of the religious, idealistic and Zionist destination ... I always knew that a realistic political plan would include the marking of borders, and that's why I was deterred from it.

It stood and stands in opposition to our ideological being. I see it as very bad, but if you have to choose between utter destruction of the settlements and leaving some of them, I will certainly choose the lesser evil.[29]

Conclusion

In the aftermath of Rabin's assassination, one noted observer of Israel's political scene remarked, 'If [ideo-theology] combated in its own terms, with interpretations of Jewish tradition that make Judaism the friend of democracy, pluralism and life over land – not the enemy of those values – then Judaism can still save the Jewish State.'[30] But the ideo-theology of religious nationalism remains exclusive in both tone and outlook, only able to compromise *in extremis* and certainly reluctant to embrace a Judaism where attachment to the land has only secondary or symbolic meaning. Indeed, the emergence of the *Hardal* and its counterculture suggests a growing rift from the State and with it, a sense of isolation and grievance that carries the potential for internecine conflict between those who see themselves as the authentic 'Jew' and Israelis. Such a scenario might seem far-fetched, but as the attack on Zeev Sternhall illustrates, it is certainly more than just a chimera. Under pressure from the Obama administration, the limited freeze in settlement construction agreed to by the government of Benjamin Netanyahu in late 2009 saw the *Hardal* once more take to the hills and establish a rash of new outposts while Defence Minister Ehud Barak was the reported recipient of death threats from extreme right-wing elements.[31] Such actions may not enjoy the support of most settlers; after all, the construction of the security fence and its implications for the future borders of the State suggest an acceptance that the messianic era will certainly not be achieved in their lifetimes. Even so, many settlers certainly admire the principles of the *Hardal*, whose ardour remains undimmed by the outward trappings of comfort, if not modernity, that now define many of the settlements. The *Hardal* may find themselves increasingly alienated from the Israeli mainstream but they may, ironically, continue to draw strength from the words of that most influential of early Zionist thinkers, Theodore Herzl: *Im tirtzu ain zo agada* – if you will it, it is no dream.

Notes

1. Macintyre, D. 2008. 'How I became a target for Israel's Jewish terrorists', *The Independent*, 2 October.

2. Yiftachel, O. 1997. 'Israeli Society and Jewish-Palestinian Reconciliation: "Ethocracy" and its Territorial Contradictions', *Middle East Journal*, 51 (4), pp.506–510.

3. See for example Zertal, I., and Eldar, A. 2007. *Lords of the Land: The War over Israel's Settlements in the Occupied Territories*; Gorenberg, G. 2007. *Occupied Territories: The Untold Story of Israel's Settlements*.

4. Gurr, T.R. 1970. *Why Men Rebel*.

5. Sprinzak, E. 1988. 'Fundamentalism, Terrorism, and Democracy: The Case of Gush Emunim', *New Outlook*, 31, (9), September-October, p.9.

6. This point is made forcefully by Hall-Cathala, D. 1990. *The Peace Movement in Israel 1967–87*. Macmillan/St Anthony's: Oxford. pp.4–5.

7. For a useful collection of essays dealing with *Gush Emunim* see Newman, D. (ed.) 1985. *The Impact of Gush Emunim: Politics and Settlement on the West Bank*.

8. Quoted in Sprinzak, E. 1991. *The Ascendence of Israel's Radical Right*, p.116. Amital has since renounced his links with *Gush Emunim* and was a founding member of *Meimad* (Dimension), a religious-nationalist movement but one takes a more benign view towards the issue of territorial compromise.

9. Ben Meir, Y. 2005. 'The Disengagement: An Ideological Crisis', *Strategic Assessment*, 7(4), March, p2. Accessed on www.tau.ac.il/jcss/sa/v7n4p2Ben-Meir.html.

10. Morag, N. 2005. 'Measuring success in coping with terrorism: the Israeli case', *Studies in Conflict and Terrorism*, 28 (4), p.310.

11. Before his collapse Sharon was reportedly the recipient of a number of death threats even before the Gaza withdrawal. See Macintyre, D. 2005. 'Israel on alert as Rumours Circulate of Right Wing Plot to Assassinate Sharon', *The Independent*, 21 June.

12. Ben Meir, Y. 2005. 'The Post-Disengagement Anguish', *Strategic Assessment*, 8 (3), November, pp.2–3. Accessed at www.tau.ac.il/jcss.sa/v8n3p6BenMeir.html.

13. Ibid., p.2.

14. Kimmerling, B. 2006. 'The Fence will never be a Border', *Ha'aretz* (in Hebrew), 23 January.

15. Author's interviews with youth leaders from the settlements of Elkana, and Elon Moreh, 3 and 4 March 2008.

16. Gurr, op.cit., pp.83–84.

17. Sprinzak, E. 1992. 'Violence and Catastrophe in the Theology of Rabbi Meir Kahane: The Ideologisation of Mimetic Desire', in Juergensmeyer, M. (ed.) *Violence and the Sacred in the Modern World*. pp.48–49.

18. See *Exodus*, Chapter 17, Verses 8–16; *Deuteronomy*, Chapter 25, Verses 17–19. *Amalekh*, though a collective name used to describe a warring tribe, was actually the son of Esau, an opponent of Jacob. Renowned for their under-hand methods of combat, the tribe of the *Amalekh* were eventually defeated in battle. The grandson of Amalekh, Agag was captured by Saul and con-demned to death. Saul allowed him to live for one day, during which time, so tradition has it, he impregnated two women, one of whom gave birth to Hanon. Consequently, the enemy of the Jews continued to reproduce and multiply every generation. This story fits it neatly with those who regard Arabs as the modern day *Amalekh* who must to be destroyed if God's glory is to be revealed.

19. This point is made forcefully in a profile of Goldstein. See the editorial 'Hazvavah' (Disaster) *Ma'ariv*, 27 February 1994.

20. 'Israel's Religious Right and the Question of Settlements' *International Crisis Group*, Middle East Report No.89, 20 July 2009, pp.8–9.

21. Pedahzur, A., and Perliger, A. 2010. *Jewish Terrorism in Israel*, p.114.

22. Rapoport, M. 2006. 'Religious Zionism without Zionism', *Ha'aretz* (in Hebrew), 2 February.

23. Burston, B. 2006. 'The Brushfire Civil War: Israel, the New Enemy of the True Jew', *Ha'aretz* (in English), 2 February.

24. Ben Meir, 'The Post Disengagement Anguish', p.6; Sheleg, Y. 2006. 'After Amona: When 'Absolute Truths' are Undermined', *Ha'aretz* (in English), 13 February.

25. Eldar, A. 2010. 'Poll: 21 per cent of settlers resisting evacuation 'by any means', *Ha'aretz,* 31 March.

26. Press, E. 2010. 'Israel's Holy Warriors', *The New York Review of Books*, LVII (7), 29 April-12 May, pp.33–35.

27. Pedahzur and Perliger, op.cit., pp.111–113 and pp.116–122.

28. This assumption appears to have determined the route of the security bar-rier for at least three years. See Farell, S. 2003. 'Israel's great divide redraws occupied lands', *The Times*, London, 27 October. Between October 2001 and October 2002, 20,000 settlers returned to Israel, citing a mix of economic

and security considerations as responsible for their migration. See Elizur, Y. 2003. 'Israel Banks on a Fence', *Foreign Affairs*, 82 (2), March/April, p.118.

29. Rapaport, M. 2006. 'Religious Zionism, without Zionism', *Ha'aretz* (in Hebrew), 2 February.

30. Friedman, T. 1995. 'Land or Life?', *The New York Times*, 19 November.

31. Harel, A. 2010. 'Barak gets death threat over West Bank Settlement freeze', *Ha'aretz* (in Hebrew), 6 January.

Bibliography

Cohen, S. 2010. *Israel and its Army: From Cohesion to Confusion.* Routledge: London.

Gorenberg, G. 2007. *Occupied Territories: The Untold Story of Israel's Settlements.* I.B.Tauris: London.

Gurr, T.R. 1970. *Why Men Rebel.* Princeton: Princeton University Press.

Hall-Cathala, D. 1990. *The Peace Movement in Israel 1967–87.* Palgrave Macmillan: Oxford.

Juergensmeyer, M. (ed.) 1992. *Violence and the Sacred in the Modern World.* Frank Cass: London.

Lustick, I.S. 1988. *For the Land and the Lord.* Council on Foreign Relations: New York.

Newman, D. (ed.) 1985. *The Impact of Gush Emunim: Politics and Settlement on the West Bank.* Croom Helm: London.

Pedahzur, A., and Perliger, A. 2010. *Jewish Terrorism in Israel.* Columbia University Press: New York.

Shafir, G., and Peled, Y. 2002. *Being Israeli: The Dynamics of Multiple Citizenship.* Cambridge University Press: Cambridge.

Sprinzak, E. 1991. *The Ascendence of Israel's Radical Right.* Oxford University Press: Oxford.

Zertal, I., and Eldar, A. 2007. *Lords of the Land: The War over Israel's Settlements in the Occupied Territories.* Nation Books: New York.

10

SOWING DRAGONS' TEETH: RADICALISATION IN THE IRAQI THEATRE OF OPERATIONS

James Spencer

While 'radical' and 'radicalisation' have always been loose descriptive terms, in the Conservative lexicon they have always had an additional, pejorative resonance. As Sanders notes 'Conservatives frequently deployed "radical" as a blanket term of abuse.'[1] This use extends to modern times too, for example, conservatives in America opposed to Sonia Sotomayor's nomination as a supreme court judge described her as a 'radical'.[2] In the context of the invasion and occupation of Iraq, this definitional vagueness was exploited to maintain fictions[3] useful to the public relations campaign[4] of the Bush administration.

In this chapter, 'radicalisation' will be defined as taking up arms against the governing power, and fighting to install a fundamentally different form of government will be regarded as 'extremism'. This definition immediately runs into difficulty, since according to some of the speculation over the American intent in invading Iraq (as part of its project to reshape the Middle East),[5] it might be argued that the most radical, if not extreme, actor in the Iraqi drama was the United

States itself. We shall, however, confine ourselves to the domestic situation in Iraq in what follows, highlighting the ways in which these terms have been abused.

The Situation in Iraq

The situation inside Iraq in the wake of the American invasion in 2003 evolved quickly and in ways that the United States had not anticipated. The new provisional administration had to cope with both radicals and extremists in unexpected numbers and with agendas for which it was ill-prepared. Nor, as time went on, were all its opponents Iraqi or related to the former Saddam Hussein regime. Ironically enough, one factor that exacerbated the problems it faced was the fact of its own lack of readiness, both in the political and the security fields. One way in which it responded was to claim, in pejorative terms, that its opponents were 'radicals'. Often, this was little more than misleading abuse as the discussion below demonstrates.

'Radical' Politicians

Two obvious examples of such abusive use of the term are given here. Muqtada' al-Sadr was regularly described as a 'Radical Iraqi Shi'a cleric'.[6] Yet far from being a radical, he is part of the Iraqi Establishment, the scion of the eminent clerical al-Sadr family. As his black *imamah* (turban) denotes, he is a *sayyid* – a descendant of the Prophet – and, as his title of *Hujjat al-Islam* made clear in 2003, Muqtada' al-Sadr was midway up the Shi'a clerical hierarchy. Further, as his own frequent use of colloquial Iraqi Arabic (in pointed contrast to Grand Ayatollah Ali al-Sistani's Persian-accented Arabic), and his followers' derisive dismissal – as not 'made in Iraq'[7] – of many other Shi'a politicians made clear, Muqtada' al-Sadr makes much of his solid Iraqi nationalist credentials.

Muqtada' al-Sadr could accurately be described as being 'radical' in one theological respect. While Twelver Shi'ism requires anyone not certified as a *mujtahid* (able to reason independently) to follow a *marja' al-taqlid* (a source of emulation), Muqtada' al-Sadr may[8] have formulated the novel idea that he would follow his (dead) father's example,[9] an anathema in Twelver Shi'ism. Since Muqtada' al-Sadr is said now to be an Ayatollah, which accords him the financial benefits of the *khums* tax, he may eschew this radical idea.

The same inaccurate designation of 'radical' has been applied to many Sunni Arabs – for example, 'The radical Sunni cleric Harith al-Dhari urged Arab governments and the United Nations (UN) to withdraw their support from al-Maliki's government.'[10] Yet, like Muqtada' al-Sadr, Harith al-Dhari is a member of the Iraqi establishment through and through: he is a senior shaykh of the al-Zawba tribe (and lived in the eponymous Khan Dhari). He holds a doctorate from al-Azhar (the premier Sunni university in Cairo), and subsequently taught at Baghdad University. Shaykh al-Dhari, too, comes from a politically active family; his grandfather murdered Colonel Leachman in 1920 and was a leader of the Sunni uprising thereafter. Harith al-Dhari's explicit demands have been remarkably consistent.[11] As he said in 2005:

> This solution [to the crisis in Iraq] must be based, first, on an announcement by the US and its allies of a timetable for withdrawing their troops. Second, it would entail replacing the occupation forces with a UN force whose main task would be to fill the security void. This would be followed, thirdly, by the formation of an interim Iraqi government for six months under the supervision of the UN in order to conduct genuine parliamentary elections in which all parts of the Iraqi population would take part. Finally, the duly elected Iraqi government would take charge of the task of rebuilding the country's civil and military institutions.[12]

The withdrawal of the occupiers, incidentally, later included *al-Qa'ida* when the movement appeared to wish to replace the Multi-National Forces. Shaykh al-Dhari also includes the Iranians and, implicitly, their affiliated Iraqi parties – the Islamic Supreme Council in Iraq and *Hizb al-Da'wa* – whom he would also like to see leave. Al-Dhari has held to his demand even when the 'Sons of Iraq', a Sunni militia, swapped sides, and threatened him.[13]

So why have Harith al-Dhari and Muqtada' al-Sadr acquired the stock epithet 'radical'? The answer is, that they have been the political face[14] of armed insurrection against the invading Multi-National Coalition in Iraq (MNC-I) and the Iraqi Governing Council and, subsequently, the government, whose legitimacy (if not legality) was dubious. Muqtada' al-Sadr and al-Dhari have been rabble-rousing and rebellious, but little more radical – although certainly more violent – than Lech Wałęsa or Vaclav Havel. While both al-Dhari and Muqtada' al-Sadr are clerics (and thus prefer Islamic governance) both have stood on a nationalist cause. As Sami Moubayed pointed out in 2005:

> The US and Muqtada's enemies at home accuse him of wanting to create a theocracy in Iraq, similar to the model in Iran. Muqtada claims that this is untrue, saying that this is the objective of his rival, the Iran-backed Hakim. What he wants, he has often said, is to create an Islamic democracy.[15] [16]

In practice, too, Muqtada' al-Sadr and his *Jaysh al-Mahdi* movement have demonstrated such nationalist credentials. For example, the kangaroo court which sat during Muqtada' al-Sadr's occupation of al-Najaf in 2004 had more similarity to the Provisional IRA's 'Civil Administration' teams in Northern Ireland during the Troubles than to any Shari'a court[17].

The two main radical parties in Iraq are *Hizb al-Da'wa al-Islami-yya* (to which the current prime minister Nuri al-Maliki, belonged up to 2010 when he formed his own political movement) and the Supreme Council of the Islamic Revolution in Iraq (now the Islamic Supreme Council in Iraq). Both of these hold to the theologically dubious *velayat-e faqih* doctrine, yet have been close allies of the United States and its partners. Both have previously used violence, in terrorist attacks against Ba'athist Iraq and the United States in Kuwait[18], while the Islamic Supreme Council in Iraq retains a formally disarmed, formerly military, wing – the 'Badr Organisation' – which had fought with Iran against Iraq. Whether the Badr Organisation has actually been disarmed is moot: many Sunni Arabs believe that it was absorbed wholesale into Iraqi security organisations, yet remains under the control of the Islamic Supreme Council in Iraq, alongside its new official status. According to the New York Times in 2005:

> One Iranian-backed Shiite religious party [...], the Supreme Council for the Islamic Revolution in Iraq, or Sciri, has controlled the Interior Ministry under the transitional government that took office in May. The minister, Bayan Jabr, is a senior Sciri official. He has been widely accused by Sunni Arabs of infiltrating hundreds of members of the paramilitary wing of Sciri, the Badr Organisation, into the police force, and allowing them to form death squads and to run torture centres.[19]

'Radical' Fighters

While the term 'radical' was much bandied about in the media, two other terms were used at lower levels with similar intent: 'Former Regime Extremist' (sometimes 'Loyalist') and 'Anti-Iraqi Forces'. These two ideas were Strategic Communication (STRATCOM) terms, the former was intended to suggest that anyone resisting the occupation was a violent Ba'athist, while the latter was to suggest that resistance was traitorous.[20] The implication was that both were irreconcilable, and neither could be resolved by negotiation. The term 'Former Regime Extremist' certainly had some currency – as the Saddam-era document cited below and numerous newspaper reports at the time showed.[21]

> Top Secret. To all state agencies listed below. Secret emergency plan:
>
> * Security [Agencies]
> * Military Intelligence
> * Secret Services
>
> Following on our secret letter No. (3870) of 1/19/2003. In the event of the downfall of the Iraqi leadership in the hands of the

American, British, and Zionist forces, God forbid, it is incumbent on all the members of the agencies listed above to act in accordance with the instructions listed below:

- Looting and burning of all state agencies connected with our directorates and other [government agencies]
- Changing residence from time to time
- Destroying power generating stations
- Destroying water installations
- Mobilising of dependable elements and bringing them into mosques
- Joining the religious centres in Najaf
- Joining the nationalist and Islamic parties and groupings
- Cutting off internal and external communications
- Purchasing stolen weapons from citizens
- Establishing close ties with those who are returning from outside the country
- Assassination of imams and preachers of mosques.
    Copies to:
    Secret Service Bureau – Baghdad
    Secret Service Bureau – [unclear]
    Secret Service Bureau – [Basra]
        [Signed] – 'Comrade Head of Secret Services'.[22]

Saddam Hussein anticipated the 'Shock and Awe Campaign' directing and resourcing his loyalists to cause mayhem and carnage after the attack had passed through. Saddam was probably basing this strategy on the alleged post-Vietnam casualty aversion of the United States, as exemplified by the Blackhawk Down debacle in Mogadishu in Somalia in which the loss of 18 American soldiers resulted in the withdrawal of the United States Task Force there. Saddam (like many others) had misread the stiffening of American resolve, in the wake of the events of 11 September 2001, and the ideological drive of President G.W. Bush. As *The New York Times* reported in 2006: 'The United States was seen as a lesser threat, mostly because Saddam Hussein believed that Washington could not accept significant casualties.'[23]

However, this concept – that all Sunni Arab activity was solely the responsibility of the Tikriti clique of Saddam Hussein, trying to return the situation to the status quo ante — was clearly awry. Many in the Sunni Arab community had been profoundly alienated from the regime and would not have wished to support it. While more limited and lower in profile than the massacres of the Kurds or the Shi'a Arabs after defeat in 1991, Saddam Hussein's weeding of the Sunni Arabs who formed the backbone of the Armed Forces and Security Services was ruthless – they were, after all, the most credible threat to his power.[24] Many of those who took up arms were doing so to resist the invaders, as they had done against the British in 1920–21 and 1941. Such resistance is a legitimate right (under certain specific conditions, which were not always fulfilled by Sunni Arabs[25]) as evidenced by the terms of Article 4A of the Third Geneva Convention, 12 August 1949:

> Prisoners of war, [include:] (2) Members of other militias and members of other volunteer corps, including those of organized resistance movements, belonging to a Party to the conflict and operating in or outside their own territory, even if this territory is occupied, provided that such militias or volunteer corps, including such organized resistance movements, fulfil the following conditions: [. . .] [26]

Like most Iraqis, many of these Sunni Arabs had completed their military service, yet to conflate them with 'Former Regime Extremists' was inaccurate. The weight initially given to the designation was, however, helped by the fact that many of the Sunni Arab resistance used existing familial or military networks, as did the real Former Regime Extremists, although for different ends.

Given the fact that the Sunni community had usually denied the full demographic weight of Shi'a Arabs inside Iraq, after the January 2005 elections many Sunni Arabs continued to fight – to safe-guard their privileged positions, to forestall the dominance of Shi'a *fiqh* in Arab Iraq, and to prevent the anticipated vengeance of the Shi'i parties. For hard-line Sunnis, Shi'a power is a bitter pill. [. . .] 'Those Shiites were servants,' one man told another [. . .]. 'They wiped our shoes. Now they are going in front of us.'[27]

Yet from the beginning, Sunni Arab leaders had tried to negotiate with the coalition and (subsequently) with the Multi-National Force in Iraq to achieve a compromise solution, 'The Sunni insurgents had offered to come to terms with the Americans thirty months earlier, in the summer of 2004, during secret talks with senior American officials and military commanders'.[28]

As 'Sons of Iraq' (the STRATCOM antonym of 'Anti-Iraqi Forces'), the Sunni Arabs' cooperation against al-Qa'ida[29] as part of the 'Surge' initiative in 2008 was a similar strategy, at a time when many in the United States were openly calling for withdrawal. It was predicated on the promise that the militias which supported the Surge would subsequently be integrated into Iraq's new security forces, a promise that the Shi'a-dominated government subsequently proved reluctant to honour – a decision which, in turn, could still lead to the militia anti-regime violence. The possible return to violence by elements of the Sons of Iraq is therefore an equally logical choice if this promise were not to be eventually honoured. They would have to act while American combat forces (and political attention) remained focussed on Iraq, in order to leverage American influence to force the Shi'a Arabs to fulfil their part of the Sons of Iraq agreement: adequate Sunni access to *wusta* (power and patronage) through the promise of integration into the security services.

These are calculated actions, which, however unpleasant it was to be on the receiving end of them, are age-old strategies. They were certainly not extremist acts, since they proposed no significant change to the status quo. Can they even be described as 'radical' since often they distinguish between attacking foreign personnel and attacking Iraqis? As one commentator noted, this distinction was commonly made. 'Mr. Juburi said that he opposed Al Qaeda's use of suicide bombers to kill Iraqi civilians but was soliciting support for Iraqis intent on killing American troops.'[30] Perhaps the less pejorative term 'militant' is analytically more apt here, rather than 'radical' or 'extremist'?

Financial Incentives

It should also be noted that many of those who took part in violent actions against the occupation forces were not motivated by politics, or religion, but rather by money. In a country which had been degraded by 12 years of sanctions, had seen the major employer – the state – suddenly cease to pay salaries, and where private enterprise had been nearly suffocated by the security situation, finding enough money to survive was an uphill struggle particularly after the invasion. As a result, any stratagem to obtain it became commonplace, as *Newsweek* reported in 2009:

> Powers likes to point out that when he served in Iraq [2004] the going rate to have an IED planted was $1,000, with another $1,000 paid for killing an American. Now [2007], he says, kids will set bombs for as little as $20.[31]

The rapid deflation the country experienced was probably symptomatic of the continuing deterioration in the economic situation of many former military men, now dismissed and many other former Ba'athists and state employees who had spent their savings and sold their possessions[32]. While Jerry Bremmer's decision to dissolve the Iraqi Security Forces put 400,000 Iraqis out of a job, the refusal of the Shi'a-dominated Iraqi government to re-employ many of the rank-and-file Sunni Arabs in the new security forces – at $340/month[33] – did much to add to their anger. As *The New York Times* reported in the wake of the 2005 elections on 27 December 2005:

> It has been suspected that Sunni Arabs are underrepresented in the new military and police. [...] In the special tally [from the Dec. 15 vote] – [...] – about 7 per cent of the votes were cast for the three main Sunni Arab parties. Across the whole population, though, officials have estimated, Sunni Arab candidates won about 20 per cent of the seats in the new Parliament. [...] And the estimation seems to be a sign of how complete the reversal of fortune has been for Sunni Arabs, who dominated security forces under Saddam Hussein.[34]

For women with no male breadwinner, the age-old alternative of prostitution was an even bleaker alternative, redolent of shame and ostracisation.[35]

'Foreign Fighters'

There have been many accounts of foreign fighters journeying to Iraq to fight: some reports date from before and during the Invasion,[36] certainly before transnational Jihadis such as those involved in al-Qa'ida made their presence known. Yet here, too, the grain of reality is masked by terminology. Some 'foreigners' were members of the same tribe or family, merely living on the other side of the 1921 borders. A Sunni Arab from Dayr al-Zawr fighting the coalition forces in al-Anbar would legally be regarded as 'foreign', but was he a 'radical'?

Similarly, while some fuss was made of the decision to cover up the Guernica Tapestry on the occasion of US Secretary of State Colin Powell's presentation to the United Nations Security Council, the question suggested by the subject of the tapestry does not seem to have been posed. Were international participants in the Spanish Civil War 'radicals'? If not, can foreign fighters in the Iraq theatre of conflict be so termed? The answer is both 'yes' and 'no' – even within the mujihadin. There were those who came to expel the occupying forces from Iraq, as well as those who sought to turn the 'Land of the Two Rivers', an allegorical name for Iraq, into the kernel of a vast Islamic state. While the latter are surely 'radicals' and extremists according to our terminology, the former are not extremist, and possibly not radicals either, since many sought to attack the multinational force[37], but not Iraqis. As Neil MacFarquhar reported of one individual in *The New York Times* on 2 November 2004, 'he volunteered to steer a vehicle into any United States military target, but did not want to kill Iraqis – even Iraqi soldiers.'[38]

So what motivated Arabs from across the Middle East[39] to commit such acts? Pan-Arab nationalism, in particular in opposition to the United States, compounded by suspicion as to American motives was certainly a major reason.

As columnist Mahmoud Mubarak wrote in *al-Hayat* on 20 April [09], 'the seven years that have passed since Durban 1 have been some of the most racist in recent history'. From an Arab perspective, the US is to blame for much of this: the war on terror, Iraq, Afghanistan, Abu

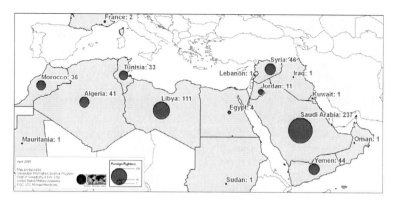

Foreign Fighters by country of Origin[41] Source: CTC Sinjar Documents

Ghraib, urinating on the Qur'an in Guantanamo, have all been products of a resurgent neo-colonialist USA under President Bush. Add to that the Muhammad cartoons, Israel's indiscriminate wars on Lebanese and Palestinian civilians, the continued occupation of Palestinian territories, and the racist ideology that underpins it.[40]

This is an issue of which President Obama has been acutely conscious, but one of which President Bush was either oblivious, or recklessly ignored. His was an attitude that was also shared within the Middle East itself. Typifying apparent American attitudes to the Middle East – and a major motivator of Arab nationalist and Islamist attacks on the United States and sympathetic regional governments are – the roles and attitudes of Israel in the region, where it is widely seen – and hated – as a colony of the United States. As Neil MacFarquhar reported in 2004 in *The New York Times*:

> The moneychanger said many men in the region had long dreamed of joining the Palestinians fighting Israel, but that border is impenetrable. The road to Iraq is open, he noted, and killing American soldiers is the next best thing.[42]

Even amongst transnational Jihadis, whilst some did indeed go to Iraq to kill and die, many more came to gain combat experience in order to return to their homelands and take up the fight there. It is no coincidence that many came from the less democratic states of the region – one radical in a Palestinian refugee camp in Lebanon has estimated that he had 50 militants from Saudi Arabia and other Arab countries, fresh from fighting with the insurgency in Iraq, under his command.[43]

Radicalisation

Did genuine radicalisation actually happen? Certainly it did, both within Iraq and without, and was exacerbated by '[t]he exodus of middle-class Iraqis – some two million refugees now live outside the country -[which] eviscerated the least sectarian slice of society.'[44] One of the main factors that caused radicalisation was the high-handed conduct of occupying troops. Harith al-Dhari reported in the Guardian in 2005 that:

> The occupation troops have resorted to excessive force, indis-criminate killing and collective punishment of the population. They have besieged entire towns, storming into them, instill-ing fear and horror among residents and destroying their homes. Iraqis have been humiliated and stripped of their basic human rights; they have been subjected to brutal and ghastly forms of torture, as the infamous Abu Ghraib prison case and the British troops' abuse of detainees in Basra have shown.[45]

This conduct rapidly produced the phenomenon known to occupying forces as the 'Pissed Off Iraqi',[46] or POI for short, the exact opposite of what had been intended by the alleged campaign for 'hearts and minds'. According to *The Washington Post* in 2006:

> 'Hearts and Minds,' the soldiers shrug. They joke like this often. The few Iraqis still living in Ramadi have had their homes raided and streets patrolled for three years now. Every time a window is broken, a bedroom is trashed or husbands are ques-tioned, the glares become harsher. Compliance with US troops turns to hatred.[47]

The reasons behind this are many and various: the pro-Israel evangelical attitudes of many American troops; the low socio-economic strata from which infantrymen were recruited and above all the callousness resulting from overexposure to the horrors of war. Whatever the reasons, the reporting of such attitudes[48] was consistent,[49] and the result the same. Newsweek reported in 2007 that:

> Jumaa, the Fallujah high-school student, was himself detained by the Americans in September 2005, when he was 16 years old. US forces raided his house searching for his father, a Baath Party member and insurgency sympathiser. In his absence, they took Jumaa instead. He says the Americans handcuffed him, blindfolded him and held him at a nearby US base. According to him, the Americans left him alone for 24 hours with no food or water. He ended up staying there for two months, until he was transferred to the Iraqi security forces, who, he says, tortured him for three months until he was released. Now he longs to kill Americans. 'I will carry a weapon,' he declares. 'I will fight them to defend my land, country and religion.'[50]

This should not have come as a surprise to readers and politicians alike, as it replicates experience in a myriad of military theatres throughout history, going back as far as the Ancient Greeks. As Diodotus, son of Eucrates, pointed out in Athens in the fifth century BC:

> The right way to deal with free people is this – not to inflict tremendous punishment on them after they have revolted, but to take tremendous care of them before this point is reached, to prevent them even contemplating the idea of revolt, and if we do have to use force with them, to hold as few as possible of them responsible for this.[51]

Extremism

The Middle East is certainly a more religious place than Europe – although not more than the United States. It has been overtly so for at least the last century, partly as a result of colonialism. However even the religiously-motivated[52] transnational Jihadis had to have their background religiosity actively focussed and distilled to make them first effective radicals and then extremists, often through education and conditioning. According to several journalisrs, this took place within Iraq:

> Diyala residents and officials say, militants from Al Qa'ida in Mesopotamia have worked to instil their radical Islamist vision in the population. Almost immediately after moving in four years ago, they began holding religion classes for men and women.[53]

and outside:

> Before leaving for Iraq, he said, he first studied at an ad hoc academy for jihad. The classes, under clerical tutelage, gave some of the many men from the area who wanted to fight an understanding of the religious basis for expelling infidel invaders from Muslim lands.[54]

The perceived injustice of the various occupations of Arab and Muslim lands has proved to be a powerful motivator for radicalisation, itself the starting point towards extremism. According to the New York Times in March 2007:

> 'Today's youth, when they see what is happening in Palestine and Iraq, it enthuses them to join the way of the right and jihad,' he said. 'These people have now started to adopt the right path.'[55]

This self-evident initiation into radicalisation can be subtly and incrementally transformed by recruiters for extremist causes from nationalist anger into religious self-righteousness. Once dependency on recruiters and teachers is established, this mechanical fury can be turned on the object of extremist ire: the occupying forces, the Shi'a, or even secularists nationalists. This process – isolation, indoctrination and dependency – is much the same as is carried out by anybody anxious to recruit for a cause, whether ideological, political or criminal. It occurs both in the strangely intimate sphere of cyberspace, and in personal contact. According to one potential suicide bomber:

> We keep listening lessons in how to use weapons and the right way to use the belt filled with the bombs to attack the invader. From these long hours we stay praying at least forty per cent of them as we have to be really close to God before holding our destiny. My day is coming and I have been told that I should have my special day soon. I had to leave my family three months ago to keep in a special place to be trained.[56]

Detention

The point where radicalism and extremism intersect, where constructive interference produces the perfect storm of violence, is often in detention facilities.[57] This should have come as no surprise to America and its allies since it has long been observed in military campaigns,[58] and in civil prisons[59] as well. It is the combination of boredom, resentment, isolation and dependency that recruiters thrive upon. *The New York Times* reported in March 2007 that:

> Mr Ani and other former detainees described the sprawling complex of barracks in the southern desert near Kuwait as a bleak place where guards casually used their stun guns and exposed prisoners to long periods of extreme heat and cold; where prisoners fought among themselves and extremist elements tried to radicalise others; and where detainees often responded to the harsh conditions with hunger strikes and, at times, violent protests.[60]

Uninvolved 'men of military age' who were rounded up by ill-chance became 'POI', while radicals were either confirmed in their views, or were perverted[61] into Islamist extremism. In all cases, their resentment increased and their technical proficiency grew, as did the networks of like-minded individuals which they could exploit if or when they were released. This experience was identical to Britain's experience in Ulster, where the Maze Prison acquired the soubriquet of the University of Terrorism.

Since the day-to-day operations of the detainee programme were within the ambit of the American military and had limited political visibility to the outside world, this was an aspect that the American forces were able to change, for the better, once alerted to it. In one initiative, the United States combined elements from the Discharge Wing programme of Britain's Military Corrective Training Centre at Colchester (where inmates were taught useful trade-skills and literacy) with orthodox religious studies, as pioneered by Judge Hitar in Yemen,[62] with other elements, in a complex programme. This sophisticated programme reduced both the boredom factor, and the opportunity for Jihadis to convert detainees into extremists in prison. The results were unprecedented: 'Of the 8,000 detainees released since last September [2007], only 21 have been recaptured as a result of suspected insurgent activity',[63] the New Post reported in 2008.

Suicide Attacks

It is incontrovertible that that many foreigners who travel to Iraq (and increasingly to Afghanistan) do so with the intention of killing themselves (and others) for religious reasons. *Times Magazine* noted in 2005 the views of one local observer,

> He says foreign fighters 'come a long way from their countries, spending a lot of money and with high hopes. They don't want to gradually earn their entry to paradise by participating in operations against the Americans. They want martyrdom immediately.'[64]

However, this self-centred motivation does not fit easily within either the radicalism or the extremism scenario, since the aim of those involved is not to avenge themselves, or to affect the government, but rather to attain Paradise. Some of the strongest opponents of such terrorism are other Islamists, who object both to the killing of innocent Muslims[65] – even Twelver Shi'a, whom many Salafis castigate as *rafidhin* (rejectionists) – as well as on the standard grounds of all Abrahamic theologies, namely that suicide is a sin.

As the *reductio ad absurdum* of extremism, it might be thought that suicide attacks were all the work of extremists and religious fanatics. Yet the evidence from survivors suggests otherwise: for many[66] who intend to kill themselves, revenge or despair – radicalism? – is the motive:

> The women who become suicide bombers often have lost close male relatives – a husband, a brother, a son – in fighting, because they became suicide bombers themselves or because they were detained by American or Iraqi security forces.[67]

This would suggest that any religious element in the justification for such an attack was often a form of self-justification and comfort ('a day [. . .] of God's forgiveness'[68]), rather than the cause. Coupled with the often ill-educated nature of many women in the Middle East, for example, this makes rational and doctrinal avenues of countering such events[69] far harder. Such non-religious aspects to suicide attacks are seen in other reports as well: several cases of mentally handicapped people being exploited in this fashion have been reported[70], whilst there have been complaints from foreign Jihadi amirs that their trainee 'soldiers' have been turned into suicide bombers, rather than returning as veteran mujahidin. At least one 'suicide' bomber was unwitting: Ahmad Abdullah al-Shaya was blown up by his handlers outside the Jordanian Embassy in Iraq on Christmas Eve 2004. He reported that:

> They asked me to take the truck near a concrete block barrier before turning to the right and leaving it there. There, somebody will pick up the truck from you,' they told him. 'But they blew me up in the truck' he says.[71]

There is a final reason why some foreigners may agree to carry out a suicide attack – desperation. As several different reports recount, many facilitators are acting for commercial reasons, not out of 'charity'. Would-be mujahidin are expected to bring various items with them, including cash. Neil MacFarquhar related in *The New York Times* in 2007 that:

> The Arabs were told that if they wanted to fight Americans, they would have to pay $200 for their military kit, including a machine gun, rocket-propelled grenade launcher and 10 hand grenades. They also had to pay for food.[72]

With their identity documents confiscated, once the money ran out, they had little alternative but to comply with the suggestion of their handlers, and become the guidance system for explosive attacks.

Conclusion

The discussion above would suggest that radicals and extremists are far less numerous, and far less radical, than security pundits would have us believe. Instead, many who resort to violence are acting from rational motives, such as resisting invasion and occupation. This should be an encouraging finding, as there is usually a political solution to a rational grievance, as demonstrated by the example of the al-Sahwa/'Sons of Iraq' militia during the 'Surge' in 2007.

Similarly, many of those who are radicalised might never have reached that stage were it not for conduct by Western forces which they deeply resented. Here, too, radicalisation can be reduced by more sensitive predeployment training, less use of area weapons, and perhaps shorter tour lengths: what is lost in area familiarity is gained in reduced callousness towards the local population.

There is also much that can be done to counter the extremism against the West felt in much of the Middle East. The suppurating sore of the Israeli-Arab problem is one major issue, as is the encouragement of democratic governance and economic stimulus for job creation. Above all, however, a 'Dialogue between Civilisations' on the basis of mutual respect will do much to reset the toxic relationship between Middle East and West so current at present. Currently, many in the Middle East hark back to the days when they were taken seriously, to the days of the Ottoman Empire. When the Caliphate was abolished, they believe the Middle East's temporal prestige declined. The extremists interpret this religiously: their solution is to bring back Islam and thus the world's respect – a solution with a potentially Delphic outcome.

Notes

1. Sanders, M. (ed.) 2001. *Women and Radicalism in the Nineteenth Century (Subcultures and Subversions)*. Routledge: London. p.XIX.

2. Marcus, R. 2009. 'The 'Radical' who isn't', *The Washington Post*, 3 June. http://www.washingtonpost.com/wp-dyn/content/article/2009/06/02/AR2009060202969.html?wpisrc=newsletter&wpisrc=newsletter.

3. Principally that there was a direct link between Saddam Hussein and al-Qa'ida, and inferring that the former had assisted the latter in the attacks of 9/11.

4. Hayes, S.F. 2003. 'Case close: *The US government's secret memo detailing cooperation between Saddam Hussein and Osama bin Laden*', *Weekly Standard*, 24 November. http://www.weeklystandard.com/Content/Public/Articles/000/000/003/378fmxyz.asp?ZoomFont=YES accessed 26 May 2009.

5. Donnelly, J., and Shadid, A. 2002. 'Iraq war hawks have plans to reshape entire Mideast', *Boston Globe*, 10 September. Cited here: http://www.commondreams.org/headlines02/0910-01.htm.

6. Anon. 2009. 'Iraq: Radical cleric becomes "ayatollah"', *Adnkronos International*, 5 May. http://www.adnkronos.com/AKI/English/Religion/?id=3.0.3277106453 accessed 12 May 2009.

7. Moubayed, S. 2006. 'Iraqi visions on the road to Damascus', *Asia Times*, 10 February. http://www.atimes.com/atimes/Middle_East/HB10Ak03.html, 27 May 2009.

8. Cole, J. 2004. 'Patel on Muqtada al-Sadr', *Informed Comment*, 9 April, http://www.juancole.com/2004/04/patel-on-muqtada-al-sadr-david-patel.html accessed 12 May 2009.

9. This was probably an effort to have no religious superior to control him. MAS may have been making a statement about his father's traditional Iraqi Twelver Shi'a philosophy, rather than that of his father's nominated successor Kadhim al-Ha'iri, a follower of Khomeini's *Velayet-e Faghih* (like ISCI/Hizb al-Da'wa).

10. Bazzi, M. 2006. 'A delicate tug-of-war in Iraq', *Newsday*, 25 November. http://www.newsday.com/news/nationworld/world/ny-woanal1126,0,4831513.story accessed 13 May 2009.

11. Worth, R.F. 2005. 'Sunni leader insists on timetable for U.S. withdrawal', *The New York Times*, 29 March, http://www.nytimes.com/2005/03/29/international/middleeast/29sunni.html, accessed 13 May 2009; see also 'Iraqi Muslim Scholars leader interviewed on US withdrawal, other issues', *Al-Jazeera*, 28 May 2009.

12. al-Dhari, H. 2005. 'No elections will be credible while occupation continues', *The Guardian*, 15 December 2005, http://www.guardian.co.uk/politics/2005/dec/15/iraq.iraq1 accessed 27 May 2009.

13. Khalil, L. 2006. 'Harith al-Dari: Iraq's most wanted Sunni leader', *Jamestown Terrorism Monitor*, 26 December, http://www.jamestown.org/single/?no_cache=1&tx_ttnews%5Btt_news%5D=997 accessed 27 May 2009.

14. Sh al-Dhari operates in the political sphere (albeit not formally), and on the fringes of the insurgent one.

15. This 'Islamic Democracy' may be MAS's version of the *Wilayat al-'Umma* (Governance of the people) concept of his father-in-law Gr Ay Muhammad Baqr al-Sadr.

16. Moubayed, S. 2005. 'The US and that man Muqtada again', *Asia Times*, 24 September, http://www.atimes.com/atimes/Middle_East/GI24Ak01.html accessed 27 May 2009.

17. Anon. 2004. 'Tales of brutality in al-Sadr's religious court', *Fox News*, 10 September, http://origin.foxnews.com/story/0,2933,131978,00.html.

18. Anon. un-dated. 'Terrorist attacks on American 1979–1988', *PBS*, http://www.pbs.org/wgbh/pages/frontline/shows/target/etc/cron.html accessed 27 May 2009.

19. Burns, J.F. 2005. 'The struggle for Iraq: prisons; to halt abuses, U.S. will inspect jails run by Iraq', *The New York Times*, 14 December, http://query.nytimes.com/gst/fullpage.html?res=9F0DE3DD1F31F937A25751C1A9639C8B63 accessed 1 June 2009.

20. Use of the term 'resistance' was problematic, as it implied an element of legitimacy. Further, it was said that to the post-Star Wars generation which comprised much of the US Forces, if the Iraqis were the Resistance, that made the other side (i.e. the MNC-I) the Evil Empire.

21. Ballout, A. 2003. 'Is Saddam Hussein's post-war plan unfolding?', *Daily Star*, 21 August.

22. Sookhdeo, P. 2003. 'A political, ethnic and religious analysis of Iraq in the post-Saddam era', ISIC (September 2003); Appendix A.

23. Gordon, M., and Trainor, B. 2006. 'Even as U.S. invaded, Hussein saw Iraqi unrest as top threat', *The New York Times*, 12 March, http://www.nytimes.

com/2006/03/12/international/middleeast/12saddam.html, accessed 1 June 2009.

24. Baram, A. 2003. 'The Iraqi tribes and the post-Saddam system', *Brookings Institute*, 8 July, http://www.brookings.edu/papers/2003/0708iraq_baram.aspx, 26 May 2009.

25. By contrast, Muqtada' al-Sadr's Jaysh al-Mahdi met most of the conditions.

26. Convention (III) relative to the Treatment of Prisoners of War, Geneva, 12 August 1949, http://www.icrc.org/ihl.nsf/7c4d08d9b287a42141256739003e636b/6fef854a3517b75ac125641e004a9e68 accessed 26 May 2009.

27. Tavernise, S. 2006. 'Iraq power shift widens a gulf between sects', *The New York Times*, 18 February, http://query.nytimes.com/gst/fullpage.html?res=9E02EFDA103EF93BA25751C0A9609C8B63, accessed 1 June 2009.

28. Rose, D. 2009. 'Heads in the sand', *Vanity Fair*, 12 May 2009, http://www.vanityfair.com/politics/features/2009/05/iraqi-insurgents200905?printable=true&currentPage=all accessed 20 May 2009.

29. al-Qa'ida was itself a foreign organisation, and had begun to threaten entrenched Sunni Arab interests, and to kill Sunni Arabs who opposed the radical form of Islam it espouses.

30. Moss, M., and Mekhennet, S. 2007. 'Jailed 2 years, Iraqi tells of abuse by Americans', *The New York Times*, 18 February, http://www.nytimes.com/2007/02/18/world/middleeast/18bucca.html?th&emc=th accessed 19 February 2007.

31. Caryl, C. 2007. 'The next jihadists: Iraq's lost children', *Newsweek*, 22 January, cited in http://www.military-quotes.com/forum/next-jihadists-iraqs-lost-children-t31735.html accessed 12 May 2009.

32. Of detainees 'Some 78 per cent said they'd participated in attacks against Coalition forces to feed their families, and 79 per cent have children. Only one in three said that they had a strong religious belief. Some 64 per cent are illiterate'. Miller, J. 'What I Learned At 'Anti-Jihad U'', *New York Post*.

33. Shanker, T. 2006. 'Elite Iraqi unit seeks footing as it fills U.S. boots', *The New York Times*, 20 February, http://www.nytimes.com/2006/02/20/international/middleeast/20training.html?fta=y 1 June 2009.

34. Oppel, R. 2005. 'Iraq vote shows Sunnis are few in new military', *The New York Times,* 27 December, http://query.nytimes.com/gst/fullpage.html?res=9405E3DB1230F934A15751C1A9639C8B63 accessed 1 June 2009.

35. Sarhan, A. 2007. 'Nafisa Ridwan, Iraq: "Mine is a dirty and miserable life"', *IRIN*, 21 May, http://www.irinnews.org/report.aspx?ReportID=72262.

36. Anon. 2003. 'A bus ride to martyrdom', *The Economist*, 3 April, http://www.economist.com/world/mideast-africa/displaystory.cfm?story_id=E1_TGRNSJR accessed 22 May 2009.

37. UKN. 2007. 'Saudi youth infiltrated into Iraq across Syria', *al-Hayat*, 11 April, www.mideastwire.com.

38. MacFarquhar, N. 2004. 'An Arab "martyr" thwarted', *The New York Times*, 2 November, http://www.nytimes.com/2004/11/02/international/middleeast/02lebanon.html?ex=1180584000&en=c0b645247080b834&ei=5070 accessed 27 May 2007.

39. For a full breakdown of origins, see the Sinjar Documents, http://www.ctc.usma.edu/harmony/FF-Bios-Trans.pdf

40. Haugbolle, S. 2009. 'Arab reactions to Durban II: the ghost of colonialism' *CUMINet blog*, 21 April, http://cuminet.blogs.ku.dk/2009/04/21/arab-reactions-to-durban-ii-the-ghost-of-colonialism/ accessed 21 May 2009.

41. Fishman, B. (ed) 2008. *Bombers, bank accounts and bleed-out: al-Qa'ida's road in and out of Iraq*.Countering Terrorism Centre, 22 July, http://www.ctc.usma.edu/harmony/pdf/Sinjar_2_July_23.pdf accessed 24 July 2008.

42. MacFarquhar, op.cit.

43. Mekhennet, S., Moss, M., and Mazzetti, M. 2007. 'In Lebanon camp, a new face of jihad vows attacks on U.S.' *The New York Times*, 16 March, http://query.nytimes.com/gst/fullpage.html?res=9C00E0D61E31F935A25750C0A9619C8B63 accessed 8 May 2009.

44. Caryl, op.cit.

45. Op. cit.

46. White, W. 2006. 'An oversight hearing on pre-war intelligence relating to Iraq', *Senate Democratic Policy Committee,* 26 June, http://democrats.senate.gov/dpc/hearings/hearing33/white.pdf accessed 19 April 2009.

47. Bruce, A. 2006. 'On a mission in a hard place', *The Washington Post,* 27 December. http://www.washingtonpost.com/wp-dyn/content/article/2006/12/26/AR2006122600830.html 23 April 2007.

48. Schmitt, E., and Marshall, C. 2006. 'In secret unit's 'black room,' a grim portrait of U.S. abuse', *The New York Times,* 19 March, http://www.nytimes.com/2006/03/19/international/middleeast/19abuse.html accessed 1 June 2009.

49. von Zielbauer, P. 2007. 'Civilian claims on U.S. suggest the toll of war', *The New York Times,* 12 April, http://www.nytimes.com/2007/04/12/world/middleeast/12abuse.html?th&emc=th.

50. Caryl, op.cit.

51. Thucydides. *A History of the Peloponnesian War,* Bk III, Ch 9.

52. In a region where democracy and civil society is functionally absent, but Islam is universally accessible, much political activity runs through religious channels. While most secular terrorist organisations have detailed political manifestos, few Islamist terrroist groups have a manifesto, except for adopting 'the Shari'a'.

53. Rubin, A.J. 2008. 'Despair drives suicide attacks by Iraqi women', *The New York Times*, 5 July, http://www.nytimes.com/2008/07/05/world/middleeast/05diyala.html?emc=tnt&tntemail1=y.

54. MacFarquhar, op.cit.

55. Mekhennet, op.cit.

56. Sarhan, A. 2008. 'Iraq's female bombers', *Islamon-line*, 1 July, http://www.islamonline.net/servlet/Satellite?c=Article_C&cid=1213871459730&pagename=Zone-English-News/NWELayout accessed 27 May 2009.

57. Pincus, W. 2007. 'U.S. working to reshape Iraqi detainees', *The Washington Post*, 19 September, http://www.washingtonpost.com/wp-dyn/content/article/2007/09/18/AR2007091802203.html accessed 26 May 2009.

58. Anon. 2009. 'Stone-throwers in glass houses', *Economist*, 21 May, http://www.economist.com/world/europe/displaystory.cfm?story_id=13702749.

59. Wakin, D.J. 2009. 'Imams reject talk that Islam radicalises inmates', *The New York Times,* 23 May, http://www.nytimes.com/2009/05/24/nyregion/24convert.html 26 May 2009.

60. Moss, M., and Mekhennet, S. 2007. 'Jailed 2 years, Iraqi tells of abuse by Americans' *The New York Times*, 18 February, http://www.nytimes.com/2007/02/18/world/middleeast/18bucca.html?th&emc=th.

61. Chandrasekaran, R. 2009. 'From captive to suicide bomber', *The Washington Post,* 22 February, http://www.washingtonpost.com/wp-dyn/content/article/2009/02/21/AR2009022101234.html?wpisrc=newsletter.

62. Whitaker, B. 2004. 'Treat the cause, not the symptoms', *The Guardian,* 2 March, http://www.guardian.co.uk/world/2004/mar/02/worlddispatch.yemen.

63. Miller, J. 2008. 'What I learned at 'Anti-Jihad U'', *New York Post,* 2 May, http://www.nypost.com/seven/05022008/postopinion/opedcolumnists/what_i_learned_at_anti_jihad_u_109130.htm.

64. Ghosh, B. 2005. 'Professor of death', *TIME Magazine,* 16 October, http://www.time.com/time/magazine/article/0,9171,1118370–1,00.html.

65. Haykel, B. 2005. 'Muslims and martyrdom', *The World Today*, 61(10), October, http://www.chathamhouse.org.uk/files/5792_wt051004.pdf accessed 14 June 2007.

66. Most male suicide attackers are foreigners, while most female attackers are Iraqis.

67. Rubin, op.cit.

68. Anon. 2007. 'Killings drive women to become suicide bombers', *IRIN,* 8 March, http://www.irinnews.org/report.aspx?ReportID=70582.

69. Spencer, R.J. 2008. '"Do as I Say, Not as I Do": Towards a Pro-Active Exposure of Opposition Failings', Strategic Insights, April, http://www.ccc.nps.navy.mil/si/2008/Apr/spencerApr08.asp.

70. Anon. 2007. 'Mentally handicapped children used in attacks', *IRIN*, 10 April, http://www.irinnews.org/report.aspx?ReportID=71257.
71. Komarow, S., and al-Anbaki, S. 2005. 'Would-be suicide bomber angry at those who sent him', USA Today, 4 February, http://www.usatoday.com/news/world/iraq/2005–01-24-suicide-bomber-revenge_x.htm 29 May 2007.
72. MacFarquhar, op.cit.

Bibliography

Hayes, S.F. 2003. 'Case close: *The US government's secret memo detailing cooperation between Saddam Hussein and Osama bin Laden*', *Weekly Standard*, 24 November. http://www.weeklystandard.com/Content/Public/Articles/000/000/003/378fmxyz.asp?ZoomFont=YES accessed 26 May 2009.

Sanders, M. (ed.) 2001. *Women and Radicalism in the Nineteenth Century (Subcultures and Subversions).* Routledge: London.

Sookhdeo, P. 2003. 'A political, ethnic and religious analysis of Iraq in the post-Saddam era,' ISIC, September 2003, Appendix A.

Thucydides. *A History of the Peloponnesian War,* Bk III, Ch 9.

11

ETHNIC RADICALISATION: KURDISH IDENTITY AS EXTREMISM IN THE HEGEMONIC DISCOURSES OF TURKEY

Ayla Göl

History teaches us clearly that the battle against colonialism does not run straight away along the lines of nationalism.[1]

Since the terrorist attacks of 11 September 2001 in New York and Washington and 7 July 2005 in London, the latest trends in the study of violence prioritise the mono-causality of religion in order to explain the role of either Islam or the individual in radicalisation. In contrast, this chapter explores the multi-causality and complexity of radicalisation and then applies its findings to an empirical case, namely the radicalisation of Kurds in Turkey. The case of the Kurds presents a unique historical and sociological example through which to understand the causes of radicalisation and the transition of the struggle from non-violence to terrorism. Kurds in the Middle East are the 'invisible nation', representing the largest ethnic group, divided between Turkey, Iran, Iraq and Syria (see Map 1).[2] The Kurdish people of the Middle East form a stateless nation, which is in

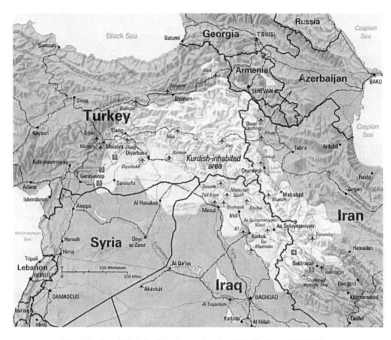

Map 1: Kurdish inhabited area in the Middle East, CIA Maps

search for identity. This case study, therefore, particularly seeks to explain the complex relationship between ethnicity, identity and radicalisation or extremism.

Moreover, the case of the Kurds in Turkey has non-religious dimensions that challenge the basic assumptions in the burgeoning literature on the study of terrorism and radicalisation. These challenges are as identified by Critical Terrorism Studies (CTS) which contrast orthodox studies on terrorism on three basic epistemological and ontological assumptions: the dominance of state-centric perspectives and the pre-eminence of ahistorical and problem-solving approaches.[3] Furthermore, the methodology of CTS demonstrates that an ahistorical approach to understanding the Kurdish issue is necessarily incomplete, hence the resurgence of PKK (*Partiya Karkaren Kurdistan* – the Kurdish Workers Party) terrorism needs to be historicised and contextualised. The underlying assumptions of this chapter are threefold: first, that a mono-causal explanation – the emphasis on the role of religion – fails to appreciate the complexity of radicalisation and terrorism; second, a multi-causal analysis of each phenomenon is necessary; and third, such an analysis must be placed within broad historical, sociological and political contexts.

The first part of the chapter offers a new definition of 'ethnic radicalisation' based on Tarik Fraihi's typology of radicalisation and the Weberian concept of ethnicity. The second part highlights the historical context, within which the multi-causality and complexity of the radicalisation of Kurds with reference to identity politics is explained; then the Kurdish question is sociologically examined with reference to how Turkish state ideology is based on the discourse of assimilation of Kurds and the corresponding denial of their existence as an ethnic group. The last section engages with the political context by focusing on the rise of PKK terrorism. The chapter concludes by examining the feasibility of non-violent solutions for the future of the Kurdish question in Turkey and the Middle East.

Ethnic Radicalisation and Identity Politics

Since the 7 July 2005 terrorist attacks in London, there has been an increased usage of, and a shifting meaning attached to, the term 'radicalisation' in Britain. According to Breen-Smyth, within this new trend 'radicalisation' has become synonymous with particular political-religious orientations that dehumanised Muslims as a 'suspect community'.[4] Furthermore, it has (mis)informed specific government programmes and perspectives on 'de-radicalisation'. In order to challenge this trend and contribute to current debates on radicalisation, CTS has suggested the following: to explore alternative frameworks for understanding contemporary forms and processes of radical – violent and non-violent – activism; to strive towards a discourse within which real and perceived threats to security might be identified and better understood; and, hence, to provide an imminent critique of the way in which the term 'radicalisation' is used in the literature.[5]

In this chapter, I offer an alternative definition of radicalisation with reference to an example of ethno-nationalism (Kurdish nationalism), and the rise of political violence (PKK terrorism). The socio-political causality between ethnicity and violence are intensively studied with reference to nationalism, but neither theoretical debates nor empirical studies formulate a comprehensive definition of 'ethnic radicalisation'.[6] In twenty-first-century politics, while ethnicity is generally coupled with nationalism,[7] radicalisation is usually associated with Islam and Muslims.[8] This chapter argues that these mono-causal approaches to radicalisation, significant and interesting as they are, often miss the complexity of the relationship between Islam, radicalisation, ethnic nationalism and identity.

To begin with, 'identity' is under-theorised in existing debates and prevailing theories of radicalisation studies.[9] While I cannot develop fully in this chapter why a critical engagement with identity has been so conspicuously missing in the studies of radicalisation, the analysis of this research shows from a socio-historical perspective that identity politics is the best point of departure in establishing the link between ethnicity, religion and radicalisation. In particular, *'ethnies'* (ethnic communities) are 'named human populations with shared ancestry myths, histories and cultures, having an association with a specific territory and a sense of solidarity'.[10] The identity dimension of ethnicity has been at the centre of sociological concerns:

> An 'ethnic group' refers to those human groups that entertain to subjective belief in their common descent...this belief must be important for the propagation of group formation: conversely, it does not matter whether or not an objective blood relationship exists. Ethnic membership (*Gemeinsamkeit*) differs from the kinship group precisely by being a *presumed identity* .... (emphasis is mine)[11]

In Weberian parlance, 'the sentiment of ethnic solidarity' by itself does not always lead to the process of constructing a 'nation'.[12] Ethnicity is related to a complex web of socio-historical characteristics. Ethnic identity is not the only factor but one among many, which can act as social cement to form national unity. Religion, culture, language, history, homeland and national myths are all commonly employed by nationalist ideologies; so, the existence of an ethnic group itself is not sufficient to claim nationhood and statehood.[13] For example, the ethnic origins of Turks were discursively transmitted towards imagining a homogenous Turkish nation whereas the same cannot be claimed in the case of Kurds. Furthermore, the search for nationhood and the radicalisation of Kurds overlap at the centre of identity politics.

According to Tarik Fraihi, radicalisation refers to a process when 'an individual's convictions and willingness to seek for deep and serious changes in the society increase'.[14] Being 'radical' does not necessarily have negative connotations. In the *Oxford English Dictionary*, the first three descriptions of 'radical' indicate the following: 1) relating to or affecting the fundamental nature of something; 2) advocating thorough political or social reform; politically extreme; 3) departing from tradition; innovative or progressive. When individuals act as agents of changes – radical or not – they can contribute to the progress of society. In the main literature, the term radicalisation is described as 'a process of personal development whereby an individual adopts ever more extreme political or politico-religious ideas and goals, becoming convinced that the attainment of these goals justifies extreme methods'.[15] Nevertheless, the positive implications of being radical were overshadowed by the September 2001 and July 2005 terror attacks and the definition of 'radicalisation' shifted to the negative connotations that highlight the violent nature of radical Islam.

Despite this alarming evolution, radicalisation is still a 'marginal phenomenon'.[16] Radicalisation should not be seen as a natural product of Islam's violent characteristics but that of specific historical, social and political causes. The following three types of radicalisation are particularly relevant to this research: political Islam, radical Islamic Puritanism and ethno-centric radicalisation.

First, political Islam or Islamism as an ideology refers to the use and abuse of religion for ideological causes.[17] Islam as a belief system is presented as a monolithic and homogenous entity despite all its complexities, contradictions and cultural differences in the Middle East, Africa, Asia and Asia Pacific. Hence, Islam as a monolithic identity is seen as a violent religion. This was partially the product of the misjudgements of the radical Islamists of the New York, Washington and London attacks, who confused political Islam as a modern ideology with Islam as faith by judging the use of religion as advantageous to their cause against the West. Islam as the primary referent of violence and radicalisation in theory and praxis has become the primary focus of the Western media.[18]

Second, 'radical Islamic Puritanism' differs from political Islam by a strong emphasis on returning to a 'pure' or 'fundamental' Islam. The search for 'pure' religion is not necessarily negative, but indicates distancing oneself from outside influences and society in a puritanical way. Nevertheless, this type of radicalisation creates serious problems when it is accompanied by intolerance towards 'Others' (including people of the same faith).[19]

Third, ethnic radicalisation is a particularly important way to understand the differences between religious and ethno-national causes of the radicalisation process. In this process, 'ethnicisation' indicates an increasing solidarity with the 'imagined community' that is constructed as a nation and in which the collective identity formation is based on the negation of 'Others'.[20] The notion of others can sometimes include people who belong to the same religion (as in the case of Kurds and Turks who are both Sunni Muslims in Turkey). Islam as a religion is not the cause of the radicalisation process but being a Muslim and showing solidarity with the *umma* (religious community) support the radicalisation of an individual or ethnic group. Nevertheless, it is important to highlight that those who belong to a specific ethnic group, which is marginalised and suppressed by the majority, can be radicalised along the lines of ethno-nationalism, not necessarily religion, i.e. Islam. One can have both 'Muslim and secular' identities as in the example of Turkey.[21] Even if one disregards the theoretical separation between religion and nationalism in general by accepting the existence of 'religious nationalism', Mark Juergensmeyer's arguments seem to be convincing. As he points out, the issues of minority rights and the assertion of identities are not 'peculiar to religious nationalists; they are fundamental problems in secular societies as well. In fact, secular nationalism is unable to deal easily with any kind of collective identity except those defined by geography'.[22]

In light of these theoretical concerns, the radicalisation of Kurds and the rise of PKK terrorism in Turkey provide an interesting case study to challenge the common understandings of the 'radicalisation' process in an Islamic society. The majority of debates in the literature focus on Kurdish nationalism, Kurdish terrorism and its impacts on Turkey-EU relations, but none offer a comprehensive study of the correlation between ethnicity, identity, radicalisation and violence.[23] Furthermore, in some of the most recent research,[24] the social correlation between identity and radicalisation is examined with reference to British Muslims. Although there is no direct reference to ethnicity, the following five key points are important for the analysis on this chapter even though they are drawn from the British experience:

1. the path to radicalisation often involves a search for identity at a moment of crisis;
2. underlying the identity crisis is a sense of not being accepted or belonging to society;
3. as part of this process, individuals seek to construct a sense of what it means to be Muslim in Britain today;
4. a lack of religious literacy and education appears to be a common feature among those that are drawn to such groups; and
5. the discourse of 'European/British-Islam' is emerging as a powerful response to 'radical Islam'.[25]

The first two points are particularly relevant to the empirical study of Kurds: a search for identity and constructing an alternative sense of belonging at a moment of identity crisis. It is also crucial to understand how the forces of assimilation, discrimination, racism and a sense of blocked social mobility reinforce the intensity of the identity crisis. Under these circumstances, individuals might be radicalised while in their search for identity to resolve the crisis of not belonging to a larger ethnic group. If they are included in a homogenised society the search remains at individual, cultural and non-violent level of crisis. However, if they experience the politics of assimilation, exclusion and the denial of identity as imposed by state ideology and hegemonic discourses, individuals either alone or collectively (for example, Kurds in Turkey) tend to become radicalised.

For theoretical clarification, I suggest the following working definition: 'ethnic radicalisation' is a socio-historical process with consequent political behaviour, whereby members of an ethnic group (acting individually or collectively) become convinced of the need to improve their social, cultural and political position within the existing *status quo* and take action to achieve this.[26] The next section engages with the historical context of ethnic radicalisation of Kurds and how they resist the hegemonic discourses of the Turkish state.

Kurds as a Stateless Nation and Hegemonic Discourses

In the contemporary Middle East, Kurds are the largest stateless nation, divided along the borders of Turkey, Iraq, Syria and Iran after the collapse of the Ottoman Empire. There is, however, no ethnic unity among Kurds. Historically, the traditional Ottoman identity was based on the *millet* (religious community) system, characterised by the religious autonomy of different groups rather than ethnic ties or language.[27] Each religious group was allowed free practice of its religion. Muslim *millets* of the Empire (Turks, Kurds and Arabs) were differentiated from non-Muslim *millets* (Christians – Greeks and Armenians – and Jews) but there was no official differentiation within the Muslim *millet* by ethnicity or language. In contrast to Greeks and Armenians who were separated by their internal differences, Turks, Arabs and Kurds were united as one within the Muslim *umma* (religious community). Kurds as part of Muslim subjects of the Ottoman *Millet* system did not ethnically distinguish themselves from Turks. Within the unity of Islam and the modernising reforms of the Ottoman Empire during the nineteenth century, the use of the Kurdish language was not banned and the first book comprised of poetry in Arabic, Persian and Kurdish was published in Istanbul in 1844.[28] The first Kurdish newspaper, called *Kurdistan*, was published in Cairo as a bilingual Kurdish-Ottoman paper in April 1898.[29] Under Ottoman rule, about 20 books were published in Kurdish between 1844 and 1923.[30] When the Ottoman army was defeated during the World War I, the Kurdish notables in Istanbul established their organisations as a response to the weakness of the Turks. The idea of Muslim solidarity united Kurds with Turks against the Christian Greeks and Armenians to defend the empire during the World War I. Almost half of the Kurdish books published during the Ottoman era materialised in 1918–19. The press and printed work are important not only for a standardisation of a language but also for the spreading of nationalist ideas. Ekrem Cemilpasa was the first Kurdish nationalist who bought a printing house in Diyarbekir and published the *Gazi* newspaper in 1918.[31]

The Kurds in Anatolia supported the Turkish nationalist movement under the leadership of Mustafa Kemal, rather than fighting for the Kurdish independence and eventually a Kurdish state, for three main reasons. It was initially believed that the Kemalist movement aimed to save the Ottoman state and preserve the caliphate. Hence, there was no discussion or vision of replacing the Ottoman Empire with a new Turkish Republic based on a homogenised nation under the hegemony of Turks. Second, Kurds were told that Turkish nationalists were determined to preserving the unity of eastern Anatolia – the Ottoman Kurdistan – and to recovering the *vilayet* (province) of oil-rich Mosul (considered by Kurds today to be part of present-day Iraqi Kurdistan) from enemies. Third, Mustafa Kemal as the charismatic leader of the Turkish nationalist movement emphasised the importance of Turkish-Kurdish brotherhood in a series of declarations and diplomatic communications.[32] Consequently, Kurdish tribes and sheikhs opted for the alliance with Turks in order to protect the empire and the homeland of Kurds and Turks rather than aiming for Kurdish nationalism and an independent state.

The Ottoman Empire lost the World War I and one of the most important impacts of the empire's collapse was that the idea of *Kurdistan* was revisited. For the first time, Kurds were introduced to the idea of nationalism via Woodrow Wilson's famous 14 points, one of which recognised the self-determination of 'minorities' living in Ottoman lands.[33] In 1920, the Treaty of Sevres promised an independent Kurdish state: the territory known as Kurdistan, east of the Euphrates, was to gain autonomy with the right to opt for independence within a year if the Kurds wished (Articles 62 to 64) while an independent Armenian state was recognised in Eastern Anatolia, with its borders to be demarcated by arbitration on the part of President Wilson (Article 83 to 93).[34] The promised land for a Kurdish state would reflect the area of the ancient Kurdistan, which dates back as far as the third millennium BC. The Treaty of Sevres was never ratified, hence, neither an Armenian nor a Kurdish state in Eastern Anatolia was implemented.

In 1923, the declaration of the Republic of Turkey and the Treaty of Lausanne a year later invalidated the promises of a free Kurdistan. While northern Kurdistan remained within the borders of new Turkey the British established control in southern Kurdistan and French in western Kurdistan. Despite the diplomatic efforts of the Kemalist group, the new Turkish state was compelled to accept the annexation of the oil-rich Kurdish *vilayet* of Mosul to Iraq then under the British mandate. With the decolonisation of the Middle East after the Second World War the borders were re-drawn and the Kurdish area was divided among Turkey, Iraq, Iran and Syria (see Map 2). To this day there is no official and authoritative source on the distribution of the Kurdish population in the Middle East.

Kurds constitute approximately 23 per cent of Turkey's population, 20 per cent of that in Iraq, 15 per cent in Iran and 9 per cent in Syria.[35] Demographic and linguistic unity, which usually plays a key role in nation-building, is lacking among Kurds (see Map 2). Kurdish

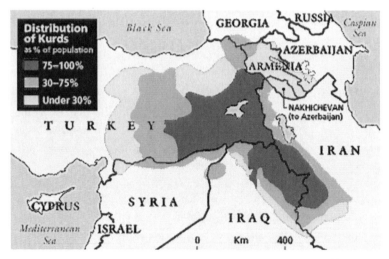

Map 2: Demographic distribution of Kurds in the Middle East[36]

is generally accepted to stem from the Indo-Iranian branch of the 'Indo-European' language group[37] but it is divided into three major dialects – *Kurmanci*, spoken in Turkey and Syria, *Sorani* in Iraq and *Zaza* in Iran.[38] There is little religious unity among Kurds, not only due to the major division between Sunni and Shi'a Islam but also due to the existence of Jewish, Christian, Alevi and Yazidi sects.[39] Hence, the 'imagination' of a Kurdish nation based on ethnicity has been historically disadvantaged due to a lack of a united language, religion, homeland, publications or a charismatic leader.[40] Kurds have been not only the *object of* historical imperial designs but also *subject to* modern assimilation policies of strong nationalist states – Turkey, Iran, Iraq and Syria.[41]

Paradoxically, Kurds are historically one of the oldest indigenous people of the Middle East but still an 'invisible' nation in the twenty-first century.[42] Under these historical and socio-political circumstances Kurds are a stateless nation and they continue the search for the recognition of Kurdish identity. The subsequent political destiny of Kurds led to different paths in parallel with political developments in Turkey, Iraq, Iran and Syria, and the next section focuses on Turkey.

Three Phases of Ethnic Radicalisation of Kurds in Turkey

After the establishment of the Republic of Turkey the Turkish state exercised even greater restriction on languages than the Ottoman Empire. The idea of creating an independent Kurdish state at the expense of Turkey's territorial integrity was perceived a real threat and this influenced the way in which the Turkish state constituted its hegemonic discourses. The aim of these discourses was to deny Kurdish existence, language and identity since the 1920s. To begin with, the new state was called the Republic of Turkey, which indicated the ethno-cultural identity of the Turkish majority and the implicit denial of other identities, such as Kurds, Lazis and Alevis. In the following years, the Kurdish ethnicity, including identity, language and culture, was suppressed in three phases of new policies and discourses between the 1920s and the 1990s: the politics of denial and resistance; the quiet assimilation of Kurds; and the decades of silence and oppression of Kurdish cultural rights. It was the establishment of the

PKK as a Marxist-Leninist terrorist organisation and the resurgence of political violence that led to the recognition of the 'Kurdish question' in the 1990s after the then president, Suleyman Demirel, spoke of a 'Kurdish reality' in the 1991.

The first phase was shaped in the early stages of Turkish state-building during the 1920s and the 1930s. It was based on the politics of 'denial and resistance'.[43] Under the Ottoman rule, a few Kurdish newspapers and magazines were banned for political reasons but the Kurdish language was not banned after the Young Turk Revolution in 1908. However, with the establishment of the Turkish Republic in 1923 all references to 'Kurdistan', where Kurds lived under the Ottoman rule, were extracted from official documents and maps. In 1924, the use of the Kurdish language, traditional Kurdish dress and music was forbidden. Kurds responded to this systematic erasure and the suppression of difference through local uprisings. Sheikh Said-i Nursi led the most famous revolt in 1925. The uprising was savagely suppressed and its leader, who was subsequently elevated into a religious symbol and hero among Kurds, was hanged. Subsequent Kurdish uprisings in 1927–30 in Dersim and in 1936–38 were again forcefully suppressed. During this period, martial law was imposed in the Kurdish region and thousands of Kurds were killed or subjected to forced displacement.[44] Nevertheless, it was not the aim of these early Kurdish insurgencies to gain independence or create separatist ethnic nationalism. They were against the state's suppression of difference and the erasure of their cultural history, language and identity. In addition, Kurds were not content with the secularisation policies of Turkish state-builders under the banner of Kemalism. They particularly rejected the idea of translating the Arabic call-for-prayers into the Turkish language.[45] Afterwards, the construction of hegemonic discourses determined Turkey's policies towards the denial of the existence of Kurds in Turkey. As explained earlier with reference to the discursive link between identity and radicalisation, the denial of identity, minority language and belonging to a forcefully 'assimilated' ethnic group often leads to radicalisation. The Kurdish insurgencies and revolts of the 1920s were a response to the denial of the existence of Kurdish language and identity.

In the 1930s, a new period of 'quiet assimilation' of Kurds and Kurdish identity started. It was part of the Turkish nation-building project that assumed the complete homogenisation of the population (Turks and Kurds) in Anatolia. The Turkish state developed the official theories of the 'Turkish History thesis' and the 'Sun-Language theory', which claimed that the crucial stage of the nationalist project was the homogenisation of all Muslims within the borders of the Turkish state into a new concept of citizenship. In the official state ideology, every 'citizen' was officially a Turk. The sense of 'Turkishness' was represented as an identity of choice and it was commonly associated with 'modernity, progress, and pride' in the achievement of the young Turks.[46] For example, the tenth anniversary of the Turkish Republic was concluded by Atatürk's famous phrase, which became the official motto of Turkish nationalism: *'Ne mutlu Türküm diyene!'* [Happy is one who calls oneself a Turk!]. The interpretation of this phrase, however, varies depending on how ethnicity and identity is understood. One leading sociologist, Metin Heper, denies the forced assimilation of Kurds on the basis that Turkey is a Jacobinist 'state-nation' rather than a 'nation-state'. The notion of 'state-nation' indicates the civic character of Turkish nationalism that rejects the existence of a hegemonic ethnic community. The consequences of this have been the absence of 'forceful assimilation' of Kurds and other ethnic minorities.[47] However, from the perspective of Kurdish scholars, the Turkish nationalist discourse as encapsulated in the official motto was based on the homogenisation of people that implied mass deportations (Greeks, Armenians, Assyrians) and forced assimilation (Kurds and Alevis) in order to create a homogenous Turkish nation.[48]

The third phase of Kurdish radicalisation was a consequence of three 'decades of silence' between the late-1930s and the 1960s. The nationalist ideology of the Turkish state served to reproduce a hegemonic discourse and self-censorship that highlighted 'the *mission civilisatrice of* Kemalist nation-building'[49] and the personality cult of Mustafa Kemal (Atatürk) as the leader of Turks and Kurds within the borders of the Republic of Turkey. After the last Kurdish rebellion in the 1930s, it was forbidden to even mention the words 'Kurd', 'Kurdish' and 'Kurdistan'.[50] Although everyone in public and political realms knew that Kurds existed in the country, the existence of a Kurdish minority was not to be openly spoken of as a 'social reality'.[51] Instead, a complete denial of Kurdish identity took place not only on a discursive level but also at the political level. All references to Kurds and Kurdishness were deliberatively avoided in official documents and in the media.

In the early 1960s, the Kurdish people began to emerge from the 'decades of silence' but their struggle for recognition did not become radical and violent until 1974.[52] During the 1960s, a number of Kurdish intellectuals published a few short-lived journals that focused on the problems of the 'East' (the current euphemism for Kurdistan in Turkey) and occasionally used Kurdish words. Avoiding explicit nationalism, these publications demonstrated an awareness of the Kurds as a distinct group with a distinct ethnic identity and interests, which in itself was felt as a threat to the state. These publications were banned and editors punished, but new publications kept appearing. The Turkish sociologist Ismail Beşikçi published studies of contemporary Kurdish society, the first writings in Turkey to openly mention the Kurds and to speak of 'national oppression'.[53] In the realm of public discourse, 'Kurdishness' as anything related to Kurds and Kurdistan had become taboo and Turkish governments carefully avoided engaging with the Kurdish issue as a social reality.

The non-violent phase of Kurdish radicalisation was ended with the establishment of the PKK group in 1974.[54] This was a response to earlier politics of the quiet assimilation of Kurds during which the Kurds were declared to be of the Turkic race, and the Kurdish language – *Kurmanci* – was declared a Turkish dialect with some Persian influence. While speaking Kurdish was forbidden, ethnic stereotypes and prejudice continued to exist in the dominant Turkish community towards people who spoke Turkish with the Kurdish accent of Eastern Anatolia. After the rise of PKK terrorism, the radicalisation of Kurds turned into a violent and brutal form that brought the 'Kurdish reality' to the centre of public awareness. The forceful attention drawn to the demands of Kurds led to the construction of new discourses such as the Kurdish 'question', 'issue' and 'trouble'. Despite their nuances in English all these terms were used interchangeably to describe the

Kurdish reality. Nevertheless, the term the 'Kurdish question' (*Kürt sorunu*) was preferred to the use of 'Kurdish reality' – (*Kürt gerçekliği* – in Turkish). This shows how the Turkish governments carefully avoided presenting the Kurdish question as a 'social reality' but only as a question to be resolved. The acceptance of Kurdish reality would have meant recognition of the existence and of the legitimacy of Kurdish cultural and political demands in Turkey. The Kurdish reality was recognised by the Turkish state only when Kurdish armed militias opted for the use of violence. To understand the turning point in the radicalisation process is, therefore, to understand how the aspirations of an ethnic group shifted from passive cultural demands to a violent phase, as I shall explain next.

From Non-violent Struggle to PKK Terrrorism

The early Kurdish insurgencies of Sheikh Ubeydullah of Nehri in 1880 and Sheikh Said in 1925 tend to be considered as 'tribally' and 'religiously' motivated revolts.[55] The establishment of the PKK, based on a modern Marxist-Leninist ideology, challenged the religious and tribal character of Kurdish rebellions. As Byman argues, ethnic terrorism is considerably different from the violence carried out for religious, ideological and material reasons.[56] Ethnic terrorists often aim to foster a new collective identity in opposition to an identity proposed by the state, as explained by Fraiqi's typology of radicalisation mentioned earlier.

As Martin van Bruinessen emphasises, Peter Waldman's comparative study of ethnic violence in Northern Ireland, the Basque country in Spain and the Quebec region in Canada is very useful in understanding why the process of Kurdish radicalisation changed from non-violent to violent. According to Waldman's study, the transition from non-violence to violence ethnic nationalism is usually correlated with a shift of the dominant element within the movement to another social stratum.[57] In Waldman's theory, the path to radicalisation and violence is rooted in the middle stratum of an ethnic group, the majority of whom tend to be accommodative towards central government, but which also includes a radical minority preaching violence and justice. When this minority reaches out to lower strata, which are, in Waldman's view, more capable of doing the actual fighting, the movement may enter a violent phase. In this new phase, according to Waldman, the leadership of the struggle is usually taken over by a new leader, who advocates 'revolutionary' violence as a means of social mobility.[58] The case of the PKK in Turkey supports Waldman's comparative study in three main ways.

First, the middle stratum of the Kurdish community consisted of both tribal sheiks and the accommodative majority towards the central state. During the 'decades of silence' between the 1930s and the 1960s, the middle stratum advocated cultural and socio-economic rights. However, they distanced themselves from the central government when their cultural demands were brutally repressed by the state. Consequently, this accommodative majority faded into the background and a minority of young Kurds, who came from a lower social stratum, took their place. Interestingly, the PKK was initially relatively insignificant among the rival Kurdish political organisations. The PKK achieved its hegemony over the Kurdish cause when it became the most violent of them. In particular, the PKK leaders 'combined the discourses of anti-colonialism and national liberation struggle with that of proletarian revolution, in which revolutionary violence had a central place'.[59]

Second, the radical turn in making the Kurdish movement more violent took place when the minority reached to lower strata by preaching violence for justice and equality under the new leadership of Abdullah Öcalan. The founders of PKK were well-educated Ankara University students from lower class backgrounds. They combined the ideologies of anti-colonialism and nationalism with that of Marxism, in which revolutionary violence had a central place. Its leaders identified the PKK with anti-tribal ideology and refrained from playing some tribes off against others for the benefit of the party. They consistently advocated the progress of minority rights and of ethnically pluralistic Kurdistan. Therefore, the Marxist-oriented PKK leaders identified two enemies which had to be defeated: the Turkish state and its coercive force was the 'enemy outside', while the backward-oriented tribal sheikhs, who either collaborated with the state or acted in their own interests, were the 'enemy within'. From the year of its establishment in 1974 to its first terrorist attack in 1984, almost all its guerrilla wars targeted other Kurdish rival organisations and 'collaborators' or 'traitors'. In order to establish the PKK as the only legitimate representative of the Kurdish cause, it deliberately used violence against fellow Kurds that would invite further state repression in the Kurdish areas. Despite the brutality of their methods, the PKK managed to make uneducated peasants aware of their 'Kurdishness' and create a resurgence of Kurdish nationalism at the expense of the 'radicalisation' of the movement.[60] Hence, the case of the PKK does not neatly fit into the category of traditional tribal or religious violence but is rather 'ethnic terrorism'.

The third factor was the revolutionary force of a new leadership that shifted from the urban elite to another social stratum when Abdullah Öcalan, a student of political science in Ankara University, escaped to Syria where he established contacts with Palestinian circles and received guerrilla training in Lebanon. Almost all scholars agree about the importance of the leadership role and extent of the 'determinability' and 'indispensability' of Öcalan.[61] Many young males from a low socio-economic stratum and with few prospects in life joined the PKK as a result of sweeping counterinsurgency operations, violence by paramilitary groups and successful guerrilla operations that demonstrated the insurgency's strength.[62] As Walkman argued, the change took place after a new type of leader, for whom revolutionary violence was acceptable and implied social mobility, replaced the leadership. This was particularly noticeable in the case of young Kurdish women, who were radicalised and joined the organisation to escape from a patriarchal social order and overcome feelings of powerlessness and marginalisation in a patriarchal society.[63]

Between 1979 and 1999 the Kurdish movement changed its character from being tribal and religious in the 1920s to becoming national and radical under Öcalan's leadership. While the minority of young Kurds were radicalised, the majority of ordinary Kurds were subjected to the asymmetrical use of violence by both the PKK and the Turkish state. During the 1990s, the state repression of Kurdish cultural rights and ethnic identity continuously reinforced the process of systematic radicalisation and anti-state violence. In 1999, the

PKK leader Öcalan was captured and sentenced to death. However, far from ending Turkey's Kurdish problem, Öcalan's capture led to a new process of discursive bargaining, the so-called democratic engagement (*demokratik açilim*) between the state and many of its citizens of Kurdish ethnic origin, represented by the radicalised members of the PKK and Kurdish political parties, in particular HADEP (the Peoples Democratic Party) and DTP (Democratic Society Party).

Meanwhile, in the denial of Kurdish ethnic identity, the Turkish state and its silent assimilation strategies were supported by three subtle legal restrictions. First, as regulated by provisions 68 and 69 of the 1982 Constitution and the Political Parties Law of 1983, regulations concerning the formation, activities, supervision and dissolution of political parties stipulated that such organisations must not support the existence of any minorities based on class or sect within the territory of the Turkish Republic, as this would undermine the 'national and territorial unity' of the state.[64] Second, the infamous Article 301 of the Turkish Penal Code notoriously made subsequent verbal or written support for Kurdish rights grounds for being charged with 'provoking hatred or animosity between groups of different race, religion, region or social class'. The Kurdish novelist Yaşar Kemal, and later the Nobel Prize winner Orhan Pamuk, were charged with 'thought crime' for violating Article 301 in 2005. Third, according to Article 8 of the anti-terror law (*Terorle Mucadele Yasasi*), written and oral propaganda and assemblies, meetings and demonstrations aimed at damaging the indivisible unity of the Turkish Republic with its 'territory' and 'nation' were prohibited, regardless of the methods, intentions and ideas behind such activities.

Under these provisions, any citizen of the Turkish Republic can be imprisoned for accepting the existence of a separate ethnic identity and advocating a political solution to the Kurdish problem – and many have been. In December 2009, the Constitutional Court decided to close down the pro-Kurdish Democratic Society Party (DTP) for its alleged links with the outlawed PKK. The Court declared that actions and statements made by the party became a focal point for terrorism against the 'indivisible integrity' of the state, as regulated by Articles 68 and 69 of the Constitution and the Political Parties Law. Hence, the invisible Kurdish nation poses a real threat to the indivisible integrity of the Turkish state – governments in Ankara remain suspicious of anything related to Kurdishness that could lead to the establishment of a 'free Kurdish' state at the expense of its territorial integrity.

The Search for a Viable Solution: Democratic Engagement

The Kurdish path to radicalisation and the subsequent rise of PKK terrorism were shaped by the repressive policies and hegemonic discourse of the authoritarian state which refused to accommodate ethnic diversity in Turkey. As Fanon remarked: 'History teaches us clearly that the battle against colonialism does not always run straight away along the lines of nationalism'.[65] The resistance of Kurds against colonialism and the hegemonic discourses of the Turkish state were reinforced by the rise of Kurdish nationalism. The subsequent policies of the Turkish state based on their 'assimilation' and the denial of Kurdish ethnic identity led to radicalisation and violence. Thus the rise of PKK terrorism did not run straight away along the lines of Kurdish nationalism and Kurdish demands for cultural rights.

This chapter has sought to offer a new definition of radicalisation in relation to ethnicity and identity as 'ethnic radicalisation'. It identified the multi-causality of Kurdish radicalisation and examined the relationship between ethno-nationalism and political violence. It then critically explored how 'ethnic radicalisation' led to the rise of PKK terrorism. Its theoretical argument was based on the iron triangle of historical, sociological and political concerns. Theoretically, it challenged the generalised definitions of radicalisation by differentiating between 'religious' and 'ethnic' forms. Historically, it examined how and why the denial of non-violent (cultural) demands of an ethnic group might lead some individuals into the path of radicalisation. Sociologically, it explored the complex interdependency between the process of radicalisation, ethnicity and identity politics in a specific society. Politically, it explained why the failure of hegemonic discourses of the state to entirely eradicate counter-hegemonic narratives and its corresponding policies contributed towards transforming the Kurdish movement from non-violence to terrorism.

Its findings also reinforce the key theoretical assumptions of CTS. The Kurdish question shows that Islam is not necessarily the main cause of either radicalisation or violent terrorism. The forces of ethnic nationalism, with its separatist tendencies and identity politics, can be stronger than religious causes. In a similar vein, the debates over the 'silent assimilation' of Kurds in Turkey and PKK terrorism feed directly into twenty-first century identity politics and the Turkish government's policy of 'democratic engagement'. As argued in this chapter, the historicised and contextualised analysis of the Kurdish radicalisation and the rise of PKK terrorism overlap with the search for non-violent solutions and, therefore, democratic engagement is the acid test of Turkish democracy. Politically, it is still too early to predict whether a democratic solution to the Kurdish question can be found, based on the experiences of Irish, Basque and Québec precursors. It is paradoxically too late to acknowledge the relationship between radicalisation, terrorism and the denial of ethnicity and identity. After all, these ethnic conflicts overlap on the same crucial dimension of identity politics: to be Irish is not to be English; to be Basque is not to be Spanish and to be Kurdish is not to be Turkish. Hence, suppressing the expression of ethnic minority rights and identities in undemocratic ways is more likely to lead to further radicalisation, violent insurgency and terrorism in the Middle East of the twenty-first century.

Notes

1. Fanon, F. 2001. *The Wretched of the Earth*, p.119.
2. Lawrence, Q. 2008. *Invisible Nation: How the Kurds' Quest for Statehood Is Shaping Iraq and the Middle East*, p.12.
3. Jackson, R., Breen-Smyth, M., and Gunning, J. (eds.) 2009. *Critical Terrorism Studies: A New Research Agenda*.
4. Breen-Smyth, M. 2009. 'Subjectivities, "Suspect Communities", Governments, and the Ethics of Research on "Terrorism"', in Jackson, R., Breen-Smyth, M., and Gunning, J. (eds.) *Critical Terrorism Studies: A New Research Agenda*, pp.194–215.
5. See the CSRV Conferences on 'Religion, Radicalisation and Terror', University of Wales, Aberystwyth, Saturday 26 November 2005; 'The Politics of Radicalisation: Reframing the Debate and Reclaiming the

Language', London Muslim Centre, Whitechapel: Thursday 18 October 2007.

6. Tezcür, G.M. 2009. 'When Democratization Radicalizes: The Kurdish Nationalist Movement in Turkey', *Journal of Peace Research* (forthcoming) Annual Meeting of the American Political Science Association; Koutroubas, T., Vloeberghs, W., and Yanasmayan, Z. 2009. *Political, Religious and Ethnic Radicalisation among Muslims in Belgium,* MICROCON Policy, Working Paper 5; Emerson, M. (ed.) 2009. *Ethno-Religious Conflict in Europe: Typologies of Radicalisation in Europe's Muslim Communities.*

7. Smith, A.D. 1983. *Theories of Nationalism*; Smith, A.D. 1991. *National Identity*; Greenfeld, L. 1995. *Nationalism: Five Roads to Modernity*; McCrone, D. 1998. *The Sociology of Nationalism.*

8. Emerson, op.cit.

9. McLoughlin, S. 2002. *Representing Muslims: Ethnicity, Religion and the Politics of Identity*; Faas, D. 2009. 'Reconsidering Identity: The Ethnic and Political Dimension of Hybridity among Majority and Turkish Youth in Germany and England', *British Journal of Sociology*, 60 (2), pp.299–320; Stolz, J. 2009. 'Explaining Religiosity: Towards a Unified Theoretical Model', *British Journal of Sociology* 60 (2).

10. Smith, A.D. 1998. *Nationalism and Modernism*, p.191.

11. Weber, M. 1968 [1920]. *Economy and Society,* vol.1, eds. Roth, G., and Wiitich, C., p.389.

12. Ibid., p.923.

13. Breuilly, J. 1999, 'Nationalism and Modernity', in Müller, J.U., and Stråth, B. (eds.) *Nationalism and Modernity*, EUI Working Paper HEC No.99/1, p.192; Romano, D. 2006. *Kurdish Nationalist Movement: Opportunity, Mobilisation and Identity,* p.5; Giddens, A. 1993. *Modernity and Self-Identity: Self and Society in the Late Modern Age*, pp.15–16.

14. Fraihi, T. 2008. '(De-)Escalating Radicalisation: The Debate within Muslim and Immigrant Communties', in Coolsaet, R. (ed.) *Jihadi Terrorism and the Radicalisation Challenge in Europe*, p.135.

15. Graff, B. de. 2007. 'The Risks of the (Overly?) Broad-Based Approach in Dutch Counterterrorism Policy' in *Radicalisation in Broader Perspective*, pp.14–21. Netherlands: The National Coordinator for Counterterrorism, p.50.

16. Fraihi, op.cit., p.132.

17. Roy, O. 2001. *The Failure of Political Islam.*

18. Said, E.W. 1997. *Covering Islam: How the Media and the Experts Determine How We See the Rest of the World.*

19. Fraihi, op.cit., p.135.

20. Ibid., p.136; Anderson, B. 1991. *Imagined Communities: Reflections on the Origin and Spread of Nationalism.*

21. Göl, A. 2009. 'The Identity of Turkey: Muslim and Secular', *Third World Quarterly*, 30 (4), pp.795–811.

22. Juergensmeyer, M. 1993. *The New Cold War? Religious Nationalism Confronts the Secular State.*

23. Kirisci, K., and Winrow, G.M. 1997. *The Kurdish Question and Turkey: An Example of a Trans-state Ethnic Conflict*; Besikci, I. 2004. *International Colony Kurdistan*; Yıldız, K. 2004. *The Kurds in Iraq: The Past, Present and Future*; Özcan, A.K. 2006. *Turkey's Kurds: A Theoretical Analysis of the PKK and Abdullah Öcalan*; Jaber, F.A., and Dawod, H. (eds.) 2006. *The Kurds: Nationalism and Politics*; Ahmed, M.M.A., and Gunter, M.M. (eds.) 2007. *The Evolution of Kurdish Nationalism*; Lundgren, A. 2007. *The Unwelcome Neighbour: Turkey's Kurdish Policy*; Olson, R. 2009. *Blood, Beliefs and Ballots: The Management of Kurdish Nationalism in Turkey, 2007–2009*; Marcus, A. 2009. *Blood and Belief: The PKK and the Kurdish Fight for Independence.*

24. Modood, T. 2003. 'Muslims and the Politics of Difference', *Political Quarterly* 74(1), p.100.

25. Choudhury, T. 2007. *The Role of Muslim Identity Politics in Radicalisation (A Study in Progress).* Communities and Local Government: London. Accessed 18 July 2010,

26. http://www.communities.gov.uk/documents/communities/pdf/452628.pdf.

27. I am grateful to Marie Breen-Smyth for her contributions to this working definition of radicalisation.

28. The Ottoman Empire was a multi-religious, multi-lingual, multi-cultural but not multi-national empire, as we understand it in modern terms. The usage of 'nation' for millet misrepresents its religious connotation. The number of millets changed throughout Ottoman history. New millets were created as a consequence of pressure from the European great powers. For instance, while there were nine recognised millets, of which six were fairly large in 1875 there were seventeen in 1914.

29. Malmisanij, M. 2006. *The Past and Present of Book Publishing in Kurdish Language in Syria,* Next Page Foundation. http://www.npage.org/IMG/pdf/Syria.pdf, p.17.

30. http://imld.i-iter.org/en/content/the-first-kurdish-newspaper-published-on-thursday-22st-of-april-1898, accessed 18 July 2010.

31. Malmisanij, op.cit., p.18.

32. Ibid., p.17.

33. Bozarslan, H. 2003. 'Some remarks on Kurdish Historiographical Discourse in Turkey (1919–1980)', in Vali, A. (ed.) *Essays on the Origins of Kurdish Nationalism*, p.41.

34. Zubaida, S. 2006. 'Religion and Ethnicity as Polticised Boundaries', in Jabar, F.A., and Dawod, H. (eds.) *The Kurds: Nationalism and Politics*, p.106.

35. Göl, A. 2005. 'Imagining Turkish Nation through 'Othering' the Armenians', *Nations and Nationalism*, 11(1), pp.121–139.

36. Vali, A. 2006. 'The Kurds and Their "Others": Fragmented Identity and Fragmented Politics', in Jabar, F.A., and Dawod, H. (eds.) *The Kurds: Nationalism and Politics,* op.cit., p.53.

37. McDowall, D. 1997. *A Modern History of Kurds,* p.3; Bruinessesn, M. Van. 1999. 'The Nature and the Uses of Violence in the Kurdish Conflict', paper presented at *The International Colloquium, Ethnic Construction and Political Violence* 2–3 July 1999, p.15; Romano, op.cit., p.3.

38. Russell D. Gray's the Anatolian Farmers theory of Indo-European origin claims that 'Indo-European languages expanded with the spread of agriculture from Anatolia around 8,000–9,500 years BP' (Gray, R.D., and Atkinson, Q.D. 2003, p.435). Gray's origins of English language theory also supports the historical existence of pre-Islamic Kurdish and Armenian language and ethnic groups in Anatolia before the arrival of the Seljuk Turks in the eleventh century.

39. Kreyenbrock, P.G., and Allison, C. 1996. *Kurdish Culture and Identity*, p.10; Malmisanij, op.cit., p.4.

40. Yıldız (2004) argues that there are believed to be over 15 million Kurds in Turkey; 7 million in Iran; over 1 million in Syria, pp.8–9.

41. Halliday, F. 2006. 'Can We Write a Modernist History of Kurdish Nationalism?' in Jabar, F.A., and Dawod, H. (eds.) *The Kurds: Nationalism and Politics*, p.15.

42. The estimated demographic distribution of Kurds in the Middle East,

43. www.mapcruzin.com/ free-kurdistan-maps.htm, accessed 23 January 2010.

44. Iraq was ruled by the Ottoman Empire from the sixteenth century to 1918. The Ottoman administrative system was based on the division of three vilayets (provinces): Mosul in the north with Kurdish majority, Baghdad in the centre with Sunni Arabs and Basra in the South with Shiite Arabs. Great Britain became the mandatory power in Iraq in 1920. Although Iraq became an independent nation-state in 1932 Britain remained a dominant power until the overthrow of the Hashemite monarchy by the nationalist General Qasim in 1958. During this period, the British never advocated an independent state for the Kurds but supported Kurdish limited political autonomy and nationalist demands to a limited degree as a counterpoise to Arab nationalism and the Iraqi government in Baghdad. General Qasim was overthrown in 1963 and the Ba'ath regime was established in 1968. Saddam Hussein came to power in 1979 and stayed in power until he was overthrown by the US-led invasion of Iraq in 2003.

45. Vali, op.cit., p.52.

46. Yildiz. 2004, op.cit., p.15.

47. Heper, M. 2007. *The State and Kurds in Turkey: The Question of Assimilation*, p.148.

48. Meiselas, S. 2008. *Kurdistan: In the Shadow of History*, p.148.

49. Heper, op.cit., p.186.

50. Bozarslan 2003, op.cit., pp.14–39.

51. Taspinar, O. 2005. *Kurdish Nationalism and Political Islam in Turkey*, p.57.

52. Chaliand, G. (ed.) 1980. *People without a Country: The Kurds and Kurdistan*, p.13.

53. Searle, J.R. 1995. *The Construction of Social Reality*.

54. Watts, N.F. 2007. 'Silence and Voice: Turkish Policies and Kurdish Resistance in the Mid-20th Century', in Ahmed, M.A., and Gunter, M.M. (eds.) *The Evolution of Kurdish Nationalism*, p.53.

55. Meiselas, op.cit. p.224.

56. White, P. 2000. *Primitive Rebels or Revolutionary Modernisers? The Kurdish National Movement in Turkey*.

57. Gunter, M. 2007. 'Modern Origins of Kurdish Nationalism', in *The Evolution of Kurdish Nationalism*, op.cit., pp.78–97; Ozoglu, H. 2007. 'The Impact of Islam on Kurdish Identity Formation in the Middle East' in *The Evolution of Kurdish Nationalism*, pp.30–31.

58. Byman, D. 1998. 'The Logic of Ethnic Terrorism', *Studies in Conflict and Terrorism*, 21, pp.149–169.

59. Waldmann, P. 1989. *Ethnischer Radikalismus: Ursachen und Folgen gewaltsamer Minderheitenkonflikte*, Opladen: Westdeutscher Verlag; Bruinessen, op.cit., p.9.

60. Ibid.

61. Bruinessen, op.cit., p.10.

62. Bishku, M.B. 2007. 'The Resurgence of Kurdish Nationalism in Northern Kurdistan-Turkey from the 1970s to the Present' in *The Evolution of Kurdish Nationalism*, op.cit., pp.84–85.

63. Özcan, op.cit., p.222.

64. Romano, op.cit., pp.88–89.

65. Buldan, N. 2004. *PKK'de Kadýn Olmak* [Being a Woman in PKK].

66. Chaliand, op.cit.; Arslan, Z. 2002. 'Conflicting Paradigms: Political Rights in the Turkish Constitutional Court', *Middle East Critique* 11 (1), pp.9–25.

67. Fanin, op.cit., p.119.

Bibliography

Ahmed, M.M.A., and Gunter, M.M. (eds.) 2007. *The Evolution of Kurdish Nationalism*. Mazda Publishers: California.

Anderson, B. 1991. *Imagined Communities: Reflections on the Origin and Spread of Nationalism*. Verso: London.

Arslan, Z. 2002. 'Conflicting Paradigms: Political Rights in the Turkish Constitutional Court', *Middle East Critique*, 11 (1), pp.9–25.

Besikci, I. 2004. *International Colony Kurdistan*. Parvana: London.

Bishku, M.B. 2007. 'The Resurgence of Kurdish Nationalism in Northern Kurdistan-Turkey from the 1970s to the Present', in Ahmed, M.A., and Gunter, M.M. (eds.) *The Evolution of Kurdish Nationalism*. Mazda Publishers: California.

Bozarslan, H. 2007. 'Kurdish Nationalism under the Kemalist Republic', in Ahmed, M.A., and Gunter, M.M. (eds.) *The Evolution of Kurdish Nationalism*. Mazda Publishers: California.

—— 2003. 'Some remarks on Kurdish Historiographical Discourse in Turkey (1919–1980)', in Vali, A. (ed.) *Essays on the Origins of Kurdish Nationalism*. Mazda Publishers: California.

Breen-Smyth, M. 2009. 'Subjectivities, "Suspect Communities", Governments, and the Ethics of Research on "Terrorism"', in Jackson, R., Breen-Smyth, M., and Gunning, J. (eds.) *Critical Terrorism Studies: A New Research Agenda*. Routledge: London.

Breuilly, J. 1999. 'Nationalism and Modernity', in Müller, J.U., and Stråth, B. (eds.) *Nationalism and Modernity*. EUI Working Paper HEC No.99/1. Badia Fiesolana: San Domenico (FI).

Bruinessesn, M. van. 1999. 'The Nature and the Uses of Violence in the Kurdish Conflict'. Paper Presented at The International Colloquium, Ethnic Construction and Political Violence, 2–3 July 1999, Fondazione Giangiacomo Feltrinelli, Cortona.

Buldan, N. 2004. *PKK'de Kadýn Olmak* [Being a Woman in PKK]. Doz: Istanbul.

Byman, D. 1998. 'The Logic of Ethnic Terrorism', *Studies in Conflict and Terrorism*, 21, pp.149–169.

Chaliand, G. (ed.) 1980. *People without a Country: The Kurds and Kurdistan*. Zed Books: London.

Choudhury, T. 2007. *The Role of Muslim Identity Politics in Radicalisation (A Study in Progress)*. Communities and Local Government: London.

Emerson, M. (ed.) 2009. *Ethno-Religious Conflict in Europe: Typologies of Radicalisation in Europe's Muslim Communities*. CEPS Paperbacks: Brussels.

Faas, D. 2009. 'Reconsidering Identity: The Ethnic and Political Dimension of Hybridity among Majority and Turkish Youth in Germany and England', *British Journal of Sociology*, 60 (2), pp.299–320.

Fanon, F. 2001. *The Wretched of the Earth*. Penguin: London.

Fraihi, T. 2008. '(De-)Escalating Radicalisation: The Debate within Muslim and Immigrant Communities', in Coolsaet, R. (ed.) *Jihadi Terrorism and the Radicalisation Challenge in Europe*. Ashgate: London.

Giddens, A. 1993. *Modernity and Self-identity: Self and Society in the Late Modern Age*. Polity Press: London.

Göl, A. 2005. 'Imagining Turkish Nation through "Othering" the Armenians', *Nations and Nationalism*, 11 (1), pp.121–139.

—— 2009. 'The Identity of Turkey: Muslim and Secular', *Third World Quarterly*, 30 (4), pp.795–811.

Graff, B. de. 2007. 'The Risks of the (Overly?) Broad-Based Approach in Dutch Counter-Terrorism Policy', in *Radicalisation in Broader Perspective*. The National Coordinator for Counter-terrorism: Netherlands.

Greenfeld, L. 1995. *Nationalism: Five Roads to Modernity*. Harvard University Press: Harvard.

Gunter, M. 2007. 'Modern Origins of Kurdish Nationalism', in Ahmed, M.A., and Gunter, M.M. (eds.) *The Evolution of Kurdish Nationalism*. Mazda Publishers: California.

Halliday, F. 2006. 'Can We Write a Modernist History of Kurdish Nationalism?' in Jabar, F.A., and Dawod, H. (eds.) *The Kurds: Nationalism and Politics*. Saqi: London.

Heper, M. 2007. *The State and Kurds in Turkey: The Question of Assimilation*. Palgrave Macmillan: London.

Jaber, F.A., and Dawod, H. (eds.) 2006. *The Kurds: Nationalism and Politics*. Saqi: London.

Jackson, R., Breen-Smyth, M., and Gunning, J. 2009. *Critical Terrorism Studies: A New Research Agenda*. Routledge: London.

Juergensmeyer, M. 1993. *The New Cold War? Religious Nationalism Confronts the Secular State*. University of California Press: Berkeley.

Katzman, K. 2010. *Iraq: Politics, Elections and Benchmarks*. CRS Report for Congress.

Kirisci, K., and Winrow, G.M. 1997. *The Kurdish Question and Turkey: An Example of a Trans-state Ethnic Conflict*. Frank Cass: London.

Koutroubas, T., Vloeberghs, W., and Yanasmayan, Z. 2009. *Political, Religious and Ethnic Radicalisation among Muslims in Belgium*. MICROCON Policy, Working Paper 5, MICROCON: Brighton.

Kreyenbrock, P.G., and Allison, C. 1996. *Kurdish Culture and Identity*. Zed Books: London.

Krishna, S. 2009. *Globalisation and Post-colonialism: Hegemony and Resistance in the Twenty-first Century*. Rowman and Littlefield: New York.

Lawrence, Q. 2008. *Invisible Nation: How the Kurds' Quest for Statehood Is Shaping Iraq and the Middle East*. Walker and Company: London.

Lundgren, A. 2007. *The Unwelcome Neighbour: Turkey's Kurdish Policy*. I.B.Tauris: London.

Malmisanij, M. 2006. *The Past and Present of Book Publishing in Kurdish Language in Syria*. Next Page Foundation, http://www.npage.org/IMG/pdf/Syria.pdf.

Marcus, A. 2009. *Blood and Belief: The PKK and the Kurdish Fight for Independence*. New York University Press: New York.

McCrone, D. 1998. *The Sociology of Nationalism*. Routledge: London.

McDowall, D. 1997. *A Modern History of Kurds*. I.B.Tauris: London.

McLoughlin, S. 2002. *Representing Muslims: Ethnicity, Religion and the Politics of Identity.* Pluto Press: London.

Meiselas, S. 2008. *Kurdistan: In the Shadow of History.* University of Chicago Press: Chicago.

Modood, T. 2003. 'Muslims and the Politics of Difference', *Political Quarterly,* 74 (1), pp.100–115.

Olson, R. 2009. *Blood, Beliefs and Ballots: The Management of Kurdish Nationalism in Turkey, 2007–2009.* Mazda Publishers: California.

Özcan, A.K. 2006. *Turkey's Kurds: A Theoretical Analysis of the PKK and Abdullah Öcalan.* Routledge: London.

Ozoglu, H. 2007. 'The Impact of Islam on Kurdish Identity Formation in the Middle East', in Ahmed, M.A., and Gunter, M.M. (eds.) *The Evolution of Kurdish Nationalism.* Mazda Publishers: California.

Romano, D. 2006. *Kurdish Nationalist Movement: Opportunity, Mobilisation and Identity.* Cambridge University Press: Cambridge.

Roy, O. 2001. *The Failure of Political Islam.* Harvard University Press: Harvard.

Said, E.W. 1997. *Covering Islam: How the Media and the Experts Determine How We See the Rest of the World.* Vintage: London.

Searle, J.R. 1995. *The Construction of Social Reality.* Penguin: London.

Smith, A.D. 1983. *Theories of Nationalism.* Duckworth: London.

—— 1991. *National Identity.* Penguin: London.

—— 1998. *Nationalism and Modernism.* Routledge: London.

Stolz, J. 2009. 'Explaining Religiosity: Towards a Unified Theoretical Model', *British Journal of Sociology,* 60 (2), pp.345–376.

Taspinar, O. 2005. *Kurdish Nationalism and Political Islam in Turkey.* Routledge: London.

Tezcür, G.M. 2009. 'When Democratization Radicalizes: The Kurdish Nationalist Movement in Turkey', *Journal of Peace Research*, Annual Meeting of the American Political Science Association, 47 (6), pp.775–789.

Vali, A. 2006. 'The Kurds and Their 'Others': Fragmented Identity and Fragmented Politics', in Jabar, F.A., and Dawod, H. (eds.) *The Kurds: Nationalism and Politics.* Saqi: London.

Waldmann, P. 1989. *Ethnischer Radikalismus: Ursachen und Folgen gewaltsamer Minderheitenkonflikte.* Westdeutscher Verlag: Opladen.

Watts, N.F. 2007. 'Silence and Voice: Turkish Policies and Kurdish Resistance in the Mid-20th Century', in Ahmed, M.A., and Gunter, M.M. (eds.) *The Evolution of Kurdish Nationalism.* Mazda Publishers: California.

Weber, M. 1968. *Economy and Society,* vol.1. Roth, G., and Wittich, C. (eds.). Bedminster Press: New York.

White, P. 2000. *Primitive Rebels or Revolutionary Modernisers? The Kurdish National Movement in Turkey.* Zed Books: London.

Yıldız, K. 2004. *The Kurds in Iraq: The Past, Present and Future.* Pluto Books: London.

—— 2005. *The Kurds in Turkey: EU Accession and Human Rights*. Pluto Books: London.

Zubaida, S. 2006. 'Religion and Ethnicity as Polticised Boundaries', in Faleh A. Jabar, and Hosham Dawod (eds.) The Kurds: Nationalism and Politics. Saqi: London.

12

WHAT IS RADICALISM? POWER AND RESISTANCE IN IRAN

Arshin Adib-Moghaddam

My basic thesis is that today's humankind is generally incarcerated within several prisons, and naturally it becomes a true human being only if it can liberate itself from these deterministic conditions.[1]

Radical or Revolutionary?

What does it mean to be radical? In European political theory, radicalism has long been associated with leftist ideas and socialist theories. 'To be a "radical"', Anthony Giddens writes, 'was to have a certain view of the possibilities inherent in history – radicalism meant breaking away from the hold of the past.' Some radicals were immersed in the idea of revolution and many were fascinated by the possibility to bring about an entirely 'new' historical sequence. 'History was there to be seized hold of, to be moulded to human purposes,' Giddens argues, 'such that the advantages which in previous eras seemed given by God, and the prerogative of the few, could be developed and organised for the benefit of all.'[2] This definition of radical politics as a revolt against the status quo is also emphasised by Fred Halliday. Halliday focuses on revolutions more specifically when he conceptualises them as 'a break with the constraints of the past, the traditional or established society.' Revolutions made it possible to imagine 'a new society, even a new world, to be constructed. This emphasis upon breaking with the past, the creation of something new,' he continues, 'was to become a prominent strain in the appeals and self-justification of revolutions.'[3]

Both Giddens and Halliday point to an important object of radical politics: the negation of the prevalent order. When Lenin said that without theory there will be no revolutionary action, Ernesto Guevara stressed the indispensable need to explain the motives, ends and methods of the revolution in Cuba, and Marx imagined the final moment of the class struggle when everything would be decided in a momentous battle for the end of history, they alluded exactly to the necessity and possibility of a systematic confrontation with the status quo that would yield a transcendent order imagined in a largely secular sense. Yet in their many pamphlets and writings, as much as in the scholarly treatment of radical politics and revolutionary action presented by Halliday and Giddens, it does not become entirely clear what the difference between 'radical politics' and 'revolution' would be. It appears that both radicals and revolutionaries attempt to overcome what they consider to be the injustices of the respective system, but that the radical would be satisfied with radical transformation, whilst the revolutionary aims at overthrowing every political, socio-economic and cultural determination all the way down to the consciousness of the individual and all the way 'up' to the constitution of History. As Giddens puts it: 'Radicalism, taking things by the roots, meant not just bringing about change but controlling such change so as to drive history onwards.'[4] From this perspective, the radical subject retains some linkage and dependency with the prevalent order; there remains a degree of complicity with the determinations of history. He/she is a 'passive revolutionary', an agent of *transformismo* to use two of Gramsci's ideal-types.[5] Conversely, such relative interdependency with the status quo is wholly unacceptable, in theory and practice, to revolutionaries for whom the 'vision of revolutionary change is that of a world restructured and regenerated in all its aspects – social, political, economic, cultural, and familial.'[6] In this sense one of the primary differences between revolutionary and radical politics, in their contemporary conceptualisation, is the degree of the transformation envisaged and implemented. This is a nuanced difference between radical reform and a total break with the past, between agonistic and antagonistic politics, between a revolt and a mass movement, between a molar digression from the temporal order and the imagination of a parallel universe: RADICALISM ↔ revolt ↔ agonism ↔ riotous violence ↔ temporal trajectory (transformative); REVOLUTION ↔ mass movement ↔ antagonism ↔ structural violence ↔ temporal break (utopian).[7] In this sense, radicalism is 'second' to revolution in the typology of demands for political change. It is followed by 'reform' that Halliday defines as 'change that is more cautious or limited, and "evolution", suggesting change that does not involve a radical break with the past.'[8]

In the following paragraphs I will move along and traverse the two types of politics espoused by radicals and revolutionaries with two principal digressions: one empirical, and the second theoretical. I will take the contemporary emergence of radical and revolutionary politics in Iran as my empirical departure point, partially in order to contribute to a comparative conceptualisation of theories of power and resistance. Both historiographers and critical theorists despite the international tremors that Iranian politics continue to provoke have largely ignored the Iranian case. Yet the recent unrest after the controversial re-election of President Mahmoud Ahmadinejad in the summer of 2009 and the crackdown of the oppositional 'Green Movement' that continues at the time of writing reveal the salience and obduracy of radical political subjectivity in Iran. Thus, delving into the dialectics between state and society in the country promises to unhinge a wealth of theoretical insights. In many ways, Iranians have never really seized to believe in 'making history' and many theoreticians of politics and comparative historiography have failed to ask why.[9] In order to address this shortcoming and to position the Iranian case more firmly in those fields, I will discuss how the contemporary radical subject in Iran emerged out of the dialectics between state and society in the late nineteenth century. I will sketch, moreover, how out of the depth of the political disillusionment with the Pahlavi monarchy, political radicalism turned to revolutionary action yielding the Islamic Republic in 1979. Throughout the following paragraphs I will attempt to identify, at once cautiously and tangentially, aspects of the Iranian case that merit theoretical deduction.

A (Short) History of Radicalism in Iran

The contemporary 'radical subject' is very different from earlier ideal-types of Iranian politics in that its political activism is systematic, institutional, (theo-)nationalistic and ideological. This is largely due to the historical syntax out of which the radical subject emerged. Radical politics developed only gradually within Iranian society, in the many institutional and organisational loci that were increasingly networked and politicised at least from the late nineteenth century onwards. A variety of agonistic political discourses were perfected by oppositional clerics, intellectuals (another 'new' subject), students, philosophers, teachers and workers who were positioning themselves both against the arbitrariness of the state and the structural violence of imperialism, at first in its British and Russian manifestation and later in its US American form.

More specifically, the contemporary radical subject in Iran emerges out of the dialectics of the first mass upheaval of Iranian history engendered by the 'tobacco revolt' of 1891. We are transferred back to a period when Iranian politics was seriously affected by the interplay of the imperial interests of Russia and Britain. In 1891, the Qajar monarch Nasser al-Din Shah granted an exclusive monopoly for the sale and export of tobacco to Major Talbot, a British citizen. The shah had to cancel the monopoly not only because of Russian opposition, but primarily due to the nationwide protests and an ensuing boycott of tobacco products. For the first time in contemporary Iranian history, different strata of society cooperated in order to bring about and sustain a radical 'counter-regime' that was intrusive enough to affect the politics of the state. The emerging discourse thus signified was uttered by a whole range of clerics, intellectuals, military personnel, merchants and Islamic 'revivalists'. The category 'society' was distanced from the category 'state' whose claim to exercise 'sovereign' power without accountability was suddenly questioned. Now some members of the *ulama* (Muslim clergy), the Islamic revivalists and nationalists created fields of political activism that were disintegrated from the formal power of the monarchy. It is in this way that in the tobacco revolt, the *fatwa* (religious verdict) of 'Grand Ayatollah' Shirazi forbidding his followers to use any tobacco based product merged with the 'anti-imperial' pamphlets of Jamal-al-din Afghani and the speeches and secret memoranda of 'nationalists' officers who called for resistance against any economic concessions that would galvanise foreign influence in Iran. Similarly, the mosques were increasingly reorganised to serve as places of political activism and resistance providing sanctuary to protesters. They did not function merely as places of worship and social activity. Rather, they increasingly became sites of communicative, mass-ideological transmission. For the first time in contemporary Iranian history diverse strata of society were equipped with both a national 'micro-geography' to organise their political agenda and the structural (religious and non-religious) legitimation to that end. The contemporary radical subject emerges out of this modified dialectic between state and society in the country. From now on resistance is not merely scattered, the radical subject does not only utter a whisper in the cacophony of Iranian politics. From now on the radical subject speaks with a voice that is simultaneously peremptory in its ideological ellipses and emphatic in its sublating demands.

Ervand Abrahamian, Homa Katouzian and Nikki Keddie, who have chronicled the contemporary history of Iran most comprehensively, rightly interpret 1891 as a precursor to the 'Constitutional Revolution' of 1905–11.[10] But the term 'revolution' to designate these events has been applied without much theoretical reflection. It is not the revolutionary subject that was dominant during this period. In Persian, the Arabic term *inqilab*, which is derived from *qleb* meaning 'to overturn' or 'to knock over', attains its ultimate revolutionary politico-cultural signification in the discourse of the Marxist-Leninist, the communist *Tudeh* party and, more significantly for the trajectory of the revolution in 1979, in the influential writings of Jalal al-e Ahmad, Ali Shariati and the clerical revisionists supporting Ayatollah Khomeini.

The revolutionary subject in Iran is a hybrid creature constituted by the tapestry of overlapping utopian-romantic ideas espoused by both the Islamic and leftist revolutionaries. This revolutionary subject had stopped to negotiate and called for a new social and political status quo at least from the 1950s onwards. Yet the radical subject, who was at the centre of the constitutional revolt, was satisfied with an amendment to the political order. The radical constitutionalists did not call for a wholesale overthrow of the political and social system (neither did they command the discursive capabilities to do so). The events leading up to the establishment of a constitutional monarchy in 1906 centred on very specific grievances: in Mashhad bread rioters agitated against high food prices; in Tehran women demonstrators protested against worsening social conditions; senior clerics deprecated the 'trade' of Iranian women who were forced into 'sexual slavery' because of the deteriorating economic conditions; *bazaaris* (merchants) contested the high taxes that were levied in order to bankroll the lavish life style of the monarch and his court; and students of the Dar al-Fanon began to translate constitutional and republican forms of governance into the political situation encompassing Iran. Consequently, the outcome of the revolt was a radical, not a revolutionary transformation of the political order in the country: On 5 August 1906, Muzaffar al-Din Shah, the fifth monarch of the Qajar dynasty, agreed to institute nationwide elections. According to the new constitution the shah's oath of office had to be made before the newly established National Assembly; he had to accept both the ministers and officials proposed by it and the bills signed into law by its elected members. At the same time, the shah would be the head of the executive, commander-in-chief, and would retain significant legislative and executive rights.[11] The *majles-e melli* was born and the discourse of democracy and republicanism emerges. But the monarch did not only remain a significant institution of the political system, in 1907 Iran was divided into Russian and British 'spheres of influence', and the country descended into a virtual civil war until the coup d'état of Reza Khan on 21 February 1921. Thus, the Pahlavi dynasty was established and the mandate of absolute monarchic authority was reconstituted – this time not around God, but around a novel, modernistic mythology which proved to be by far more susceptible to this-worldly contention.

The political culture enveloping and delivering the constitutional movement that I can only dissect rather sketchily here equipped the radical subject with extraordinarily diverse institutional and discursive powers. The new moment in Iranian society was an expansion of the geography of politics. This expansion can be discerned from two interdependent factors: first, the emergence and re-imagination of a whole new vocabulary constituting the political discourse. Terms denoting the new phenomenon of the 'masses' such as *tudeh* and *khalgh* ('the masses'); terms conscribing the idea of democracy, constitutionalism and the exigencies of the nation-state model such as *jomhuri* (republic), *mashrute* (constitutional), *melliyat* (nationality), *demokrasi* (democracy) and *vatan* (homeland); terms differentiating the newly established political field and the party competition exercised therein such as *chab* (left), *rast* (right), *melligera* (nationalist) or *sosialist* (socialist); and terms that were re-signified in order to construct a radical discourse of Islam that would depart from the quietist tradition of the orthodox Shi'a clergy. It is within this latter field that the Ayatollah establishes his (no women Ayatollahs yet) significance. From now on those senior oppositional *mujtahids* who sided with the demands of the people were referred to as *Ayat Allah*, a sign of God, a discursive challenge to the religious authority of the shah who was traditionally referred to as *ill-Allah* or the 'Shadow of God' and at times as *Ayatollah* as well. In this way the dialectics of the constitutional movement produced an important factor of the Islamicised revolution of 1979. Since the constitutionalists emphasised, in the name of equality, that no aristocratic or religious titles should be used anymore, the *Ayatollah* turned into an exclusively clerical ideal-type. It is true, as Fakhreddin Azimi recently argued, that the 'constitutional demystification of monarchy meant that the shahs could no longer claim to be shadows of God on earth, fully entitled to their patrimonial fiefdom.'[12] But it is equally true to argue that God cast another shadow: From now on, God exited the domain of the palace and wandered back into the praying rooms of the mosque. Here (s)he increasingly deified what was considered to be the ultimate form of political authority by an increasing number of Iranians and Shi'a-Muslims more generally.

Second, this political discourse was now professionally dispersed by a set of new institutional ideal-types: places of education such as the Dar al-Fanon which was established under the patronage of Amir Kabir in 1851 and which was turned into the University of Tehran in January 1935. Dar al-Fanon, whose faculty was dominated by European academics under the Qajars, further facilitated the translation of canonical European books in the fields of the human sciences and literature, including the works of Darwin, Voltaire, Dumas, Fenelon, Descartes and Verne. A whole new archive informing an 'Iranian' dialectic with European modernity was engineered during this period. Yet far from educating the 'native' population into apathy, the European presence enmeshed in the newly devised 'Iranian' narrative, provoked its own, 'native' form of resistance. Various political organisations, a whole range of *anjumans* (assemblies), stratified in accordance with 'sub-national' affiliations (Armenians, Azeris, Lurs, Kurds etc.) or, interdependently, religious preference (Muslim, Zoroastrian, Jewish, Christian, Baha'i), institutionalised their political agendas transmitting them through the pages of a burgeoning local press and publications such as *Asr-e now* (New Age), *Esteghlal* (Independence), *Eghbal* (Progress) or *Sur-e Israfil* (Israfil's Trumpet), the latter written mainly by the famed lexicographer Ali-Akbar Dehkhoda.[13] A second rather more contested factor has to be added here, that is the role of institutionalised discourses of Islam in the radical politics of this period. As Hamid Enayat notes: 'The religio-political tracts of the time denote an attitude which, while returning to the compromise of the Safavid period, is as anxious to prevent the monarchy from lapsing into despotism and corruption.'[14] Enayat points to the writings of Mullah Muhammad Kazim Khorasani and Mohammad Hussein Naini to support his argument, and to the emergence of a 'pre-constitutionalist mentality' in the chief doctrines of the *usuli* school of Shi'a-Islam with its emphasis on the necessity of *ijtihad* and critical reasoning which had become increasingly influential in Shi'a jurisprudence since the emergence of Mohammad Baqir Wahid Behbehani (1704–91).[15] The Usuli discourse equipped progressive members of the *ulama* with the critical devices to accommodate and further the constitutional demands for democratic legislation and public accountability of the state, both in the build up and in the aftermath of the constitutional revolt.[16]

The point of adding this latter factor is not to unearth the signposts of a 'truer' history of the constitutional movement. I am not interested in fighting History with History here. Yet it must be added in the name of a critical attitude towards the way History is written in general and the political economy of 'Iranian Studies' in particular that the fortunes of Islamo-centric, nationalist or socialist representations of this pivotal period do not ebb and flow in accordance with their truth value, but too often in lieu with political allegiance and/or the hegemonic political culture of the day. It is such guided cultural constellations and the discursive regimes of truth that they inform that set the conditions for the production of a 'truer' history of Iran.[17] Hence, Ahmad Kasravi, who managed to chronicle the history of the constitutional movement in sublime prose and from a staunchly anticlerical perspective, has been central to the nationalist narrative and its adherents, while the writings and pro-constitutional activities of clerics such as Naini are rather more pronounced in 'Islamist' representations of Iranian history. It is no coincidence of course that the 'Islamist paradigm' proliferated in many quarters especially after the establishment of the Islamic Republic in 1979.[18]

Such battles over the official history of Iran are too often parochial and ideologically tainted and shall not concern me beyond their value for a critical reading of the way discourse/power/knowledge constellations determine how an Iran is represented. What has been rather more central to my reading of Iran thus far is to show that at least from the latter half of the nineteenth century onwards, the radical subject revolted in the name of nationalist fervour, anti-imperial passion, socialist rationality and/or Islamic reasoning. Of course, these are all my ideal-typical 'categories' that do not exhaust the range of causes that challenged the political status quo during that period.

What can be discerned from the developments at least since the latter half of the nineteenth century is a steady growth and networking of the sites – institutional and individual – of political discourse in Iran. The radical subject was endowed with a whole new space to function and to propagate against the state. Out of the fierce nationalism and constitutionalism of this moment, many voices were raised, feminine and male, in condemnation of Iran's subservience to imperial powers and the abandonment of the constitution of 1906 by the Pahlavis, in the accent of an elite class that was adamant to constrain the power of the monarchy. At least from the latter part of the 1940s onwards, the target was Mohammad Reza Shah, who acceded to the Peacock Throne in 1941 after his father Reza Khan was forced into exile by the British on the pretext that he wanted to collude with Nazi Germany.

The primary driving force of the opposition to the shah's rule in the period 1949–53 was not only Mohammad Mossadegh, the Swiss-educated 'aristocrat' who died a great and almost 'prototypical' nationalist. The expansion of the discursive geography of politics brought with it the emergence of politically functional individuals who were introjected by a range of counter-hegemonic ideas. There emerged a mass psychology that was geared towards achieving the utopia of full independence and to constraining the authoritarianism of the state. The radical subject thinks and acts within a political counter-culture that is entirely sophisticated both in terms of its ideological vigour and its internationalist outlook. The radical subject has privileged access to socialist, Marxist-Leninist, social-democratic, nationalist and 'Islamist' discourses, all of which created their own fulminate momentum merging on the demand for radical change. Groups espousing violence as a political strategy such as the *Fedayan-e Islam* (Devotees of Islam) who were responsible for a range of terrorist atrocities in Tehran and beyond; the communist Tudeh Party which was established in 1941 and which turned increasingly pro-Soviet in the latter 1940s bowing to the irresistible ideological pressures and financial incentives of Stalinism;[19] clerics such as Ayatollah Seyyed Abol-Qassem Kashani who was sympathetic to the nationalists cause; and at the helm of it all Mohammad Mossadegh and his National Front party (*Jebhe-Melli*). Mossadegh managed to turn the prevalent mood for radical action into a popular movement that would bring about the nationalisation of the Anglo-Iranian Oil Company in 1951; two years before he was ousted by a MI6/CIA engineered coup d'état, which would reinstate the dictatorship of the shah.

Mossadegh is a singularly important figure in history, not merely because he managed to nationalise the Iranian oil economy nor because of his democratic credentials. Mossadegh demonstrated that it was possible to overthrow, on the one side, the institution of the monarchy in Iran, and, on the other side, to resist the 'superpowers' of the day. Henceforth, the new counter-culture in Iran is no longer organised around questions such as: How can we negotiate with the state? How can we pressure it to accept a particular agenda? How can we confine its authoritarianism? How can we bargain with it? How can we play the superpowers off against each other? Since Mossadegh, the dialectic between Iranian society and the state is no longer ordered around the agonistic politics, semi-ordered revolts and 'realistic' calculations of the radical subject. It is premised on revolution, on a total break of the prevalent system both within Iran and beyond – from now on utopia is not only thought, from now on it is enacted.

Licentious Power versus Revolutionary Libido

For the revolutionary subject death is salvation, justice is transcendental, martyrdom is *Erlebnis*. The revolutionary subject craves climactic events; it functions according to a 'libidinous bio-ontology'. The revolutionary subject is adamant to demonstrate political prowess, the ability to channel passion into political action. The revolutionary subject relentlessly tries to elicit as many 'ineffable' events as possible in order to establish a superior counter-discourse which would be linked, with the help of an intellectual vanguard, into a strident, ideologically charged counter-culture which would simulate the viability of a temporal break with everything that 'is'. This is what Marx called the 'sixth great power' which would overwhelm, quite inevitably, every other power in its way. In *Labour of Dionysus*, Michael Hardt and Antonio Negri allude to this transformative dynamic that drives the revolutionary subject. According to them: 'It is as if the world is unmade and reconstructed on the basis of a set of thoughts, actions, and intuitions established on the individual and collective singularity that organise it through its desire and its power.'[20] This desire and power of the revolutionary subject is organised, infused by the utopia that everything is possible. Time and being are conceived of as limitless, and the revolutionary subject is placed at the edge of that possibility, with a clear view of what is to come in the future. The revolutionary subject employs a distinctly modern, positivistic syntax that is almost impervious to disappointment taking as its primary battleground the official writing of history and the national narratives thus spun.

Charles Kurzman has recently termed the revolution in Iran 'unthinkable', a coincidence of several factors that were unpredictable and that delivered the revolution almost as a *bonne chance* of history.[21] But Kurzman does not take into account that Iranians began to 'think' the revolution at least since the late 1950s. Indeed, in the most influential writings of Iran's prototypical revolutionary intellectuals, such as Jalal al-e Ahmad and Ali Shariati, Iranian history in particular and Islam in general were rewritten to function as building blocks for a viable and uncompromising ideology that was quite overtly and explicitly revolutionary. So for the former, the thirteenth-century astronomer and philosopher Nasir ad-Din Tusi (1201–74) becomes the prototypical 'aggressive intellectual' (*rowshanfekr-e mohajem*), 'who made history' after obliterating the prevalent order seeking to 'destroy the contemporary governmental institutions in order to erect something better in their place.'[22] Whereas for the latter we find a comparable signification of revolutionary change which is likened to a golden age of justice, a classless society, social equality and the final victory of the oppressed masses against their oppressors. According to Shariati, there was no choice towards that end since the victory of the revolution was historically determined which made it mandatory for the vanguard to 'object to the status quo and to negate the ruling systems and values.'[23] With al-e Ahmad and Shariati then, an entirely new ontology for Iran is imagined and increasingly enacted.

This newly imagined Iran was not provincial, as some scholars have argued. The revolutionary subject in Iran was not confined to a nativist habitat, even if it indulged in the utopia of 'authenticity'.[24] In the writings of intellectuals such as al-e Ahmad and Shariati we hear echoes of, and see direct reference to, Che Guevara, Marx, Sartre, Marcuse, Fanon and others. It is in Shariati especially, where East meets West, and where the potentialities of a seemingly contradictory 'Islamo-socialist' discourse are exploited in order to channel what was considered to be the emancipating message of Islam and socialism to receptive constituencies within Iranian society. This internationalist cross-fertilisation was not limited only to the intellectual/theoretical realm. For instance, the nascent Iranian armed movements of the 1960s drew their inspiration from theories of guerrilla warfare developed in Cuba, Nicaragua, Vietnam, Palestine and China. '[A]long with centres for study of present and future zones of operations, intensive popular work must be undertaken to explain the motives of the revolution, its ends', Che Guevara suggests in his manual for guerrilla warfare that was translated and widely distributed in Iran in the 1960s. It is imperative, according to Guevara, 'to spread the incontrovertible truth that victory of the enemy against the people is finally impossible. *Whoever does not feel this undoubted truth cannot be a guerrilla fighter.*'[25] In Iran such 'bio-ontological' re-education towards the revolutionary subject gained momentum out of the disillusionment with the political order after the enforced downfall of Mossadegh in 1953, and more exponentially in the late 1950s. From now on the revolutionary subject plots to reverse History *in toto*. From now on, the revolutionary subject in Iran takes on a dual combat: resisting the 'bipolar' world order, dominated by the Soviet Union and the United States on the one side and combating the monarchy of the shah on the other.

So at least from the 1950s onwards something quite 'bio-ontological' occurs in Iranian politics. On the one side, politically conscious Iranians become the target of rather more systematic, certainly more consequential revolutionary agitation. On the other side, *zoon politikon*, the political 'animal', becomes the target of a formal, systematic and overbearingly paternalistic form of state-power which is entirely 'licentious'. The power of the state, that the revolutionary subject is not only attempting to resist, but to conquer, turns to a perversely excessive form of ideational self-assertion. 'Identity' becomes the major issue in the representation of Iran's national narrative and in the making of the legitimacy of the state. Now we enter the world of 'genetic' manipulation: licentious power forcefully induces, on the 'macro-level' of the state, the factor of race into the idea of what the Iranian nation 'is'. In the political biology propagated by the Pahlavis, Iranians were first and foremost 'Aryan', quite Indo-European due to the Persian language and very much distinct from the Semitic Arabs and 'their' Islamic history. Accordingly, Shah Mohammad Reza Pahlavi was to be referred to as *Aryamehr* or 'Light of the Aryans'. At the height of his megalomania, exemplified by his Napoleon-esque self-coronation in 1966 and the extravagant festivities at Persepolis in 1971, the shah changed the Islamic solar hegra calendar into an imperial one. Suddenly, Iran was in the year 2535 based on the presumed date of the foundation of the Achaemenid dynasty. In lieu with the effort to Iranianise the Persian language, which had already been pursued by his father Reza Khan, the Pahlavi state also sponsored systematic efforts to substitute Arabic terms with Persian ones. The situation in Iran was assessed, with increasing worry for the stability of the Pahlavi regime, in an intelligence report by the CIA, dated May 1972 and declassified in June 2006:

> The Shah sees himself in the role of a latter-day Cyrus the Great who will restore to Iran at least a portion of its old glory as a power to be reckoned with in its own part of the world. His coronation in 1966, 25 years after he assumed the throne, and the grandiose celebration of the 2,500 anniversary of the founding of the Monarchy were the Shah's way of publicly affirming his belief in the validity of royal rule. Although he frequently insists on the possibility of a true constitutional monarchy in Iran, his actions suggest that he does not foresee it in his time. A noncharismatic leader, he has taken on many of the trappings of totalitarianism; scarcely a town of any size does not have its Avenue Pahlavi and it is a mean city, indeed, that does not have a traffic circle dominated by a statue of the Shah or his father. Massive rallies are held, complete with giant portraits of the Shah and banners bearing quotations by him, and no politician ventures a suggestion without carefully pointing out that it fits within the framework approved by the Shah. ... The Shah is the master of what has been called the 'Pahlavism'.[26]

The ideational architecture of 'Pahlavism' was crafted around the symbolism of monarchic rule and the metaphysics of modern nationalism consisting of romantic myths about the authenticity of the 'Persian' language and the 'Iranian civilisation'. Their impact on the making of a modern 'identity' of Iran devoid of an intrinsically 'Islamic' component comes out in an article which the shah placed in *Life* magazine in May 1963: 'Geographically Iran is situated at the crossroads of the East and the West; it is where Asia and Europe meet', the shah asserts. 'On one side thrived the old civilisations of China and India; on the other those of Egypt, Babylon, Greece, Rome, and, later on, the modern Western World.' His country was not a part of any civilisation per se, but 'Iran welded her own civilisation from all those many sources.' This distinctly 'Iranian civilisation' holds a universal religion and universal art which 'have left their traces all over the world'. But this universal religion that the shah refers to is not conceptualised as Islamic. Rather, he heralds the pre-Islamic era, 'the old Iranian religion of Mithra' and the 'teachings of the mystic prophet Mani'.[27] So an Islam did not have much of a role in the making of an Iran during this period. A discourse of Islam only re-enters the re-imagination of what it means to be Iranian in the counter-culture of the 1960s and 1970s and after the Islamicised revolution of 1979.

There were more dramatic developments for the dialectic between state and society. On the micro-level the *vision* of Shah Mohammad Reza Pahlavi about the past (Aryan), present (transitionary) and future (*tamadon-e bozorg* or the great civilisation) was enhanced by a sophisticated *supervisionary* regime that extended the licentious power of the state on the very body of its object of desire, that is Iranian society. In 1957, the shah established a new 'intelligence agency' called SAVAK which employed thousands of operatives and informants across the country and beyond. SAVAK, which was created under the tutelage of the FBI and the Israeli Mossad, introduced, for the first time in Iranian history, 'professional' techniques of torture to the expanding number of prison cells in the country. Other intelligence institutions such as the Imperial Inspectorate and the J2 Bureau which functioned as the intelligence branch of the imperial army joined the supervisionary network. The budget for the military – meant to be one of the pillars of the shah's rule and hence closely supervised by him – expanded from US\$60 million in 1954 to US\$7.2 billion in 1977 (at 1973 prices and exchange rates).[28] In the latter 1970s the military budget of Iran was one of the largest in the world – as a percentage of Gross National Product. Much of this expansion of the security bureaucracy was possible because of increasing oil revenues, which skyrocketed after the OPEC boycott of 1973.[29]

At least from the early twentieth century onwards and later on abetted and catalysed by the modernisation doctrines of the Pahlavis themselves, the state in Iran was confronted with three novel social tendencies: First, the urbanisation of Iranian society, the physical concentration of persons in towns which the growth of the population of the country facilitated. Second, the social and political expansion of the geography of politics that caught more and more people into its space. And third, the emergence of new politically savvy ideal-types in society such as the *rowshanfekr* (intellectual), *kargar* (the worker), the *zan-e mobarez* (resisting woman) and the oppositional Ayatollah. All of these actors were now endowed with enough institutional space and discursive leverage to impinge on the territory of the sovereign.

This impingement on the sovereignty of the state that the expansion of the geography of politics brought about dramatised the problems of management and surveillance of an increasing numbers of persons. The state reacted by instituting a range of novel disciplinary strategies, techniques of power and knowledge that made it possible for its bureaucracy to organise the population and to make it visible; to attempt to turn society into an object of formal power (e.g. judicial and administrative), especially after the shah was reinstalled in 1953. A particularly prominent example in this regard is the so-called White Revolution launched by the shah ten years later. It did not only lead to land reform but also unprecedented levels of industrialisation and social change (women rights including the right to vote, growth of the educational sector). It was not merely an ideological device to pre-empt the revolutionary rhetoric of the burgeoning 'Left' in the country. The 'White Revolution' simultaneously territorialised Iranian society and made it visible to the 'gaze' and the disciplinary apparatus of the state. As part of the land reform which was the main pillar of the proposed changes, Iranians were professionally censused and mapped in accordance with the newly devised 'provinces'. This made possible, for the first time in Iranian history, the authoritative, 'scientific' language of the second census of the country published in 1966 which established that 'Iran had a population of 25,323,064 distributed over an area of 628,000 square miles.'[30] From now on everything and everyone within this newly delineated anatomy – the Iranian body politic – were affected by the state, at least formally: families who wanted to apply for birth certificates to enable their children to go to school or to marry; people who had to apply for a passport in order to be able to travel abroad; farmers who had to qualify for government subsidies to finance the fertilisation of their crops; students who applied for government scholarships, and so on.

But, despite this modernisation of the disciplinary apparatus of the state, it would be wrong to assume that the licentious form of power, despite its 'rational', 'scientific' pretensions and despite the FBI/Mossad torture handbooks, is equal, in status and efficiency, to the omnipresent, yet 'clandestine' power that Michel Foucault thinks. In *Discipline and Punish*, Foucault describes such 'panoptical power' as unspectacular, capillary, almost invisible. It strikes from afar, it is not immediately identifiable: 'If it is still necessary for the law to reach and manipulate the body of the convict,' Foucault writes, 'it will be at a distance, in the proper way, according to strict rules, and with a much "higher" aim.' Consequently, the executioner was relieved from his task by a whole army of technicians such as 'warders, doctors, chaplains, psychiatrists, psychologists and educationalists'. By their very immediate presence close to the prisoner these professional enforcers of the law 'sing the praises that the law needs: they reassure it that the body and pain are not the ultimate objects of its punitive action.'[31] No Iranian polity, including the Islamic Republic which reintroduced the 'spectacle' of public executions, really has been successful in instituting a micro-strategic disciplinary regime that would be as 'omniscience' as the panoptical model that Foucault ponders. That is not because the state in Iran is somehow 'primitive', but exactly because modern power, at its tangents, retains a degree of unmitigated aggressiveness towards the political enemy that is not at all 'measured' and 'capillary' as Foucault imagined. A few examples illustrate the point: On 4 May 1970 members of the Ohio National Guard entered the campus of Kent State University in the United States killing four unarmed anti-war students and injuring nine others, one of whom remained paralysed. On 2 June 1967, Benno Ohnesorg was killed by a plainclothes German policeman during a protest against the state visit of Shah Mohammed Reza Pahlavi.[32] And during the miners strike between 1984 and 1985, the Thatcher government in Britain was directly and indirectly responsible for the arrest of thousands of protesters, the jailing of hundreds of others, the injury of tens of thousands and the killing of two miners who died on the picket lines and eight more who died in related events. And of course there is the sadistic sexual violence unleashed on the inmates of the Iraqi Abu Ghraib prison complex and as a part of the international rendition regime that the George W. Bush Administration supervised. Modern state power was never as timid as Foucault believed. When the interests of the power elite are at stake, democracies will kill, if necessary with frightening arbitrariness.[33]

Perhaps I am describing what Susan Buck-Morss terms a 'wild zone of power' which she conceptualises as 'a zone in which power is above the law and thus, at least potentially, a terrain of terror.'[34] As she rightly observes this zone can never really be total; it can never really subsume all segments and particles of society. So both in the panoptical model of Foucault and beyond the wild zone of power of Buck-Morss, the possibility of escape, dissidence and an arena for rebellion – however contracted and minute – retain the promise for political transformation. Where there is power, there is resistance, Foucault was right to claim, and the points of resistance are not only 'a reaction or rebound, forming with respect to the basic domination an underside that is in the end always passive, doomed to perpetual defeat. … [N]either are they a lure or a promise that is of necessity betrayed.' Rather most of the time 'one is dealing with mobile and transitory points of resistance'.[35]

This power-resistance dialectic is an important part of the explanation why the radical subject has not been subdued until today, in Iran (and elsewhere). While the shah launched the 'White Revolution' and professionalised the disciplinary apparatus of his increasingly oppressive state, the opposition managed to extend the geography of revolutionary politics, the transitory points of resistance to the arbitrariness of the formal power of the monarch. From the late 1950s onwards all strata of Iranian society became a target of ideological agitation. This is exemplified by the range of new associations that were involved in mobilising the masses, now more visibly than before from an explicitly 'Islamic' disposition, for instance the Islamic Association of Engineers (*anjuman-e Islami-ye mohandesin*), the Islamic Association of teachers (*anjuman-e Islami-ye mo'allemin*) or the Monthly Religious Association (*anjuman-e mahanih-ye dini*). Unfazed and determined to push his policies through, the shah held a mock referendum on the 'White Revolution' and announced its 'victory' in January 1963. Ayatollah Khomeini reacted with a strongly worded declaration denouncing the shah's domestic and foreign policies. In the same month, the shah ordered the army into Qom, the religious centre of Iran and the place where Khomeini lived, taught and studied. Army units stormed the seminaries that had become a hub for revolutionary agitation and in another signpost of the 'discursive war' characteristic of this period the shah denounced the clergy as 'black reactionaries' (*irtijai-e siyah*). The confrontation cumulated in Khomeini's speech at the Feiziyeh Seminary on the afternoon of Ashura (3 June 1963), which is commemorated by Shi'a Muslims as a day of mourning for the martyrdom of Hossein (the grandson of the prophet Mohammed), his family and his followers who were killed by the forces of the Umayyad caliph Yazid at the Battle of Karbala in the year 61 of the Islamic calendar (680 AD). 'O Mr. Shah, dear Mr Shah, abandon these improper acts', Khomeini advised.

> I don't want people to offer thanks should your masters decide that you must leave. I don't want you to become like your father. When America [the United States], the Soviet Union and England attacked us [during the Second World War] people were happy that Pahlavi [the Shah's father, Reza Shah] went. Listen to my advice; listen to the clergy's advice, not to that of Israel. That would not help you. You wretched, miserable man, forty-five years of your life have passed. Isn't it time for you to

think and reflect a little, to ponder about where all this is leading you, to learn a lesson from the experience of your father? ...
You don't know whether the situation will change one day nor
whether those who surround you will remain your friends. They
are the friends of the dollar. They have no religion, no loyalty.
They have hung all the responsibility around your neck. O miserable man![36]

Two days after delivering this speech, Khomeini was arrested and
incarcerated sparking the historic uprising of 15th Khordad 1342.
Unrepentant, Khomeini continued resisting the shah especially after
the monarch pushed through the Iranian parliament what came to
be known as the 'Bill of Capitulation' in the jargon of the revolutionaries, granting US military personnel diplomatic immunity on
Iranian territory. As a consequence of his intransigent opposition,
Khomeini was exiled, first to Turkey, then to Iraq and finally to
France before he returned to lead the Islamic Republic after the revolution in 1979.

The conceptual point underlying the preceding snapshot of Iranian
history can be summed up with an analogy in reverse: if Bentham's
Panopticon is Foucault's ultimate architectural and organisational
example for the invisible, omnipresent 'carceral' complex that con-
tributes to controlling (European) society, Evin, Iran's first professionally designed modern prison, is an example for the way the state
has failed to produce politically apathetic and socially submissive
objects. Foucault witnessed for himself how the Pahlavi state failed
to discipline society, when he travelled to Iran during the revolution,
and when he wondered how Iranians produced 'a movement strong
enough to overthrow an apparently well-armed regime while being
close to old dreams that the West had known in times past, when
people attempted to inscribe the figures of spirituality on political
ground.'[37] It is very likely that the excesses of the revolution prevented Foucault from engaging with the Islamic Republic in a more
conceptual manner. Yet if Foucault would have theorised the confines
of modern power in Iran, if he would have expanded the empirical
scope of his scholarly corpus beyond Europe, he may have taken more

seriously his own proposition that resistance is inherent to power. Modern panoptical power, whether in its Iranian or western variance, can never really be all-encompassing. Political subjects continue to express agency; they continue to think political change and to put it into practice.[38]

So the absence of an all-encompassing disciplinary regime in Iran that would educate society into submission can be isolated as one of the reasons for the very success of the revolutionary subject at least from the late 1950s onwards. It is no coincidence that all of the major figures of the revolution, Khomeini, Montazeri, Taleghani, Khamenei, Rafsanjani, Motahari, Bazargan, Bani-Sadr, Shariati, had a prison experience in pre-revolutionary Iran at some stage of their life. Neither the political 'bio-ontology' espoused by the Pahlavis, nor the modern prison system 'disciplined' these individuals. Rather the contrary. If they entered the prison as notorious radicals, they exited them as angry revolutionaries. It is difficult, if not impossible, to establish a threshold according to which radicalism turns into revolutionary action, but the inability of the shah to a) socialise society with the 'bio-ontology' of Pahlavism, b) the expansion of the geography of politics in the country and c) the creation of a functional revolutionary counter-discourse within that space, can be isolated as major factors in the moulding and success of the revolutionary subject. This extraordinary devotion to a new order of things was inscribed in the names of the burgeoning militant parties, for instance the *Fedayeen-e Khalgh* ('devotees' of the masses) which employed urban guerrilla warfare tactics against the state in the 1970s, the *Mujahedin-e Khalgh* (the 'warriors' of the masses) which mixed socialist ideology with Islamist imagery, and the discourse of the aforementioned intellectuals such as Jalal al-e Ahmad and Ali Shariati who deprecated the shah's cultural and political subservience to the 'west' and who called for a return to Iran's 'true identity' which was increasingly imagined in Islamic, rather than in 'Aryan' terms.[39] To sum all of this up: the 'wild zone of power' carved out by the Pahlavi state remained 'licentiously modern'; it did not perfect a panoptical disciplinary regime that would be truly totalitarian and omnipresent.

Iran's *Zoon Politikon* Today

What is 'radical' can only be measured against what is considered to be normal in a given society. What is considered to be normal in a given society is seriously affected, if not entirely determined, by the cultural texture which sets the normative guidelines according to which society is supposed to function and deliberate. The state, due to its administrative tentacles which follow us into our very living room and its ideological power which assaults our very cognition, is a central agent of the normative consensus that is meant to keep radicals at bay, exactly because radicals are coded to question the status quo. It must follow quite logically that any increase in the number of political prisoners in a country is not indicative of the ability of the state apparatus to subdue the combatant population. Rather the contrary. It is a measure of opposition, defiance and resistance.

I have argued that the state apparatus of the shah introduced the 'modern' prison system to the country in the 1970s. This was not merely an institutional development. With the modern prison there came 'modern' interrogation techniques, a whole culture of incarceration and physical violence that was increasingly 'professionalised'. To that end, interrogators were sent to the United States and Israel so that they can learn the trait of 'scientific torture' that would not unnecessarily kill, but discipline, through nail extraction, sexual violence, water boarding, stress positions, sleep deprivation and/or mock executions.[40] This was merely one of the central excesses of western modernity in Iran. The overheating economy, the colossal socio-economic upheavals, cultural uprooting and alienation that the 'develop*mental*' ideology of the Pahlavis brought about were others. No wonder then that the country's revolutionary intellectuals expressed their antagonism to the 'west' in so vivid and at times utterly melancholic terms. They encountered western modernity at first through the politico-economic violence of imperialism and then through the psychological violence of the develop*mental* state. Both were rejected.

But the revolution in Iran also points to the impossibility of total change. Power and resistance, once reversed remain power and resistance. Revolutions as we know them, do not merge them into one;

they have not nullified *either* resistance *or* power. So after the Islamic revolution of 1979, the power of the Islamic Republic, that used to fuel the resistance to the shah, remained as licentious as the power of the Pahlavi state, if less pretentiously 'modern' in its respect for universal declarations of human rights and prohibitions against torture. If the Pahlavi state punished in the name of a royal prerogative, a monarcho-formal jurisdiction that rationalised the brutality of the state, the Islamic Republic punishes in the name of a deity. It exercises licentious power that is mandated by God. A central pathology ensues. The state turns God into an accomplice and the punished is relieved of his right to pray for mercy. The *mohareb* (enemy of Islam) and *mofsed-e-filarz* (corrupters on earth) enter the politico-judicial discourse as the archetypal enemies of the state. Both offences are punishable by death. From being a callous method to exert the sovereignty of the king, punishment is imagined as a moral necessity to safeguard humanity from itself.

I don't have the luxury here to present a comprehensive analysis of the judicial discourse after the revolution. Suffice it to say that in terms of disciplinary surveillance and the securitisation of state and society, the Islamic Republic is by far more professional (viz. modern) than the Pahlavi state ever was. This is not at least due to the mandate that the state usurped and the sovereignty that it appropriated which Khomeini, quite from the outset, did not restrict to worldly matters. If the French revolution in 1789 promised a new order for mankind and communism rendered the end of history inevitable, the Islamic revolution thrust into the transcendental space beyond mankind and History, the very space that used to be the sole prerogative of God. The humble outfit of the Iranian nation-state was not merely elevated to the level of ontological transcendence, but it was heaved higher, in close proximity to the otherworldly. In this sense, the Islamic revolution in Iran also promised to bring about the first metaphysical revolution in the history of humankind. To that end, the constitution, adopted by a plebiscite in 1979, institutionalised the sovereignty of the *velayat-e faqih*, the Supreme Jurisprudent who represents the highest institution of the political system in Iran. The faqih's mandate is both transcendental, privileged in relation to God, and transnational, mandated to rally the umma (Islamic nation) and the oppressed (*mostazafan*) masses of the world against the oppressors. No wonder then that Iran's 'enemies of the state' are not only considered counter-revolutionaries, but exactly *mohareb*, i.e. enemies of God on earth. They are considered to be enemies of *the* state that is positioned at the nexus of the here and now and the millenarian promise of a utopian tomorrow.

This hubristic extension of the sovereignty of the ruling elites in Iran, a sort of Islamic reincarnation of the Hegelian *Geist* that was meant to descend upon nation-states in nineteenth-century Europe, is safeguarded by a range of rather this-worldly institutions that have been created after the revolution in order to discipline Iranian society into accepting the ideology of the state. Henceforth, SAVAK was substituted by the Intelligence Ministry, the army units of the shah's Imperial Guard merged into the *Sepah-ye Pasdaran-e Enqelabi* (Revolutionary Guards Army) which joined the national army and the military wings of the *Baseej-e Mostazafan* (Mobilisation of the Oppressed) to constitute the defence forces of the country which were placed under the command of the *velayat-e faqih*, i.e. at first Ayatollah Khomeini and since his death in 1989 Ayatollah Ali Khamenei. In recent years, the *Sepah* has become a major economic player creating, for the first time in Iranian history, a sophisticated military-industrial complex with political clout. Moreover, today, almost every major street in Iran has its own military compound, police station, *Baseej* headquarter or Islamic 'committee building' attached to the Intelligence Ministry, and at the time of writing major streets in Tehran, Shiraz and Isfahan are being equipped with CCTV cameras. Before the revolution the Iranian police drove two-door hatchbacks, today they are equipped with E-class Mercedes and BMW motorbikes.

Moreover, the Iranian state has put the World Wide Web under surveillance as well. In December 2001, the Supreme Council of Cultural Revolution set up an inter-agency organisation called the 'Committee in Charge of Determining Unauthorised Sites' which is responsible for centralising and formalising the criteria according to which websites are filtered. The Committee is comprised of members of the ministries of Islamic Guidance, Intelligence and Communication. Additional layers of regulation have been added since then. Under one of the most central censorship legislations, voted into law by the conservative dominated parliament in 2006, it is the owner of commercial Internet Service Providers (ISPs) who would be charged if their clients break the Cyber Crimes Bill. Political agitation and pornography are particularly high on the list of censorship priorities.

Yet, despite all of these formal levers of policing and surveillance, state power in Iran remains dysfunctional. The 'wild zone of power' exists, but the radical subject continues to operate at its tangents. The disillusionment and lost causes that have punctured so disastrously radical activism in much of the late capitalist world seem like marginal impediments when compared with the continuation of radical politics in Iran, not entirely different, in audacity and vigour, from other contemporary manifestations of radical politics in the non-western world. Much of this has to do with the dialectics between state and society in contemporary Iranian history, as I have explained. The revolution of 1979 added an additional factor to this interaction: the revolutionary libido that was absorbed by the state and re-channelled onto the populace created the very social and political conditions for the re-enactment of radical politics today. On the one side, in political terms, the revolution granted Iranians the absolute right to rise up and question authority, exactly because the oppressed-oppressor dialectic espoused by Khomeini suggests and creates the conditions for an ongoing interrogation of the state and – given that the state is mandated to interpret the law of God – the realm of God itself. Yet, once this utopia of a just and transcendental state was ideologically appropriated, it set the high standard according to which the Islamic Republic is measured. As I have argued, we are not talking about merely an ideological utopia that was central to the French, Russian, and Chinese revolution here. This is a 'divine' utopia encapsulated in the millenarian promise that the twelfth Imam of the Shi'a will return to create the just rule of God on earth. Today, President Ahmadinejad and the functionaries of the Revolutionary Guards among others espouse this interpretation of the Islamic Republic. They have attempted to monopolise the custodianship of the divine utopia and reserve it for a tight clique organised around the current Supreme Jurisprudent Ayatollah Ali Khamenei. This nucleus of Iran's current power elite is by far less inclusive than the 'Khomeinists' revolutionaries during the first decade of the revolution when Khomeini successfully forged cross-political alliances. Moreover, the rather closed interpretation of the Shi'a mythology and the revolutionary heritage adhered to by the current Administration and its supporters is largely rejected by the old conservatives and the reformists. The opposition, which is galvanised by Iran's radical civil society, continues to argue that the revolution has failed to live up to its expectations, certainly in realising a rather more democratic and just political order which was thought to be possible under the banner of Islam. Consequently, a counter-discourse has emerged that is confronting the ideologised Islam of the guardians of the disciplinary state with a transformative, secularised Islam defended by the cumbersome reformists.

On the other side, social policies such as the wide-ranging literacy campaign implemented immediately after the revolution and the massive expansion of the higher-education sector in the 1990s further expanded what I have called the geography of politics in Iran. Indeed, one central reason why women's right activists are at the forefront of political dissent in the country is their central position in Iran's highly educated middle class.[41] As such, the radical subject which today speaks in an emphatically feminine voice, not at least because the female body itself has been a site of war in modern Iran, has become an integral part of the 'pluralistic momentum' in the country.[42] It is this pluralistic momentum – diffuse, scattered, molar, eclectic, yet full of political impact – which is both the effect of and the arena for Iran's burgeoning civil society and the radical democratic politics that it engenders. I offer this in cautious conclusion of the two central topics of this essay: First, as a part of the genealogy of the radical subject in Iran, who today is neither apathetic, subdued by a feeling of political paralysis, nor unduly euphoric, intoxicated by a sense of an impending triumph over its rightwing competitors. And secondly, in support of my disquisition on the centrality of the Iranian experience to a truly comparative and critical theory of contemporary power and resistance and the histories of defeat and triumphalism that they provoke. After all, what is the purpose of critical theory if not the repositioning of histories in a global context? Mustn't we finally acknowledge that History itself is a truly hybrid field that is interpenetrated by the experiences of all of us? I think we have to, not only out of empathy, but also due to analytical necessity.

Notes

1. Shariati, Ali.
2. Giddens, A. 1994. *Beyond Left and Right: The Future of Radical Politics.* Polity: Cambridge, p.1.
3. Halliday, F. 1999. *Revolution and World Politics: The Rise and Fall of the Sixth Great Power.* Duke University Press: Durham, NC, p.36.
4. Giddens, op.cit., p.1.
5. Gramsci, A. 1971. *Selections from the Prison Notebooks*, edited and translated by Quinton Hoare and Geoffrey Nowell Smith. Lawrence and Wishart: London, p.58 ff. The concept of 'passive revolution' is revisited persuasively in Morton, A.D. 2007. *Unravelling Gramsci: Hegemony and Passive Revolution in the Global Economy.* Pluto Press: London.
6. Kraminick, I. 1972. 'Reflections on Revolution: Definition and Explanation in Recent Scholarship', *History and Theory*, 11 (1), pp.30–31.
7. Similarly, Hannah Arendt emphasises the element of a complete transformation, a temporal break with the prevalent order with regard to the revolutions in France and America: 'These two things together – a new experience which revealed man's capacity for novelty' she writes, 'are at the root of the enormous pathos which we find in both the American and the French Revolutions, this ever-repeated insistence that nothing comparable in grandeur and significance had ever happened in the whole recorded history of mankind ....' 1999. *On Revolution.* Penguin: London, p.34.
8. Halliday, op.cit., p.38. Halliday argues that Theda Skocpol's theory of revolution (1979. *State and Social Revolutions: A Comparative Analysis of France, Russia and China.* Cambridge University Press: Cambridge, pp.46–47) unnecessarily prioritises war, and external factors in general, in the making and success of revolutionary movements. A similar argument against Skocpol's top-down approach is presented by Nikki Keddie (ed., 1996. *Debating Revolutions.* New York University Press: New York, p.viii) and Said Amir Arjomand (1988. *The Turban for the Crown: The Islamic Revolution in Iran.* Oxford University Press: Oxford, pp.191–192).
9. A comprehensive re-treatment of subjectivity and agency is offered by Palti, E. 2004. 'The "Return of the Subject" as a Historical-Intellectual Problem', *History and Theory*, 43 (1) (February), pp.57–82.

10. Abrahamian, E. 2008. *A History of Iran*. Cambridge University Press: Cambridge, p.39; Katouzian, H. 2006. *State and Society in Iran: The Eclipse of the Qajars and the Emergence of the Pahlavis*. I.B.Tauris: London, p.33 ff.; and Keddie, N. 1966. *Religion and Rebellion in Iran: The Tobacco Protest of 1891–1892*. Frank Cass: Abingdon, p.131.

11. Abrahamian, op.cit., pp.45–49.

12. Azimi, F. 2008. *The Quest for Democracy in Iran: A Century of Struggle against Authoritarian Rule*. Harvard University Press: Cambridge, MA, p.3.

13. Abrahamian, op.cit., p. 46.

14. Enayat, H. 1982. *Modern Islamic Political Thought: The Response of the Shi'i and the Sunni Muslims to the Twentieth Century*. I.B.Tauris: London, p.174.

15. Ibid., p.167.

16. See further Algar, H. 1980. *Religion and State in Iran, 1785–1906: The Role of the Ulema in the Qajar Period*. University of California Press: Berkeley, CA; and Hairi, A-H. 1977. *Shi'ism and Constitutionalism in Iran: A Study of the Role Played by the Persian Residents of Iraq in Iranian Politics*. E.J. Brill: Leiden.

17. I have started to engage with this political economy in *Iran in World Politics: The Question of the Islamic Republic*. Columbia University Press: New York, 2008.

18. Kasravi, A. 2008. *Tarikh-e mashrute-ye Iran* [History of the Iranian Constitution]. Tehran: Negah Publications; and Naini, M.H. 2003. *Tanbih al-ummah wa tanzih al-millah* [Advising the Muslim community and purifying the religion]. Bustan-e Ketabe Qom Press: Qom.

19. On the history and politics of the Iranian 'Left' see Cronin, S. (ed.) 2004. *Reformers and Revolutionaries in Modern Iran: New Perspectives on the Iranian Left*. Routledge: Abingdon.

20. Hardt, M., and Negri, A. 1994. *Labor of Dionysus: A Critique of the State-Form*. University of Minnesota Press: Minneapolis, pp.286–287.

21. Kurzman, C. 2004. *The Unthinkable Revolution in Iran*. Harvard University Press: Cambridge, MA.

22. Quoted in Pistor-Hatam, A. 2007. 'Writing Back? Jalal Al-e Ahmad's (1923–69): Reflections on Selected Periods of Iranian History', *Iranian Studies*, 40 (5) (December), p.565.

23. Quoted in Rahnema, A. 2000. *An Islamic Utopian: A Political Biography of Ali Shariati*. I.B.Tauris: London, p.305.

24. Boroujerdi, M. 1996. *Iranian Intellectuals and the West: The Tormented Triumph of Nativism*. Syracuse University Press: Syracuse.

25. Guevara, C. 1969. *Guerrilla Warfare*. Penguin: Harmondsworth, p.21, emphasis in original.

26. CIA, Directorate of Intelligence. 1972. *Intelligence Report: Centres of Power in Iran*. Available from: http://www.state.gov/documents/organization/70712.pdf, p.11, accessed 24 December 2009.

27. Pahlavi, M.R.S. 1963. 'A Future to Outshine Ancient Glories', *Life*, 31 May, p.66.

28. Stockholm International Peace Research Institute. 1977. *World Armaments and Disarmament Year Book for 1977*. MIT Press: Cambridge, MA, pp.228–229.

29. Abrahamian, E. 1982. *Iran between Two Revolutions*. Princeton University Press: Princeton, pp.435–436.

30. The first census in Iran was undertaken in 1956, but it was largely considered to be unreliable or 'unscientific'. See further Firoozi, F. 1970. 'Iranian Censuses 1956 and 1966: A Comparative Analysis', *Middle East Journal*, 24 (2) (Spring 1970), pp.220–228.

31. Foucault, M. 1991. *Discipline and Punish: The Birth of the Prison*, trans. Alan Sheridan. Penguin: London, p.11.

32. Subsequently, Karl-Heinz Kurras who shot Ohnesorg in the courtyard of Krumme Strasse 66 in Berlin was cleared of all charges in two trials.

33. See further my *A Metahistory of the Clash of Civilisations: Us and Them beyond Orientalism*. Columbia University Press: New York, 2011, Chapter 3.

34. Buck-Morss, S. 2002. *Dreamworld and Catastrophe: The Passing of Mass Utopia in East and West*. MIT Press: Cambridge, MA, pp.2–3.

35. Foucault, M. 1998. *The Will to Knowledge: The History of Sexuality, Volume 1*, translated by Robert Hurley. Penguin: London, p.96.

36. Khomeini quoted in Moin, B. 1999. *Khomeini: Life of the Ayatollah*. I.B.Tauris: London, p.104. On Israel, Khomeini was particularly uncompromising declaring elsewhere that Iranians, Muslims and the oppressed of the world would never accept the state of Israel and that Iranians would always support 'their Palestinian and Arab brothers'. Khomeini, R. 1373 [1994]. *Ain-e enghelab-e Islami: Gozidehai az andisheh va ara-ye Imam Khomeini*. moasses-ye tanzim va naschr-e assar-e Imam Khomeini: Tehran, p.200.

37. Foucault, M. 2002. *Power: Essential Works of Foucault 1954–1984, Volume 3*, trans. Hurley, R., et al., ed. Faubion, J.D. Penguin: London, p.451.

38. On this 'lapse' in Foucault's theory see Fitzhugh, M.L., and Leckie, W.H. Jr. 2001. 'Postmodernism, and the Causes of Change', *History and Theory*, 40 (4) (December), especially p.63ff.

39. See further Adib-Moghaddam, *Iran in World Politics*, part 1.

40. See further Abrahamian, E. 1999. *Tortured Confessions: Prisons and Public Recantations in Modern Iran*. University of California Press: Berekely, CA, p.106; and Halliday, F. 1979. *Iran: Dictatorship and Development*. Penguin: London, 75 ff.

41. See further Adib-Moghaddam, *Iran in World Politics*, part 4.

42. Ibid.

Bibliography

Abrahamian, E. 1982. *Iran between Two Revolutions.* Princeton University Press: Princeton.

—— 1999. *Tortured Confessions: Prisons and Public Recantations in Modern Iran.* University of California Press: Berkeley.

—— 2008. *A History of Iran.* Cambridge University Press: Cambridge.

Adib-Moghaddam, A. 2012. 'What Is Radicalism? Power and Resistance in Iran', *Middle East Critique,* xx (xx), pp.xxx–xxx.

—— 2011. *A Metahistory of the Clash of Civilisations: Us and Them beyond Orientalism.* Columbia University Press: New York.

—— 2008. *Iran in World Politics: The Question of the Islamic Republic.* Columbia University Press: New York.

Arendt, H. 1990. *On Revolution.* Penguin: London.

Arjomand, S.A. 1988. *The Turban for the Crown: The Islamic Revolution in Iran.* Oxford University Press: Oxford.

Boroujerdi, M. 1996. *Iranian Intellectuals and the West: The Tormented Triumph of Nativism.* Syracuse University Press: Syracuse.

Buck-Morss, S. 2002. *Dreamworld and Catastrophe: The Passing of Mass Utopia in East and West.* Massachusetts Institute of Technology Press: Cambridge, MA.

CIA, Directorate of Intelligence. 1972. *Intelligence Report: Centres of Power in Iran.*

Cronin, S. (ed.) 2004. *Reformers and Revolutionaries in Modern Iran: New Perspectives on the Iranian Left.* Routledge: London.

Enayat, H. 1982. *Modern Islamic Political Thought: The Response of the Shi'i and the Sunni Muslims to the Twentieth Century.* I.B.Tauris: London.

Fakhreddin, A. 2010. *The Quest for Democracy in Iran: A Century of Struggle against Authoritarian Rule.* Harvard University Press: Cambridge, MA.

Firoozi, F. 1970. 'Iranian Censuses 1956 and 1966: A Comparative Analysis', *Middle East Journal,* 24 (2), pp.220–228.

Fitzhugh, M.L., and Leckie, W.H., Jr. 2001. 'Postmodernism, and the Causes of Change', *History and Theory,* 40 (4), pp.58–81.

Foucault, M. 1991. *Discipline and Punish: The Birth of the Prison,* trans. Alan Sheridan. Penguin: London.

—— 1998. *The Will to Knowledge: The History of Sexuality, Volume 1,* translated by Robert Hurley. Penguin: London.

—— 2002. *Power: Essential Works of Foucault 1954–1984, Volume 3,* trans. Robert Hurley et al., Faubion, J.D. (ed.). Penguin: London.

Giddens, A. 1994. *Beyond Left and Right: The Future of Radical Politics.* Polity: Cambridge.

Gramsci, A. 1971. *Selections from the Prison Notebooks,* edited and translated by Quinton Hoare and Geoffrey Nowell Smith. Lawrence and Wishart: London.

Guevara, C. 1969. *Guerrilla Warfare.* Penguin: London.

Hairi, A.H. 1977 *Shi'ism and Constitutionalism in Iran: A Study of the Role Played by the Persian Residents of Iraq in Iranian Politics*. E.J. Brill: Leiden.

Halliday, F. 1979. *Iran: Dictatorship and Development*. Penguin: London.

—— 1999. *Revolution and World Politics: The Rise and Fall of the Sixth Great Power*. Duke University Press: Durham.

Hamid, A. 1980. *Religion and State in Iran, 1785–1906: The Role of the Ulema in the Qajar Period*. University of California Press: Berkeley.

Hardt, M., and Negri, A. 1994. *Labor of Dionysus: A Critique of the State-Form*. University of Minnesota Press: Minneapolis.

Kasravi, A. 2008. *Tarikh-e mashrute-ye Iran* [History of the Iranian Constitution]. Negah Publications: Tehran.

Katouzian, H. 2006. *State and Society in Iran: The Eclipse of the Qajars and the Emergence of the Pahlavis*. I.B.Tauris: London.

Keddie, N. (ed.) 1996. *Debating Revolutions*. New York University Press: New York.

—— 1966. *Religion and Rebellion in Iran: The Tobacco Protest of 1891–1892*. Frank Cass: London.

Khomeini, R. 1994. *Ain-e enghelab-e Islami: Gozidehai az andisheh va ara-ye Imam Khomeini*. Moasses-ye tanzim va naschr-e assar-e Imam Khomeini: Tehran.

Kraminick, I. 1972. 'Reflections on Revolution: Definition and Explanation in Recent Scholarship', *History and Theory*, 11 (1), pp.26–63.

Kurzman, C. 2004. *The Unthinkable Revolution in Iran*. Harvard University Press: Cambridge, MA.

Moin, B. 1999. *Khomeini: Life of the Ayataollah*, I.B.Tauris, London.

Morton, A.D. 2007. *Unravelling Gramsci: Hegemony and Passive Revolution in the Global Economy*. Pluto Press: London.

Naini, M.H. 2003. *Tanbih al-ummah wa tanzih al-millah* [Advising the Muslim community and purifying the religion]. Bustan-e Ketabe Qom Press: Qom.

Pahlavi, M.R.S. 1963. 'A Future to Outshine Ancient Glories', *Life Magazine*. 31 May.

Palti, E. 2004. 'The "Return of the Subject" as a Historical-Intellectual Problem', *History and Theory*, 43 (1), pp.57–82.

Pistor-Hatam, A. 2007. 'Writing Back? Jalal Al-e Ahmad's (1923–69): Reflections on Selected Periods of Iranian History', *Iranian Studies*, 40 (5), pp.559–578.

Rahnema, A. 2000. *An Islamic Utopian: A Political Biography of Ali Shariati*. I.B.Tauris: London.

Skocpol, T. 1979 *State and Social Revolutions: A Comparative Analysis of France, Russia and China*. Cambridge University Press: Cambridge.

Stockholm International Peace Research Institute. 1977. *World Armaments and Disarmament Year Book for 1977*. Massachusetts Institute of Technology Press: Cambridge, MA.

13

POLITICAL ISLAM IN THE GULF REGION

Abdullah Baabood

Political Islam in the Gulf region is not an entirely new phenomenon.[1] Historically there have been, at least, three major political Islamic movements that continue to have an enduring influence on the contemporary Gulf and regional politics. These are namely, the Abadhi (Ibadi) movement in Oman, Shi'a Islamism and the Sunni Salafi Wahabbi movement in Saudi Arabia. This chapter will discuss contemporary political Islam in the Gulf region and especially the countries of the Cooperation Council for the Arab States of the Gulf (GCC)[2] with reference to the evolution of the main political Islamic movements there.

Oman became an Abadhi state, ruled by a leader, the Imam who has been chosen by consensus from the early years of Islam apart from some periods of interruption in the late 1950s when the last Imam was defeated by the Sultan, aided by British forces. Abadhism, a form of Islam distinct from Shi'ism and the 'Orthodox' schools of Sunnism, had become the dominant religious sect in Oman by the eighth century AD. Today, Oman is the only country in the Islamic world with a majority Abadhi population. Abadhism is a movement stemming from a minority doctrine in Islam and is known for its 'moderate conservatism.' One distinguishing feature of Abadhism is the choice of ruler the 'Imam', by communal consensus and consent.[3]

Like Abadhism, Shi'sm affirms the merging of religious and political authority. It was initially a legitimate movement born from a quarrel over the succession to Prophet Mohammed in the seventh century.[4] Shia's have come to account for roughly one-tenth of the Muslim population but represent about 70 per cent of the population of the Gulf, of which the bulk reside on the Iranian shore.[5]

Wahabbism, a conservative, non-violent movement, is firmly rooted in Saudi society today and among the religious scholars, the *ulama*. The term '*Wahabbi*' refers to a religious tradition developed over the centuries by the *ulama* of the official Saudi religious establishment.[6] This revivalist movement initiated in Najd (Central Arabia) in the early eighteenth century by Muhammad Ibn Abd al-Wahhab has been continued by its followers who consider themselves to be the legitimate guardians of the Tradition. Indeed, in seeking to spread his *da'wa* (preaching), Abd al-Wahhab found an ally in Muhammad Ibn Saud, head of the small town of Dir'iyya (near modern-day Riyadh). Their pact in 1744 marked the foundation not only of the first Saudi state,[7] but also of a local religious establishment entrusted with developing and spreading Abd al-Wahhab's puritanical ideas.

Political Islam in the Gulf region is thus best seen in the context of the historical establishment of these Islamic movements as well as in the current rise in global religiosity including Islamic revivalism and resurgence in the Third World. However, political Islam in the Gulf region has its own flavour, with its own added local characteristics and idiosyncrasies.[8] This chapter will provide an overview of the historical development of political Islam in the Gulf region and consider the reasons and causes for its rise by providing a survey of the range of the contemporary Islamic movements in the region and their goals and aspirations.

Reasons for the Rise of Political Islam

In addition to the muddle amongst observers on theorising and conceptualising political Islam, there is also no consensus over explaining its reasons and causes and especially on accounting for the extraordinary pace and speed of its evolution and ascendance into what is probably the fastest moving force in the politics of the Muslim world. The gathering power and reaffirmation of the Islamic faith have causes internal and external to Islam itself. There is a wide-ranging general acceptance in the literature that the surge in Islamism appears to be an outcome of a host of historical, political, economic, cultural and social developments in Muslim countries. The colonial legacy,[9] the accountability of rulers, rapidly deteriorating social conditions, the marginalisation of large sections of society, intergenerational conflict, globalisation, cultural hegemony and the fear of losing identity and values, together with rising inequalities and the failure of earlier attempts to address these issues, such as Arab nationalism, have been among the main causes of the appeal of political Islam. The failure of capitalist modernity and the promised social utopia have made the language of morality, articulated through religion, a substitute form of politics.[10] While these developments constitute the background for the rise of political Islam in the Gulf region and other Arab and Muslim countries, other domestic, regional and global factors have also played a central role.

The governments of the Gulf States have mastered the art of co-optation and manipulation of religion and its ideas for the purposes of bolstering state power and for consolidating national identity as an additional attribute for the legitimacy of ruling dynasties.[11] Indeed, all GCC governments have constitutions or basic laws that explicitly proclaim Islam as the official religion of the state as well as the main, if not the sole, source of legislation. Religious teaching at schools and mosques is a central element of educational curriculi, while preaching at mosques and other social and religious gatherings has become a socio-political phenomena aimed at Islamising the population to counter the spread of other ideological concepts such as communism, socialism or even Arab nationalism. Given the lack of other venues for public speeches, gatherings and political congregations, mosques have become the only channel open to the population for public assembly. This is an essential issue, as far as political development in the Muslim world is concerned, and has much to do with the politicisation of religion, both by the regimes and by opposition groups.

Meanwhile, Gulf States governments have used Islamic tenets to create their own ideology and self-avowed identity in order to enhance their own legitimacy and to fend off other ideologies. Moreover, Gulf regimes have sought to respond to challenges from Islamic groups by using the same ideology as they do and by lending support to their activities both at home and abroad, in an effort to out-manoeuvre these groups and to tame and to co-opt them.

To many Islamists, the governments of the Gulf States fall short in their strict application of Islamic principles and shari'a law and are regarded as being tainted by human reasoning and by being unfaithful to the true teachings found in the Qur'an and in the *Sunna* ('The Way of the Prophet').[12] This calls into question the legitimacy of ruling regimes that by their very nature are mainly autocratic monocracies dominated by hereditary royal families. Opposition groups judge the performances of the Gulf States exposing what are perceived as their unacceptable shortcomings in both domestic and foreign policies. The question of legitimacy is, moreover, compounded by what they perceive as incompetent governance involved in corruption and mismanagement of state resources.

In foreign policy-making, domestic opposition to these regimes stems from their inability to ease the sufferings of the Palestinians and to resolve the Arab-Israeli conflict. The defeat of Arab armies at the hands of Israel and the continual Israeli occupation of Arab land including that of Jerusalem, Islam's third holiest site, as well as unchecked and unchallenged Israeli intransigence, have exposed the ineptness of these regimes and demonstrated their failure to defend Arab and Islamic causes. The policies of Western governments – and especially the United States – which unequivocally and uncritically support Israel is seen by many as applying double standards and is perceived as being directed against Arab and Islamic interests. The utility of the close relations Gulf States government have with the United States is, therefore, questioned by the restive populations and especially by Islamic groups. Governmental relationships with the West have become a liability and a burden for the Gulf States who have become defensive in response, while Islamic groups who call for more action and oppose such close relations have become popular and their message attains wider public appeal.

As the Gulf States gradually expanded their contacts with the outside world from the 1960s onwards, they exposed their citizens to broader political debates at a time of regional radicalisation and politicisation. Moreover, because of pragmatic considerations and regional politics the Gulf States urgently needed well-trained professionals at a time of rapid, oil-induced modernisation. Amongst those who emigrated to the Gulf in response were mainly members of the Muslim Brotherhood. The Muslim Brotherhood came to play a key role in the new and expanding administrations of the region, especially in education where they designed school and university curricula and formed the bulk of faculty members too. Gulf State regimes were also host to a large number of Syrian and Egyptian Muslim Brothers, who had been persecuted in their home countries by the Ba'athist and Nasserist regimes there.[13]

Syrian and Egyptian religious leaders were welcomed in the Gulf States and were the main reason for creating organised groups of the Muslim Brotherhood there in the 1950s and 1960s. Subsequently, they played a major role in the rise of the ancestral Salafi movements of the 1980s. The Gulf States also used the Muslim Brothers' politicised version of Islam as a weapon in their political and ideological disputes with their Nasserist and Ba'athist neighbours.[14]

In the Gulf, perhaps more than in any other part of the world, globalisation, modernisation and economic development have surpassed social and political development. As the socio-cultural fabric began to unravel under such pressure, the ensuing disaffection gave rise to a quest for familiar traditional values. Both the champions of official Islam and of popular Islam – those who defend the system and those who challenge the system – justify their policies and their demands in terms of the Islamic faith because of the reaffirmation of such familiar values that it provides.

In addition, empowered by oil wealth, the Gulf States embarked on consolidating state power and expanding state welfare programs throughout the region in an attempt to buy popular legitimacy in return. However, the benefits of these initiatives have been unevenly distributed, making material inequities and social imbalances greater and more visible than ever before. As population growth has also outstripped the economic prosperity of these rentier states, since their economic well-being is largely dependent on the vagaries of the oil market, the unwritten social contract – generous welfare for political acquiescence – has begun to be put into question.

Furthermore, falling oil prices in the 1980s and 1990s resulted in economic austerity and stagnation, as well as rising unemployment especially among youth. With the lack of successful economic diversification, less disposable income was available for governments of the Gulf States to distribute among their citizens and to finance welfare programs. Failure of other ideological forces to solve equity and distribution issues has invariably forced Islamic groups to take on that role and followers of other failed ideologies quickly converted to its appeal. Deteriorating socio-economic conditions at times of growing demography, highly skewed towards a young population with rising expectations, caused both social unrest and an ideological void which encouraged demands for political participation and stimulated opposition to government. In addition, the appeal of political Islam has been partly due to a popular reaction against official corruption and repression which, in the minds of many citizens, have reached intolerable levels. Issues of inequality and injustice are debated across the Gulf by those who contrast the sometimes objectionable realities of everyday life with the Islamic ideals of equality, justice and charity. Political Islam has become the means through which to express discontent and Islam's social promise suddenly has a political relevance.[15] This was accentuated by the official support that the religion has gained from governments, for quite different reasons, and the political space and sanctuary available for Islamic activism.

Although Iran was Shi'a in sectarian affiliation, and thus different from the dominant Sunnism in the Gulf States, the Iranian revolution in 1979 succeeded in inspiring religious advocates and in triggering religious organisation throughout the region. The Iranian revolution presented a model of revolutionary Islam, in contrast to the conservative model of the regimes in the Gulf States. To respond to the perceived threat of exporting Iran's Islamic version of revolution, conservative Gulf governments gave an extra dose of support to the Sunni camp at a time when political Islam was gathering momentum.

The Soviet invasion of Afghanistan in the early 1980s and the subsequent support from Gulf States with Western backing to *Jihad* in Afghanistan against the Red Army and the Communist regime in the country built up considerable support for activist Islam and a wide network of Islamic groups and organisations fighting against the Soviet occupation. These institutions received large financial, logistical, political and moral support from the Gulf States, whose citizens were recruited as *mujahidin* to participate in the struggle in Afghanistan where Osama bin Laden and his al-Qa'ida organisation were located. These groups were emboldened by the success of the *mujahidin* in Afghanistan. Later, the global experiences Islamists have had in Afghanistan, Bosnia and Chechnya, in their struggle in areas where Islam and Muslims were seen to be under attack, gained them much popular support, especially among alienated youth.

Other regional events aided this process and catalysed the attitudes of those who pursued Islamic ideas in the Gulf. Among such events are the civil war in Yemen and the emergence of Yemen's Islamist Movement for Reform (*Islah*), established in September 1990, which combined tribal influences along with those of the Yemeni Muslim Brotherhood and more radical Salafi groups.[16] The party, headed by Abdallah al-Ahmar, the leader of Hashid tribal confederation who was also elected speaker of Parliament, was invited into the ruling coalition, and the presidential council was altered to include one Islah member. It later played a role in the Yemeni war of re-unification in 1994. Moreover, the arrival of Islamists into government in Sudan in the 1980s had given another impetus of optimism for other Islamist organisations in the Arab world, since it was the first time for groups close to the Muslim Brotherhood to head an Arab country, even though it was through a military coup.[17]

The Iraqi invasion of Kuwait in 1990 resulted in a growing non-Muslim American troop presence in the region, particularly in Saudi Arabia – home to Islam's most holy sites – which was seen as heretical and undermined Gulf regimes. It also augmented the case of the opposition, especially Islamists.[18] The Gulf States were portrayed as American protectorates, a view which highlighted the dependence of these states on foreign protectors and their vulnerability to suggestions, insinuating that the billions spent on arm purchases and large defence contracts had been mismanaged. Washington's Middle East policies, especially those relating to the Arab-Israeli conflict, Palestine and Iraq damaged its allies in the region. Thus, in the eyes of the opposition, the Islamic credentials of these states was called into question and the continual presence of Western troops in the region – despite the subsequent US redeployment out of Saudi Arabia and into Qatar – was viewed as support for illegitimate governments.

The final blow was provided by the Bush Administration's policy of 'the war on terror', in the wake of the al-Qa'ida attack on American soil on 11 September 2001 and the subsequent American attack on Afghanistan to destroy the al-Qa'ida network and its host government, the Taliban. The subsequent treatment of detainees at the detention camp in *Guantánamo Bay* was perceived in the Arab world as a 'crusade' directed against Muslims. This belief was fuelled by the rise of xenophobia and Islamophobia in the West in response, which also coincided with neo-conservative policies warning of the rise of Islam and the looming clash of civilisations.

American sanctions against Iraq and the subsequent invasion in 2003 necessitated Gulf participation by providing land and logistical support to the United States and its allies to enforce sanctions and to mount the invasion. The drastic consequences of the invasion of Iraq, in terms of the loss of life and the suffering of the Iraqi people and the destruction of an Arab and Muslim country along with the treatment of Iraqi prisoners in Abu Ghraib prison fuelled further public anger throughout the Arab world, leading to a further rise in the appeal of political Islam. Indeed, the resulting Shi'a takeover of control of Iraq and Iranian involvement in this gave rise to more radical Sunni elements from the Gulf States joining the Iraqi resistance to the American occupation.

Unlike other ideologies in the Arab region, Islam forms an essential part of people's consciousness and is inherently embedded in the very fabric of Arab Muslim society. On a personal level, Islam as such constitutes a crucial element of identity. Political Islam, however, was initially held at bay by Arab nationalism which reigned supreme as the dominant ideology in the 1950s and 1960s until June 1967, when Arab armies were defeated in the Six Day War by Israel. In their search for alternative models to this increasingly discredited secular movement, Islam provided a ready answer as it reoriented people's vision to the glory of the past, to Muslim *esprit de corps* and to an authenticity untouched by corrupting foreign values. The public became more contemptuously dismissive of the Western concept of modernity, with its alien ideas of 'sovereignty' and 'nationalism', rejecting such notions as imported ideas (*hulul mustawrada*). 'The only solution is Islam' ('*al-Islam huwa al-hal*') became the operative slogan for political Islam. With the threat of globalisation and its cultural impact in the age of mass communication, political Islam gained more appeal in defending the identity and values of Arab Muslims.

Survey of Movements in Political Islam

Islamic groups and movements, as mentioned earlier, are not new phenomena; they existed in the region in one form or another well before the 1980s. However, they were mainly quietly occupied in teaching, preaching and proselytising. While other political and ideological forces such as Liberalism, Socialism, Nationalism, Baathism or Nasserism were the mode, Islamists groups were confined to providing community work and building up their socio-political bases. They barely existed at the political level and were largely confined to the fringe of the political and ideological arena. Islamic groups, nevertheless, began to take centre stage as other competing secular ideologies began to wane, helped by the changes in the new environment, as explained above.

Although they share some common ground, beliefs and aspirations, Islamic groups are far from being monolithic or homogeneous with a central organisation or hierarchical structure. Far from taking on uniform appearance, they appear in various forms depending to local conditions and particular needs and circumstances. They are commonly loose, fragmented and decentralised groups divided between different religious sects and factions, with diverse aims and objectives with means and methods that are often poles apart.

Nevertheless, with Islamic principles as their common source of inspiration, these groups share a similar historical context and operate in similar environments. Their goals and demands vary from the call for such ambitious aims as the overthrow of incumbent governments and ruling elites, or the creation of an Islamic state under shari'a law in opposition to official corruption, and calls for good governance, social justice and political reform.

The growing power of political Islam in the Gulf region is not monolithic in character either, for it emanates from the three main sects of Islam: Sunnism, Shi'ism and Abadhism, the latter being specific to Oman. Adherents of political Islamic groups are composed of a varied mix of workers, university students, intellectuals, religious scholars, businessmen and even royal princes.[19] Women, although not active participants, still play an important supporting role in the Islamisation of society.

Sunni Groups

The Sunni, with the largest number of followers, constitute the main group and is itself divided. There are generally three major Sunni movements extending from mainstream movements to traditional fundamentalism. They can be categorised into:

1. The Muslim Brotherhood: The Ikhwan (note changes)

The Muslim Brotherhood groups consist of *al-Ikhwan* as the mainstream and most accommodating; *al-Salafi* (traditional/ancestral) as the most extreme; and slightly less dogmatic is the *al-Islah* reform trend.[20] All three Sunni movements share a strong dislike for Shi'a Islam. In the words of a leading Sunni fundamentalist theoretician in Kuwait: 'Although the Shi'is do share some of our social and political goals, they have distorted Islam beyond imagination. We cannot and will not communicate and cooperate with them.'[21]

The Ikhwan, the mainstream Muslim Brotherhood, now has a small but active following among urban, educated Gulf citizens. Unlike the early Abadhi and the Salafi Wahhabi which respectively brought religion to the forefront of politics in the early eighth and eighteenth centuries, the Ikhwan was the start of the new wave of political Islam in the Gulf, which began in the 1980s. The Muslim Brotherhood began after the migration of its leaders from Nasserist-Egypt and Ba'athist-Syria to the Gulf where Gulf rulers welcomed them, co-opted its leaders to take over religious education and to confront new revolutionary ideas emanating from Arab Nationalist, Liberal and Leftist circles.

The Ikhwan adopted the method of directing, preaching and carrying out philanthropic activities while working alongside incumbent governments to achieve gradual reform and the transformation of society to Islamic principles. It, however, began to lose appeal for restive youth because of its long-term strategy for gradual change and the charge that it appeased rulers in exchange for senior government posts for its leaders who were thereby corrupted.

The Muslim Brotherhood still has followers in almost all of the Gulf States despite its waning. In Saudi Arabia, although its main pillars still remain, it has gradually given place to conservative Salafi and neo-Salafi movements, as many of its former members have moved to Salafism. However, it still has its followers among urban, educated Saudis.

In Qatar, it is no longer an organised movement. The Brotherhood was mainly active through the Youth of Doha Society which it subsequently dissolved, but it is still well represented within Islamic banking and Islamic financial services organisations. It has influence in media, education and religious institutions. Given its small Qatari following, it did not represent a political opposition and its former leaders enjoy high status and wide influence as well as close government relations.

In the UAE it was represented by the Society of Social Reform (*al-Islah al-Ijtimai*), which was dissolved in the mid 1990s. It concentrated on preaching and charitable work. It used to have sway in the education sector before the government decided to curb its influence. Despite some interesting initiatives by cadres and youth of the Brotherhood, intense security obstacles prevented them from doing much by way of modernising their views or engaging in popular action.

In Bahrain, the Brotherhood is active through the Reform Movement (*al Islah*), and its political wings, the Al-Menbar Islamic Society and the National Islamic Forum. Prominent members of Al Menbar include Dr Salah Abdulrahman, Dr Salah Al Jowder, and outspoken MP Mohammed Khalid. Following the parliamentary elections in 2002, Al Menbar had become the joint largest party with seven seats in the 40-seat Chamber of Deputies. However, in the 2010 elections, it only succeeded in securing three seats.[22] The party has generally backed government-sponsored legislation on economic issues but has sought a clamp down on other social issues such as pop concerts, sorcery and soothsayers. It has strongly opposed the government's accession to the International Covenant on Civil and Political Rights on the grounds that this would give Muslim citizens the right to change religion.[23] More recently, however, the Salafi trend has overwhelmed the movement – to the point of achieving hegemony over the Sunni Islamist arena.

In Kuwait the Muslim Brotherhood, which was created in the 1920s in part as a reaction to the growth of missonary activities in the region, used to maintain a low profile and had a secretive existence there. In 1991 it created the Social Reform and the Islamic Constitutional Movements (ICM) as it needed a new political front.[24] Kuwaiti Brotherhood members also established two women's civil society organisations;[25] Bayader al-Salam and the Islamic Care Society, to represent the emerging Islamic voice in Kuwaiti politics. Their goals covered a wide range of issues such as charity, ethics and morality and contributing to the global Islamic project of a comprehensive process of Islamisation to state and society across the Islamic world. However, their agenda and mandate went far beyond Kuwait to include Islamic causes worldwide such as Palestine, Afghanistan, Lebanon and Muslims in Africa, as they were part of the international Islamic Brotherhood movement which is dedicated to accomplishing 'the Islamic Project'. The invasion of Kuwait proved disastrous for the Kuwaiti Brotherhood, causing a rift with the international movement, which had tried to play a mediating role with Saddam Hussein.

In Oman, where political association is not allowed, the government uncovered in 1994 an Islamic cell of about 130 people believed to be members of the Muslim Brotherhood.[26] It was made up of high-ranking government officials together with security and army personnel. They were charged with forming an illegal political party to undermine state security and subversion. A state security court sentenced them to imprisonment and also issued some death sentences but the Sultan reduced these to imprisonment and finally freed them in 1995. Its followers, once freed, were not absorbed by government and some lost their official jobs. Many, however, found opportunities in the private sector where they enjoyed some success. After the security crackdown, the organisation went through a transitional period effectively in hibernation. It has, however, made a historic decision by refusing to be dragged into a sectarian conflict with the Ibadhis and the Shi'a despite efforts to push it in that direction.

2. The Salafi Movement

Although the Salafi movement had begun as long ago as the early eighteenth century in Saudi Arabia, it has been mainly an official movement and largely controlled by the government. Its revival since the 1970s, although influenced by regional events, was also due to the blurring of the Brotherhood and official Salafi ideas and teaching and because of the shortcomings and lack of their credibility. However, while the Muslim Brotherhood had begun in a different environment in Egypt and the Levant and was generally flexible and tolerant, dealing with women's rights and other social issues, the Salafi, mainly Wahhabi movement in the Arabian Peninsula, was generally scriptural and intolerant and some of its elements were even violent. It is made up of a number of groups.

Wahabbism

Wahabbism and the Saudi religious establishment historically constitute the core of the Saudi intellectual field. The influence of Wahhabism extends far beyond the religious establishment's official role. Since the state's foundation, the movement has shaped its religious culture, education and judiciary.[27] As a result, it has had to some degree an impact on all the kingdom's Sunni Islamist trends.

However, after decades of relative autonomy, the religious establishment has developed a noteworthy political pragmatism. To preserve its alliance with the rulers, it supports Saudi policy even if it diverges from their religiously held convictions.[28] It has also been used by the ruling elite to rubber-stamp official decisions, by issuing religious rulings to validate the regime's political stands.[29] Among these, the *fatwas* authorising the presence of foreign troops in 1990[30] and peace with Israel in 1993[31] cost the Wahhabi establishment much credibility – to such an extent that many Saudis now view it as a mere extension of the regime. However, while it continues to provide indispensable legitimacy to Saudi rule and acts as guardian of the country's official Wahhabi doctrine, its perceived alliance with the ruling elite has caused a neo-Wahabbism to emerge. The movement's pragmatism has repeatedly led to 'radical Wahhabis' opposing the official religious establishment and accusing it of being corrupt and subservient to the regime.[32] While early Wahhabism was unified it has now, in short, disintegrated into different strands.

The Salafi Reformers: al-Sahwa al-Islamiyya

The term *al-Sahwa al-Islamiyya* (the Islamic Awakening) refers to the eruption of religious activism that gripped Saudi universities in the 1970s and 1980s, not to any defined sub-movement per se. Ideologically, the young *Sahwa* Islamists advocated a blend of the traditional Wahhabi outlook (mainly on social and cultural issues) and the more contemporary Muslim Brotherhood approach (especially on political issues). They distinguished themselves from the Wahhabi establishment, which concentrates on abstract theological debates, by their readiness to discuss issues of contemporary significance. Unlike their official counterparts, they also were open to modern technology, such as the cassette tape, which rapidly became their principal means of communication, faxes and the extensive use of cyberspace.

A turning point in the *Sahwa* evolution was the 1979 take-over of the mosque in Mecca by Juhayman al-Utaybi and his group of Neo-Salafis, who were motivated to a large extent by anger at the perceived immorality and societal changes in Saudi Arabia, which the conservative and moderate religious establishment could not handle.[33] The regime, rather than using the opportunity to initiate long-overdue political and social changes, responded by strengthening the religious establishment and pouring additional money into religious institutions as a means of co-opting its critics and bolstering its legitimacy. The unintended consequence was to strengthen the *Sahwa*, which was not at that time considered to be an autonomous movement and had been largely assimilated into the margins of the official establishment. The *Sahwa* used their significant presence in the educational sector to take advantage of the government support.

With this new-found impetus, *Sahwa* clerics grew increasingly confident and began to participate in public debates. They took issue both with liberals, who they accused of undermining Saudi society through secularisation,[34] and with the Wahhabi establishment, who they criticised for its lack of interest in contemporary issues and – albeit still in veiled terms – its unconditional support for the regime.

This *neo-Wahabbi* reformist strain was made of the self-styled '*ulama* of the centre' – centrist religious scholars – who had emerged from the Islamic awakening. These were personalities such as Salman al-Awdah and Ayad al-Qarni. In the 1990s and beginning with the Gulf War, *Sahwa* clerics, such as Salman al-Awdah, Safar al-Hawali, Ayidh al-Qarni and Nasir al-Omar became more vocal, denouncing the state's failure to conform to Islamic values, and its corruption and subservience to the United States, whilst condemning official Wahhabi clerics for their silence on these matters.

Sahwa clerics had never, however, constituted a uniform group. From the outset, and because of their background, they have displayed a variety of undercurrents, some closer to Wahhabism, others to the Muslim Brotherhood.[35] Such divisions to this day are still manifest in their conflicting positions on issues such as relations with liberal reformers, Shi'as or Sufis, and attitudes towards al-Qa'ida and other violent Islamists.[36]

Both the *Sahwa* and the *neo-Sahwa* (Sahwaism) accepted the legitimacy of the Saudi state as a political structure and would only demand, after the second Gulf war in 1990, a reform of its policies. In

Kuwait, Salafism was more marginal and had its base in the Revival of Islamic Heritage Society (RIHS) – an influential Islamic association group that had been gaining strength since the 1970s, and in *al-Tajammu' al-Islami al-Sha'bi* (the Popular Islamic Grouping) after Kuwait liberation in 1991, better known as *al-salaf* (ancestors), which has its roots in the Society for the Rebirth of the Islamic Tradition. This group, which has been attracting followers since the 1980s, is more literal than the Constitutional Movement in its interpretation of Islam.[37] While Salafis traditionally shunned politics for ideological reasons, they became more involved after the liberation of Kuwait. For example, the Popular Islamic Grouping joined other political groups in demanding that the ruling family reinstate the constitution and parliament, increase popular participation in government and maintain the independence of the judiciary, as well as to participating in local elections.[38]

The Salafi Rejectionists

Rejectionist Islamists (sometimes referred to as neo-Salafists) first appeared in the 1970s on the margins of the *Sahwa*; however they regarded the *Sahwa* as overly interested in politics, just as they considered the *Jihadists* to be ignorant on religious affairs. Unlike *Sahwa* reformers who were dominant in schools and universities, rejectionists avoided official education altogether, seeking religious teaching opportunities elsewhere. They focused on questions of individual faith, morals and ritual practices, as opposed to broader social, cultural or political issues. They were not only hostile to the very concept of the nation-state, they regarded the state as illegitimate, seeking not to modify it but to break with it – most often through withdrawal but at times through revolt.

Rejectionist Islamists are also not a homogenous social or political movement. Indeed, there was far more diversity among them in approach and organisational structure than among the *Sahwa*. Saudi rejectionist Islamism, for example, has been variously represented by organisations such as the one led by Juhayman al-Utaybi, which seized Mecca's Great Mosque in 1979; fringe communities, which typically withdrew from society and adopted a very conservative, puritan lifestyle; and informal religious study circles, which rejected both the mosque-based Wahhabi and school and university-centred *Sahwa* teachings.[39]

Juhayman al-Utaybi founded a movement known as the *al-Jamaa al-Salafiyya al-Muhtasiba* (JSM). The JSM movement was one of the Saudi rejectionists' most visible and organised manifestations. The JSM began in Medina in the mid 1970s and was inspired in part by the views of Nasr al-Din al-Albani (1909–99), a Syrian scholar.[40] JSM rejected all schools of Islamic jurisprudence (*fiqh*), including Wahhabism, insofar as they involved a degree of human judgement, adhering instead to a literal reading of the *hadith* (traditions of the Prophet's sayings) as the sole source of religious truth. Disagreements with the Wahhabi establishment initially turned on ritual questions; over time, however, JSM evolved into a full-fledged socio-political protest movement with vast significance.

For example, a radicalised faction of JSM under the leadership of Juhayman seized the Mecca mosque in the 1979 uprising. The significance of the mosque take-over itself is that while some of Juhayman's followers were persuaded that his companion, Muhammad al-Qahtani, was the Mahdi (the Islamic equivalent of the messiah), and that the Mecca operation would bring about the end of the world, many others took part in order to precipitate radical political and social change.[41]

Juhayman and his companions were either executed or imprisoned and the JSM as an organisation disappeared after the Mecca events, but the bulk of its basic ideas, notably the critique of social corruption and moral decadence in Juhayman's writings, outlived him.[42] JSM remnants sought refuge in Kuwait, Yemen and northern Saudi desert regions in the 1980s. A decade later, groups of young Islamists who called themselves 'students of religious knowledge' (*talabat 'ilm*) and viewed themselves as direct JSM heirs still could be found seeking out remaining Juhayman companions among desert Bedouins. Shunning mosques and universities, they formed religious study groups in their homes and they had for all practical purposes withdrawn from a society they deemed sinful. Juhayman al-Utaybi's letters were re-published in Kuwait years later and inspired a younger generation of neo-Salafi ideologues. One of those who had been introduced to Juhayman's writings in Kuwait was Abu Muhammad al-Maqdisi, who in the 1990s became a leading ideologue of the so-called salafi-*jihadi* trend.[43]

Another faction was the *Madhakhila*, the followers of Saudi scholar Rabi' al-Madkhali. Certain adherents of this thought, including al-Madkhali, initially opposed the Saudi state, but were co-opted by it following the 1979 events in Mecca. Led by al-Madkhali, they subsequently became the Al Saud's staunchest apologists.[44] This tendency rejects any challenge to the authority of rulers no matter how deviant their behaviour. It also considers *manhaj* (methodology) and *'aqida* (doctrine) to be inseparable, thus precluding the adoption of innovative political practices such as participation in political parties and parliaments. Moreover, those engaged in such activities are often targeted as unbelievers. Several prominent figures within the Kuwaiti Salafi movement came to adhere to this school, separating themselves from the politicised Salafi majority.[45]

The Committee for the Defense of Legitimate Rights

As a direct challenge to the Saudi authorities, in May 1993, six prominent Islamists announced the formation in Riyadh of Saudi Arabia's first human rights organisation – The Committee for the Defence of Legitimate Rights (CDLR). It is a loosely-knit political reform group that began expressing itself after the 1991 Gulf War. Its intention was to place the Islamic group's struggle against the regime within the context of worldwide human rights movements. Although the CDLR declarations did not define human rights in terms of generally accepted universal standards accepted by global human rights organisations – they were defined within the legitimate confines of shari'a law in a strict Islamic interpretation (*al-huquq al-shar'iyyah*), international human rights groups rushed to support the Saudi association.[46] It was, however, disbanded by the authorities two weeks after its formation and its spokesman, Mohammed al-Mas'ari, was jailed. However, CDLR members were among the signatories of the 1992 memorandum of advice calling for the eradication of corruption and the application of shari'a law. Mas'ari was freed in 1993 and clandestinely went to London where he re-founded the CDLR with Sa'ad al-Faqih in

April 1994. Through a series of communiqués faxed to Saudi Arabia and elsewhere, the CDLR sought to mobilise public opinion against the Saudi regime and its human rights record. Despite attacks, the CDLR advocated moderation and peaceful change in the kingdom on the basis of Shari'a principles. In 1996 the CDLR split because of disputes between its UK-based founders, Mas'ari and al-Faqih, and the latter created the Movement of Islamic Reform in Arabia (MIRA), which followed more radical approaches.[47] Until this split, the CDLR had been one of the most organised and professional of Saudi political opposition groups.

Salafi Jihadists

Salafi jihadism is a loose description used to designate an outlook that invokes Wahhabi theology to advocate resort to violence. In effect, Wahhabism provided *jihadists* with a more sophisticated theological framework for their activism. This violent version, with followers among radical youth, enjoyed (overt and covert) support of some of the *ulama*.[48] While both Salafi reformers and Salafi rejectionists are at pains to distinguish themselves from those they refer to as *jihadists*, there were instances of rejectionists gravitating towards *jihadi* circles and their activism occurred with increasing frequency from the early 1990s onwards.[49] In the mid 1990s, the *Jihadi* movement, of which al-Qa'ida is the most prominent radical group, was split into two main branches: the 'classical *jihadists*' and the more radical and marginal 'global *jihadists*'.[50] The distinction between the two branches is that classical *jihadists* prefer to wage semi-conventional warfare within confined theatres of war, while global *jihadists* were prepared to use all means in all locations to attain their ends. This was the main reason for the separation of Abu Khattab, the Saudi commander of the Arabs in Chechnya, from Osama bin Laden, the Saudi *jihadist* leader in Afghanistan.[51]

The origins of current *jihadism* can be traced back to the participation – actively encouraged and facilitated by Gulf regimes and Western governments at the time – of thousands of Saudis and, to a lesser extent, other Gulf nationals who participated in the Afghan war against the Soviet Union. These governments offered logistical and financial assistance to prospective *mujahidin* – for example, subsidised flights to Pakistan – and the official religious establishment declared it a collective duty (*fard kifayah*) for Muslims to fight in Afghanistan.[52]

There is no satisfactory comprehensive analysis of the motivations and socio-economic background of Saudis and other Gulf nationals who went to Afghanistan in the 1980s and 1990s. Although their motivation was not clear, they appear not to have been driven by any particular political project or religious belief. For most of them – mostly teenagers – participation was purely symbolic; the trip rarely lasted more than the summer holidays, and many never made it across the border from Pakistan to Afghanistan. For those who remained, the experience was profoundly transformative, as they became part of the romanticised culture of violent resistance that flourished within the Arab contingent in the Afghan *mujahidin* war.[53]

These militants developed an ultra-masculine, militaristic and violent worldview, and they experienced their initial political awakening outside their own country. Moreover, the so-called Afghan Arab *jihadists*, who retained a home base, were given virtually free access in and out of their country during the 1990s and were in a position to influence Gulf youth.[54]

By the end of the Afghan war against the Soviet Union, a global *jihadist* culture had already spread in many Gulf Islamist circles while many of Gulf youth continued to leave their countries in search of military training and to gain combat experience throughout the 1990s, particularly once al-Qa'ida had established a training camp infrastructure in Afghanistan in the mid 1990s.[55]

The US-led invasion of Afghanistan in the aftermath of 9/11, the fall of the Taliban and the 'global war on terror' denied al-Qa'ida its safe haven, thus removing the basis of its unique organisational concept and resulting in a decentralised and multipolar version of the global *jihadist* movement.[56] With *mujahidin* recruits returning home, al-Qa'ida began to change its tactics and perspectives and started its war against the 'crusaders' in the Arabian Peninsula. Additionally, the US-led invasion of Iraq in March 2003 gave the global *jihadist* movement a strategic and emotional focal point at a time when the movement was strategically disoriented, having lost its territorial base in

Afghanistan. A splinter group of al-Qa'ida known as 'al-Qa'ida in the Arabian Peninsula' (AQAP) launched a terrorist campaign in 2003 with a series of large-scale attacks against Western targets in Saudi Arabia, pitting them against Saudi security services and undermining and diverting attention from another al-Qa'ida splinter group in Iraq known as *al-Qa'ida fi Bilad al-Rafedain* 'al-Qa'ida in the land of the Two Rivers'. The latter was involved in fighting against American troops and Shi'a dominance in Iraq. This rekindled the ideological conflict between classical *jihadists* and global *jihadists* as it was considered to drain crucial human and financial resources away from individual campaigns.[57] The invasion and occupation of Iraq led to a channelling of radical forces to Iraq, possibly at the expense of other *jihad* fronts. It also changed the *jihadist* notion of the enemy and placed the Gulf countries and even Europe more clearly in the spotlight, which explains the number of terrorist attacks in Europe and the increase in the number of violent incidents in Gulf countries such as Kuwait and Qatar.[58]

Shi'a Islamists[59]

The Shi'a Islamist presence as a political movement in the Gulf is more recent than the Sunni Ikhwan. Its political framework and evolution began to emerge with the creation of the al-Daawa Party in Iraq in 1958, which was eager to create branches in the Gulf and other Arab countries in the 1960s and 1970s.[60] Learning from the Ikhwan's organisational and political experience, the al-Daawa Party started to open affiliate branches in Bahrain, the Eastern Province of Saudi Arabia and Kuwait. While political openness in Kuwait helped it to operate in a relatively public manner, political conditions in Bahrain and Saudi Arabia prevented it from doing so, despite the fact that some of al-Dawaa leaders came from these countries.[61]

Where Sunni Islamism has fragmented into rival tendencies with distinctive worldviews as well as different strategies and forms of organisation, Shi'a Islamism has remained impressively integrated. However, there is no such thing as Pan-Shi'ism, or even a unified leadership.[62] In contrast to Sunnis, Shi'as are better organised and share coherent religious views. They have also developed a distinct conception of Islamic laws and practices. Specifically, Shi'ism is not differentiated into separate political, missionary and *jihadi* forms of activism. This is ultimately rooted in its historic status as the minority form of Islam. More immediately, activism is closely connected with a remarkable feature of Shi'a Islamism, namely the leading political role of the *'ulama*. Historically, the *'ulama's* influence has been based on their autonomy vis-à-vis the state. But their authority within the Shi'a community also owes a great deal to the fact that, unlike their Sunni counterparts, the mainstream Shi'a *'ulama* have never stopped practicing *ijtihad*, the intellectual effort involved in the interpretation of scripture. Notwithstanding the images of bearded and turbaned clerics, the activist Shi'a *'ulama* have been far more modernist in this sense than most of their Sunni counterparts. The result is that the divisions within Shi'a Islamism are quite different from those in Sunni Islamism in their origins, nature and implications.

Although reliable data is unavailable, three Gulf States have sizable Shi'a populations. They are estimated to be roughly around 10 per cent of the overall population in Saudi Arabia, 30 per cent in Kuwait, 15 per cent in UAE, something between 50–70 per cent in Bahrain and smaller percentages in the remaining Gulf States.

Because of their status as the minority and as politically marginal or even oppressed communities (whether or not they have been absolute numerical minorities) in most of the states in which they have found themselves, communalism – the defence of community interests in relation to other populations and the state – has become the most natural form of Shi'a political activism.[63] This has been the case for Shi'a activism in both the Gulf States of Kuwait, Saudi Arabia and the United Arab Emirates, and even Lebanon and Pakistan. It has also been the tendency in states where Shi'as have become the numerical majority, such as Iraq and Bahrain.

Although Shi'a movements in some of the Gulf States were relatively active in the past due to socio-economic and political grievances, it was the Iranian revolution that gave a strong political and moral velocity to the movement. The success of the Shi'a revolution in Iran was a turning point not only for all of the political Islam movements in the region but had even more relevance to the Shi'as. The revolution introduced an entirely new lexicon – the use of religion as a political tool – and inspired more populist movement throughout the region where the Shi'a now had a more powerful neighbour, Iran, to support their cause. Khomeini's promise to export Iranian-style revolution to the Gulf monarchies gave the Shi'a an ally and a supporter so that Shi'a uprisings began to gather momentum throughout the Gulf States.

In Saudi Arabia, the Shi'as are mainly concentrated in the oil-rich Eastern Province, which was integrated into the Saudi state in 1913. Since then, Shi'as have complained about not being allowed to practice their faith freely and of being treated as second-class citizens.[64] In fact, Shi'a Islamist organisations began to emerge in the Eastern Province in the 1970s, enraged by the socio-economic and political marginalisation of the Shi'a. The process accelerated with the 1979 Iranian revolution and, invigorated by that uprising, thousands celebrated the Shi'a Ashura festival despite an official ban. The resulting heavy-handed response led to violent confrontations and disturbances in 1979 and 1980 which were crushed by the Saudi National Guard.[65] Few Shi'a activists remained in Saudi Arabia thereafter and those who did were co-opted and silenced by the regime. Most fled to Syria, Iran, Britain or the United States. Significant mass civil disobedience lasted less than a decade, but the leadership gradually moderated its views, recognising the limitations of agitation and violence and seeking improved ties with a regime whose legitimacy it came to acknowledge and whose role as a bulwark against more extreme Sunni militants it came to accept. By the late 1980s, many leaders had moderated their views, distancing themselves from Khomeini-style agendas and embracing principles of political pluralism and democracy.[66] In 1993, the Saudi government reached an agreement with the exiled activists, pursuant to which many returned.[67]

The 11 September 2001 attacks and the al-Qa'ida in the Arabian Peninsular's subsequent terror campaign inside the Kingdom focused government attention on the most militant forms of religious extremism. They also spurred rapprochement between non-violent Islamists and liberal Sunni and who, faced with the threat of violent Sunni militancy, joined in calling for political and religious reform. But if al-Qa'ida's activities offered a chance to improve sectarian relations, the war in Iraq has pulled in the opposite direction. Emboldened by the example of Iraqi co-religionists, some Saudis believed they ought to press further, while the sight of Shi'a dominance in yet another neighbouring country has heightened Sunni suspicion. A rising number of Saudi Sunni *jihadi* militants have been seeking new battlefields and threatening Western and governmental targets, as well as the minority drawn to Iraq and motivated by opposition to the United States but also to the increased role of the Shi'a there.[68]

Activists there periodically express community grievances yet are at pains to make clear their loyalty to the nation. They openly display their hostility to any alliance with an outside power, and – in an effort to pre-empt an obvious regime concern – show their determination not to take advantage of the situation in Iraq. Some explicitly deny the existence of a 'question', insofar as 'the problems affecting us are those that affect the Saudi nation as a whole'.[69] Thus, in April 2003, three weeks after the fall of Iraq's Ba'athist regime, 450 activists signed a letter to the Saudi Crown Prince requesting an end to religious discrimination and the establishment of a religious authority to regulate their affairs in Saudi Arabia. Equally, by demonstrating their clear nationalist stance, fifteen Shi'a intellectuals, mainly Islamists, were able to join the centrist coalition that issued the January 2003 petition. Among them were Jaafar al-Shayeb, a long-time rights campaigner and Muhammad al-Mahfuz. Hasan al-Saffar, the long-time leader of the Saudi Islamist movement, welcomed the initiative. While some liberals balked at the December 2003 petition's overly 'Islamist' tones and the presence among the signatories of prominent Sunni Islamists from the *Sahwa*, the latter remained part of the movement. This represents a significant evolution in Saudi Islamism, insofar as *Sahwists* and Islamists had traditionally considered each other enemies and avoided any cooperation on political issues.[70]

Anxious about the centrists, but far more fearful of any potential Shi'a separatism, the regime appears to view the centrist/Shi'a rapprochement as the lesser of two evils. This explains why it has for the most part spared Shi'a Islamists during the recent crackdown: none of their leaders were arrested, and the only Shi'a who remains in jail, Ali al-Dumayni, is a liberal activist who has not formulated his political demands within a Shi'a framework.

By most accounts, community leaders such as al-Saffar have persuaded the vast majority of the Shi'a movement of the wisdom of this conciliatory approach. More radical factions have in effect been silenced. Modest as they may be, the achievements of the Shi'a community – most notably the right to celebrate Ashura in relative freedom, gained in March 2004 – strengthened al-Saffar and the moderate leadership while winning over some residual sceptics. The Saudi Government has accepted more rights, most importantly by promoting inclusive national dialogues and bringing key members of the Sunni clergy along.

Informal Shi'a Networks

Activists who helped transform religious and political authority in the late 1970s and share personal bonds and a common experience in confronting the regime now lead The Islamic Reform Movement, the most powerful and popular religious-political network. It is a loose network, lacking central coordination, or an official membership. While its popular support cannot be precisely assessed, its unofficial candidates swept the 2005 municipal elections in predominantly Shi'a communities. The group has abandoned its 1970s radicalism and focus chiefly on education, charities, counselling programs and mosque maintenance. The most prominent leaders, including al-Saffar, also aspire to a national role as interlocutors between the rulers and the Shi'a. In recent years, they registered some success in carving out space for Shia's.[71]

Saudi Hizbollah (*Ansar Khat al-Imam*) is the next largest Shi'a Islamist group and is also known locally as the Followers of the Line of the Imam 'Khomeini'. Founded in 1987 by several prominent clerics, it is a clergy-led, religious-political organisation whose leaders come from the Eastern Provinces.[72] Saudi Hizbollah is distinguished from the Islamic Reform Movement in two important ways. First, it espouses Khomeini's principle of *vilayat-e-faqih* (Leadership by the Jurisconsult), and most members emulate the *marja'iyya* (religious leadership) of Iran's Supreme Leader, Ayatollah Khomeini. There is also a small yet important difference in juridical theory. While the Islamic Reform Movement calls for greater clerical involvement in politics, it does not insist that the clergy supervise political affairs. Secondly, the Followers of the Line of the Imam reject the Islamic Reform Movement's more conciliatory approach, wholly distrusting the ruling al-Said family and government. For the most part, that sentiment has translated into isolation (as opposed to al-Saffar's engagement with government) though the Islamic Reform Movement reportedly has slipped into periodic violence as well. The Khobar attack of 1996 is typically highlighted, despite continued uncertainty as to whether that organisation was behind the bombing and whether, assuming the perpetrators belonged to Hizbollah, they directed the actual attack. The government cracked down in the wake of the Khobar bombing which led Hizbollah/The Followers of the Line of the Imam to focus on social and cultural activities to the exclusion of politics resulting in its increased influence.

'Traditionalists and Rejectionists' is the smallest Islamist political grouping. It is composed of a limited number of independent clerics who, lacking any genuine organisation, play a marginal role as opponents of the Shi'a Islamic Reform Movement and other advocates of national integration. They include quietist religious figures displaced by followers of other Shi'a religious and political tendencies who fundamentally distrust the Sunni-dominated regime, hold that the community ought to avoid national politics altogether and opt for an exclusive focus on community affairs.[73]

The Shi'a community in Kuwait accounts for about 20–30 per cent of the population, including thousands of Iranian origin, who form the majority, while the rest originate from the Eastern Province of Saudi Arabia.[74] Iraqi and Lebanese Shi'a who had connection to Iran were arrested following the bombings in Kuwait in 1983 and the attempted assassination of the Emir. Domestic extremists groups sparked off violence in January 1987 after eleven Kuwaiti Shi'as were arrested following bomb attacks on oil installations. Sixteen Kuwaiti Shi'as, a majority of whom were of Iranian origin, were executed in Saudi Arabia in September 1989 after being convicted by a Shari'a court of causing bomb explosions in Mecca during the Hajj of July

1989. Inter-communal tension eased following a Shi'a demonstration of loyalty during the Iraqi occupation of Kuwait in 1990–91. The 'National Coalition' (*al-iatilaf al-watani*) is the main framework under which the Shi'a have functioned since the liberation in 1991 and the 'Society of Social Culture' (*Jamiyat al-thaqafa al-ijtimyah*) is the social and cultural front for the coalition. The few Shi'a who are susceptible to Iranian influence include *Hizb al-Da'wa* (the Islamic Call Party). The National Coalition claims to be independent from any outside influence and, as a framework, allows for differences within its membership with no hierarchy of authority. It shares many views with Sunni groups with few ideological and religious differences, and it calls for respect for the constitution and reform, as well as women's rights.[75]

In Bahrain there are relatively far more Shia's than in any other Gulf State making up more than half of the population. Therefore, the Shi'a religious movement there occupies a far more important role in the social context because of its nature, its relation to the state and its history, compared to its Sunni counterparts.[76] Its relative autonomy from the state gives it more credibility and impact. The Shi'a movement in Bahrain is divided into two main groups: the first is more conciliatory and more integrated within the system and the second is in opposition to and critical of the Sunni-dominated government and resorts to political discourse rather than religious preaching. There is an extensive use of mosques, *Hussainyat* (meeting centres) and *Ashura* (the main Shi'a festival) in disseminating its ideology and in exerting its influence.

The Shi'as in Bahrain have repeatedly protested against government policy, formulating demands for change. While some of these demands overlap with those of the secular and Sunni opposition in demanding constitutional change, in many cases, the Shi'a address social and economic concerns as well.[77] Dissident Shi'a groups such as the 'Islamic Call Party' and the 'Islamic Front for the Liberation of Bahrain' (IFLB) have periodically challenged the government. Following the Iranian revolution, a large number of IFLB members were arrested in December 1981 on charges of supporting an Iranian-backed plot to overthrow the Sunni regime and subsequent plots have been forestalled. Since then many Shi'as have been arrested or killed by riot police, most notably at the start of 2011.[78]

Since the Gulf Crisis in 1990–91, the Shi'a have agitated mainly over human rights and democratisation issues using persuasion and advocacy, operating through international media and human rights organisations such as Amnesty International, to protest their grievances. The Shi'a religious leadership has also established substantial organisations inside and outside the island state but not without developing contradictory political and religious stances amongst them. The largest such organisation is *Jam'iyat al-Wifaq al-Watani al-Islamiyyah* (*al-Wifaq* – The Islamic National Reconciliation Society), which is an amalgam of a variety of personalities and movements with different ideologies and outlooks. Although it may appear to be representative of the Shi'a community as a whole, its confrontational stances seem to demonstrate problems associated with inherent differences in its leadership which resulted in its boycotting the 2002 elections.[79] Despite its shortcomings, *al-Wifaq* generally calls for equality among citizens, fair and equitable power sharing, redistribution of national wealth and fair employment opportunities.

Similarly, the *Jam'iyat al-Amal al-Islami* (Islamic Action Society), whose chairman calls for a real democracy, is geared towards embodying the rule-of-law in the institutions of the state. It aims to promote constructive dialogue between the Bahraini king and the people and a return to the 1973 constitution, as well as resolving problems of unemployment and discrimination. Outside Bahrain, two political organisations dominate. The first is the *Harakat Ahrar al-Bahrayn al-Islamiyyah* (the Islamic Freedom Movement of Bahrain) which was founded in 1981 and is based in London, headed by Dr al-Shihabi and Mansour al-Jamri. The 'Bahrain Freedom Movement', as it is known in the West, has moderate Islamic views and does not call for shari'a law but for the application of the 1975 constitution and for a fair distribution of wealth amongst Bahrainis. The second group, founded in 1976, is *al-Jabha al-Islamiyyah li Tahrir al-Bahrain* (the Islamic Front for the Liberation of Bahrain) with offices in Damascus, London and Tehran. The Front advocates more radical views, calling for shari'a law and the replacement of the Al-Khalifah royal family if they refuse to accept a constitution limiting their powers. A smaller organisation called the 'Committee for Human Rights in Bahrain' operates in England and Denmark.[80]

Other Gulf States have small unorganised Shi'a groups which are not necessarily active or are not in opposition to national governments. For example, in Oman, the Shi'a community, which consists of three main tendencies: *al-Liwatiyah*, *al-Baharnah* and *al-Ajam*, forms one of the richest elites in Omani society. Its members often assume government positions and a good number of them are considered top traders in the Sultanate, with a high percentage of their children being highly educated. However, in December 1987, the Omani government arrested of a group of Shirazi Shi'a inspired by the Islamic Republic of Iran and the state security court sentenced eighteen people to jail terms of between two and eight years on charges of 'communicating with external parties to overthrow the regime'. Following their terms in prison, most of the Shirazi Shi'as live today normally and practice normal economic activities. Their activities now focus on the personal practice of religion and the simple traditional interest of the requirements of the Shi'a sect.[81]

Abadhi Islamists

Oman is the only country in the world with a sizable Abadhi community that constitutes the majority of the population. The rest of the population is made up of different Sunni schools of thought with a small number of Shi'as. Abadhism rejects primogeniture as a legitimate process of political and asserts the leadership of Islam should be provided by an Imam in whom both religions and political leadership a vested and who is elected by the people in the Sultanate.[82] The ruling al-Said family, in fact, comes from the Abadhis.

Given the nature of Omani internal politics, where no parties or political associations are allowed, there are no political groups to speak off. However, some Abadhi conservatives still harbour dreams of the restoration of the Imamate as the religiously dominated but elected form of government which preceded the establishment of the present al-Said dynasty in 1741 and which operated in the interior of Oman until the decisive establishment of al-Said rule over the whole of the country in the 1950s.[83]

Moreover, some Abadhis fear that the tenets of the sect are under attack, especially from Sunni extremists from Saudi Arabia.[84] Others object to the speed of modernisation and the loss of values and national identity in what is a conservative country. Hence in late December 2004 and early January 2005, a plot was reported to have been discovered whereby thirty-one civil servants, military personnel, preachers, Islamic scholars and university professors were detained. They were charged with joining a secret organisation first set up in 1982; forming the *al-Bashaer* military group, raising funds, conducting military training, convening secret meetings, arms smuggling and possession of arms, and seeking to overthrow the regime. In May 2005, in an open public court they were convicted and given sentences ranging from one to twenty years. The Sultan subsequently pardoned them in June 2005.[85]

Conclusions

Political Islam in the Gulf region is a multi-branched movement that began to gain momentum in the 1980s, after Gulf governments failed to secure economic independence, prosperity and good governance. Although the movement is heterogeneous and largely homegrown and responds to a range of domestic, regional and international issues in each country, there are some commonalities in its causes and its manifestations.

The movement is part of the resurgence of religion in the Third World where modernisation, westernisation and secularism had been adopted at the expense of traditional Islamic values. Frustration over post-independence aspirations, the effects of the demographic explosion in the region, the impact of rapid urbanisation, imbalances in the distribution of wealth, poor governance and problems derived from external economic exploitation and cultural domination, all created opposition to all manifestations of secularism. Globalisation coupled with the impact of consumer society and social permissiveness were seen to be corrupting Islamic morality, destroying the social fabric and threatening the identity of Islamic countries.

Within this general trend towards a rise in political Islam, there are other national peculiarities that have contributed to the spread and the growth of this phenomena in the Gulf. The nature of the political systems and the rentier economic structures resulting in unfair distribution of wealth and unfulfilled aspirations of a young and growing population have added to the momentum for change. Other regional factors have played a role in the rise of political Islam in the Gulf, including the Arab defeat in 1967 and the consequent collapse of Arab nationalist ideology, as well as the Iranian revolution in 1979 which inspired both variants of political Islam, Sunni and Shi'a alike. The perceived attack against Islam and the occupation of Arab Muslim lands have also been motivating factors for using Islam as a unifying force. This call has gained resonance in the traditional and conservative societies of the Gulf, where groups to challenge government because of political, social or economic discontent used political Islam. However, given the division of Islam into Sunni, Shi'a and Abadhi schools of doctrine there have been clear differences in the approaches of each of the three sects. There have even been vast differences within each of these Islamic schools over their own goals and methods.

The majority, however, aspire to more reform and political and economic participation, as well as social equality and good governance. These groups, drawn from all the Islamic sects tend to work within the existing political system to achieve a peaceful transformation of it according to Islamic principles. Other minority Islamic groups, although more vociferous, wish to change the status quo as well and are not reluctant to use violence and force to achieve their goals. Where there is sufficient political space and more freedom of action, even radical groups have moderated their views and participated in the political process. The contrary is also true; repression has led to more subversion and violence. However, the resilient regime of the Gulf have been largely able to co-opt Islamic opposition groups, open up the political arena through national dialogue and grant more political participation. They appear, in short, to be riding the Islamist wave successfully.

Notes

1. It is generally accepted that 'political' Islam has proved to be problematic for difficulties begin at the conceptual level. There is a problem with the definition of the phrase 'political Islam'. Scholars have attempted different definitions and the literature on Islam and politics attributes various labels to the phenomenon: revivalism, resurgence, reform, Islamism, radical, militant, revolutionary, fundamentalism, extremism, terrorism, to name but a few. These labels and the ensuing definitions underline the problem at the conceptual level and create ambiguity and misunderstanding of the term 'political Islam'. The definition of 'political Islam' used here is that it denotes 'Islam used to a political end'.

2. The GCC member states are Bahrain, Kuwait, Qatar, Oman, Saudi Arabia and the United Arab Emirates.

3. Ghubash, H. 2006. *Oman: The Islamic Democratic Tradition*. Routledge: London, New York, p.1; for a background on the tradition see also Wilkinson, J.C. 1987. *The Imamate Tradition of Oman*. Cambridge University Press: Cambridge.

4. The succession of Prophet Mohammed is clearly the key question in Shi'i Islam and the principal factor separating Shi'a from Sunni. The question is not only who was the successor to Mohammed but also the nature of his role, for it is on both these points that Shi'a and Sunnis disagree. Contrary to the Sunni, the Shi'a believe that Mohammed explicitly designated his successor in the linage of Ali, his cousin and the husband of his daughter Fatima, who became the fourth caliph. In contrast to other schools of thought, Shi'a Islam holds that Mohammed's family, the *Ahl al-Bayt* ('the People of the House'), and certain individuals among his descendants, who are known as Imams, have special spiritual and political authority over the Islamic community. For a background see, Momen, M. 1985. *An Introduction to Shi'i Islam*. George Ronald Publisher and Yale University Press, especially Ch.2.

5. Within the GCC States Shi'a are said to constitute 70 per cent of the Bahraini population, 7 per cent of Saudi population and 35 per cent of Kuwaiti population. See, pp.6–7.

6. For more on Wahhabism and the history of Saudi Arabia, see Vassiliev, A. 2000. *The History of Saudi Arabia*. New York University Press: New York; and al-Rasheed, M. 2002. *The History of Saudi Arabia*. Cambridge University Press: Cambridge. The term Wahhabi is now 'overused and devoid of analytic significance, serving to describe disparate groups and (individuals) across time and space, so long as they adhere to an austere or conservative view of Islam'. ICG Middle East Report, 28, *Can Saudi Arabia Reform Itself?* 14 July 2004.

7. Although both the first (1744–1818) and second (1823–91) Saudi states eventually collapsed as political entities; the alliance between the Al Saud and the Wahhabi preachers remained the basis for the formation of the modern Kingdom of Saudi Arabia in 1932.

8. Thomas, S.M. 2010. 'A Globalized God: Religious Growing Influence in International Politics', *Foreign Affairs*, November/December, Special Issue, 89 (6), pp.93–101; Haynes, J. 1993. *Religion in Third World Politics, Issues in Third World Politics*. Open University Press: Buckingham, Philadelphia.

9. Including the spread of Christian Missionaries in the Gulf.

10. Bayat, A. 2007. *Making Islam Democratic: Social Movements and the Post-Islamist Turn*. Stanford University Press: Stanford, California.

11. Nevo, J. 1988. 'Religion and National Identity in Saudi Arabia', *Middle Eastern*, 34 (3) (July), pp.34–53.

12. Among the precepts of Islam that govern the relationship between the ruler and the ruled are such issues as the duty of hearing and obedience (*al-Sama wa al-taa*), the pledge of allegiance (*al-Bayah*) and the promotion of virtue and the prevention of vice (*al-amr bi al-marruf wa al-nahy an al-munkar*), the obligation of applying the *Sharia'h* (God's Law) and the concept of the holy war (*Jihad*). Governments have used such politico-ideological concepts to Islamise populations and spread religion. Opposition Islamic groups occasionally used the same ideas to challenge regimes.

13. Dawisha, A. 2003. *Arab Nationalism in the Twentieth Century from Triumph to Despair*. Princeton University Press: Princeton and Oxford, p.278.

14. Abukhalili, A. 2004. *The Battle for Saudi Arabia: Royalty, Fundamentalism, and Global Power*. Seven Stories Press: New York, p.104.

15. Benard, C., and Khalilzad, Z. 1984. *The Government of God: Iran's Islamic Republic*. Columbia University Press: New York, p.25; Noreng, Ø. 1997. *Oil and Islam: Social and Economic Issues*. Wiley: Oxford, p.272.

16. Hamzawy, A. 2009. 'Between Government and Opposition: The Case of the Yemeni Congregation for Reform', Carnegie Papers, Carnegie Middle East Center, 18 (November), available at: http://carnegieendowment.org/files/yemeni_congragation_reform.pdf.

17. Omar Hasan al-Bashir led the revolution for national reform in Sudan, with the support of the National Islamic Front against the Prime Minister al-Sadiq al-Mahdi in 1989. The Islamic Front evolved from the Muslim Brothers and was under the leadership of Hasan al-Turabi. Said Bin Sultan al-Hashimi Islamic Movements in Oman 1970–2010, 'Navigating the Milestones of a Nebulous Road', unpublished paper handed to the author.

18. Saddam's invasion to Kuwait in 1990 also caused great controversy within the international circles of the Muslim Brotherhood. Such controversy

resulted in the withdrawal of the Brotherhood in Kuwait from the main organisation and in tension in the relationship between the Kuwaiti branch and the main organisation.

19. Sagar, A.O. 2005. 'Political Opposition in Saudi Arabia', in Arts, P., and Nonneman, G. (eds.) *Saudi Arabia in the Balance, Political Economy, Society, Foreign Affairs*. Hurst and Company: London, pp.234–270.

20. There is also a fourth Sunni group that is part of resurgent Populist Islam in the Gulf. This is Populist Sufism represented by mystical movements such as the al-Rifa'i brotherhood in Kuwait. This mystical component of Sunni Populist Islam is especially strong in North Africa but has only a limited presence in the Gulf at this time. The Sufi groups that do exist are sharply opposed both to the Salafi movement and to Shi'ism.

21. Quoted in Bill, J.A. 1984. 'The Persian Gulf: Resurgent Islam', *Foreign Affairs*, 63 (Fall), pp.108–127.

22. See http://www.ikhwanweb.com/article.php?id=26979.

23. For example, municipal councilor, Dr Salah Al Jowder, has campaigned against people being able to look into other people's houses, changing the local by-laws in Muharraq to ensure that all new buildings are fitted with one-way glass to prevent residents being able to see out.

24. '"We don't want to box Islam in": Kuwait's Islamists, officially unofficial'. 2002. *Le Monde diplomatique*, English Edition, June, available at http://mond-ediplo.com/2002/06/04kuwait.

25. Al-Mudaires, F.A. 1999. 'Jamaat al-ikhwan almuslameen fi al Kuwait' (Islamic Brotherhood Group in Kuwait) (in Arabic). Qurtas Publishing: Kuwait; see also Ghabra, S.N. 1997. 'Balancing State and Society: The Islamic Movement in Kuwait', *Middle East Policy*, 5 (2) (May), pp.58–71.

26. Janardhan, N. 2006. 'Islamist Stay Clear of Terrorism in Oman', *Terrorism Monitor*, 4 (5), 9 March, available at: http://www.jamestown.org/single/?no_cache=1&tx_ttnews%5Btt_news%5D=698.

27. Wahhabism is by no means the only Muslim denomination in Saudi Arabia. In fact, the country's population is one of the most diverse in the Middle East in this respect: Saudi Arabia has Sunnis belonging to all four jurisprudential schools, Sufis and separate branches of Shi'ism.

28. Steinberg, G. 2005. 'The Wahhabi Ulama and the Saudi State, 1745 to the Present in Political Opposition in Saudi Arabia', in Arts, P., and Nonneman, G. (eds.) *Saudi Arabia in the Balance, Political Economy, Society, Foreign Affairs*. Hurst and Company: London, pp.11–34.

29. The nomination of Shaykh Ibn Baz as the head of the Wahhabi establishment in 1967, under the reign of King Faysal (1964–75), may be considered the turning point in its subordination to the regime.

30. This first ruling was given in August 1990, a few days after Saddam Hussein's invasion of Kuwait, by the Council of Senior Ulama (*hay'at kibar al-ulama*), the highest institution in the Wahhabi religious establishment.

31. This ruling was provided by the Kingdom's top *mufti*, Shaykh Ibn Baz himself, on 13 September 1993.

32. Steinberg, op.cit.

33. Hegghammer and Lacroix, op.cit.

34. The 1980s were marked by the so-called modernism debate, which opposed a group of writers and poets calling for a reform of Islamic literary tradition and the *Sahwa*, which accused them of trying to destroy the foundations of Saudi society. See Fandy, M. 1999. *Saudi Arabia and the Politics of Dissent.* Palgrave Macmillan: Basingstoke, p.48.

35. Among the latter are sub-divisions between so-called Bannaists and Qutbists. Bannaism and Qutbism refer to the two main ideologues of the Egyptian Muslim Brotherhood, Hasan al-Banna and Sayyid Qutb. See ICG Middle East Briefing, *Islamism in North Africa II: Egypt's Opportunity*, 20 April 2004.

36. 'Saudi Arabia backgrounder: who are the islamists?' International Crisis Group, *ICG Middle East Report*, 31, 21 September 2004, available at: http://www.crisisgroup.org/library/documents/middle_east___north_africa/iraq_iran_gulf/31_saudi_arabia_backgrounder.doc.

37. Ghabra, S.N. 1997. 'Balancing State and Society: The Islamic Movement in Kuwait', *Middle East Policy*, 5 (2) (May), pp.58–71.

38. 'Talal Al-Rashoud, An Unlikely Reformer? Kuwait's Salafi "Ummah Party"'. 2010. Paper presented at the 'Islamism in the Gulf workshop' at the Gulf Research Meeting, Cambridge, 6–8 July, p.9.

39. Hegghammer, T., and Lacroix, S. 2007. 'Rejectionist Islamism in Saudi Arabia: The Story of Juhayman al-'Utaybi Revisited', *International Journal of Middle East Studies*, 39 (1), pp.103–122.

40. Nasr al-Din al-Albani was a Syrian scholar of Albanian origin who was born in 1914. He founded a school of Islamic thought that views the *hadith* as the sole basis for religious decisions. Al-Albani taught at the University of Medina in the late 1950s but was compelled to leave due to his many disagreements with Saudi scholars, notably on ritual issues. Nevertheless, he maintained close ties with Saudi Arabia, and particularly with the city of Medina, until his death in 1999. 'Saudi Arabia backgrounder: who are the Islamists?' International Crisis Group, available at: http://www.crisisgroup.org/library/documents/middle_east___north_africa/iraq_iran_gulf/31_saudi_arabia_backgrounder.doc.

41. Hegghammer and Lacroix, op.cit.

42. While living in the desert, Juhayman wrote a series of articles known as 'the Seven Letters of Juhayman', to justify the attack, as well as much religious poetry. He also made tape recordings of his speeches, some of which still circulate in Saudi Arabia. See, 'Saudi Arabia backgrounder: who are the Islamists?' International Crisis Group, available at: http://www.crisisgroup.org/library/documents/middle_east___north_africa/iraq_iran_gulf/31_saudi_arabia_backgrounder.doc

43. Lacroix, S. 2005. 'Islamo-Liberal Politics in Saudi Arabia: In Political Opposition in Saudi Arabia', in Arts, P., and Nonneman, G. (eds.) *Saudi Arabia in the Balance, Political Economy, Society, Foreign Affairs*. Hurst and Company: London, pp.35–56.

44. Lacroix, S. 2009. 'Between Revolution and Apoliticism: Nasir al-Din al-Albani and His Impact on the Shaping of Contemporary Salafism', in Meijer, R. (ed.) *Global Salafism: Islam's New Religious Movement*. Columbia University Press: New York, pp.74–77

45. al-Rasheed, M. 2007. *Contesting the Saudi State: Islamic Voices from a New Generation*. Cambridge University Press: Cambridge, pp.75–78; 'Talal Al-Rashoud, An Unlikely Reformer? Kuwait's Salafi "Ummah Party"'. 2010. Paper presented at the 'Islamism in the Gulf workshop' at the Gulf Research Meeting, Cambridge, 6–8 July, p.11.

46. Dekmejian, R.H. 1994. 'The Rise of Political Islam in Saudi Arabia', *Middle East Journal*, 48 (4) (Autumn), pp.627–643.

47. Sagar, op.cit.

48. Ibid.

49. 'Saudi Arabia backgrounder: who are the Islamists?' International Crisis Group, ICG Middle East Report No.31, 21 September 2004, available at: http://www.crisisgroup.org/library/documents/middle_east___north_africa/iraq_iran_gulf/31_saudi_arabia_backgrounder.doc

50. Hegghammer, T. 2008. 'Islamists and Regime Stability in Saudi Arabia', *International Affairs*, 84(4), pp.701–715.

51. Ibid. p.706.

52. For example, Abd al-Aziz bin Baz, the Mufti of Saudi Arabia at the time, issued a fatwa decreeing *jihad* in Afghanistan a collective duty.

53. 'Saudi Arabia backgrounder: who are the Islamists?' International Crisis Group, ICG Middle East Report No.31, 21 September 2004, available at: http://www.crisisgroup.org/library/documents/middle_east___north_africa/iraq_iran_gulf/31_saudi_arabia_backgrounder.doc.

54. So long as they were not involved in domestic militant activities with some notable exceptions such as Osama bin Laden – they were rarely prosecuted. Saudi officials acknowledge this; see 'Interview with Jamal

Khashoggi, 7 July 2004, available at www.jamestown.org/images/ pdf/ tm_002_014-ftinterview.pdf.

55. In addition to attending training camps in Afghanistan, global *mujahidin* fought in places such as Bosnia and Somalia in the early 1990s and in Chechnya in the late 1990s.

56. Hegghammer, T. 2006. 'Global Jihadism After the Iraq War', *The Middle East Journal*, 60 (1) (Winter), pp.11–32.

57. Hegghammer. 2008. op.cit.

58. Hegghammer. 2006. op.cit.

59. Shi'ism originated in the dispute over Prophet Mohammed's succession. Ali, the Prophet's cousin and son-in-law (as husband of the Prophet's daughter Fatima) claimed to be the rightful successor but was repeatedly passed over before eventually becoming the fourth Caliph. Mu'awiyya, the founder of the Umayyad dynasty, soon challenged his position and Ali was killed in 661 CE His supporters, the 'Shi'at Ali' ('the partisans of Ali'), were those who accepted the argument that the leadership (*al-imama*) of the Muslim community combined spiritual and temporal responsibilities, required divine inspiration, and should, therefore, be drawn from the Prophet's line alone. They subsequently supported the claims of Ali's sons, Hassan and Hussein, as his rightful successors, in opposition to the line of Sunni rulers; both sons led unsuccessful revolts against the Umayyads and were killed (Hassan in 671 and Hussein in 680 CE). Thereafter, the Shi'as regarded all Sunni rulers as illegitimate usurpers and recognised only their own imams in the line of descent from the Prophet through Ali's children.

60. Al-Najjar, B.S. 2007. *Islamic Movements in the Arabian Gulf*. Saqi: London, p.61.

61. Ibid.

62. Nasr, V. 2006. 'When the Shi'ite Rise', *Foreign Affairs*, 85 (4) (July/August), pp.58–74.

63. 'Understanding Islamism', International Crisis Group, ICG, Middle East/ North Africa Report No.37, 2 March 2005.

64. Ibrahim, F. 2007. *Al-Shi'a fi Al-Saudiya* (Shi'a in Saudi Arabia) (in Arabic). Saqi: London, p.7.

65. See al-Rasheed, M. 1998. 'Saudi Arabia: A Minority in Search of Cultural Authenticity', *British Journal of Middle Eastern Studies*, 25 (1).

66. ICG interviews, Eastern Province.

67. In a 1993 meeting, King Fahd promised Shi'a leaders to relax political restrictions in exchange for their ending active opposition from abroad. See Fandy, M. 1999. *Saudi Arabia and the Politics of Dissent*. Palgrave Macmillan: Basingstoke, pp.198–199.

68. 'The Shi'ite Question in Saudi Arabia', Middle East Report No.45, 19 September 2005, International Crisis Group, available at: http://www.crisis-group.org/home/index.cfm?id=3678&l=1.

69. Ibid.

70. Ibid.

71. Through its leader al-Saffar's efforts, notably, Shi'as have been permitted to observe Ashura publicly (albeit only in predominantly Shi'ite towns and villages, not in mixed cities such as Dammam).

72. Including Sheikh Hashim al-Shukus, Sheikh Abdulrahman al-Hubail and Abduljalil al-Maa, current leaders include Sheikh Hashim al-Hubail, Sheikh Hassan al-Nimr and Sayyed Kamal al-Sada.

73. One such rejectionist cleric, Sheikh Nimr al-Nimr, head of a mosque in the village of 'Awamiyya north of Qatif', typically speaks against any engagement with the al-Saud.

74. Al-Mudaires, F.A. 1996. *Kuwaiti Political Groups: The period after liberation* (in Arabic). Second Edition, Al-Manar: Kuwait, p.25.

75. Ibid., pp.28–29.

76. Al-Ansari, A. 2008. 'Religious groups and their impact on Political Stability (the Gulf Region as an example)'. Conference Paper delivered at Religion and Society in the Arab World, Al-Itihad Annual Forum 2008, Abu Dhabi 20–21 October 2008.

77. Bahry, L. 1997. 'The Opposition in Bahrain: A Bellwether for the Gulf', *Middle East Policy*, 5 (2) (May), pp.42–57.

78. Ibid.

79. Al-Ansari, op.cit.

80. Bahry, op.cit.

81. al-Hashimi, S.B.S. undated. 'Islamic Movements in Oman 1970–2010: Navigating the Milestones of a Nebulous Road', unpublished paper handed to the author.

82. For a background see *Mamiri, A.H.* 1989. *Oman and Abadhism*. Lancer Books, New York, NY.

83. Jones, J., and Ridout, N. 2005. 'Democratic Development in Oman', *Middle East Journal*, 59 (3) (Summer), pp.376–392.

84. Katz, M. 2004. 'Assessing the Political Stability', *Middle East (Review of International Affairs (MERIA)) Journal*, 8 (3) (September), available at: http://meria.idc.ac.il/journal/2004/issue3/jv8n3a1.html.

85. See Janardhan, op.cit.

Bibliography

Abukhalili, A. 2004. *The Battle for Saudi Arabia, Royalty, Fundamentalism, and Global Power.* Seven Stories Press: New York.

al-Ansari, A. 2008. 'Religious groups and their impact on Political Stability', Conference Paper delivered at Religion and Society in the Arab World, Al-Itihad Annual Forum, Abu Dhabi.

Asef, B. 2007. *Making Islam Democratic, Social Movements and the Post-Islamist Turn.* Stanford University Press: Stanford, California.

Bahry, L. 1997. 'The Opposition in Bahrain: A Bellwether for the Gulf', *Middle East Policy,* 5 (2), pp.42–57.

Benard, C., and Khalilzad, Z. 1984. *The Government of God: Iran's Islamic Republic.* Columbia University Press: New York.

Bill, J.A. 1984. 'The Persian Gulf: Resurgent Islam', *Foreign Affairs,* 63.

Dawisha, A. 2003. *Arab Nationalism in the Twentieth Century from Triumph to Despair.* Princeton University Press: Princeton.

Dekmejian, R.H. 1994. 'The Rise of Political Islam in Saudi Arabia', *Middle East Journal,* 48 (4), pp.627–643.

Fandy, M. 1999. *Saudi Arabia and the Politics of Dissent.* Palgrave Macmillan: Basingstoke.

Ghabra, S.N. 1997. 'Balancing State and Society: The Islamic Movement in Kuwait', *Middle East Policy,* 5 (2), No.2, pp.58–72.

Ghubash, H. 2006. *Oman: The Islamic Democratic Tradition.* Routledge: London.

Hamzawy, A. 2009. 'Between Government and Opposition: The Case of the Yemeni Congregation for Reform', Carnegie Papers, Carnegie Middle East Center, Number 18, November 2009.

Haynes, J. 1993. *Religion in Third World Politics, Issues in Third World Politics.* Open University Press: Buckingham, Philadelphia.

Hegghammer, T. 2008. 'Islamists and Regime Stability in Saudi Arabia', *International Affairs,* 84 (4), pp.701–715.

Hegghammer, T., and Lacroix, S. 2007. 'Rejectionist Islamism in Saudi Arabia: The Story of Juhayman al-'Utaybi Revisited', *International Journal of Middle East Studies,* 39 (1), pp.103–122.

Ibrahim, F. 2007. *Al-Shi'a fi Al-Saudiya* [Shi'a in Saudi Arabia]. Dar al-Saqi: London.

Janardhan, N. 2006. 'Islamist Stay Clear of Terrorism in Oman', *Terrorism Monitor,* 4 (5), 9 March 2006.

Jones, J., and Ridout, N. 2005. 'Democratic Development in Oman', *Middle East Journal,* 59 (3), pp.376–392.

Katz, M. 2004. 'Assessing the Political Stability', *Middle East Review of International Affairs Journal (MERIA),* 8 (3).

Lacroix, S. 2005. 'Islamo-Liberal Politics in Saudi Arabia, in Political Opposition in Saudi Arabia', in Arts, P., and Nonneman, G. (eds.) *Saudi Arabia in the Balance: Political Economy, Society, Foreign Affairs.* Hurst: London.

_____ 2009. 'Between Revolution and Apoliticism: Nasir al-Din al-Albani and His Impact on the Shaping of Contemporary Salafism', in Meijer, R. (ed.) *Global Salafism: Islam's New Religious Movement*. Columbia University Press: New York.

Louer, L. 2008. *Transitional Shi'a Politics, Religious and Political Networks in the Gulf*. Hurst and Co. Ltd.: London.

Mamiri, A.H. 1989. *Oman and Abadhism*. Lancer Books: New York.

Momen, M. 1985. *An Introduction to Shi'i Islam*. George Ronald Publisher and Yale University Press: New Haven.

al-Mudaires, F.A. 1999. *Jamaat al-ikhwan almuslameen fi al Kuwait* [Islamic Brotherhood Group in Kuwait]. Qurtas Publishing: Kuwait.

al-Najjar, B.S. 2007. *Islamic Movements in the Arabian Gulf*. Dar Alsaqi: London.

Nasr, V. 2006. 'When the Shi'ite Rise', *Foreign Affairs*, 85 (4).

Nevo, J. 1988. 'Religion and National Identity in Saudi Arabia', *Middle Eastern*, 34 (3), pp.34–53.

Noreng, Ø. 1997. *Oil and Islam: Social and Economic Issues*. Wiley: Oxford.

al-Rasheed, M. 1998. 'Saudi Arabia: A Minority in Search of Cultural Authenticity', *British Journal of Middle Eastern Studies*, 25 (1), pp.121–138.

—— 2002. *A History of Saudi Arabia*. Cambridge University Press: Cambridge.

—— 2007. *Contesting the Saudi State: Islamic Voices from a New Generation*. Cambridge University Press: Cambridge.

al-Rashoud, T. 2010. 'An Unlikely Reformer? Kuwait's Salafi "Ummah Party".' Paper presented at the 'Islamism in the Gulf workshop' at the Gulf Research Meeting, Cambridge, 6–8, July 2010.

Sagar, A.O. 2005. 'Political Opposition in Saudi Arabia', in Arts, P., and Nonneman, G. (eds.) *Saudi Arabia in the Balance: Political Economy, Society, Foreign Affairs*. Hurst and Co. Ltd.: London.

Steinberg, G. 2005. 'The Wahhabi Ulama and the Saudi State, 1745 to the Present', in Arts, P., and Nonneman, G. (eds.) *Saudi Arabia in the Balance: Political Economy, Society, Foreign Affairs*. Hurst: London.

Thomas, S.M.A. 2010. 'Globalized God, Religious Growing Influence in International Politics', *Foreign Affairs*, November/December 2010.

Wilkinson, J. 1987. *The Imamate Tradition of Oman*. Cambridge University Press: Cambridge.

Vassiliev, A. 2000. *The History of Saudi Arabia*. Saqi: London.

INDEX

T

U